MILITARIZING THE NATION

.

Militarizing the Nation

THE ARMY, BUSINESS, AND REVOLUTION IN EGYPT

Zeinab Abul-Magd

Columbia University Press

New York

Columbia University Press
Publishers Since 1893
New York   Chichester, West Sussex
cup.columbia.edu
Copyright © 2017 Columbia University Press
Paperback edition, 2018
All rights reserved

Library of Congress Cataloging-in-Publication Data

Names: Abul-Magd, Zeinab, 1976- author.
Title: Militarizing the nation : the army, business, and revolution in
Egypt / Zeinab Abul-Magd.
Description: New York : Columbia University Press, 2016. | Includes
bibliographical references and index.
Identifiers: LCCN 2016032821 | ISBN 9780231170628 (cloth)
| ISBN 9780231170635 (pbk.) | ISBN 9780231542807 (e-book)
Subjects: LCSH: Egypt—Armed Forces—Political activity. | Egypt—Politics and
government—20th century. | Egypt—Politics and government—21st century. | Egypt—
Economic conditions—1952–
Classification: LCC DT107.827 .A29 2016 | DDC 962.05—dc23
LC record available at https://lccn.loc.gov/2016032821

Cover Design: Rebecca Lown
Cover Image: AP Photo/Bill Foley

Contents

Abbreviations

ACA	Administrative Control Authority
AFLPO	Armed Forces' Land Projects Organization
AOI	Arab Organization for Industrialization
ASA	Accountability State Authority
ASU	Arab Socialist Union
CSF	Central Security Forces
EAAF	Engineering Authority of the Armed Forces
FMF	Foreign Military Finance
FMS	Foreign Military Sales program
GAO	U.S. Governmental Accountability Office
MISO	Maritime Industries and Services Organization
MoD	Ministry of Defense
MoMP	Ministry of Military Production
MTS	Maritime Transport Sector
NDP	National Democratic Party
NSPO	National Service Projects Organization
SCAF	Supreme Council of Armed Forces
VO	Volunteer Organization

MILITARIZING THE NATION

Introduction

The Officer Has Saved the Nation

Defense of society is tied up with war by the fact that . . . it is thought of in terms of "an internal war" against the dangers arising from the social body itself.

—Michel Foucault, *Security, Territory, and Population*

U pon the graduation of new cadets in the summer of 2015, the director of the Egyptian war college proudly asserted that these young officers were the country's "future leaders . . . the ministers, governors, ambassadors, presidents, and managers."[1] At this time, ex-generals were already the leaders of the country's present. Besides the newly elected president who used to be the minister of defense, other retired officers headed the Suez Canal and all seaports, along with the governmental authorities of agriculture, housing, foreign trade, telecommunication, and much more. Many others managed state-owned companies of water and sewerage, Internet services, land reclamation, and so forth. After all, the military had saved the nation twice recently by deposing two dictators in the previous few years. Unfortunately, many of those military administrators had difficulties with their new civilian jobs. The ex-general who headed the River Transportation Authority was sacked after a public ferry sank in the Nile and tens of poor passengers drowned with it. Meanwhile, the ex-general heading the public authority of Greater Cairo's underground metro system struggled with reoccurring crises of crashed or broken trains.[2] In another realm, however, managers of the military's vast business enterprises in a liberalized market were doing well. A uniformed general who chaired the Queen Pasta Company—part of a gigantic manufacturing conglomerate owned by the Ministry of Defense— affirmed that his nine factories produced quality and healthful assortments of macaroni. The Ministry of Military Production sold its manufactured goods of kitchenware and home appliances to families at national fairs.[3]

In Egypt's postcolonial history, the army saved the "nation" and served as its faithful guardian three times. The first was six decades ago, in 1952, when a group of young officers kicked out the British colonizer, deposed the monarch, and established a liberated republic. The second took place more recently, in 2011, when the armed forces decided to take the side of mass protests to overthrow an autocratic president, an ex-general himself who oppressively ruled the country for thirty years. The third was two years later, in 2013, when the armed forces again sided with protesting masses to overthrow an Islamist regime. But saving the nation was insepa- rable from militarizing it. Each time, the saviors assumed full power over the state and amassed immense economic privileges. This book follows how Egypt's semiautonomous military institution has been visibly, or often invisibly, hegemonizing the country's politics and economy throughout the past six decades. It traces the genealogies of military penetration into the urban spaces of all social classes of the population toward their full sub- jugation. It reveals how the officers in recent history deployed neoliberal means both to make business profits and to establish constant surveillance and omnipotent control over docile or rebellious masses. While propagat- ing nationalistic rhetoric about guarding it, the Egyptian army has milita- rized the nation for long decades in the past and diligently continues to do so in the present.

Uniquely in its regional context, the Egyptian Army adapted to and benefited from crucial moments of change and survived old and new waves of revolutionary shifts in the country. It weathered fundamental moments of transition to socialism in the 1960s, market consumerism in the 1980s, and neoliberalism from the 1990s onward, while successfully enhancing its political supremacy and expanding a mammoth business empire. Recently it has survived hard times during two popular uprisings, retained full power, and increased its wealth. While adjusting to these difficult shifts, the of- ficers have successfully turned the urban milieus of the population into an ever-expanded military camp: into sites of their permanent armed presence, continuous gaze, and control of everyday life. The military institution's busi- ness enterprises tapped into consumerist realms of rich and poor citizens alike, for both unaccountable profit and optimized social command. In the meantime, military bureaucrats securitized local urbanities to watch over the subordinated masses during times of peace or rebellious turmoil.

After the sweeping wave of the "Arab Spring" uprisings that erupted in 2011, the Egyptian Army stood among a few Arab militaries that not only remained intact but also succeeded in restoring command over its crumbling state. Military regimes and military-backed autocrats were born across the Middle East ever since its states gained independence from European colonialism in the mid-twentieth century. Tens of military coups d'état took place in the region and gave birth to officer-dominated regimes in post-colonial Arab states such as Syria, Libya, Iraq, Algeria, Tunisia, Yemen, and Egypt. These authoritarian regimes lasted for decades, until many of them finally collapsed under mass unrest in 2011. This wave led not only to overthrowing old military dictators such as Muammar al-Qadhafi of Libya or Ali Abdullah Saleh of Yemen, but also to dismantling many of their military institutions. Next door to Egypt in Syria, the son of a military dictator who inherited his father's security state, Bashar al-Assad, has not yet been deposed, but his army has been similarly severely fractured. In Egypt, however, the aging military autocrat, Hosni Mubarak, was overthrown, but his army was kept fully intact and managed to shortly reinstate the military regime anew amid cheering masses. This book follows the historical roots of the Egyptian Army's political and economic might and how it survived the Arab Spring to restore absolute dominance.

When President Abdel Fattah al-Sisi swept elections in the summer of 2014, he was the fourth officer to take off his uniform and rule Egypt since its independence. Before him, Gamal Abdel Nasser (r. 1954–1970), Anwar Sadat (r. 1970–1981), and Mubarak (r. 1981–2011) were all ex-officers who uninterruptedly controlled the country through always obtaining landslide victories at ballot boxes. After Mubarak was deposed, the Supreme Council of Armed Forces (SCAF) ruled the country for a year and a half until it delivered authority to a civilian, Islamist president. Eventually al-Sisi returned the presidential seat to his institution after its loss for a brief one year in six decades.

During these long decades, the army has militarized everyday life of its subjugated and manipulated citizens across social classes. It has baked them subsidized bread, built affordable apartments, opened wedding halls, constructed football stadiums, and sold all sorts of consumer goods. The banners of military-owned expansive farms, manufacturing conglomerates, or construction companies are visibly installed atop their supermarkets, large shopping malls, toll highways, bridges, luxury hotels, summer resorts, and even parking lots. Moreover, retired generals have taken charge of state authorities and public-sector companies that provide citizens with basic services from water and sewerage, transportation, and road maintenance to telephone lines and the Internet. Above all this, the military has penetrated into the daily life of every family through compulsory conscription of male youths for a period between one and three years. A young man cannot travel, get a job, or even get married without finishing his military service first. In the meantime, the army produces popular songs about heroic officers, makes documentaries about brave soldiers, opens museums displaying great battles from pharaonic to modern times, and distributes charitable items to the poor in big festivities celebrating its sacrifices for the nation.

While adapting to change and adjusting to transformations, the Egyptian military switched ideologies and socioeconomic alliances, and altered external allies. The first military president, Nasser, opted for socialism, favored the middle and lower classes, made friends with the Soviet Union during the Cold War, and made enemies of conservative Arabian Gulf regimes. On the contrary, his successor, Sadat, decided to embrace an open-market economy, partner with a class of local business tycoons, switch Cold War camps to the United States, and revive relations with the oil-producing Gulf states. Mubarak followed Sadat's footsteps to encourage big consumerism in the 1980s, until he fully transformed the country into neoliberalism in the 1990s and the 2000s. Within these changing environments, the military as an institution positioned itself to maximize its power and profit at every moment of transformation. It was an army that fought for Arab liberation and socialism in the 1960s, fully embraced market consumerism through venturing into civilian production in the 1980s, and finally adopted neoliberalism to expand a business empire in collaboration with local and foreign capital throughout the 1990s and 2000s. Moreover, during the last ten years of Mubarak's reign, retired generals occupied numerous key bureaucratic positions managing his neoliberal state, which was infamous for clientelism, corruption, and inefficiency. When the wealthy Muslim Brothers rose to power in 2011, the military quickly allied itself with the new elite and expanded its business enterprises under their regime. But the officers soon switched domestic alliances again to other discontented political stances and social groups to take down the Islamist regime. Toward this end, they relied on the indispensable help of oil-producing Arab Gulf states, displeased the United States, and revived old ties with Russia.

Militarizing the nation was justified when the army was fighting big wars. But the Egyptian military fought its last war and signed a peace treaty with its main enemy, Israel, four decades ago. Thus, as it almost lost importance and relevance in society, the military had to reinvent its image and forge new nationalistic myths in order to maintain its omnipotent presence in the nation. The Egyptian Army generally fought wars that matched with the ideological choices and external alliances that the incumbent military presidents made. Based on an anti-imperial and Arab nationalist agendas in the 1950s–1960s, it fought in the Suez Crisis, supported the Algerian freedom fighters against French colonialism, and backed republican Yemenis. After the 1967 and 1973 wars against Israel, it never fought big conventional wars of its own again—it only contributed to regional battles. During times of war, an omnipotent presence for the military within society was justified and popularly consented to through propaganda campaigns. After signing the peace accord with Israel in 1978, the Egyptian military was required to reduce its size and budget and keep to its barracks. Nonetheless, it continued to impose compulsory conscription, enjoy a considerable budget, and intensively occupy the socioeconomic realms of the masses.

In the time of peace, the Egyptian military reinvented its role in society. It claimed that its new duties now were to contribute to the country's economic development. In reality, it turned the whole society into a big military camp under its constant surveillance. Through business ventures and civilian positions, the military sustained its uninterrupted gaze over the urban milieu and securitized the everyday life of subjected citizens. The guardians of the nation had already been living outside of their barracks for a long time when they offered their help to save the country in the past few years.

By tracing the history of the Egyptian military institution from the 1950s until the present day, this book applies political economy and Foucauldian approaches to deconstruct how the officers have repeatedly saved and long militarized the nation. It attempts to decipher the mysteries of the institution's ability to constantly adapt to change by reinventing its image, altering its doctrine, redeploying its patriotic rhetoric, and reforging its socioeconomic alliances in order to maintain power and hegemonize the citizens as their only trusted guardian. While contextualizing it within the domestic, regional, and global environments, the book investigates transformations in the Egyptian military institution and the distant and near roots of its rise to full supremacy today.

The book poses four main arguments in this regard. First, it argues that the military institution that exists in Egypt today is not the same as the one that created the country's first military regime sixty years ago. A fundamental rupture took place in this institution in the 1980s, which gave birth to the new army that rules the country today. Old and new armies differ in their socioeconomic composition, their doctrine, and the way they militarized society. Whereas the old army was led by lower- to middle-class soldiers who rose into an affluent ruling elite and militarized society through war and socialism, the new army is controlled by a class of managers of military business enterprises, or "neoliberal officers," and militarizes society through market hegemony. Whereas the old army's ambitious doctrine adopted an Arab nationalist identity and a socialist ideology and was externally oriented to regional affairs, the new army's less ambitious doctrine focuses on narrow Egyptian patriotism and is internally oriented toward domestic matters. The book follows the genealogies of this rupture and the birth of the neoliberal officers who enjoy leverage in Egyptian politics today. Their birth took place alongside Egypt's transformation into the market economy under Mubarak. The neoliberal officers do not necessarily believe in the dicta of the free market; in fact, they function against them as their enterprises enjoy privileges far above those of the private and public sectors. However, they take advantage of the openness of the market for institutional and individual gains.

Second, the book argues that before the uprisings of 2011, the officers were an integral part, or rather makers, of Mubarak's neoliberal regime. This regime was deposed owing to its failure to deliver social justice and was plagued by patron-client relations, conspicuous corruption, overall decadence of public services, and acute social disparities. Throughout the 2000s, as he accelerated the pace of transforming to neoliberalism, Mubarak hired an ever increasing number of retired officers in civilian positions in order to "coup-proof" his regime. While he maintained a civilian face for the state in Cairo by appointing cabinets of civilian technocrats, retired generals were the de facto rulers of most of provincial Egypt through occupying the seats of local governors. More important, retired officers were major participants in running a dysfunctional market economy, as they were hired heads of numerous government authorities responsible for the key economic activities of the liberalized state. Thus they were evidently contributors to the fallacies of the regime that eventually collapsed under public rage in 2011. The fact that the army acted as the savior of the state from Mubarak falls under close scrutiny here.

Third, the book argues that the Egyptian military is a product of its regional and global contexts and has changed with major transformations in these wider surroundings. The Egyptian Army came to power in the middle of the Cold War and, like many other Third World, newly independent, anti-imperialist global armies, opted to join the Soviet camp. It also supported other Arab militaries to follow suit. Before the end of the Cold War, when most global armies could no longer choose between camps of superpowers, the Egyptian Army joined them in voluntary migration to the U.S. side. Many global and Middle Eastern armies also established business enterprises to overcome economic crises and budget cuts that they had to face with the post–Cold War global mass transition to the market economy. These businesses helped them maintain a superior status of power and control over their respective milieus and populations. The book draws comparisons between the Egyptian military and other Middle Eastern and global armies to detect patterns of transformation that they all shared and undertook in a parallel manner, which renders the Egyptian officers as no exception in the wider context.

Finally, the book argues that the Egyptian military's engagement in business and the bureaucracy was not simply to generate profit and amass resources. There is a Foucauldian twist to the story. By tapping into the consumerist markets of all social classes and governing their urban milieus, the officers managed to establish their constant surveillance over the population with an eye toward full control. The Egyptian military is a modern institution in a modern state. According to Michel Foucault's deconstruction of the modern state's mechanisms of power, this state developed the practice of closely observing the society in order to make it a disciplined and docile population. Foucault illustrates how the state adopted the model of a military camp, that is, of keeping a permanent gaze over the hierarchized dwellers of the camp, as a perfect structure in urban development, toward disciplinary control over every individual body.[4] In *Security, Territory, and Population*, Foucault indicates that the modern state aimed at structuring its urban institutions in the military camp's "panoptic" shape, which "basically involves putting someone in the center—an eye, a gaze, a principle of surveillance—who will be able to make its sovereignty function over all the individuals [placed] within this machine of power. To that extent we can say that the panopticon is the oldest dream of the oldest sovereign: None of my subjects can escape and none of their actions is unknown to me."[5] In the Egyptian case, the military institution that exercises state power by itself has turned the whole society into an infinite, long-lasting camp where everyday life is subjected to the officer's visible or invisible watch, yet with allegations of achieving security or guarding the nation.

In this introduction I embark on three tasks. The first is to *describe* the Egyptian military institution and historicize its edifice. The second is to *contextualize* it within its larger regional and global milieus, with their big theoretical questions, interpretive approaches, and common patterns of transformation. The third is to explain how this book plans to *scrutinize* it, and particularly what forms of conventional and unconventional sources it utilizes to carry out such a challenging mission.

Described

Briefly described, Egypt's military institution is a typical modern army that inherently carries legacies of its postcolonial structure, ideological choices, and the wars it fought in the twentieth century. It is a military that is considerably oversized, imposes compulsory conscription on hundreds of thousands of youth annually, enjoys a large budget, adopts an ultranationalistic rhetoric in its doctrine, and runs a sophisticated propaganda apparatus for continuous militarization of society. It is traditionally trained to engage in conventional wars and owns a large defense industry whose production is both for national consumption and for exportation abroad. It keeps a publicly unaccountable business empire whose secretive size and profits are unfeasible to estimate, and combines this with dominating the country's bureaucratic apparatus that facilitates this business.

In 2011 the Egyptian Army was ranked tenth largest in the world.[6] In 2015 it had 438,500 active personnel, 397,000 paramilitary forces, and 479,000 reservists. Although the Egyptian population conspicuously grew in the past three decades, almost doubling from around 50 million in 1985 to 90 million in 2015, the military did not seek to expand its size accordingly and remained largely at a fixed size during the past three decades. Active and reserve personnel together were about 3 percent of the population in 1986, and this fell to 1 percent in 2015. In the 1960s and 1970s the army became much larger when the military regime was involved in regional struggles, and it further increased in size during the 1967 and 1973 wars against Israel. It grew from 80,000 in the mid-1950s to 211,000 in 1968–69, and again to 325,000 in 1972–73 (see table 1).[7] Signing the peace treaty with Israel did not translate into reducing the number of active personnel. In fact, the Egyptian military grew larger in the early 1980s, but it maintained relatively fixed numbers during the following decades.

The organization is composed of commissioned officers and conscripted soldiers. The former are largely a professionalized, cohesive body with no sectarian, tribal, or ethnic factions. Cadets are trained and socialized in the academies of the main branches of the military: there are war, naval, air, military technical, and air defense colleges, as well as a recently opened medical school for military doctors.[8] Attending these military academies has been an important means of social mobility in Egyptian society since the colonial period. In the 1930s the sons of lower- and middle-class families were finally admitted to them next to those of aristocratic and bourgeois origins. As a result, the three military presidents who succeeded one another in ruling postcolonial Egypt—Nasser, Sadat, and Mubarak—all came from humble origins but climbed the social ladder after being accepted into military schools. In 2014 more than 92,000 students applied to military schools and institutes, but only 2,700 were admitted.[9] Young rejected applicants over the years have complained that nepotism and high bribes are integral to the admission process, but the director of the war college denies these claims.[10] The sons of the Sinai Peninsula's tribes were exceptionally excluded from admission for decades under Mubarak out of fear of their potential connection to terrorist groups.[11]

In addition to receiving education and training at home, commissioned officers are sent to study abroad. During the colonial period they went to Western countries, but the situation changed in the 1950s and 1960s as the Soviet Union became their destination instead. They switched back to the West in the late 1970s and now go to study for graduate degrees in U.S. military schools as part of the American military aid package to Egypt. For example, both President al-Sisi and Minister of Defense Subhi Sidqi studied in the U.S. Army War College in 2006. Based on their specialty, many other officers ended up in places such as the Marine Corps University or the Naval Postgraduate School to study for a year.

To keep the pyramidal structure of the institution, the Egyptian military dismisses a significant number of commissioned officers at the ranks of colonel and brigadier general in their early forties. It promotes only a small number into the ranks of major general, lieutenant general, and chief of staff, who in turn usually retire in their early fifties. Most of the latter are placed in civilian positions after retirement and receive both military pensions and high salaries in their new government jobs. Depending on the rank at which they leave service and the degree of loyalty to the leadership, an officer can receive anything from a prestigious position like a governorship to a middling bureaucratic position in, for example, public relations in a ministry. This generates income and class differences among officers who retire early and those who rise into higher ranks and receive civilian appointments afterward. However, the armed forces remain a highly monolithic bloc with an extensive degree of loyalty among active and retired officers because of the other perks that young and middle-aged officers enjoy and their high pensions after retirement.[12]

As for conscripts, their numbers are of course much larger than those of commissioned officers. Every young male Egyptian citizen between eighteen and thirty years old compulsorily serves in the military for a period of one to three years, based on his level of education. While college graduates must serve for one year, those with lower degrees of education serve for two or three years. After completing service, soldiers are placed on reserve lists for nine years. In 2015 the number of conscripts reached around 290,000–320,000 draftees out of the total of 438,500 military personnel, in addition to 325,000 allocated to the anti-riot paramilitary forces in the Ministry of Interior. The state expanded the draft to include large numbers of college graduates after the 1967 defeat and through fighting the 1973 war because of the army's need for their technical expertise. After the peace treaty was signed with Israel, a law in 1980 reduced service time to only one year for those who hold degrees from colleges and other higher institutions, and two to three years to holders of other lower degrees.[13] Aside from those, conscripts who are illiterate or barely educated are separately sent to the Ministry of Interior's Central Security Forces (CSF), the anti-riot paramilitary that Mubarak conspicuously enlarged in the 1980s. Generally all soldiers suffer from harsh conditions while in service, but those at CSF suffer the most, which led them to riot as well in 1986 (see table 1).

Conscripts have been used in military business enterprises as free or cheap labor. This practice started when Field Marshal Abdel-Halim Abu Ghazala, Egypt's minister of defense in the 1980s, deployed illiterate conscripts who were not "medically, culturally, technically, or psychologically fit" as free laborers in commercial activities such as farming and baking bread. Some local critics called these soldiers "slave labor."[14] But since the expansion of military business into large industries, draftees who hold higher technical degrees have been similarly used in factories, hotels, gas stations, hospitals, trading companies, and more.[15] "A conscript goes into the army less for training, and more for working in one of the military factories or business schemes," prominent economist Ahmed El-Naggar stated.[16] Their remarkably low monthly salaries were raised to between $34 and $35 in 2013.[17] It is worth mentioning here that many Egyptian youths have recently launched campaigns against compulsory conscription in which they criticize forced work at the military businesses, calling it "corvée labor" (a'mal sukhra) that wastes years of their lives without fair payment and under inhumane conditions.[18]

The Egyptian Army's budget is large and constantly increases. Right after the officers assumed power in 1952, defense expenditures consumed only 4.9 percent of the country's gross national product (GNP). In Nasser's first year as president in 1954–55, the percentage increased to 5.7, and it rose to 12.5 after the defeat in the 1967 war. Understandably it was very high in the 1970s—as much as 40 percent of government spending on the eve of signing the peace treaty—but this amount was immediately reduced to 22.5 percent after the peace accord of 1979. In the 1980s Mubarak maintained military expenditures at an average of 20 percent of all government expenditures. However, after liberalizing the economy and reducing public spending in the 1990s, he drastically reduced the level to an average of only 10 percent. The military faced more budget cuts after 2004, when Mubarak accelerated the pace of liberalization, until expenditures reached 6.1 percent in his final fiscal year in power. Although the percentage decreased after the 2011 uprisings to 4.9 percent of government spending in fiscal year 2015–16, the actual amount of money the military received from the public budget noticeably increased from that year onward. While it received LE25,397 billion ($4.4 billion) in fiscal year 2010–11, the amount rose to LE43,205 billion ($5.6 billion) in 2015–16 (see table 2).

The military doctrine of Egyptian officers has witnessed considerable shifts from one period to another, depending on who has been identified as the country's enemy. Under Nasser it was an offensive doctrine that viewed the capitalist West as the major enemy. After Sadat signed a peace treaty and became a U.S. ally, it switched to a defensive one with an internal rather than external focus. It changed again during the past few years to counterterrorism goals.

During the 1950s and 1960s, the period of decolonization and striving for political and economic independence from the West in the Arab world and the Third World at large, the Egyptian military adopted an Arab nationalist discourse combined with Soviet weapons and doctrine.[19] Signing a unilateral peace treaty with Israel and subsequently receiving an annual amount of $1.3 billion in military aid from the United States brought substantial change in the doctrine in response to U.S. requirements. The army ought to take Israel off the list of the country's enemies and focus on defensive armament and activities only. Engaging in civilian economic activities became part of its reorientation to internal affairs.

A major doctrinal shift took place in the 1980s. Field Marshal Abu Ghazala adopted a strong anticommunist and pro-U.S. rhetoric. For instance, he considered Qadhafi's Libya, then a Soviet ally, the first threat to Egypt and was on the verge of war with it. Israel was officially no longer identified as a foe in his statements. In addition, the security of other Arab states against external aggression continued to be part of the Egyptian military doctrine, but it was mainly the conservative, oil-producing Gulf states that were U.S. allies.[20] More important, as Abu Ghazala initiated large commercial enterprises, he perpetuated rhetoric about the army's new duty to assist with the state's developmental plans in the time of peace. Whenever he opened a new project for the army, he reiterated that such activities were designed to increase the armed forces' self-sufficiency as well as to help the government with pressing economic crises.[21] His successor, Field Marshal Hussein Tantawi, used the same discourse as he expanded the military business empire, emphasizing the army's contribution to economic development and the welfare of the lower classes.[22]

Another critical doctrinal shift took place in the past few years as a counterterrorism discourse was adopted. Although Islamic fundamentalism has been a main threat in the country since jihadists assassinated Sadat in 1981, the military did not amend its doctrine then to add fighting Islamic fundamentalism to it. Combating terrorism remained the duty of other security apparatuses, especially the Ministry of Interior. The United States pressured the Egyptian military to change its doctrine and adopt counterterrorism after September 11, 2001, but it strongly resisted the idea. The Egyptian Army insisted on continuing with its conventional training and procurement and did not clash in unconventional battles with terrorist groups domestically or regionally during Mubarak's years. However, as terrorist organizations proliferated in the Sinai Peninsula in the past few years and launched systematic attacks against soldiers there—especially after the Muslim Brothers were deposed from power in 2013—the Egyptian military had to officially put "eliminate extremism and terrorism" at the top of its agenda and change its rhetoric accordingly.[23] Satisfied with such change, the United States pledged to reorient military aid to Egypt toward armaments used to combat insurgency enclaves in Sinai.[24]

The Egyptian military continues to own the oldest, largest, and most advanced defense industry in the Arab world, although large parts of it were converted to civilian production. Egypt has twenty-five overt military factories: sixteen function under the Ministry of Military Production (MoMP) and nine under the Arab Organization for Industrialization (AOI). They were mostly built between the 1950s and the 1970s and were used to produce heavy ordnance. Egypt's arms industrial complex witnessed a golden age in the 1980s as it received enormous state support, obtained advanced technology from various sources, and made great profits from exports on the regional market.[25] But the factories' production declined, for various regional and domestic reasons, and now they mainly produce light weapons. One factory is still engaged in the coproduction of M1A1 tanks with the United States as part of an agreement initiated in the 1980s. These military industrial conglomerates partially converted to civilian manufacturing from the early 1990s onward. By 2011, 70 percent of AOI's production was for the civilian market, and the remaining 30 percent was still military. Meanwhile, 40 percent of the MoMP's outcomes were civilian, and the other 60 percent were still military.[26]

In terms of foreign procurement, the United States is the main source of weapons—sent in the form of military aid. For the two decades of the 1950s and 1960s, the Soviet Union and the Eastern bloc were the source of Egyptian arms. When Egypt severed its ties with the Soviet Union, switched alliances to the United States, and signed the peace treaty, it started to receive a constant and fixed annual flow of American military aid. In the beginning it was in the form of heavy loans, but these were later converted fully into grants. From 1986 onward Egypt has received an uninterrupted annual $1.3 billion in military aid from the United States. This includes sending Egypt F-16 fighter jets and Apache helicopters, and the coproduction of M1A1 tanks. It also includes training Egyptian officers in U.S. military schools. Most recently, when the United States suspended some aid shipments for a brief period after the army reseized power in 2013, al-Sisi successfully sought procurement from Russia and France. The United States has recently decided that grants would be redirected to send Egypt equipment mainly used in "counterterrorism, border security, Sinai security, and maritime security."[27]

One of the most frequently asked questions about the military business empire in Egypt involves its exact size: how many enterprises developed, how much profit they generate annually, and their proportion of the national economy. Because military enterprises are untaxed and unaudited by either the parliament or public accountability agencies and are not listed in the stock market with publicly open company profiles, it is almost impossible to estimate their precise number and gain access to their annual profit figures. Robert Springborg estimates their size to be anywhere between 5 and 40 percent of the country's economy and asserts that they make billions of dollars.[28] Economist Ahmed El-Naggar calculated them at only 1.8 percent in 2013. Al-Sisi also presented an estimate, asserting that they made up only 2 percent of the national economy in 2014.[29] Whereas the higher estimates take into consideration the military's formal and informal control over state land and other sectors, the lower estimates mostly depend on materially counting the visible commercial facilities that the military owns.

Generally, the military business enterprises that exist today fall under the umbrellas of eight different conglomerates and organizations: (1) the Ministry of Defense's (MoD) National Service Projects Organization (NSPO), which was created with the peace treaty in 1979, began engaging in civilian production during the 1980s, and now owns eleven gigantic firms with subsidiaries; (2) the MoMP, which was created in the 1950s and grew into a conglomerate of sixteen factories now involved in defense conversion; (3) the AOI, which was created in 1978 and has nine defense factories that have also been converted to civilian production; (4) the Engineering Authority of the Armed Forces (EAAF), which functions as a gigantic parastatal contractor for government and military construction projects; (5) the Maritime Industries and Services Organization (MISO), which owns four companies for shipbuilding and river transport; (6) the Department of Social Clubs and Hotels, which manages wedding halls, restaurants, cafes, and other facilities; (7) the Department of Medical Services of the Armed Forces, which builds and manages military hospitals admitting civilians for fees; and (8) the Armed Forces' Land Projects Organization (AFLPO), which uses military-owned land in construction projects. Furthermore, the military informally placed its hand over quarries.

It is similarly impossible to reach an exact number for how many ex-officers occupy civilian positions in the state's labyrinthian bureaucratic apparatus. Whereas some retired generals are appointed in top and visible positions, others occupy hidden locations inside the numerous offices of the country's mammoth bureaucracy. Generally, each corps in the armed forces dominated high appointments in a certain sector of civil service that may or may not have matched its expertise. Generals originally coming from the ground forces in the army, such as infantry, artillery, and air defense corps, were mostly appointed as governors. Meanwhile, ex–navy rear admirals and admirals swept positions as heads of ports, as well as government authorities of maritime navigation and safety, and chaired relevant state-owned companies. Military engineers flooded the ministry of housing and its various authorities responsible for distributing state land or building affordable housing. Finally, ex–air force pilots controlled the sector of civil aviation, all the way from the seat of the minister to the heads of relevant authorities and holding companies. In mid-2012 a group of young revolutionaries created a Google map locating workplaces where officers occupied civilian or business positions and managed to identify 447 locations at top and medium administrative levels in Cairo and across provincial areas.[30]

Finally, for propaganda purposes in and outside the armed forces, the Egyptian military keeps a public relations body called the Department of Morale Affairs. It is a typical modern army's propaganda apparatus that deploys media to disseminate messages for mass mobilization purposes. It funds the production of popular songs and documentaries that glorify and celebrate the heroic actions of the army during times of war and peace. Mubarak appointed a former director of this department to be the head of the Cairo Opera House in the early 2000s.[31] Right after deposing Mubarak, the ruling officers appointed a member of this department to run state-owned television and radio.[32] Moreover, the department today persistently appears on the public scene by filling the country's streets with gigantic billboards displaying kind-looking yet strong officers, producing patriotic songs, and making videos to encourage citizens to vote in elections. Most recently the department took charge of producing videos about the officers' heroic efforts to counter terrorism in Sinai and displaying scenes from their operations.[33]

Contextualized

When a group of young officers took over power in Egypt in 1952, their movement was part of an already growing trend of military coups d'état in the Middle East. After World War I and throughout the Cold War era, Arab and Middle Eastern soldiers led numerous coups that they often labeled as nationalist revolutions. They either targeted European colonial or conservative postcolonial administrations to replace them with republics or overthrew one another to replace one military regime with another. In the period between the 1940s and the 1980s the region witnessed about fifty-five coups or coup attempts.[34] Although Israel saw no officer takeover after its independence, its army already played such a pervasive role in the civilian arena that the country was dubbed a "nation-in-arms."[35] Coups resulted in placing the Turkish Army above civilian governments and gave birth to famous pan-Arab military autocrats such as Nasser in Egypt, Assad in Syria, and Qadhafi in Libya. Military leaders presented themselves as "guardians" of their newly born nation-states, and ruling armies assumed themselves "vehicles of modernization" in society. In a Cold War context, most Arab military regimes opted for socialism to reach this dream of modernization, whereas states like Turkey and Israel stayed on the Western side. Eventually the number of coups declined in the 1980s, especially after military autocrats consolidated power.[36]

Early literature on Middle Eastern armies highlighted the age, socioeconomic background, ideological underpinnings, and radical reform policies of officers who formed regimes. Inspired by the charismatic officer Mustafa Kemal Ataturk, generations of young Arab officers would follow the Turkish model of military guardians and modernizers of the independent nation and the rule of a "benevolent despot." Their leadership mostly came from middle- to lower-middle-class backgrounds or the petite bourgeoisie. They originally had various ideological orientations, from the far left to the far right, but agreed on adopting the rhetoric of social justice on issues such as agrarian reform and adhered to secular nationalism.[37] Later literature classified the Turkish officers and their Egyptian fellows among those military elites that undertook "revolutions from above," similar to others in Japan and Peru. Although they seized power without mass mobilization, their actions went beyond simple coup d'états. Their "military bureaucrats" embarked on top-down revolutionary reforms uprooting the ancien régimes.[38] Generally in Third World countries during this period, societies sought development, and military institutions posed as the most organized, educated, and technologically advanced agents to carry out such a task.[39]

Middle Eastern armies were surrounded by similar experiences in other Third World regions during the Cold War era. Latin American militaries also occasionally undertook coups that installed ruling juntas and formed authoritarian regimes.[40] In colonial and postcolonial Latin American states, militaries intervened in politics as the "saviors" of their nations as early as the nineteenth century. Generals and colonels claimed to be neutral arbiters of political conflicts between civilians, especially in times of civil war. In the 1960s and 1970s a wave of military coups took place in South America, giving birth to dictatorial regimes that repressively governed through the 1980s. During the Cold War, as opposed to Arab military regimes that chose the socialist side, Latin American military juntas ruling countries such as Brazil, Argentina, Peru, Chile, Guatemala, and Bolivia received U.S. support in order to contain or fight communism. Comparing Latin America and Turkey in particular, David Pion-Berlin argues that the militaries of these two regions "intervened in defense of common propositions: that the armed forces are guardians of their nations; that only they can judge how, whether or when the nation's core values and interest have been endangered. Militaries in Latin America and Turkey have a self-inflated sense of their own historical worth, reinforced by feelings of professional superiority over civilian leaders." Pion-Berlin points out parallel change in civil-military relations in the two regions in the 2000s, after a wave of democratization pushed the new generation of officers to keep to the barracks, submit to civilian control, and focus more on security duties.[41]

From the viewpoint of Samuel Huntington, none of these Middle Eastern militaries could qualify as "professional" institutions. Professionalism for Huntington simply meant civilian control over the army and the nonintervention of officers in politics. A professional officer corps should acquire specialized expertise, act responsibly, and enjoy corporateness or a sense of unity. It should keep political neutrality, with clear separation between the military and the civilian government.[42] Revisionists of Huntington's traditional view insist that it is mainly derived from the American model of civil-military relations and ignores other political cultures. Rebecca Schiff asserts that in non-Western states, civil-military relations are not always based on full separation between the soldier and the civilian. Rather, institutional and cultural conditions might encourage or obstruct officers' intervention in politics based on the agreement and harmony between three partners: the military, the political elite, and the citizenry. Schiff has developed this vision into the "concordance theory" and applies it to Israel with commendable insight. She argues that "the military institutional and cultural influence over Israeli society is so great that the entire concept of civil is inappropriately applied to this nation." In Israel, officials undertake military and political duties interchangeably, army officers affect politics without a need for coups, there is a lack of parliamentary authority over the security sector, and officers retire early to find second careers in the government or private organizations.[43]

Egypt is part of a region where societies are mostly tainted by manifest "militarism." The militarization of a nation could take various forms and shades. Describing the Turkish case, Ayşe Gül Altınay defines militarism as

> a set of ideas and structures that glorify "practices and norms associated with militaries." In this sense, militarization is "a step-by-step process by which a person or a thing gradually comes to be controlled by the military *or* comes to depend for its well-being on militaristic ideas." Militarization is successful when it achieves a discourse of "normalcy" in public discussions surrounding the power of the military in civilian life, politics, economics, and people's self-understandings. . . . Militarism is an ideology that has become intertwined with nationalism, as well as militarization is a process that *shapes* culture, politics, and identities in Turkey.[44]

Through a focus on universal male conscription, Altınay investigates intimate links between nationalism, military service, and images of good citizenship in Turkey from the early formative years of the republic through the 1990s. She deconstructs the discourse of the Turkish nation as a "military-nation," where state ideology established compulsory service for young men as a cultural practice for the ideal citizen. Society was indoctrinated into such ideology through education and obligatory textbooks. The public accepted the idea of the military-nation as a cultural given. In addition, Altınay explains that as women are not conscripted, masculinity became an integral component of nationalism.[45]

The process of militarizing the Israeli nation does not differ much.[46] Baruch Kimmerling argues that "Israeli militarism tends to serve as one of the *central organizations principles* of the society." He identifies three general dimensions of militarism and indicates that they could exist separately or be combined to shape various patterns of militarization. The first is the violent-force dimension, which is formed when the military takes power to rule directly or indirectly for a long period of time using coercive force. The generals build a form of legitimacy that a sufficient segment of society collectively perceives as unproblematic and self-evident. The second is the cultural dimension, which relies on persuasion rather than coercion. The armed forces pose as a symbol of the collective identity, and the masses are engulfed by ceremonial practices celebrating the disciplined soldier. The third is the cognitive dimension, in which the civilian elite and populace alike internalize the priorities of the military as the crucial political and social needs of the whole country. This is a situation of "civilian militarism," where the cultural and institutional state of mind is tuned toward continuous preparation for war. When the three dimensions are combined, the military prevails over weak civilian institutions and penetrates all "social and state networks, such as bureaucracy, economy, education, and culture. . . . The military prohibits the existence of an autonomous civilian society." [47] Kimmerling sees Israel as a case of "civilian militarism," where civilians are voluntarily oriented for constant military preparedness. Recent literature detects social attitudes breaking this long-established militarism in Israel. For instance, many youth no longer take compulsory conscription as an unconditional duty for the nation. There is a "motivation crisis" that has put pressure on the Israel Defense Force (IDF) to revise its recruitment and socialization methods to draw interest in service again.[48]

Models of militarism were originally set in Western states during the first half of the twentieth century, with Nazi Germany as the roughest illustration. Militarism disappeared from today's Europe but has come back to the United States, as recent literature indicates. The prolonged Cold War followed by the war on terrorism and the invasion of Iraq have generated a shade of militarization in American society. Chalmers Johnson indicates:

> The onset of militarism is commonly marked by three broad indicators that suggest its presence. First is the emergence of a professional military class and the subsequent glorification of its ideals. This began to occur in the U.S. after the Vietnam War. . . . The second is the preponderance of military officers or representatives of the arms industry as officials of state policy. During 2001, the administration of George W. Bush filled many of the chief American diplomatic posts with militarists, including the secretary of state. . . . The third . . . is devotion to policies in which military preparedness becomes the highest priority for the state. . . . There is no nation that has the capability to challenge the United States military. [49]

Alluding to the invasion of Iraq and its aftermath, Andrew Bacevich asserts, "Americans in our own time have fallen prey to militarism, manifesting itself in a romanticized view of soldiers, a tendency to see military power as the truest measure of national greatness, and outsized expectations regarding the efficacy of force. To a degree without precedent in U.S.

history, Americans have come to define the nation's strength and well-being in terms of military preparedness, military action, and the fostering of (or nostalgia for) military ideals."[50]

When the Egyptian officers decided to establish a business empire, their move was part of a larger global trend that made its way to the Middle East. By the end of the Cold War, authoritarian regimes that were once socialists transformed their economies into neoliberal markets, and their military institutions ventured into economic activities for profit. Whether in Russia and Eastern European states or in Asia and Latin America, economic reform plans required substantial cuts in government spending, including military budgets. To compensate the officers for budgetary losses and avoid potential coups d'état, authoritarian regimes allowed their armies to engage in legal or illicit business activities. Military business, or "Milbus" as it is called by Jörn Brömmelhörster and Wolf-Christian Paes, emerged when international financial institutions (IFIs) and the donor community pushed governments transforming to the market economy to adhere to more conservative fiscal policies. But fearing security threats or officer mutiny, many of these governments sustained their sizable armies with their old large budget by hiding military expenditures in "a complex web of budgetary and off-budgetary transactions, often incorporating elements of military business." Brömmelhörster and Paes add that Milbus globally could be anything from producing medicine in China and shrimp in Honduras to running airlines in Ecuador, ferries in Indonesia, hotels in Southeast Asia, or banks in Pakistan.[51]

Investigating the Pakistani case, Aisha Siddiqa defines Milbus as "military capital that is used for the personal benefit of the military fraternity, especially the officer cadre, but is neither recorded nor part of defense budget." Both the officers and their clients from the economic and political elite benefit from it, with few challenges from civil society.[52] Comparing Pakistan to China and El Salvador, Kristina Mani explains: "Military entrepreneurs are doubly powerful: not only do they have a near monopoly on the state's power of coercion, but they are also stakeholders in lucrative nonmarket enterprises run with minimum oversight from government officials or society at large." She illuminates that military entrepreneurs "follow the market" instead of resisting it; they are capable of adjusting to the market conditions, survive economic and political shifts, and achieve "durability."[53]

Several Arab armies started to invest in the civilian sector in the 1980s. They attempted to build on the 1950s and 1960s legacy and infrastructure of their defense industries. For example, Saddam Hussein's military industry in Iraq produced for the civilian market items such as electronics, pesticides, plastic, and engines.[54] Philippe Droz-Vincent argues that the organizational abilities and technical expertise of the Arab armies allowed them to transform into successful entrepreneurs. However, he describes them as "parasitic" businessmen who know the rules of the game and how to manipulate the market to gain monopolistic privileges in crucial sectors. "In other words, the military knows how to make use of its comparative advantages, such as the cheap manpower of its conscripts, its access to technology and highly qualified civilian engineers, its heavy equipment infrastructure, its privileges (e.g., disguised subsidies, tax exemptions, and absolute financial autonomy), its monopolistic rights to produce goods of strategic interest, and its sheer size, which enables it to alter market conditions and circumvent regulations."[55]

Syria was an important case. Hafiz al-Assad allowed fellow officers from his own Alawite sect to assume an elite stratum in the army. The army was anyway inseparable from his Baath ruling party. Despite his anti-Western rhetoric, Assad did undertake market reform policies from the 1980s onward. Thus he allowed the officers to profit in order to maintain their loyalty to the regime, and he distorted the market in order to support military business activities. The Syrian military not only received around 30 percent of the state budget but also created economic organizations that established semimonopolies over fields such as construction, agricultural production, and manufacturing. Compared to the Egyptian military, the Syrian Army invested in basic and less technologically sophisticated industries.[56] Frank Mora and Quintan Wiktorowicz note that military business could happen at either an institutional or an individual level, and Syrian officers practiced it more individually for immediate personal and family profit. They assert that "unlike China and Cuba, most military involvement in economic activities [in Syria] was at the level of *individuals* rather than institutions. . . . Several hundred officers with personal connections to the regime used their relationships to evade regulations, garner favors, and generate vast personal wealth." [57]

Under the regime of officer Ali Abdullah Saleh in Yemen, a tribally composed army heavily engaged in business. Saleh's military functioned through a patronage network at whose center were loyal officers from the president's Zaydi clan in the North. Before unification of the North and the South in 1990, the armed forces enjoyed economic influence in Saleh's northern state. After the brief civil war of 1994 in which Saleh militarily triumphed over the South, his armed forces penetrated into more sources of wealth across the country. Yemen's Military Economic Corporation (MECO) was originally created in the 1980s to supply the army with boots, uniforms, and foodstuffs, but it quickly established control over civilian sectors such as real estate, import licenses, and oil. When Saleh applied economic liberalization policies and privatization in the 1990s, the military conglomerate changed its name to the Yemeni Economical Corporation (YECO). Adam Seitz indicates that it seized southern privatized companies and expanded its activities into the private sector, in fields from agricultural production and construction to pharmaceuticals. It was a main player in the "tribal-military-commercial complex" of Saleh's regime.[58]

The Turkish military initiated its business activities long before its Arab counterparts did the same. The powerful military institution led several coups to protect the Kemalist republic against leftists and Islamists alike, until the latter finally took over power in the 2000s. During the decades in which the Turkish military enjoyed absolute superiority over civilian politics, it amassed a large budget and expanded a sophisticated arms industry. It started its investments in the civilian sector after the 1960 coup and has expanded them with the neoliberal transitions in the country since the 1980s. It continued to do so under AKP's Islamist form of neoliberalism in the 2000s, despite losing absolute political hegemony. Through its holding company called the Armed Forces Trust and Pension Fund (OYAK), the Turkish military is engaged in numerous economic activities. OYAK was founded in 1961, and it has grown into one of the five biggest business conglomerates in the country. İsmet Akça argues that through its own business ventures, the Turkish military has been totally integrated into the neoliberal market. In Turkey's "capitalist-militarist structure," OYAK's "investments are concentrated in the automotive, cement, and iron-steel industries and are also distributed across the following sectors: finance, energy, mining, agricultural, chemicals, food, construction, transportation-logistics, domestic foreign trade, private security, technology-IT, and tourism."[59]

Iran has a more complicated narrative in this regard. Iran's Islamic Revolutionary Guards Corps (IRGC) developed an "economic empire" with gigantic investment conglomerates in civilian sectors in the 1990s and 2000s. This process took place as the postrevolutionary Islamic regime ideologically shifted from the left to economic liberalism and applied a privatization policy under both reformist and conservative presidents. Kevan Harris argues that Iran experienced a pseudo-privatization process in which the ownership of state-owned enterprises was transferred to "parastatal" organizations, which are run as private firms but undertake public projects funded by the government. IRGC is one hegemonic owner of these parastatals. For instance, its Khatam al-Anbia Construction Base is a domineering contractor taking charge of major infrastructure projects for the state such as developing oil and gas fields, highways, and tunnels, but it also engages in its own private business with local and foreign companies.[60] While Harris asserts that IRGC's economic might does not translate into absolute political influence, as Western media perpetuates, Ali Alfoneh insists on the opposite. Alfoneh argues that its business empire and intervention in domestic politics turned the state from a theocracy to a military dictatorship.[61] Next to IRGC, the paramilitary volunteer militia known as Basij participates in profitable business. Saeid Golkar argues that the Basij is "paramilitarizing" the Iranian economy. For example, he traces its formal and legally operated enterprises in banking, tourism, construction, manufacturing, import/export activities, and more.[62]

Israel's globally famed military-industrial complex also ventures into civilian business. The Israeli defense industry is mainly concentrated in two conglomerates: Israeli Military Industries (IMI) and Israeli Aerospace Industries (IAI). Although the two are public companies and not owned by the IDF, individual officers benefit from them as "there is a 'revolving door' through which former officers pass from staff positions in the armed forces to executive roles in the arms companies." By the 1980s Israel's arms industry was already "the largest and most sophisticated outside the industrialized countries," which rendered the state "the largest Third World arms exporter."[63] Alex Mintz asserted that Israel's national economy then came to depend on the defense industry. "More than 40% of the labor force, about 30% of the exports, and some 18% of the total income of commercial government corporations originate in the defense sphere."[64] By the late 2000s the country's arms exports reached $6 billion per year, but military expenditure declined to around 6 percent of Israel's GDP.[65] Facing budget cuts and a shrinking arms market, the Israeli defense industry adapted part of its research for civilian products. The country's boom in high-tech industries is based on civilian applications of military technology.[66] Interestingly, in 2015 the government started privatizing IMI by selling up to 90 percent of its shares to foreign investors. As part of a recent accelerated wave of privatization, the government also plans to sell IAI.[67]

About a decade before the Arab Spring, Mehran Kamrava drew a typology of civil-military relations in the Middle East that identified four categories in the region. The first existed in tribal monarchies that own oil, namely, Arab Gulf states such as Saudi Arabia, UAE, and Bahrain. They kept small armies owing to their small populations but recruited foreign soldiers to serve for high financial rewards and purchased sophisticated weapons from Western countries. Within such a model, officer mutiny was very unlikely. Under the same type existed less affluent monarchies whose legitimacy is based on historical "civic myths," namely, Jordan and Morocco. Their armies are highly loyal to the king, benefit from his effort to professionalize them, and receive prestigious perks. The second type existed in authoritarian states led by "officer-politicians" or officers who turned into civilians and depended on security apparatuses to keep control. This included Egypt, Syria, Yemen, Algeria, Sudan, Tunisia, and the Palestinian Authority (PA). Leaders of these states observed complicated relations with their armed forces, full of fear of the return of coups and officer perks. The third type was found in states with "dual" militaries—a regular army and ideologically indoctrinated paramilitaries and militias affiliated with the ruling elite—namely, Iran, Iraq, and Libya. The fourth was found in "military democracies," that is, Israel and Turkey. They are democratic systems but with politically dominant militaries.[68]

Ten years later, on the eve of the Arab Spring, this typology witnessed significant change. First, the U.S. invasion of Iraq led to complete dismantling of the Iraqi Army of Saddam Hussein and persecuting its Baathist officers. In Israel, the second Intifada that erupted in 2000, Hamas's victory in elections and formation of the government, and subsequent wars in Gaza increased the militarism in state and society. In Turkey, the Islamists finally seized full political power through repeatedly sweeping elections, and the ruling Islamist party, AKP, marginalized the military in politics. It even put many generals on trial because of old interventions and allegedly a new coup attempt. AKP swept three consecutive elections between 2002 and 2011, and the success of its neoliberal policies and attempts to join the European Union (EU) made it difficult for the military to retain its decades-long political supremacy in the Turkish republic. In Iran, the economic and political influence of IRGC increased vis-à-vis the regular army, and its economic domination and influence over various elections grew. Finally, in Egypt, Mubarak's plan for the political succession of his son led him to tremendously increase the privileges of generals and ex-generals in the state apparatuses and the economy.

Again a decade before the Arab Spring, many authoritarian regimes in the region adopted "coup-proofing" strategies to prevent potential renewal of coups d'état.[69] As Holger Albrecht lists, such strategies included three main tactics:

> the establishment of strong personal loyalty between officers and incumbents through ethnic, religious and personal bonds; divided security apparatus, pitting regular armed forces against militias and special security forces; the frequent rotation of officers to avoid emergence of alternative power centers; and buying off the officer corps by granting them economic privileges and opportunities for self-enrichment.[70]

In Syria, for example, Hafiz al-Assad depended on the loyalty of the 'Alawite officers in the army who came from his own minority religious sect. In addition, Assad kept a mixture of parallel militaries, which he played against each other for his security. In Iraq, Saddam survived on the loyalty of officers from his hometown of Tikrit and from those affiliated with his ruling Baath Party, in addition to the loyalty of some Sunni tribal groups. Besides the regular army, he formed the Republican Guard and the Presidential Guard, and the latter's job particularly was to protect the regime from the other two forces. The kings of Saudi Arabia secured the loyalty of the al-Saud family and other tribes to sustain the monarchical system. They kept three parallel armies: a regular army, the National Guard to protect oil production in the Shi'i-populated province in the East, and the Royal Guard to protect the house of Saud. All three countries kept special security forces, such as the notoriously oppressive *mukhabarat* or intelligence agencies of Assad and Saddam, and the religious police forces in Saudi Arabia. All three also granted extensive perks to officers.[71] Mubarak's Egypt was believed by many scholars to be coup-proofed, but the events of 2011 proved otherwise.[72]

Once the Arab Spring uprisings hit in January 2011, these coup-proofing strategies proved of little use as the autocrats had hoped in serious times of trouble.[73] In many Arab states that witnessed mass protests, the armed forces either sided with the protesters or responded to them in a myriad of chaotic ways, and in other cases they bloodily crushed them. Historically, the way in which the military responds to a revolutionary movement is crucial and decisive for its success or failure. Zoltan Barany asserts, "The army's response is far from the *only* predictor of whether a revolution will succeed in supplanting the status quo regime. Yet the military's backing of or at least neutrality toward the revolution is a *necessary* condition for revolutionary success." Generally, the army's response is motivated by complicated factors, including the military's own attributes and composition; the state structure and the place of the army within it; the society and its relation to the armed forces; and surrounding international conditions.[74]

When the Arab Spring protests started in Tunisia, the Tunisian Army's behavior toward the protesters formed an ideal model for civil–military relations in the region. The country's autocrat, Zayn al-'Abidin Bin 'Ali, was a former army officer and minister of interior at the time he seized power in a smooth coup in 1987. During the 2011 protests he asked the military to help the police repressively end the chaos, but officers abstained from taking action. Instead, they sided with the peaceful protesters. Hicham Bou Nassif argues that such behavior was due to an existing tradition of officer respect for the republican culture and civilian rule in Tunisia. More important, Bin 'Ali had already alienated the army within the structure of his authoritarian state as opposed to the powerful police forces, which rendered the military less of a stakeholder in saving the regime.[75] Mass protests went to Egypt next, where the military reacted in a slightly different way. It also sided with the protesters to depose a former officer, but only to later install another, younger officer in his seat.

Protests reached Libya in their following stop, against the aging military dictator Qadhafi. The reaction of the military here took bloody directions. Derek Lutterbeck explains that Qadhafi's military was highly politicized, patrimonial, fragmented, and tribally based. Qadhafi kept a regular army and multiple other security agencies for his own protection. The commanders of the elite units in the regular army were Qadhafi's close relatives, including his own sons. Other security forces were the Revolutionary Committees, the Revolutionary Guards, and the People's Guards—all commanded by members of Qadhafi's tribe and his relatives. As soon as protests erupted, many officers defected and joined the opposition. But the loyal units fiercely fought bloody battles against the armed rebels for many months. NATO airstrikes finally ended the war, and the rebels humiliatingly murdered Qadhafi.[76]

When Syria's protests erupted, Hafiz al-Assad's civilian son, Bashar, had been ruling the country for a decade by relying on notorious security apparatuses. Initially, the protesters were peaceful youth and oppositional groups, which the regime's multiple military forces brutally crushed with the help of armed civilian thugs or *shabbiha*. But the Syrian Army did not remain intact in the process, as a large number of officers defected and joined the opposition to form the Free Syrian Army (FSA). Islamists soon entered the revolutionary scene, which turned it into a highly militarized, sectarian conflict between the army of the 'Alawite president and militias of Sunni jihadists who are funded by conservative regional actors such as Qatar and Saudi Arabia—with the latter shortly creating the notorious Islamic State in Iraq and the Levant (ISIL). The Lebanese Shi'i militia of Hezbollah joined Assad's remaining troops and Iran backed them, which soon rendered the Syrian revolution a sectarian civil war of the 'Alawite and Sunni jihadists with external or foreign fighters and funds on both sides.[77]

Yemen's Arab Spring similarly turned into a sectarian civil war. When peaceful protests erupted against former officer and long-dictator Saleh, his loyalists in the armed forces harshly repressed protesters. In one incident they stormed into a university campus and fired at random at students camping in a sit-in. Although Saleh was removed after suffering an assassination attempt, his army was part of the postrevolutionary arrangements. His elected successor, Abd-Rabbu Mansour Hadi, was an ex-general and Saleh's vice president. He allied himself with Yemen's Muslim Brothers, a conservative Sunni group whose political domination angered the Shi'ite Houthis in the North. The Houthis invaded Sanaa and other major cities to seize power, in alliance with Saleh and the remnants of his tribally based army. Thus another sectarian civil war erupted with profound external interventions. On the one hand, Saudi Arabia militarily supported Hadi and the brotherhood through airstrikes and ground operations, and on the other, Iran supported the Houthis.[78]

In Arab Spring states where protesters did not succeed in removing the rulers, the military played decisive roles in terminating unrest. In the small, oil-producing kingdom of Bahrain, the armed forces are commanded by members from the al-Khalifa royal family and composed of the loyal tribes. Although Shi'a make up the majority of the country's population, the Sunni royal family excluded them from military service and other security agencies. Instead, al-Khalifas recruited foreign soldiers, especially those with a Sunni background, who received high salaries and perks and were granted Bahraini citizenship. The Shi'i majority suffered from general marginalization. Thus it was mainly Shi'i youth who initiated the protests in early 2011.

In response, the army and other forces engaged in bloody clashes with protestors, killing and injuring many. Saudi Arabia and United Arab Emirates (UAE) sent troops to assist the Bahraini security forces in the process.[79]

Meanwhile, Algeria's military regime entirely escaped the Arab Spring. Throughout its postcolonial history, Algeria has been ruled by a class of nationalist warriors who fought in the war of independence against the French. Officers took over power through either coups or elections and applied socialism. When they liberalized the economy and democratized it, Islamists swept elections and a civil war erupted in 1992, when the army canceled elections and violently clashed with Islamists. Ex-officer Abdelaziz Bouteflika was elected president in 1999 and successfully embarked on a reconciliation process that ended the civil war. When the Arab Spring uprisings hit the neighboring states, small protests did emerge in Algeria. However, Bouteflika's long-reigning regime quickly used its rich oil resources to appease public demands. In addition, the recent memories of the violent civil war discouraged most Algerians from joining a regional wave in which Islamists were prominent.[80]

Thus after many decades of major transformations and calamities experienced by Middle Eastern armies, the Egyptian Army remains among the most powerful in the region. More important, it still exists, unimpaired, with its vast business empire and full control over the state, when many of its Arab counterparts are either no longer around or fundamentally fractured and devoid of political supremacy after recent shaking waves of unrest.

Scrutinized

Mainly owing to an acute dilemma of sources, published literature on the Egyptian military institution has been scarce over the past few decades. Studying Egyptian and Arab armies at large was a popular topic when military coups were repeatedly occurring between the 1940s and 1970s, but research in this area declined with the gradual disappearance of this phenomenon. Furthermore, the secretive nature of the Egyptian Army's structure and economic activities and the lack of transparency in its official records have rendered a systematic scrutinization of the institution unfeasible for a long period. For instance, Robert Springborg published the last English monograph covering the Egyptian Army and its economic interests in 1989, and Ahmad Abd Allah edited the last Arabic volume on relevant topics in

1990.[81] Almost two decades later, in 2007, Steven Cook updated the field by undertaking a comparative study on the militaries of Egypt, Turkey, and Algeria.[82] After the 2011 uprisings Hazem Kandil published a new book on the ruling officers, with a chief focus on Nasser's period.[83]

Nevertheless, the paucity of sources witnessed a considerable breakthrough after January 2011. The months that followed the uprisings saw a rare moment of opening wide windows for public criticism of the ruling officers owing to their oppressive handling of protests and overall mismanagement of the fluid political scene. An exceptional moment of openness in media and social networks materialized for a brief period, with an unprecedented number of journalists and the masses alike seizing their freedom of expression. Printed newspapers during this period took great advantage of the revolutionary influx and published endless stories undermining existing journalistic taboos on subjects such as the military budget and business profit. Discontented youth, workers, government employees, and local communities all created Facebook pages or YouTube channels to voice their grievances against old and new hegemonic officers. This led to an unrestricted publishing of a wealth of critical information necessary to decipher the clandestine realities of the Egyptian military. This book capitalizes on this fortune of information to unearth evidence on long-hidden matters such as the army's civilian business and relevant repression of workers. Heavily relying on postrevolutionary printed press and online social media records, as well as a wide range of conventional archival sources, the book attempts to reconstruct the enigmatic history of the Egyptian military institution. Recollecting voices of dissent, it mainly scrutinizes the army's economic means of militarizing the nation.

Thus this book utilizes conventional and unconventional primary material. It relies principally on published Arabic material and purposely avoids oral accounts and cites a limited number of interviews. In terms of conventional sources, it uses memoirs of officers; speeches; published interviews with upper-echelon officers; government documents such as the state budget; military companies' profiles, pamphlets, and websites; verdicts of the Cassation Court; laws and decrees; constitutional texts; and newspapers such as the state-owned *al-Ahram*, the leftist *al-Ahali*, and the independent *al-Masry al-Youm*. It also uses English archival sources such as U.S. congressional records on military aid to Egypt, U.S. Government Accountability Office (GAO) records, the U.S. Army War College online library, and archives of the *New York Times*. As for unconventional sources, it draws analysis from novels, popular television series, movies, songs, and so on. It also collects published narratives on social media, especially Facebook and YouTube, where various social groups voiced their old and new grievances against generals and ex-generals after 2011.

Conducting interviews with officers, workers at military businesses, or employees in government entities that ex-officers run was not always feasible —especially given that the army classifies the sites of its civilian production and services as "secretive military zones." I obtained an exceptional interview with Lieutenant General Hamdi Wahiba, former chief of staff and head of the manufacturing conglomerate AOI, as well as interviews with striking workers at some of his factories. In reaction to a series of articles I published in Egyptian newspapers covering stories of alleged corruption in the twelve factories of AOI—which are engaged in both civilian and military manufacturing—Wahiba invited me to visit the headquarters of the organization to speak to him and other top officials and granted me access to two of its plants in the outskirts of Cairo to interview workers.[84] Furthermore, I traveled to Upper Egyptian provinces in the South, where retired officers occupy numerous governmental positions and dominate key economic sectors, and interviewed members of local communities and private businesses harmed by military economic hegemony. As mentioned, this book relies to a minimum extent on oral accounts because of its sensitive subject and the risks involved in citing undocumented data.

Each of the five chapters that follow explores a different historical period and relies on a set of primary sources unique to the period. Chapter 1 covers the 1950s to the 1970s, when a group of young officers embarked on a "revolution from above." The chapter argues that the first military regime in the country maintained a system of "socialism without socialists." The charismatic leader of this regime, Nasser, built a socialist state, and his successor, Sadat, fully reversed it back into the market economy. The chapter portrays how, under heavily securitized state capitalism, the regime used the system of a single ruling party to constantly observe and tightly control the factory workforce, the cooperative, public office, the syndicate, and so forth. The discussion relies on published memoirs of Free Officers representing different political stances and ideological backgrounds, such as Muhammad Naguib, Khalid Muhi al-Din, Abd al-Latif al-Baghdadi, and Ali Sabri. It also uses archives of state-owned newspapers and magazines, such as *al-Jumhuriyya*. It draws on books authored by Nasser and Sadat, especially Nasser's *Falsafat al-Thawra* and Sadat's *al-Bahth 'an al-Dhat*. It utilizes available interviews with civilian bureaucrats in the cabinets of Nasser and Sadat. These primary records are supplemented by secondary sources written by scholars who were contemporaries of this period, such as Majid Khadduri, Anouar Abdel-Malek, Samir Amin, and Robert Springborg. Moreover, it uses novels, movies, and television series to deconstruct the images that different social classes maintained about their socialist and liberalizing ruling officers.

Chapter 2 covers the 1980s, or the first ten years of the country's third military president, Mubarak. These are the years when Mubarak's charismatic minister of defense, Field Marshal Abu Ghazala, initiated the army's business empire. The Egyptian Army then enjoyed the "good 1980s," with open access to U.S. arms, Arabian Gulf markets, and large profits from civilian enterprises. Taking advantage of the open market (*infitah*) state policies, the Egyptian military continued practicing its methods of war—the already finished war—within peacetime urbanities. It created gigantic parastatal business entities that securitized consumer goods and public services. Abu Ghazala was the almighty mastermind behind this winning battle, but he lost his career to "politics of scandals." The chapter relies on the archival dossier of Abu Ghazala titled *al-Malaff al-Watha'iqi li-l-Mushir Muhammad 'Abd al-Halim Abu Ghazala*, compiled by *al-Ahram*, and published interviews with the field marshal. It also relies on laws and decrees issued to establish economic privileges for the army in land acquisition and tax breaks. It utilizes the archives of the leftist newspaper *al-Ahali,* which scrutinized the army's economic interests. For issues of American military aid, the chapter draws on U.S. congressional records and the archives of the *New York Times, Washington Post*, and other Western newspapers. Moreover, it uses novels such as Sonalla Ibrahim's *Zaat* and television series such as *Layali al-Hilmiyya*. Two indispensable secondary sources for this period are Robert Springborg's *Mubarak's Egypt* and Ahmed Abd Allah's *al-Jaysh wa-l-Dimuqratiyya fi Misr*.

Chapter 3 covers the rise of a class of "neoliberal officers" and the mammoth expansion of the military business enterprises during the 1990s and 2000s. It traces how the Egyptian military converted large parts of its defense industry into civilian manufacturing and added vast new business enterprises to them. It follows the birth of those neoliberal officers amid the country's full transformation into the market economy, and it argues that they did not necessarily believe in the dicta of the free market but took advantage of it to build military institutions' business empire. It investigates how they made big money in partnership with local and foreign capital, while seizing privatized public-sector enterprises, appropriating immense plots of land, enjoying tax breaks, ignoring labor rights, and generally functioning above public accountability. It explores how their products and services penetrated into consumer sites and urban spaces of all social classes across the country, converting the whole society into a de facto military camp where all citizens are under the invisible security eye of profit-making officers. The chapter relies mainly on official laws and decrees; legal records from the Cassation Court and the Supreme Constitutional Court; and published profiles of military-owned companies and other foreign companies that deal with them. It also relies on the archives of the state-owned newspaper *al-Ahram* and other independent press.

Chapter 4 focuses on the ex-generals whom Mubarak hired into top bureaucratic positions, especially throughout the 2000s. It asserts that Mubarak then turned Egypt into a "republic of retired generals" as a part of his coup-proofing strategies with accelerated neoliberalism. It argues that those hires were major participants in running a dysfunctional market economy as heads of numerous government authorities responsible for the main economic activities and provisions of public services of the liberalized state. Thus they were contributors to the fallacies of Mubarak's autocratic neoliberalism that eventually collapsed under public rage in 2011. The securitization of provincial towns, ports, trade, agriculture, transportation, water and sewerage services, garbage collection, and so on across the country allowed the military to run watched urbanities as sites of potential war—particularly internal war of economically deprived local dissidents. The chapter profiles some prominent retired generals who occupied civilian positions for long years. Before the 2011 uprisings little was known about these figures. Luckily, the widespread wave of protests that followed Mubarak's deposal encouraged many employees who worked under them or citizens who were harmed by their policies to voice their grievances by filing lawsuits and public complaints or telling their stories of oppression on Facebook and YouTube. The chapter draws on those published narratives of discontented civilians as a main source.

Chapter 5 covers the period between 2011 and 2014, which includes deposing Mubarak, the government of SCAF, the rise and fall of an Islamist regime, and the election of a new military president. The system of military privileges almost fell apart immediately after the fall of Mubarak. Labor protests erupted to demand the demilitarization of the state and the economy. But the military quickly adapted to revolutionary change and once more survived a difficult moment of transformation, mainly through oppressive means. Amid turmoil, the officers succeeded in further expanding their business enterprises and seizing more bureaucratic positions, which meant maximized surveillance over and subordination of citizens. The military eventually managed to restore the presidential seat after losing it for a brief one-year period. In an attempt to decipher the mysteries of such triumph, the chapter investigates the tactics through which the officers salvaged their privileges and hegemony. Like the previous chapter, this final chapter relies on the wealth of information published in newspapers and on social media criticizing the military amid the revolutionary fervor of these three years. Activists from all backgrounds in big cities or small local communities registered their rage against military incumbents and businesses on Facebook and YouTube, which turned these social media sites into essential sources of documenting discontent against the officers. Moreover, printed newspapers during this period published endless reports on the alleged incompetence of old and new military administrators.

Finally, the conclusion discusses the possibilities of "demilitarizing" the nation today. Under al-Sisi's regime, the ever-expanding military hegemony over the country's economy and the intensified securitization of civilian realms have only generated more crises and severe discontent. Is it feasible to allow civilian, democratic control of the armed forces and "civilianize" the state in the foreseeable future in Egypt? The conclusion attempts to answer this question.

CHAPTER 1

Socialism Without Socialists (1950s–1970s)

The absolute monarch is born at the moment when the military form of
power and discipline begins to organize civil rights.
—Foucault, *Society Must Be Defended*

For decades since it was produced in 1957, state television has shown
the movie *Rudda Qalbi* (My Hurt Is Returned) every July 23, celebrating the anniversary of the 1952 revolution when a group of
young officers liberated Egypt. The epic romance film narrates the story of
Ali, son of a poor gardener, who was admitted to the military academy out
of mere luck and later joined the Free Officers and participated in the heroic events of deposing the monarch and kicking out the British colonizer.
Ali's childhood sweetheart, Inji, was the daughter of the landowning prince
who employed his father. The prince, of course, refused Ali's proposal to
marry Inji with much fury and scorn. After overthrowing the ancien régime, the new military regime assigned Ali the difficult task of going to the
palace of the prince to confiscate his properties, but there he reunited with
disgraced Inji. Now powerful Ali finally married the dispossessed daughter
of the old aristocrat. The movie was based on an epic two-part novel depict-
ing the nationalist struggles of the Free Officers and portraying Ali's ethics
and high morality, while detailing his illicit relation with a belly dancer.
Interestingly, outside of fiction and movie theaters, both the novelist and
the filmmaker were ex-officers themselves who switched to civilian careers,
like most of the military personnel who took off their uniforms and flooded
top civilian positions in the postrevolution government. Moreover, the two
were far from being poor like Ali: they came from well-to-do families but

successfully forged an image that lived for long decades about humble officers delivering social justice to the masses.[1]

Militarizing the postcolonial nation of Egypt began in July 1952. As soon as the young officers took power, they declared the country an independent republic. For the following two decades, ex-officers would occupy every important position in the state, from the president to prime ministers, ministers, diplomats, chairmen of public-sector companies, and more. The radical, populist president of the nascent military regime, Gamal Abd al-Nasser (r. 1954–1970), devised his own model of "Arab socialism" with a pivotal single ruling party and strove to implement it. Nonetheless, this chapter argues that it was socialism without socialists: the very ex-officers, bureaucrats, and socioeconomic groups that managed the state and ran the party did not in fact believe in socialism. They cheered for Nasser but were not particularly the faithful ideologues that he envisioned molding. Thus not only did socialism drastically fail but also the regime converted out of it once Nasser abruptly died. At the hands of the second military president of the country, Anwar al-Sadat (r. 1970–1981), the liberalization of the Egyptian economy received the enthusiastic support of the same officials and social groups that had previously undertaken state capitalism.

Constructing and then undoing a revolutionary socialist system went through many stages over the course of three decades. These stages unfolded gradually as the military regime altered existing structures. During their first decade in power, the officers applied an uncertain economic policy that mixed encouraging private capital with a social justice agenda, but they finally embraced full-fledged socialism at the turn of 1960. Nasser adopted ideas of Arab socialism during the difficult years of unity with Syria, between 1958 and 1961. He eventually issued the socialist National Charter and created the Arab Socialist Union (ASU) as a single ruling party in 1962. Implementing the new system, civilianized ex-officers administered the bureaucratic apparatus along with technocrats, and every single citizen in the nation had to be a member of the ruling party. ASU assimilated trade unions in public factories, agricultural cooperative in villages, professional syndicates in cities, and so forth to make their members its cadres. Finally, after the defeat in the war of 1967, Nasser reduced the socialist grip. Sadat followed this by gradually dismembering ASU, privatizing parts of the public sector, and demilitarizing the regime throughout the 1970s.

Viewing the same problematique from a Foucauldian vantage point, Nasser's regime of ex-officers introduced a heavily securitizing version of state capitalism, which applied diffused surveillance over its managers and submissive workforce alike. Most fled the system en masse upon the commander's sudden death. According to Foucault, modern capitalism makes relations of domination in the workshop possible through surveillance that followed the model of a military camp.[2] He indicates: "The massive projection of military methods onto industrial organization was an example of this modeling of the division of labour following [the] model laid down by the schemata of power."[3] The ex-officer regime perceived and ran every state-owned enterprise or public institution as a huge camp, where the individuals inside should keep full obedience and be watched by the almighty commander in the middle of the walled camp. It constantly observed and tightly controlled civilian labor in the public workshop, the rural cooperative, the government office, the professional syndicate, the public newspaper, and so on. The single ruling party, ASU, was the omnipotent machine watching over every one of those institutions and disciplining its members. The entire economy functioned in a complicated web of security apparatuses that competed with one another over collecting localized intelligence on and repressively controlling every civilian individual, on the top of which was the all-inclusive ASU.[4] When Nasser died, many of the fake socialists hurried to break loose from the entangled circuits of surveillance by fleeing the one-party system's edifices and dismantling state capitalism as a whole.

As for the military institution itself, that is, officers in service, it played a problematic role within Egypt's weak socialist system and its diffused securitization. The traditional conflict between "the commander and the commissar," or chiefs of the army and leaders of the ruling party in communist states, did emerge in Egypt. Building socialism took place amid many major wars that the country endured, and the army always enjoyed a superior status and access to economic privileges that other state institutions lacked. The regime faced its first war in the Suez Crisis of 1956, after Nasser nationalized the Suez Canal. The second major war the regime fought was in Yemen between 1962 and 1967, to help overthrow a conservative imamate backed by Saudi Arabia. Finally, it faced a humiliating defeat by Israel in 1967 when it lost the Sinai Peninsula. During these war encounters, the army received a considerably high budget for an underdeveloped, industrializing country, and its military factories obtained privileges over the public sector. More importantly, the military enjoyed autonomous political powers and further militarized the economic and social spheres. The Egyptian Army never submitted itself to Nasser's ASU; on the contrary, it functioned in

competition with the ruling party as another apparatus of population observation and control. After the defeat, it had to endure a period of exclusion
from politics and the economy.

In terms of the time and the global context, the Egyptian officers' attempt at socialism was another "revolution from above," as sociologist Ellen
Trimberger has called it. The ruled masses played little role in making the
revolution and forging the system but were mobilized to execute it. In
comparison to other "military bureaucrats" who embarked on schemes of
economic development in modern states such as Japan, Turkey, and Peru,
Egyptian officers undertook a top-down revolution that controlled means
of production and distribution. Trimberger indicates that the masses in these
countries barely participated in either the officers' takeover or initiation
of economic change.[5] Nazih Ayubi explains that other armies that seized
power in the postcolonial Middle East and applied socioeconomic reforms
similarly initiated revolutions from above. He explains that many societies in
the 1950s and 1960s already perceived armies as vehicles of modernization
and capable of delivering such revolutions. While developing countries in
general during this period were on a quest for modernity, military institutions figured as the more organized, educated, and technologically advanced
entities to carry out such a task. Ayubi adds that "the military themselves
have tended to justify their intervention . . . by citing nationalistic reasons
(fighting colonialism or confronting a foreign threat), the need for national
unity above ethnic and tribal lines, the need for order, discipline and organization, or the need for prompt socio-economic reform."[6]

It is important to note here that the masses' submission to such a militarized form of socialism in Egypt initially took place through voluntary
consent, especially by the lower classes that benefited from measures of
social justice. Although the officers' movement was a "military coup," it was
far from being an ordinary one, as Trimberger puts it. It quickly turned into
a social revolution. Nasser's officer regime immediately reached popular approval through rhetoric on social justice and economic independence from
Western imperialism, and his charismatic persona assisted him in building
populist support. This coup embarked on radical social and economic reforms in the interest of the lower classes while also consolidating a stable authoritarian regime. Trimberger draws similarities between Nasser and Juan
Velasco of Peru in this regard and asserts that they both "turned a political
and nationalist coup into a social and economic revolution."[7] However, the

wide, voluntary submission to the system in Egypt gradually turned into detestation of and desertion from the socialist order.

This chapter utilizes a wide range of published memoirs, biographies, and oral accounts of main players in Nasser and Sadat's states to explore its arguments. These include testimonies of the first military president, Muhammad Naguib, the ex-military prime minister and head of ASU, Ali Sabri, and Sadat, in addition to those of civilian figures such as Minister of Industry Aziz Sidqi, Minister of Agriculture Sayed Marei, the wife of Minister of War Abd al-Hakim 'Amir, and many more. However, it must be noted that their accounts carry divergent political biases, ranging all the way from Marxism to conservative Islamic tendencies. These figures held different, and sometimes contradictory, views about the period's critical events, which render it difficult to draw consistent narratives about them. Nevertheless, these figures mostly share similar stories regarding the main arguments addressed in this chapter: that the ruling officers were not all originally on the leftist side of politics; nonideologues ran state capitalism; ASU penetrated into and continuously observed the workforce; the autonomous army did not submit itself to the ruling party; and en masse flight out of securitized socialism to the liberalized market was the choice of the very elite and party cadres who once ran the socialist regime. Moreover, the chapter seconds these testimonies with scholarly records of contemporary social scientists analyzing the unfolding of the period's critical moments of transformation. It also utilizes contemporary novels, movies, and television series to supply a more vivid depiction of the various social groups that took part in making these transitional moments.

The four sections that follow trace the history of three decades. The first section investigates the social and ideological roots of the Free Officers and the gradual evolution of their military regime toward socialism in the 1950s. The second moves to the 1960s, exploring the profiles of key ex-officers, technocrats, and socioeconomic groups that applied Nasser's state capitalism under the close surveillance of the single ruling party. The third section focuses on the army's privileged status in the system and the problematic relation between the commander and commissar within a milieu of intensive securitization. Finally, the fourth section follows the process of converting out of Arab socialism starting from the late 1960s through the 1970s.

Long Road to Socialism

The first decade of the newly born military regime was marked by contested ideological stances among the ruling officers, which generated unclear economic policies. The Free Officers were far from being a homogenous group: they came from various socioeconomic backgrounds and were inconsistent in their ideological underpinnings, stretching from religiously conservative to communist views. Thus while the Free Officers, conservatives and leftists alike, flooded state positions, they applied uncertain economic plans mixing liberal visions with social justice procedures for many years in the 1950s. It was only when Nasser, their top leader, who was from a lower-class background, crystallized his socialist ideas and consolidated his charismatic grip over power that his leftist stance triumphed over others. This section attempts to draw the socioeconomic and ideological map of the Free Officers and deconstruct Nasser's persona. It traces how all this was reflected in the mixed economic policies the military regime applied during its first few years, and the gradual shift to the left until Nasser radically ended the uncertainty when his tailored version of socialism prevailed.

It is true that the majority of the Free Officers were from nonaristocratic origins, but they were not exactly poor. The young officers were mostly sons of well-to-do urban and rural families and civil servants. The kings along with the British colonial administrations allowed only the sons of the Turkic and Egyptian aristocracy to be admitted into the military academy and denied those of middle- and lower-class native Egyptian families the same opportunity. The Anglo-Egyptian agreement of 1936 finally altered the situation and granted the latter a chance for social mobility and prestige.[8] Coming from lower-class families, Nasser and Sadat were in the first class that joined the military academy as a result of this agreement; they both joined in 1937. However, other Free Officers who entered the academy around the same time descended from rather affluent families. The most prominent example among them was 'Amir, Nasser's closest friend and his army's commander-in-chief, whose father was a large landowner and a village mayor and whose uncle was the king's minister of war. Other important examples are the cousins Khalid and Zakariyya Muhi al-Din along with Abd al-Latif al-Baghdadi, who also came from well-off families.

Apparently the social background of the officers had little impact on their ideological choices. While all of them were naturally drawn to nation-

alist ideas about Egyptian independence in a milieu of resistance against colonialism, they adopted various ideological stances that did not always reflect
their social roots. Many were attracted to the Muslim Brothers' religious
dicta, some supported the liberal ideas of the influential Wafd Party whose
leadership was mostly aristocratic landowners, and a few went to Marxism.[9]
On the lower-class side, whereas Nasser had leftist tendencies, Sadat was a
conservative liberal and sympathizer with the Muslim Brothers. On the affluent side, whereas Khalid Muhi al-Din was a Marxist, his cousin Zakariyya
in addition to Abd al-Latif al-Baghdadi held a conservative stance.[10] Nonetheless, the officers had no firm roots in any ideology except for Egyptian
nationalism—combined with political and social reform ideas.[11]

Compared to surrounding Middle Eastern armies leading coups around
the same period, the Egyptian officers were the only group to ally themselves with conservative Islamists to reach power. In the years before the
Egyptian coup, military coups had already taken place in three other Middle
Eastern countries: Turkey with two coups in 1908 and 1909, Iraq with seven
between 1936 and 1941, and Syria with four between 1949 and 1952. Egypt
had its own coup in 1881.[12] In an article published in 1953, contemporary
political scientist Majid Khadduri noted that the Palestine war and the defeat of Arab armies by Israel in 1948 was the main trigger behind the sudden wave of coups in Syria and Egypt because of officers' grievances against
civilian governments, and Kemal Ataturk of Turkey was already a popular
model for Arab officers to follow.[13] Khadduri indicated that most Middle
Eastern officers held ultranationalistic views and sought collaboration with
nationalist and liberal groups, but religious movements hesitated to back
ruling armies "either because they had come to terms with former regimes
(as in Turkey) or because their ideas proved to be too reactionary to be tol-
erated by the army (as in Iraq). In Syria the Muslim Brotherhood . . . failed
to give support to the military."[14] In Iraq for instance, pan-Arab groups
played an important role, and in Syria the army emphasized liberalism and
gave little attention to religion. But this was not the case in Egypt, where
the officers actively sought the support of the brotherhood.[15]

In fact, young Egyptian officers were culturally conservative and internal-
ized religious beliefs, which explains their initial openness to collaborate with
the Muslim Brothers. Sociologist Morroe Berger observed in 1960 that "socially . . . the army officers have not transcended their conservative middle-
class origins and upbringing. Their wives and families . . . are seldom seen
in public. . . . There is also among these leaders a certain tendency toward

puritanical attitudes which is compounded of the sexual modesty enjoined by Islamic doctrine."[16] Their cultural orientation was reflected in contemporary novels. The main protagonist of *Rudda Qalbi*, Ali, preached morals and ethics, despite keeping a secret liaison with a belly dancer. A religious officer with a puritanical mission appears in another epic novel that turned into a popular TV series in the 1970s—albeit with a critical, sarcastic rather than glorifying tone. In *Zaynab wa-l-'Arsh* (Zaynab and the Throne), the pious officer Diyab was appointed editor-in-chief of a newspaper, where he gave much attention to fixing the morality of his employees and harassed them about their personal affairs. Ironically, he had an illicit relation with a belly dancer as well, with whom he had an illegitimate daughter. The real world of the officers was not very far from fiction. In her memoirs about 'Amir, a soft-porn star whom Nasser's commander-in-chief secretly took as a second wife made proud references to the fact that the field marshal was an observant Muslim who diligently prayed and fasted, never drank alcohol, had deep knowledge of the Qur'an and classical Islamic sources, and always spoke on morality. In his office he hung the word Allah and a Qur'anic verse decorated in large frames above his desk, and he opposed hiring women as ministers.[17]

Upon leaving the barracks to form the new ruling elite, the Free Officers dominated top civilian positions and enjoyed the social and economic luxuries that came with high bureaucratic jobs. Whereas top members of the Revolutionary Command Council (RCC) occupied the cabinet seats, second-tier Free Officers took charge of restructuring the civil service, reforming newspapers and arts, administering nationalized companies, serving as ambassadors abroad, and so on.[18] In 1960 former diplomat and historian Keith Wheelock wrote:

> The military was gradually "civilianized"; the *foule* sandwiches eaten at the office desk, the bread and cheese wrapped in newspapers, the .45 automatic pistol lying on the desk as a symbol of authority— these were giving way to well-tailored suits, an occasional American or British car, and membership at the Gezira Sporting Club. A new society was taking shape, but it was a far cry from Nasser's original conception of a new order. The young captains, majors, and colonels were creating their own elite, and they were loath to surrender their newly gained privileges. In a way, it might be said that the revolutionaries of 1952 were the political conservatives of 1955.[19]

As a result of these socioeconomic transitions, a new class of "military technocrats" gradually took form and spread its influence. They were officers who switched careers after studying technical fields such as engineering, physics, journalism, law, history, and political science and earned degrees to occupy bureaucratic positions in the state. In the early years of 1950s, coup leaders seized vital government positions of president, prime minister, and minister of interior, in addition to sweeping the posts of diplomats abroad and seats as editors-in-chief at newspapers. It was hard for the officers to take responsibility in posts requiring high technocratic expertise, such as the Ministries of Finance, Housing, and Trade, but they made sure to control them. Nonetheless, by the late 1950s military technocrats who finished studies in relevant fields grew in number and power to replace many civilians and fellow military figures. In 1962, "underneath ministers and deputy minsters, there were about 5,766 bureaucratic positions, of which 3,714 were occupied by army officers (and police) in different ministries," Majdi Hammad counted in a sociological survey.[20]

Nasser himself was not immune to the evolution that other Free Officers experienced—albeit in his own "dreamy" way. The most important figure among the young officers, Nasser, whose father was a postman, was from the start on the leftist side of politics. However, he deployed contradicting leftist and conservative ideologies alike to plot the coup. After taking over, he fiercely cut ties with the Muslim Brothers but maintained a complicated relationship with the communists. Nasser was active in an underground communist cell before moving to join the brotherhood and then quitting it, and he collaborated with both groups in planning the overthrow of the king, as Marxist officer Khalid Muhi al-Din relayed in his memoirs. In this regard, General Naguib—whom Nasser unseated and placed under house arrest for the rest of his life—indicated that Nasser had an "adaptive" personality that adjusted to different conditions and moved between ideologies, but he was loyal only to his own ideas.[21] Nasser was originally an intellectually enlightened, emotional, and dreamy personality—as Tawfiq al-Hakim, a prominent Egyptian writer, put it in his 1972 text criticizing the defeated despot two years after his sudden death. Nasser was more like a writer or an artist, always "dreaming and loving," than a seasoned politician, al-Hakim added. He even wrote some fiction in the beginning of his life, and he lived his life like the protagonist of one of his stories: a "nationalist, emotional, and impulsive figure."[22]

Nasser's book *The Philosophy of the Revolution* (1954) probably reflected what al-Hakim meant about the populist hero's persona. This book was a literary more than a political text: composed of poetic, emotional prose on hopes and dreams; frustrations and success; near and far history of people's resistance; close companions; the soul; and ethics of self-denial. Although published after Nasser had been in power for two years, the book merely recorded the leader's free memoirs full of metaphors without drawing a distinguished ideology for the author or laying out defined policies for his regime. It only addressed hearts in the newly born nation. He called the July 23 movement a popular revolution and asserted that the army took it as its own duty to act as the "vanguard of the freedom fighters (*fida'iyyin*)" to liberate the country. After fulfilling this "holy task," the army looked around to disappointedly see that civilian forces were disunited and fragmented, so it inevitably had to stay in power and carry on with the task of building the nation. Nasser commended the Free Officers for their self-denial and hard-working character and accomplished professional careers and contrasted them with many unethical civilians. The officers then had to lead two parallel revolutions: a political revolution against tyrants and a social one for social justice.[23]

Nasser's ambitiously leftist dreams did not tolerate the conservative Muslim Brothers for long after the success of the revolution. Naguib asserted that the brothers supported the army's movement at first under the impression that it would work for their interests, since many Free Officers were in contact with them. The brotherhood's supreme guide asked Nasser to consult his group before making any decisions if he desired for their support. Naguib indicated that Nasser initially did recognize the help that the brothers gave for the movement. For instance, when the regime issued laws restricting the work of political parties, Nasser asked to exempt the brothers from these codes. In addition, he invited them to take share in the first cabinet by calling the supreme guide and asking him to nominate three ministers. But the Muslim Brothers quickly fought the new regime after realizing that it had secular orientations. They refused to nominate any ministers in order not to strengthen the nascent regime with their base of loyal members, and they even fired their only member who accepted a ministerial position in the cabinet. More important, the brothers objected to the officers' land reform law and suggested raising the maximum size of property.[24] Two years after assuming power, in 1954, the officers embarked on a violent campaign to prosecute and imprison the brothers for years to come.

On the opposite side, Nasser maintained a complicated relation with the communists that fluctuated between relying on their professional expertise in running the economy and sending them en masse to jail. Generally, Nasser dealt cautiously with the communists and viewed them as a "major internal threat" that received foreign assistance from the Soviet Union and plotted disorder and anarchy. A leftist whom Nasser hired as the first minister of industry in 1956, Aziz Sidqi, explained that Nasser was not against communism per se but rather against dependence on a foreign power in any form. Sidqi adds that despite believing that the leftist path was the best choice for Egypt, Nasser thought that adhering to communism would have meant reducing Egypt to a mere follower of the Soviet Union. Moreover, he was an Arab nationalist, and the communist USSR sought to eliminate nationalisms. Sidqi explains that Nasser wanted the Soviet Union's help in development but without its domination. Thus he feared that the Egyptian communists might take advantage of the state's relation with the Soviets and assume a privileged position to expand their recruitment efforts.[25]

The regime arrested communists inside and outside the army and purged many Marxist army officers, including Free Officer Khalid Muhi al-Din, between 1954 and 1956. In reaction, the communists tried to ally themselves with the Muslim Brothers, but the latter were not very responsive. After being purged, Muhi al-Din was appointed as editor-in-chief of a leftist newspaper that functioned as an intellectual venue for Egyptian Marxists, al-Misa, and won a seat in the parliament in 1957. In his memoirs he opined that the conflict was primarily the responsibility of the communists, who committed mistakes that triggered Nasser to prosecute them.[26] Muhi al-Din's testimony on the two communist workers who were tried in a military court and executed in late 1952, after leading a major strike and violent protests in a cotton plant in northern Egypt, was not on their side. He asserted that the two laborers were not connected to the main communist parties or labor unions in the country at the time and that these organized groups viewed them suspiciously.[27] When communists opposed unity with Syria, inspired by Arab nationalist ideas in 1958 because of the Soviet Union's ideological detestation of nationalism, this further troubled their relation with Nasser.

In the meantime, Nasser's regime hired many professional Marxists in top economic positions in the state. He hired economist Isma'il Sabri 'Abdullah as an advisor to the prime minister for economic and financial affairs between 1954 and 1955, before putting him in jail for a while. In 1957 Nasser hired 'Abdullah as the head of the newly established Economic Agency, which was vital for the creation of the public-sector enterprises, and another communist economist, the renowned Samir Amin, joined him in the same organization. But Nasser again imprisoned 'Abdullah between 1959 and 1964, then released him and appointed him as the head of the National Institute of Planning in the late 1960s. Interestingly, like most communists who served time in Nasser's jails, which were notorious for vicious torture, 'Abdullah admired Nasser and considered him a real leader. He appreciated the fact that Nasser was deeply knowledgeable but not a doctrinaire and that he detested dogmatic thinking.[28]

Within this ideologically blurred milieu, Nasser and the officers adopted an indefinite approach to economic reform during the 1950s. They mixed capitalist with leftist ideas, on the one hand encouraging local and foreign capital and on the other hand applying land reform laws and venturing into creating the public sector. Meanwhile, they maintained good relations with both the Soviet Union and the United States—the latter at least for a while.

Interestingly, encouraging foreign capital preceded agrarian reform in the officers' scheme for change. Moreover, the land reform laws did not exactly give land for free to peasants, and they exempted companies. Only one week after taking over, on July 30, the nascent regime modified article 6 of the corporation law of 1947 to reduce the required share of Egyptian capital versus foreign capital in joint stock companies from 51 to 49 percent and allow the latter percentage to include existing corporations where foreigners owned shares. This modification aimed at attracting more foreign capital investment in the country. Several weeks later, on September 9, the regime issued agrarian reform law no. 178, according to which the government was to requisition thousands of acres, or *feddans*, from the rural aristocracy and redistribute them to landless peasants. This law limited the landholdings of individuals to 200 *feddans*, with additional 100 *feddans* for children, and they were to receive compensation in the form of government bonds that paid an interest rate of 3 percent over the course of thirty years. Industrial companies and individuals who owned fallow or desert lands for reclamation were allowed to exceed this limit. Land was to be allotted primarily to farmers who were tenants of the requisitioned tracts with a maximum of 5 *feddans* for a family, with seasonal laborers excluded from the process, and farmers paid the price in installments over thirty years with an annual interest rate and additional 15 percent requisition fee. As for agricultural workers who did not benefit from this law, the government was to set their minimum wage to secure them fair payments. In the private capital realm, a 1953 law granted a five-year tax exemption to new industries.[29]

In the meantime, the regime attempted to keep friendly relations with the two ideological poles of the global Cold War, the Eastern and Western blocs alike. Its relations with the West worked much better in the first two years, as Nasser and the young officers sought an understanding with the United States as a superpower that could exert influence on Britain. As Laura James stated:

> Certainly, there was great goodwill between the Free Officers and the US Embassy immediately after the Revolution. On 20 August, [U.S. ambassador] Caffery was invited to dine with the regime's figureheads . . . the local CIA station assisted the Egyptian internal security forces. . . . Nasser's own association with the United States at this time was so strong. . . . He developed particular friendship with the Embassy's second secretary. . . . Nasser also got on well with the US Secretary of State John Foster Dulles, whom he met in May 1953. At this stage, the United States was not naturally ranked among Egypt's enemies—indeed, Nasser had deliberately avoided mentioning the Americans in such a context in either the original Free Officer's manifesto or his subsequent book, *The Philosophy of the Revolution*. He still saw the US as representing the non-imperialist future.[30]

The United States did show interest in supporting the new regime, and the Egyptian government encouraged American capital by, for example, granting an oil concession to the Colorado Oil Company in early 1954. Meanwhile, the Soviet Union attacked the officers, accusing them of being agents of the United States, and most Egyptian communist parties refrained from supporting them.[31]

In this early stage of uncertain visions, Nasser was perhaps influenced by a neighboring Syrian ruling officer and learned many harsh lessons from his unfortunate fate. In 1949 Colonel Adib al-Shishakli led the third postcolonial coup in Syria, and he became president between 1953 and 1954. Much like Nasser, Shishakli fought in the Palestine war in 1948, announced his coup on national radio, delivered fervent speeches, and was elected president with 99 percent of the vote. The United States found him trustworthy and offered to assist—especially to counter the considerable communist influence in Syrian society, but Shishakli cared more for fighting Zionism than for resisting communism. Nasser's regime followed the footsteps of Shishakli in many reform policies: distribution of agricultural land to landless peasants, outlawing the Muslim Brothers, founding the single ruling party, controlling newspapers, launching national irrigation projects by negotiating a World Bank loan, and supporting Arab nationalism and socialism through the Baath Party. Ambitious Shishakli concluded a friendship treaty with Iran's popular prime minister Mohammed Mosaddeq, whose radical decision to nationalize the Anglo-Iranian Oil Company was met by a CIA staged coup deposing him in 1953. Shishakli still kept good relations with the West by buying weapons from France and Britain and seeking U.S. military assistance. Eventually realizing that the U.S. administration was hesitant to grant him military support because of his position against Israel, Shishakli turned to the Soviet Union in 1954. In the same year he was overthrown by massive protests.[32]

Facing the same dilemmas as Shishakli's, Nasser's regime was keen on remaining on the capitalist side and keeping the United States content, but this proved impossible. Anouar Abdel-Malek, a Marxist sociologist whom the regime persecuted in 1950s, explained that after the series of laws issued in the first year to support private investment, foreign and local capitalists held back. Figures on investment and growth of industrial production increased "too slowly" between 1954 and 1956. "Everything, it seemed, was auspicious for an invitation to the big Western powers, but also the Egyptian capital, to take up the responsibilities for economic development. . . . But big Egyptian capital, chiefly in the landed wing, which had just undergone the agrarian reform, refused to invest in industry . . . and banks [mostly foreign capital] were hesitant to provide the development of the new economy, which was predominantly industrial, with the capital that it vitally needed."[33] On another front, Nasser negotiated with the United States for three years to receive arms, but the Pentagon placed conditions in a mutual defense treaty that Egypt was not willing accept. Nasser still attempted to maintain a neutral position by contributing to the creation of the Non-Aligned Movement, along with other Third World leaders. Eventually, in dire need of weapons and under domestic pressure, he resorted to the Eastern bloc and concluded a Czechoslovakian arms deal in late 1955.[34]

When the new constitution of the republic was promulgated a year later, in 1956, it showed progression toward the left. Although it still reflected ideological uncertainty and the mixed nature of the economy, it articulated a reserved tendency toward private capital and a desire to subjugate it to ideas of planning. The constitution guaranteed protection for private property along with emphasizing social justice and introducing government planning. With an Arab nationalist orientation, the first article stated: "Egypt is an independent, sovereign Arab state . . . and the Egyptian people are part of the Arab nation." Then, with the culturally conservative spirit of the officers, article 3 stated that Islam was the official religion of the state, and article 5 asserted that the family was the foundation of society and its bases were religion, morality, and patriotism. Having said that, article 7 asserted that the national economy would be organized through state "plans" aiming at social justice, development, and raising the standard of living. The next four articles encouraged private capital as long as it served national goals:

> 8. Private economic activities are free, provided that they do not harm the society's interest. . . . 9. Capital is to be used to serve national economy in ways that must not conflict with public good. 10. Law guarantees harmony between public and private economic activities toward social goals and people's prosperity. 11. Private property is protected . . . and it should not be confiscated except for public benefits and with just compensation in accordance with law.[35]

Soon afterward, a steadier shift to the left took place more distinctly. The famous story of the Suez Crisis in 1956 was integral to this shift. When the military regime set the ambitious plan to build the High Dam for agricultural and industrial development in the country, it preferred a U.S. and International Bank for Reconstruction and Development (IBRD) loan to offers from the Soviet Union. Secretary of State John Foster Dulles delivered the bad news of U.S. rejection of the proposal to the Egyptian ambassador in Washington, D.C., on July 19, 1956. Only a week later Nasser nationalized the Suez Canal, which triggered the triple military attack by Britain, France, and Israel on the canal area. The United States condemned the attack and the three countries withdrew.[36] Nasser had no choice but to resort to the Soviet Union's financial and technical assistance to construct the High Dam. Shortly afterward, the U.S. Congress approved the Eisenhower Doctrine to contain Nasser and Arab nationalism. Already two years earlier, the United States had backed forming the Baghdad Pact with the membership of five

allies—Iraq, Iran, Turkey, Pakistan, and Britain—to limit Nasser's expanding regional influence. Thus the relationship between Nasser and the West
became unbridgeable.[37]

Emerging out of the Suez Crisis with an extremely high degree of
popularity and consolidation of his charismatic power in Egypt and across
the Arab world, Nasser decided to make his ideological orientation toward
socialism manifest. It successfully eclipsed other remaining stances among
the Free Officers. Not long after the end of the crisis, in January 1957, the
regime issued laws 22, 23, and 24 to Egyptianize foreign banks, insurance
companies, and commercial agencies, putting them under Egyptian management. Many British, French, and Turkish banks were seized and sold to
state-owned banks newly created for this purpose. Also founded in January 1957, the Economic Agency took charge of creating new public-sector
companies and later managed Egyptian companies that were nationalized.
As mentioned above, Nasser placed this crucial agency under the administration of Marxist economist 'Abdullah. Venturing into centralized planning in industries, Nasser created the Ministry of Industry and assigned it
to leftist engineer Aziz Sidqi in mid-1956. At the turn of the new decade,
in 1960–61, the state moved on to nationalize Egyptian capital. It started
by nationalizing the two largest locally owned conglomerates in the country: Bank Misr Complex, which owned twenty-nine companies dealing in
textiles, petroleum, iron and steel, fertilizers, and so forth, allegedly with
monopolistic powers; and Ahmed Abboud Group, which owned mail lines,
a sugar refinery, a chemical-fertilizer plant, and so on, and where labor
repression and strikes were common. The head of the Economic Agency
controlled the two conglomerates.[38]

The short-lived unity with Syria around these years certainly helped
crystallize Nasser's version of Arab socialism. During the 1950s the Baath
Party was predominant in Syrian society. Established in the 1940s and
guided by Michel Aflaq, the party managed to create a base of mass fol-
lowers, recruiting army officers, students, civil servants, and more in Syria.
The party's inspiring motto was "struggling for Arab unity, freedom, and
socialism," and Aflaq coined and theorized on the term "Arab socialism"
years before Nasser in his book *Fi Sabil Ba'th* (1946).[39] In 1958, after visits
from Damascus to Cairo by Baathist army officers, the unity agreement was
concluded between Nasser and Syria's Baathist foreign minister, Salah Bitar,
and another Baath leader, Akram Hourani, was appointed vice president

of the United Arab Republic. Nasser asked to disband all parties in Syria, including the Baath, and they happily responded, and he transferred most Baathist army officers to Egypt. Shortly afterward the party found itself enjoying little influence vis-à-vis many security apparatuses and conflicting cleavages of power. The Baathist ministers in the government resigned, and Aflaq supported the separation, accusing Nasser of being an expansionist dictator who sought personal glory using Arab unity. A Syrian Army coup took place against Egypt, and the Baathists endorsed a separation document in September 1961. Nasser attacked the Baath for years to come, but he was undoubtedly influenced by Aflaq's theoretical notion of Arab socialism.[40]

Nasser initiated bold socialist measures during the union's final year and decisively carried on after the split. In July 1961 the regime issued a series of laws, nos. 117, 118, and 119, to nationalize all banks, insurance companies, and hundreds of other companies and factories in textiles, transportation, export, and many other sectors; promulgate state ownership of 50 percent of the shares of hundreds of other economic institutions that were later fully nationalized in 1962; limit the shares of an individual in a group of companies to only LE10,000; abolish the capitulations enjoyed by foreign companies in water, electricity, and tramways; and nationalize the Shell petroleum company. The agricultural bourgeoisie was also affected in the same month, as law no. 127 modifying the land reform law of 1952 further reduced the ceiling of landed property to only 100 instead of 200 *feddans* and provided for the state confiscation of any additional lots not sold within a year after the law was promulgated.[41] Such radical legislation shocked the historically well-established industrial and commercial bourgeoisie in Syrian society, and the union was broken two months after the laws were enacted, but Nasser carried on in Egypt.

By the tenth anniversary of the revolution, Nasser published the National Charter in May 1962, in which he spoke of the "inevitability of the socialist solution." In this long text, Nasser set his choice aside and distinct from both capitalist and Marxist systems and reaffirmed Arab nationalism and unity. At the same time, he inaugurated the Arab Socialist Union as the single ruling party, whose law of creation stated that the organization would be the "socialist vanguard that will lead the masses and express their will . . . and effectively *monitor* the path of national work."[42]

Socialism Without Socialists

Upon fully applying socialism, Nasser's state structure and the socioeconomic groups tied to it took entirely new shapes. At the official level, the state had three main civilian institutions underneath the presidency: ASU, with an ex-officer leadership; an elected parliament controlled by ASU; and the bureaucracy, also hegemonized by ASU. As for the social groups, Nasser divided them in a corporatist way into different interest groups lined up within various organizations, including labor unions, agricultural cooperatives, and professional syndicates. The members of these organizations also had to be members of ASU, and they were profoundly penetrated by the ruling party and subjected to its close mechanisms of surveillance. Interestingly, none of the above institutions or social groups were true or even good adherents to Nasser's socialism—even ASU. Most of their members only went along with what the populist leader wanted, in extensively securitized urban and rural spaces. These state institutions and interest groups will be investigated here.

Let's begin with ASU itself. Nasser designed the single ruling party to contain a coalition of all workforces (*tahaluf quwa al-sha'b al-'amil*), including peasants, workers, professionals, intellectuals, soldiers, and small private businessmen. But the members of the supreme executive committee that initiated ASU and its general secretariat were Nasser's close entourage of Free Officers, which lent the party a conspicuously securitizing nature. The founding officers included notably conservative figures such as Sadat. One of them, 'Abd al-Latif al-Baghdadi, who descended from a bourgeois rural family, raised objections about the socialist measures as a whole and eventually resigned and quit politics altogether.[43] As opposed to Nasser's original vision about the party's membership empowering the dispossessed classes, it was rural and urban petite bourgeoisie who constituted the key cadres in ASU. Ilya Harik explained: "The most prominent leaders of ASU in the countryside were well-to-do farmers, headmen ('*umdahs*), and the educated who had urban occupations but had maintained their ties with the countryside. In provincial towns, the notables, civil servants, teachers, and professionals (some of whom were also absentee landlords) were leaders of the ASU cadres."[44]

When ASU organized parliamentary elections, it approved only candidates who were closely linked to the party. "This does not mean simply that candidates . . . should be registered in the lists of ASU, but that the success of a candidate will depend upon his activity and his loyalty to the ASU," political scientist Ali Ed-Dean Hillal Dessouki, a young member of the party at that time, indicates.[45] The first parliament after the socialist charter was elected in 1964, with workers and peasants making up half of its members according to the electoral law. Sadat was nominated as the Speaker of this legislature, called the National Assembly. In his memoirs, Sadat stressed that he was against the socialist measures, especially the nationalization of the private sector. He thought that the country was heading more toward Marxism by considering "any free capitalist enterprise abhorrent," and that this resulted in people's apathy and "overdependence on the state," Sadat added.[46] At any rate, Sadat was presiding over a passive legislature whose members were granted little authority over the country's policies. The role of this parliament was "akin to that of the legislature in all single-party or single-movement regimes; i.e., decorative, symbolic, and ratifying, rather than real or effective."[47]

In the bureaucracy, every prime minister was an officer, Free or not, following the regime's golden rule of favoring the "people of trust" (*ahl al-thiqa*) over the "people of qualifications" (*ahl al-khibra*) in critical appointments. Eminent economist Samir Amin, whom Nasser appointed among other Marxists in the government, indicated that the ruling officers neither had a clear idea about socialism nor were "convinced" about its value or importance. Many of them were "reactionaries, friends of capitalism, or conservatives," Amin asserted.[48] Four officers headed the cabinet between 1961 and 1967, and after the defeat Nasser himself occupied the prime ministership.[49] The first of them was Kamal al-Din Husayn, who headed "the regional executive council of Egypt" within the unionized state in the middle of the transition to socialism from 1960 to 1962. Husayn was previously minister of social affairs, education, and local administration. However, he was intellectually influenced by the Muslim Brothers and an outspoken sympathizer with them. Husayn insisted that Egypt's socialism should be derived from Islamic shari'a rather than the ideas of Marx or Lenin. He debated incorporating the "spiritual aspect" into the country's model of socialism and supported private ownership of business. Husayn resigned in 1964 from his last position as a member of the presidential council and was placed under house arrest in the following year after criticizing the persecution of the brothers. After the 1967 defeat, he advised Nasser to mend relations with the United States and Saudi Arabia.[50]

After him came Ali Sabri, heading the cabinet from 1962 to 1965, who converted to the radical left after years of good relations with the Americans. On the night of the 1952 coup, the revolutionary officers needed somebody to pass a message to the American Embassy in Cairo, and they found that Sabri was the best candidate for the mission because he had studied military intelligence in the United States and kept a close friendship with the American air attaché. After meeting Nasser for the first time to take the oral message, Sabri—at the time the head of the air intelligence—informed his American friend about the goals of the officers' movement and asked for U.S. support against Britain. A few months later he made a trip to the Pentagon to negotiate an arms deal, though it was not concluded. Sabri asserted in his memoirs that despite his lower-class roots, he maintained good relations with the Americans and developed no socialist tendencies during this early period.[51] But Sabri later changed friends and became Nasser's man in building relations and making agreements with the Soviets. As prime minister, he took charge of applying the first five-year plan with a great deal of Soviet aid.[52] He continued on the path of socialism after leaving the cabinet, as he was the secretary general of ASU from 1962 to 1971.

Two famously conservative figures followed Sabri in heading the socialist cabinet. The first was key Free Officer and Revolutionary Command Council member Zakariyya Muhi al-Din, prime minister for a year from 1965 to 1966. Before that he was the founding father of the notorious General Intelligence Directorate in 1955 and was minister of interior many times. In a tense meeting with Nasser while initiating the socialist policies in 1961, Zakariyya raised profound concerns about the unclear path the regime was taking and how it generated instability. Again after the 1967 defeat, he expressed full rejection of the socialist system and the desire to convert back to capitalism.[53] In his testimony about the events as a minister of industry, Aziz Sidqi recounted how Zakariyya often spoke of the worsened economic conditions and that many ministers supported his views on switching from socialism. When Nasser announced he was stepping down after the defeat, he named Zakariyya as a successor—a sign of submitting the country to the liberalization camp.[54] Zakariyya was followed for another year by a nonideologue, Muhammad Sidqi Sulayman, who was originally only a military engineer, not a Free Officer, but was entrusted with numerous high-profile economic missions, including minister of the High Dam. After Nasser died, Sulayman equally and sincerely served Sadat's liberalized state first as his advisor and then as the head of the state accountability authority.

Civilian technocrats appointed in the bureaucracy as ministers and ad-ministrators of the public-sector companies were not very different in terms of their ideological inclinations. Nasser brought on board a good number of urban upper- and upper-middle-class technocrats who earned high de-grees from Western universities and favored them with prestigious positions and high salaries—as opposed to regular government employees. In the meantime, they all had to serve as important cadres in ASU. Most of those had liberal tendencies, but they were "pragmatic and adaptable" so they became "socialists by Presidential Decree"—as Raymond Hinnebusch puts it. However, Hinnebusch adds, "although prepared to serve in and favored by the Nasir regime, this elite was not happy with Nasserism as it evolved in the sixties and almost unanimously welcomed the victory of Sadat over the left-wing Free Officers."[55]

One must begin here with Sayed Marei. Ironically, a liberal technocrat with a rural bourgeois background implemented one of the principal poli-cies of the socialist system: agrarian reform. Originally from a notable rural family and a parliament member in the 1940s advancing a liberal party's agenda, agricultural engineer and industrial businessman Marei served as minister of agriculture from 1956 to 1961 and came back to this position again in 1967. He was a top member of ASU and a parliament member on its list. While in the pre-1952 parliament he advocated limited agrarian reform in setting minimum wages for agricultural workers and regulating land rents, but he resented radical proposals to restrict landownership. He took charge of this latter task as a minister for many years. His biographer, Robert Springborg, relayed that he first entered the regime when conser-vative Zakariyya nominated him to the Higher Committee of Agrarian Reform; Nasser initially rejected his name because of his elitist appearance but eventually gave him the job. Marei soon consolidated his control over the agricultural sector as a whole, controlling even village cooperatives and the agricultural bank.[56] Marei's management carried inherent fallacies con-tradictory to the very goals of agrarian reform: it did not benefit the rural lower classes but rather enhanced medium properties and gave birth to a new rural petite bourgeoisie, as contemporary economist Mahmoud Abdel-Fadil recorded.[57] After Nasser died, Marei turned into a key implementer of Sadat's economic liberalization. He was Speaker of the Parliament under Sadat, and his son married Sadat's daughter.

Another liberal technocrat with an interesting persona led Nasser's key ministries of economy, finance, trade, and planning and was deputy prime minister at different times between 1954 and 1968. Abd al-Mun'im al-Qaysuni was born in Cairo's bourgeois neighborhood of Heliopolis, but he switched careers and studied economics in London and worked for a British bank and the International Monetary Fund (IMF) in the 1940s. Ironically, Qaysuni was the official who declared before the parliament Sadat's open-market decisions in his capacity as deputy prime minister for economic and financial affairs in 1977.[58]

Another intriguing character was Hasan 'Abbas Zaki, minister of economy, treasury, and public supply at different times between 1957 and 1972 and the architect of implementing nationalization. Zaki asserted that Nasser suddenly informed him about his idea of nationalizing the private sector at an Alexandria resort in the summer of 1961, but he disagreed and suggested progressive taxation instead. "I was not convinced. How to rob people of the ownership of their private businesses and convert them into public properties managed by the people of trust rather than those with qualifications?! This was the crisis," Zaki stated. Eventually he had to apply the socialist measures in his capacity as the minister of economy.[59] In his late years, he turned into an Islamic thinker and Sufi shaykh and supported privatization.[60]

An important exception within this group was Aziz Sidqi, a civilian architect with a PhD from Harvard University. A technocrat who believed in the value of the socialist policies, Sidqi was minister of industry from 1956 to 1964 and again from 1967 until Nasser died. Nasser entrusted him with creating this ministry from scratch and the whole ambitious plan of industrialization, and Sidqi brought professionals who similarly earned graduate degrees abroad to work with him on this successful mission. He established more than three thousand factories. In a lengthy interview in 2004, Sidqi asserted that the 1950s–1960s were the best years in Egypt's modern history: the development rate increased at the same rate as the population. "Nasser was fair and clean from corruption and nepotism. . . . He read economic theories and used to have discussions with Abd al-Mun'im al-Qaysuni on them. . . . He read because he wanted to reach the right decisions."[61] Sidqi later served as Sadat's prime minister in 1972, but he quit with the transition to the market. Sidqi asserted: "Socialism had trouble, but Sadat could have fixed the mistakes instead of altering everything abruptly. He blindly responded to the U.S., which had a goal to terminate everything that 1952 brought about."[62]

Underneath these premiers and ministers there was a large class of government employees appointed in an ever-inflated bureaucracy to administer on a daily basis the expanding economic and social activities of the state. This class was composed of managers and technocrats—civilians or former officers—in public-sector projects and hierarchically complex government offices, and they owed their social mobility into a secured middle class to state capitalism, enjoying stable salaries and subsidized apartments, education, health care, and food. All government employees had to join ASU. Their offices overlapped with those of ASU, as the morning bureaucrats were the same as the afternoon cadres of ASU in their localities. Nazih Ayubi argues that the main reason for the expansion of the bureaucracy with frail ideological underpinnings was that "the development strategy that the regime followed in general had a technical rather than an ideological tendency . . . the development programs (although valuable) were imposed from above and the 'socialist' policies most times were applied without socialists. Thus, the public sector and the comprehensive national plan were required to function without the support of a crystallized political ideology or an active political party."[63]

At the front of the workers and their unions in state-owned factories, ASU similarly mostly controlled nonideologues. With the expansion of state capitalism, a new labor "elite" arose in the public sector. The socialist laws granted industrial workers the right to share a percentage of annual profits and be elected board members in their state-owned factories— next to technocratic managers. With this came great opportunities for social mobility for many of them. They were fully dependent on the state for stable wages, social housing, and subsidized food and services.[64] The regime first forged a romantic image of the workers when it commenced the High Dam project in the late 1950s, as poets and singers praised the hardworking laborer who was eager to learn how to work new technologies and advance his country's national development and economic independence away from imperialist capitalism. For the rest of the 1960s, celebrated romantic singer Abd al-Halim Hafiz praised the nation's expanding factories and their dedicated laborers in many cheerful, highly motivating, state-produced songs for socialist propaganda.[65]

However, this rosy image had many dark sides. Labor unions had to work within the boundaries set by ASU, and their leaders had to be loyal to the party's securitized structure. They all had to be aligned under the party's secretaries and committees of workers in the corporatist system. The Ministry of Labor, which controlled labor unions, and ASU's statutes declared that these unions were to "implement the policy drawn up by ASU."[66] Former officer Sabri, prime minister and ASU secretary general, supported the latter doctrine when he affirmed that in a socialist system the duty of unions was to enhance production rather than fight against the capital owner—in this case the state itself.[67] Ayubi indicates that the socialist system followed two parallel strategies with workers: granting them a set of financial and administrative rights, on the one hand, and organizationally controlling them by subjugating their unions to government laws and party control, on the other. The number of registered unions was restricted, they all had to be part of the Egyptian Trade Unions Federation (ETUF), and ASU controlled their cultural organs.[68] In his testimony about the period as chairman of El-Nasr Automotive Manufacturing Company, engineer Adil Jazarin described the confusing status of the workers inside his own factory: "The high politicization of the workers through ASU led to that each factory had three different bodies for workers: an ASU unit with its head, a labor union with its head, and the labor members of the board. Often times all three of them conflicted with each other, and they all conflicted with the technocratic managers."[69]

In socialist factories run like military camps, ASU recruited labor leaders who were loyal to the party yet were opportunist figures.[70] Samir Amin observed that the military regime "tried to corrupt labor leaders and board members by giving them direct and indirect privileges."[71] In *Layali a-Hilmiyya* (Nights of Hilmiyya), the most popular TV series in the late 1980s, we follow the life trajectory of Rayyis Zakariyya, who worked at a pasha's textile factory in the 1940s and was a nationalist figure who participated in popular resistance against Western colonialism. After the nationalization of his factory, Zakariyya was elected a board member and suddenly experienced social mobility that made his companions, including a communist fellow, uncomfortable with his new lavish lifestyle and frustrated with his careless attitude about their rightful demands—especially with the intelligence services he presented to ASU inside the factory.[72] We see a more complex, dramatic portrait of the period's workers in the above-mentioned novel and TV show *Zaynab wa-l-'Arsh* of 1972. In a nationalized newspaper, a former army officer administered secret cells as part of an ASU underground organization whose mission was to indoctrinate select groups.[73] One cell was for the printing workers, and its few members varied: an opportunist who saw joining the cell as a chance to get closer to power and collect favors, an anxious one who agreed to join only out of fear of authorities, and a critic who always questioned the contents of the "secret" pamphlets being handed out.[74]

At the front of the peasants, the situation was not very different. In village cooperatives that were similarly run like military camps, a new rural class of medium landowners benefited the most from the land reform laws and constituted the docile members that ASU recruited and gave seats in the parliament. Economist Abdel-Fadil revealed that rural change was limited mainly to redistributing large properties of the old aristocracy to small peasants, without affecting the medium properties between 5 and 50 *feddans*, which remained intact and even expanded. Middle peasants came to own one-third of the country's land by 1965, when they composed only 5 percent of the total number of proprietors. Generally and beyond the old aristocracy, Abdel-Fadil divided farmers in this period into five different classes: (1) landless, destitute peasants working as seasonal laborers; (2) the poor who owned less than 2 *feddans* and made up more than 50 percent of propertied families; (3) small peasants owning between 2 and 5 *feddans*; (4) middle-class owners of between 5 and 20 *feddans* who enjoyed better living conditions based on commercial farming; and finally (5) the rich who owned between 20 and 50 *feddans* and applied capitalist means of advanced cultivation. Abdel-Fadil asserted that it was this last class of "agricultural capitalists," to which most village mayors and notables belonged, that enjoyed ASU's positions in the villages and cooperatives.[75]

As for the political role of small peasants who received land from Nasser, ASU practically recruited them for public cheering. In his harsh critique of Nasser titled *'Awdat al-Wa'i* (Return of the Consciousness), al-Hakim described a scene that he witnessed where lower-class peasants were brought to Cairo in trains in large numbers by local ASU officials, on a trip the government funded. The main task of those poor peasants was to cheer for Nasser in the capital as he returned from abroad. The chanted slogans were printed on pieces of paper and handed out to them to memorize. The villagers were divided into groups, each with a cheerleader standing in an assigned location to signal the initiation of chanting upon Nasser's passing.[76] Other literary works depicted such peasants as being subjugated by oppressive and corrupt managers of the agricultural cooperatives—whose board members were all ASU local leaders.[77] Romantic novelist Ihsan Abd al-Quddus drew a critical portrait of rural political/social relations on the eve of and after the 1967 defeat. In *al-Rusasa la Tazal fi Jaybi* (The Bullet Is Still in My Pocket), Abd al-Quddus narrated the story of Fatima, daughter of a village notable who allied himself with the crooked manager of the local cooperative, 'Abbas. While depriving helpless small peasants of their shares in the subsidized goods the state distributed through the cooperative, 'Abbas illicitly favored Fatima's father with fertilizer, seeds, and machinery. But he eventually raped and abandoned Fatima. Her poorer cousin, also an army solider, restored her lost honor by marrying her after restoring the country's honor by bringing the 1973 war victory.[78]

Professional syndicates likewise received a military camp's treatment and were full of submissive nonideologues. ASU tried to assimilate the syndicates of lawyers, journalists, doctors, engineers, teachers, cinema and stage actors, musicians, accountants, and so forth through different mechanisms, including using the localized intelligence services of its loyal members. Most of these syndicates—especially that of lawyers—were created during the colonial period with largely elite memberships and enjoyed long institutional traditions. Springborg gave careful consideration to the relation between ASU and the fourteen syndicates in Egypt at the time. They were "assigned a suitable role in the new socialist society, but attempts to dilute their bourgeois character and to make them more active, mobilization-oriented organizations never progressed beyond rhetoric," Springborg asserted.[79] In ASU's crackdown on syndicates after 1964, for instance, the party made sure that their elected presidents and vice presidents were party loyalists. It particularly gave much closer attention to the lawyers syndicate by making lists of candidates for all board positions. ASU also created an internal "higher council for press" to control the journalists syndicate and demanded that all publications of societies should go to the council to monitor their content first. Soon afterward, Nasser probably realized that such policies did not bring about the ideologically faithful professionals he expected, so he issued new instructions for his deputies: "Look for men who believe in the people . . . sincere and loyal to socialism and the Revolution." He suggested creating vanguard cells of ten to twenty "dedicated socialists" with "ties to the masses" in each syndicate.[80] Nonetheless, as Springborg illustrated, this vision faced members' active resistance against ASU and its control in general, especially after 1967.

Among the state institutions that needed to adhere to socialism was the military, namely the officers in service. The army not only was never socialist but also hindered the whole process of transforming to socialism and further securitized the civilian realms for its own interests.

The Commander and the Commissar

The Egyptian Army was not the same as the one in 1952 by the time socialism was applied. Most first- and second-tier Free Officers had already moved to prestigious civilian positions. Moreover, meeting the revolutionary goals of social justice, military academies opened their doors wide to equally admit cadets from all social classes, free of fees throughout the 1950s.[81] But Nasser then felt the need to coup-proof his regime from the rapidly changing military institution, so no other enthusiastic young officers would overthrow it. He certainly looked around at the enormous number of military coups taking place in surrounding Arab countries during his eighteen years in power. As Ayubi puts it: "Up to the end of the 1960s or so, the Arab world was notorious for the frequency and scope of the intervention of its military in politics. In the three decades from the 1940s to the 1960s, there were at least three dozen actual and abortive coups observed in the region."[82] This was particularly true in Syria and Iraq, with the Baath Party ideologically recruiting army officers and backing them to overthrow regimes. But Nasser was indeed successful in coup-proofing his regime: Egypt did not have a single military coup after 1952. Nonetheless, this came at a heavy price. Nasser allowed the military institution to expand its privileges and develop a domineering position within society, in conflict with the socialist party and hindering his socialist scheme itself.

The relationship between Nasser and his long-serving minister of war, Abd al-Hakim 'Amir, was one of the most mysterious in Egyptian modern history. It was a close friendship that guaranteed no coups but resulted in catastrophic events. Under continuous "emotional" and other kinds of pressure, Nasser involuntary allowed 'Amir to create an autonomous status for the armed forces. But 'Amir grabbed a degree of authority equivalent to that of the president himself and went way beyond the military into various civilian areas, including the economy and even sports. Moreover, military factories enjoyed a far superior status to the public sector and its socialist laws.

Hailing from a notable rural family and the second man in RCC after Nasser, 'Amir was promoted from major directly to general and appointed the commander-in-chief of the armed forces in 1953, adding the title of minister of war in 1954. 'Amir's army was defeated in the first military encounter it entered during the 1956 Suez Crisis.[83] Unable to purge him or his circle of commanders after their inefficiency in this war, Nasser reconciled with 'Amir and promoted him to field marshal in 1958. 'Amir not only kept a professionally poorly developed army but also greatly expanded the military's political influence: he created an intelligence agency in tense competition with Nasser's security apparatus; hired officers in numerous civilian positions; and increased salaries and lavish perks of the officers, fostering a patron-client relation with them. The 1958 union with Syria was probably Nasser's chance to send 'Amir away, so he appointed him as the governor of Syria. 'Amir mismanaged relations with the Syrian Army and minister of interior and eventually faced a coup that detained him in his Damascus office and tore apart the united republic in 1961. After 'Amir's humiliating return from Syria to Cairo, Nasser made another failed attempt to remove him and purge his patronage circle in the officer corps by inviting him to join the newly created Presidential Council. 'Amir refused, knowing that he enjoyed engrained loyalty and support of the officers. Nasser once more had to reconcile with him and kept him as commander-in-chief, even shockingly promoting him to vice supreme commander of the armed forces—sharing authority over war decisions with the president.[84]

Thus during the drafting and issuing of the socialist National Charter, there was a severe situation of "duality of power" between Nasser as the president, on the one hand, and 'Amir and his close circle of officers running a security web, on the other.[85] We hear Nasser expressing his concern about this in Abd al-Latif al-Baghdadi's memoirs by wondering: "Are there two states here—the army and the state? This situation is not right."[86] Hazem Kandil argues that Nasser's very decision to create ASU was in order to build a political organization with a social base to enable him to balance 'Amir's power. A far-reaching ruling party that directly mobilized the masses was Nasser's solution to counter military domination over public life, Kandil asserts. 'Amir resisted the plan by launching a war against ASU. "And because 'Amir was aware of this, he fought the new organization fiercely. A good example is the Alexandria summer camp incident of 1964, when the . . . [party's] youth branch (the Socialist Youth Organization) chose the following topic for its cadres to research during their stay: 'How should ASU youth resist a possible coup?' When the MID [Military Intelligence Department] reported the episode to Amer, he was naturally furious."[87]

Generally in single-party systems, tension usually persists between the commander and the commissar, or military chiefs and party leaders—and Nasser's Egypt was no exception. As much as the one ruling party's leadership needed a professional army to build its domestic control and international strength, it often perceived this army as a threat to its monopoly over power. In the Soviet Union, civil-military relations experienced a communist elite trying to ideologically subjugate the Red Army with bloody episodes of resentment on the side of the latter. In fact, during the years when Nasser was tailoring his own one-party system and was close to the Soviet Union, Nikita Khrushchev was leading the Soviet Communist Party and state, from 1958 to 1964, and his model of party-military relations was troubled. Khrushchev struggled with an inner conflict and split in the army between one group that fought for autonym and another willing to submit to the party's ideology and its political interference.[88] Nasser faced a military institution whose commander-in-chief insisted on remaining fully autonomous and in constant dispute with the party over territories of political influence.

Upon promulgating the socialist charter and constitution, the army was required to adopt socialism as its official ideology. Originally in the 1950s, military education and indoctrination was ideology-free: it focused mainly on values of Egyptian nationalism, patriotism, and individual excellence, according to a 1958 issue of *Majallat al-Jaysh* (Military Magazine).[89] The charter necessitated developing a strong, well-equipped national army that would work as "the shield of the struggle for economic and social progress," but it asserted that the needs of defense should not overshadow the needs of development. Article 23 of the 1964 socialist constitution plainly stated that in the Egyptian Republic, "the people own the armed forces . . . and their duty is to protect the socialist gains of the popular struggle, and to protect the country, the safety of its land, and its security."[90]

But this never meant that 'Amir's military ideologically submitted itself to the socialist party's leaders—who were also the top government officials. On the contrary, the army constantly intervened in ASU's activities and restructured the party's youth organization.[91] Sabri, prime minister and head of ASU, opined that the army held "rightist self-interests" rather than leftist orientations: it adopted no ideology but allied itself with the conservatives for its own interests. But Sabri asserted that Nasser managed to overcome the conservative effect of the military and kept the upper hand in domestic and foreign policies. He denied that the army enjoyed much control over economic and political decisions and insisted that 'Amir's men did not "rule the country." A former officer himself, Sabri justified the appointment of a large number of 'Amir's men in the public sector by indicating that they were qualified and argued that there was a need to depend on the army in certain sectors at certain times—such as transportation and public outlets for subsidized goods.[92] However, Sadat, the Speaker of Parliament and top ASU member during the same period, opined otherwise. Sadat relayed that instead of focusing on professionalizing the army, 'Amir made sure to install himself in all civilian realms. 'Amir sought to hire officers or ex-officers in all "sensitive" positions in the state, such as governors of provinces and heads of state-owned enterprises. He controlled hiring and firing civilians in every state institution, Sadat asserted.[93]

As a party leader and premier, Sabri exercised little actual authority compared to 'Amir, Sadat indicated. When Nasser removed Sabri and appointed Zakariyya as prime minister instead, the latter did not stay in this position for more than a few months because 'Amir did not like him, Sadat opined. Zakariyya was succeeded by a favorite of 'Amir's, Sidqi Sulayman. 'Amir continued expanding his powers to the extent that "every public task in the country was assigned to the army or the military police. If public transportation, for instance, was in bad conditions, it was attached to the armed forces to fix. The armed forces supervised fisheries." Sadat added that "even when [social housing] apartments were vacant, the army stepped in to distribute them." 'Amir became the sole controller of peoples' lives and all the country's events, and even complaints of public authorities or individuals were referred to the army to resolve.[94]

This crucial period's minister of industry, Sidqi, agreed with Sadat regarding the military's superior economic influence and Nasser's deep dilemma with it. On the one hand, Nasser sought to hire qualified civilians in key economic positions to build the country. Sidqi himself was one of those among many others, as Nasser called on him to create the ministry after reading his Harvard dissertation on the industrialization of Egypt, when Sidqi was only thirty-six years old. On the other hand, like other Third World leaders, Nasser had to rely on the army to remain in power. So he had to please the officers by hiring them in numerous bureaucratic places, while depending on the expertise of highly qualified civilians to manage the economy. In Sidqi's opinion, the expanding economic influence of 'Amir and the military institution ruined Nasser's state. Sidqi narrated one incident in which the head of the petroleum authority died in an accident and Sidqi nominated another civilian technocrat to succeed him. But he was surprised that 'Amir had talked Nasser into hiring an unqualified lieutenant general whom he wanted to send to early retirement instead. Sidqi eventually convinced Nasser to hire an experienced candidate in this position, but he still appointed that retired officer as the head of the maritime transport authority; "he brought about destruction to it," Sidqi sadly asserted. Furthermore, Sidqi attests that the army then had its own "secret budget" outside the auditing reach of the state's accountability authority.[95]

Interestingly, even the realm of sports came under the control of 'Amir's military. Officers monopolized leadership of football clubs and the sports unions of tennis, volleyball, rowing, wrestling, fencing, swimming, shooting, squash, boxing, and rural clubs, along with the Supreme Council of Youth and Sports. Generally after 1952, the Free Officers paid special attention to football—the most popular sport in Egypt since the British colonizer introduced it to the country in the 1880s—and other athletics in order to utilize their popularity to tap into their wide base of fans. Immediately after the revolution, Naguib rode in an open car around a stadium, waving at the fans, before a game between the armed forces' football team and a civilian one—and of course the former won the match. RCC members attended important football matches with civilian masses. 'Amir, however, took this practice too far, reaching a stage of conspicuous corruption. He was a fanatic fan of the Zamalik Football Club, which was headed during the colonial period by 'Amir's own uncle, who was also the king's minister of war. 'Amir totally blurred the lines between his position as minister of war and head of the football union. When Zamalik was nationalized in 1961, 'Amir appointed his brother—who also managed public-sector enterprises—to head it. Moreover, he appointed the Zamalik players in the army to honorary ranks with salaries and perks. He infamously forced sports reporters not to criticize his favorite team.[96]

In dire need to still counter 'Amir's power against the presidency and the party, Nasser created a secret political arm within ASU called the "Vanguard Organization." Nasser created the group in mid-1963 by inviting only four security and intellectual figures—far away from 'Amir's circle—and asking each one to form a secret cell of no more than ten trusted members upon Nasser's and security approval of every person. Ironically, when 'Amir heard the news, he volunteered to form some cells inside the armed forces. Communists were invited to join, and they happily dissolved their movements for this purpose—which angered 'Amir, who was not on good terms with

Marxism. The minister of interior was appointed the secretary general of VO, which reflected its high securitization. The duties of its intensively indoctrinated cadres were to secretly report political and personal information on everybody they knew at work or home—they even reported on their own families. Its cells were first divided geographically to cover workplaces and neighborhoods and later expanded to cover all ministers, the parliament, universities, public TV, youth organizations, and so on. The experiment was not very successful, as 'Amir managed to install his loyalists in the organization's locations and penetrate its cells.[97]

Military factories under 'Amir enjoyed an exceptional status above the state budget and central planning and did not abide by the socialist laws. In his testimony about working at arms factory 54, civilian engineer Muhammad Abd al-Wahhab indicated that the state favored military factories, even in their civilian production activities, and privileged them over public-sector plants. First of all, they enjoyed priority in receiving foreign currency to purchase western or eastern technology. When military factories ventured into civilian manufacturing by utilizing some of their lines for this purpose, they had direct access to state funds without waiting in the long bureaucratic line of the government. For instance, they produced sewing machines with a Swedish license and kitchen stoves, and imported foundries to manufacture water pumps. In both kinds of production, military factories devised a different administrative system, overstepping the malfunctioning one imposed on the public sector: they had no hierarchal bureaucracy hindering innovative initiatives or manufacturing speed, they promoted workers based on productivity rather than mere seniority, and they did not have to hire redundant labor to help the welfare state with unemployment.[98]

More important, in his testimony as a public-sector manager, civilian engineer Adil Jazarin attested that socialist laws regarding labor were not applied in military factories. Workers there were not represented on the boards of directors, were prohibited from creating labor unions, and were not allowed to form ASU units on their premises. Managers of military factories who were officers or officer engineers disciplined their workers more strictly compared to those running the public sector. Furthermore, Jazarin explained that military factories that engaged in civilian production ignored government planning and did not coordinate with the ministry of industry and its public-sector companies that manufactured the exact same goods. For instance, the fighter jet factories produced heaters and fridges, which civilian factories also made. They only started to coordinate when military factories significantly expanded in civilian production and functioned as subsuppliers for the public sector, such as Factory 9 directing its foundry to provide processed parts to the El-Nasr car plant. Also military factories enjoyed the state's support in sending their employees abroad for advanced technical education in the Western and later the Eastern bloc. Overall, Jazarin confirmed that the privileges granted to military factories helped them avoid many of the problems that the public sector suffered from and that led to its decline, including delays in receiving state investments, lack of imported technology, bureaucratic conflicts, and being overstaffed with unneeded employees.[99]

The military institution hindered socialism in another way that was not entirely 'Amir's fault. Military expenditure took up a significant part of the developing state, and this was due to Nasser's strategic goals regarding his pan-Arab regional ambitions in the Cold War context. Nasser worked on developing a strong modern military both to back his revolutionary foreign policy and to face neighboring Israel. The size of the Egyptian Army grew from 80,000 in the mid-1950s to about 180,000 in the mid-1960s.[100] During the first year of the revolution in 1952–53, defense expenditures consumed only 4.9 percent of the country's GNP. In Nasser's first year as president in 1954–55, this percentage increased to 5.7. It understandably reached 8.4 during the Suez Crisis of 1955–56 but came back to 5.5 in 1957–58. There was a considerable increase from 1962 onward, with the start of the Yemen War that lasted for five years: it reached 7.1 in 1961–62; 8.5 in the following year; 11.1 in 1966; and 12.7 in 1967—when heavy capital was much needed in the rapid industrialization scheme and the expanding responsibilities of the welfare state. During his first ten years in power, Nasser managed to fund such large spending by relying on the nationalization of the private sector and state monopoly over capital.[101]

Political scientist Nazly Madkour argued in 1980 that such a large defense program was beneficial for the "socio-economic development of Egypt." Influenced by modernization theory approaches that perceived a constructive role for the modern military institutions in developing countries in Latin America and Asia, Madkour argued that armed forces were "modernizers and nation-builders." The expensive military manufacturing, for instance, played a pioneering role as a "vehicle for the transfer of modern technology" to civilian production and granted the civilian technocrats who worked in the military manufacturing firms opportunities for professional advancement and stable salaries, Madkour asserted. Concentrating on the huge number of rural conscripts—barely educated youth—she asserted that the army was "a medium through which modern characteristics were bestowed upon the Egyptian peasant." Through an "acculturation" process, compulsory conscription changed the traditional beliefs and attitudes of uneducated peasants and exposed them to cultural horizons beyond their closed village world, and they returned to civilian life with some education and vocational training to utilize. Many turned from agricultural into industrial wage laborers in the city with a much higher ratio of productivity. Madkour added that the army's increasing demand for goods and services either for the salaried officers' personal consumption or for corps supply made the foundation of many civilian industries feasible and sustainable.[102] Obviously, the socioeconomic benefits that Madkour highlighted were other facets of militarizing urban and rural spaces across the nation.

In addition, Nasser was able to afford large military expenditures to serve these modernization and other strategic goals only in the first few years of applying socialism, when state enterprises yielded rapid economic growth—especially under a successful first five-year plan. The country faced budgetary issues and a crisis with foreign currency reserves in 1964, and the army's spending in the ongoing Yemen War hindered the second five-year plan. This long war was part of Nasser's regional policy against traditional monarchies. It aimed at overthrowing the Yemeni tribal imam backed by Saudi Arabian Kings Saud and Faisal and helping create a pan-Arabist republic instead. With financial difficulties and the Soviet unwillingness to give Egyptian military factories technology necessary to produce armaments for themselves, Nasser had to become acutely more dependent on the Soviets for arms imports for the long run. The Soviets delivered discounted supplies with debts repaid after twenty years at low interest rates. However, Michael Barnett invites social concerns to this dilemma:

Although the costs of the war were not considered excessive at the rate of approximately LE40 to 60 million a year, it was enough both to restrict the implementation of the second five-year plan and shove the economy further toward deterioration. In fact, the government appeared somewhat uneasy about fully disclosing the costs of the Yemen War; the figures were underreported to forestall substantial societal resistance to the perceived economic hardship and assist Nasser's desire to maintain political control. . . . Consequently the government looked for foreign assistance to solve its balance of payments deficit.

Again, the principal Soviet role was alleviating a prime source of balance of payments difficulties—weapons imports.[103]

After his catastrophic defeat in 1967, 'Amir again refused to leave his position as the powerful minister of war. He resented resignation and allegedly plotted a coup against Nasser, but he suddenly died two months after the defeat. Whether he committed suicide as the official news reported or was poisoned by Nasser's men as his family claimed, 'Amir's abrupt departure marked a brief transition to reprofessionalize the army and demilitarize the state.

Out of Arab Socialism, 1967–1977

The end of Arab socialism in Egypt officially took place after Nasser's sudden death. After two long decades, the military regime's revolutionary era ended up with full conversion from the left to the far right. A conservative Free Officer and new president of the republic, Sadat altered Nasser's leftist polices through a bold process of economic liberalization coupled with demilitarization. As a matter of fact, what Sadat did was no more than a natural evolution of the above-mentioned situation, namely, a destined result of a socialist system run by nonideologues who were probably waiting for the opportunity to opt out of the confinements of ASU for the luxuries of an open market. Under the social pressure that followed the military defeat and economic crisis of 1967, Nasser himself loosened his radicalism and changed into a pragmatic leader by taking steps for a degree of liberalization and demilitarization. Sadat's conversion was a continuity of these measures, but he took them too far, dismantling the socialist order altogether—with the enthusiastic assistance of the very technocrats, party cadres, and social classes that Nasser had mobilized. While those elements benefited from jumping off Nasser's ship, many other social groups lost and violent bread riots were their response.

On the eve of the defeat, there was already a pressing need for economic reform. State capitalism with an import substitution industrialization (ISI) strategy, common in developing Third World countries at the time, was a success story until the mid-1960s—with the application of the first five-year plan. By 1966–67 the state had created and owned 5,259 enterprises, out of which 360 were large manufacturing plants that hired more than

500 employees. These industries focused on goods such as cars, refrigerators, chemicals, metals, and petroleum. Meanwhile, after agrarian reform, the expansion of a class of capitalist, medium-sized landowners created a lucrative market for state-produced goods such as assembled tractors, fertilizers, chemicals, and pesticides.[104] However, the infant state-owned industries enjoyed only a domestic market with the support of a protectionist government, were uncompetitive in advanced global markets, failed to generate foreign currency to finance the ambitious state planning, and were overstaffed with civil servants. John Waterbury and Alan Richards summarize the situation:

> The First Five-Year Plan . . . combining aspects of the easy (textile, sugar, automobile, pharmaceuticals) and hard (heavy engineering, steel, chemicals, and fertilizers) phases. It generated 1 million new jobs and growth rates of 6% per annum. Yet in 1965 it ended in crisis. . . . Egypt's new industries were designed to market their products in Egypt. . . . Thus, although they needed imports to function, they could not generate the foreign exchange they needed to pay for them. . . . At the same time, the state's large outlays on construction and social services drove up domestic demand without commensurate increases in surplus of goods, so that inflation reared its head. Finally, the fact that few state-owned enterprises were profitable and many were padded with redundant personnel in an effort to create jobs meant that the government had to resort to deficit financing to cover their losses.[105]

Mark Cooper asserted that the post-1967 period was the beginning of an era of economic liberalization that Nasser initiated, and Sadat's policies were but a continuation of it.[106] In February 1968 Nasser faced widespread mass demonstrations organized mainly by workers and an emerging student movement expressing angry dissatisfaction with the military, economic performance, and party repression. A month later Nasser issued the 30 March Statement that aimed at restructuring the economy and the political system. He appointed experienced technocrats in the cabinet, replaced the managers of the public sector, and "democratized" ASU through a bottom-up election system in selecting local leaders to replace the old top-down appointments.[107] Many steps followed to reform the public sector, redistribute resources between the public and the private sector, ease regulations on foreign currency transfers into and out of the country, open market opportunities for the rural bourgeoisie of large and medium landholders, and allow individual freedom to import consumer goods. However, these measures raised the criticism of ASU's gatekeepers and debates between "centrist" and "radical" stances within the regime and intellectual circles. Cooper asserted that privileged groups in the public sector and the bureaucracy in particular perceived reform as a threat to their rights and powers. For instance, workers' leaders at ASU opposed the reforms, and the minutes of the parliament recorded that for many "the rationalization of the public sector was defined as an assault on the socialist gains of the revolution."[108]

At the front of demilitarizing the government, Nasser similarly initiated a process that Sadat carried on. It was a twofold strategy: on the one hand he attempted to reprofessionalize the army and on the other he took the military out of politics. After purging many officers who exerted political influence after 'Amir's death, Nasser appointed a new commander-in-chief and a chief of staff who focused only on corps professionalism.[109] Moreover, he responded to civilian technocrats voicing opposition against officers' appointments in government occupations. Nasser replaced many ex-officers in the government, mostly with academics. Michael Barnett explained: "Nasser . . . began to strip the armed forces of those responsibilities not directly relevant to national security. These purges handed the technocrats a more visible and integral role in the decision-making process. These moves . . . marked the public emergence of a more 'pragmatic' Nasser, one who was willing to suspend radicalism at home in favor of domestic stability and military power."[110] In 1966 the cabinet had twenty-one military figures occupying 55.3 percent of the ministerial seats. In October 1968 they decreased to thirteen, making up 41.9 percent.[111]

Once he assumed power, Sadat started by accelerating this demilitarization process and then moved to focus on economic liberalization—especially after consolidating his political legitimacy by fighting the 1973 war. As vice president when Nasser passed away, Sadat succeeded him immediately as president. But other ex-officers in control of the security apparatus and the party saw themselves as the more legitimate successors of Nasser and plotted to overthrow Sadat. Through what he called the "Corrective Revolution" of May 1971, Sadat countered the coup plot and swept out the influential ex-officers remaining from Nasser's regime.[112] He arrested and sent to jail a large group of ninety-one officials, including ministers, ASU and VO leaders, parliament members, army officers in service, and more.[113]

The party's civilian opportunists were quick to support Sadat's bold movement against the hard-core ideologues, especially Sabri, who was among the arrested plotters. Some factory workers in the public sector even staged demonstrations to support the arrests—"they were fake protests by order," Sabri insisted.[114] At VO, many of the most ideologically indoctrinated and faithful cadres were among the quickest to abandon the socialist cause and convert to Sadat.[115]

Sadat followed by demilitarizing the cabinet. Springborg asserts that under the new president, "every time officers were retired [from the government], civilians occupied their positions." He explains that less than 13 percent of Sadat's ministers were military, and one-third of those had received a technical education. In his last cabinet, only two ministers came from the military: those of defense and foreign affairs. Furthermore, Sadat radically reduced the number of military governors of provinces. Whereas in 1964 there were twenty-two military governors, this number declined to only five out of twenty-six in 1980.[116] Compiling aggregate data about the process in its early stages, Cooper elaborates:

> With the January 1972 cabinet, the military declined to a level below any other cabinet since 1952 and it continued to decline. . . . Of 131 ministers who served under Nasser, 20.6 percent were officers and 13.9 percent were officer technocrats. Under Sadat, of 127 ministers, 7.5 percent were officers and 7.5 percent were officer technocrats. If we restrict ourselves to the "Sadat period ministries," officers represent only 3.8 percent while officer technocrats rise to 9.0 percent. . . . [T]wo increases in specific civilian occupations during the Sadat period are notable. First . . . lawyers rose from 12.2 percent to 23.3 percent. Second, economists rose from 9.2 percent to 15 percent.[117]

Before moving to discuss Sadat's radical economic liberalization process, it is important to delve into his persona and ideological underpinnings. Sadat is a highly controversial figure in Egyptian political culture, even decades after his assassination, and he has more critics than admirers. Nasser clearly trusted Sadat and kept him very close and influential. In 1953 RCC appointed Sadat editor-in-chief of the first state-owned newspaper, al-Jumhuriyya (The Republic). In a 1954 al-Jumhuriyya article, Sadat praised the noble objectives of the Muslim Brothers but insisted that they had members seeking power for self-interest and justified the regime's backlash against them.[118] Around the same time, *al-Jumuhriyya* published many other pieces that positively featured persecution of communist activists, and others in support of individual freedoms and rights of private business and workers alike.[119] In an English-language book that Sadat published in New York in 1957, titled *Revolt on the Nile*, with a foreword by Nasser, Colonel Sadat harshly condemned both the Muslim Brothers and the communists. He described the two as "equally dangerous forces [that] arose to take advantage of Egypt's weakness." He advanced an anti-imperialist rhetoric emphasizing "social justice" for the revolution.[120] Sadat later served as the Speaker of the Parliament between 1960 and 1968, a member of ASU's supreme executive committee, and finally vice president in 1969. But his foe Sabri claimed that Nasser did not invite him to join the VO.[121]

Many years later, in his autobiography published in 1978, President Sadat still condemned communism but spoke more positively about the Muslim Brothers. He showed his support of and good connections with rural elites, and absolute condemnation of Marxist activism in the countryside. Sadat criticized the "committee of liquidation of feudalism," created to consolidate land reform and arbitrarily managed by 'Amir.[122] In the internationally renowned Kamshish incident, in which an aristocratic family in a Delta village killed a peasants' rights activist over a land dispute in May 1967 and Che Guevara, Jean-Paul Sartre, and Simone de Beauvoir visited the struggling village in solidarity, Sadat disagreed with Nasser's support of this village's cause. This was a period when Nasser was on good terms with the communists. Sadat argued that although brutal feudalism did exist in Kamshish, "indeed the people Nasser [backed] . . . were worse than the feudalists: they were Communists and Marxists who wanted by their attack on feudalism to substitute a Marxist system."[123] On the other hand, Sadat relayed his positive experience collaborating with the brotherhood and their supreme leader, Hasan al-Banna, before 1952. He sympathetically defended their position against Nasser's persecution in the 1960s and explained how he released them from jail after Nasser died.[124]

Transitioning to a liberalized economy, Sadat officially applied an "open door" policy, called *infitah*, in 1974. A year after he declared victory in the 1973 war and retained the Sinai Peninsula, Sadat gained enough political legitimacy and popularity to alter Nasser's socialism. The plan originally included welcoming back private business—local and foreign capital alike—privatization of the public sector, eliminating subsides, floating the local currency, reversing agrarian reform in the interest of rural bourgeoisie, and eradicating the political influence of agricultural cooperatives. Moreover, Sadat dismembered ASU by dividing it into different segments, each with its own political stance, and these segments later split to create their own independent political parties. These measures were designed by the IMF and applied in response to its pressure, along with pressure from other Western and Arab money.[125] Let's take a look here at two exemplary groups that now supported infitah: technocrats and workers.

For elite technocrats, Hinnebusch argues that they originally held liberal rather than leftist stances when they joined Nasser's regime. Sadat urgently needed their support and was successful in obtaining it. They were happy to convert to infitah because Sadat preserved their privileges and opened the door for them to gain access to Western high technology, business opportunities for themselves and their families, and Western consumerism. Hinnebusch explains:

Sadat raised their salaries and lowered their taxes. . . . Nasir's nationalization measures and development program opened up many opportunities for career advancement for technocrats and administrators. But the private interests or opportunities of their families were also sometimes damaged or narrowed. . . . Under *infitah*, opportunities again began to widen. For those with political clout and connections the influx of foreign aid and business opened up opportunities, licit or illicit, for tax-free commissions and "consulting work." For those who had acquired business experience and connections in the public sector, there were now opportunities to join higher-paying private firms or go into business for themselves. Under Nasir, import controls greatly narrowed the elite's access to the Western consumer goods and life style they believed their due; under Sadat this access was restored. Under Nasir, the military domination of power was resented by civilian elites; but as Sadat pushed the military out of top elite roles, opportunities for civilians to acquire power grew.[126]

All of Sadat's prime ministers were key civil servants in Nasser's socialist state.[127] Two interesting characters were the premiers during the troubled infitah and had to face the deep public discontent it generated. Abd al-'Aziz Hijazi (1974–1975) studied trade in England, and Nasser appointed him to many important positions relevant to industrialization and military factories before entrusting him with the ministry of treasury. He worked to apply

Nasser's economic reform plan after the defeat and continued this mission when Sadat appointed him minister of finance, economy, and foreign trade in 1974. Finally he became the infamous premier who issued the Arab and foreign investment law no. 43 of 1974 known as *qanun al-infitah*. The angry masses who protested the increase in food prices chanted "Hijazi bey ya Hijazi bey, kilu al-lahma ba'a bi-ginih" (Oh Hijazi bey, oh Hijazi bey, a kilogram of meat costs one pound).[128] Mamduh Salim (1975–1978) was a police officer whom Nasser entrusted with his personal security and appointed governor of three provinces at different times. In 1977 Salim had to face massive bread riots against the elimination of subsidies.

Many other previously socialist key officials took a lead in infitah. Agricultural engineer Sayed Marei, a pre-1952 rich politician who was Nasser's minister of agriculture and applied agrarian reform laws for many years, formed one of the most important patron-client relations with Sadat. Marei served as the Speaker of the Parliament during the conversion years from 1974 to 1978. He also was Sadat's head of ASU, where he carried on the mission of eradicating remaining socialists from the party and restructuring it away from the left. Furthermore, Marei's son married the president's daughter in 1974.[129] Years before facing the 1977 bread riots, civilian economist al-Qaysuni—who studied in London and worked for the World Bank—served as Nasser's minister of economy, finance, trade, and planning in addition to deputy prime minister at different times. Sadat appointed al-Qaysuni deputy prime minister for economic and financial affairs in 1976 and then minister of planning the following year. In response to the IMF's recommendations to reduce the budget deficit, al-Qaysuni presented a government proposal at the parliament to reduce subsidies on basic goods. When the news about his action was leaked to the public in Cairo, at the night of January 16, 1977, violent demonstrations swept the country for the following two days.

As for the workers, many of them readily switched to Sadat's camp and even gave up rights acquired under socialism in return for salary increases. The open-door policy transformed many public-sector enterprises into joint companies with both state and private investments, and this required removing the labor representatives from the boards of directors of these companies. Engineer Adil Jazarin, chairman of El-Nasr car plant under Nasser and Sadat, relayed how he managed this difficult decision in his own company. As another nonideologue himself, Jazarin believed that granting the workers places in the administration, along with their politicization through ASU, was not a good policy because the workers were not qualified or trained for management roles. Jazarin is particularly proud that his company was the first to turn into a joint venture by introducing foreign investments in order to "liberate it from the public sector's constrains." Fearing protests, the prime minister then asked him to obtain the approval of the workers for losing their seats on the board, and surprisingly the union did agree and gave him written consent. Jazarin persuaded them by promises to double or triple their salaries.[130]

In parallel to this economic infitah, there was also a political infitah that included a degree of democratization. First off, Sadat welcomed back the Muslim Brothers and nourished the rise of political Islam. As for ASU and its remaining leftist ideologues, Sadat fractured the party and created a new one composed of his own loyalists. In 1974 Sadat divided ASU into three "platforms" representing the right, center, and left wings inside the party; later they became their own parties and he headed the rightist one. In 1976 he created and led the National Democratic Party (NDP) and made it into the new ruling party with the members of ASU who were close to him. Within the ruins of the dismantled party, many of the VO-indoctrinated members were happy to join the consumerist world of infitah. Novelist Sonallah Ibrahim in *al-Jalid* (The Snow) sheds light on their story. The protagonist of this novel narrated his experience in an academic exchange program in Moscow in the early 1970s. He came across many government officials and diplomats sent on missions to the Soviet Union, and they cared mainly about carrying consumer goods with them back to Egypt. A cultural attaché in the Egyptian Embassy bought a Volvo car from Finland; he was originally "a VO cadre in ASU . . . but turned into a Sadat supporter and they [the regime] sent him to Moscow to control Egyptian students abroad."[131]

Eradicating the omnipotent power of ASU, market liberalization, and demilitarization by no means meant that the masses were now free. On the contrary, the suffocating circuits of ASU's surveillance were left to other forms of Sadat's oppression: crushing social disparities and poverty. Sadat had to restore militarization and rely on the armed forces to quell the 1977 bread riots.

When the government faced pressure from the IMF and foreign banks to cut public expenditures, the cabinet considered reducing spending in many areas, including defense. It chose to begin with food subsidies, supposedly the easiest area to target.[132] Violent protests instantly broke out on January 17 and 18, primarily in Cairo and Alexandria. Frustrated, unemployed youth attacked or burned banks, government buildings, police stations, buses, trains, night clubs, and so forth and engaged in street fights with security forces. Some gathered in Tahrir Square and attempted to attack the American University in Cairo, which symbolized U.S. hegemony for them. They flooded into other squares to destroy billboards of luxury consumer goods and trams, and the hungry ones stormed into public food outlets in lower-class neighborhoods and carried off goods and money. The state-owned newspaper, *al-Jumhuriyya*, accused the communists of plotting the violence and published the Ministry of the Interior's allegedly found evidence on this "conspiracy." The paper also published statements issued by labor unions and student organizations condemning the conspiracy. Sadat called it the "the insurrection of the thief" (*intifadat al-haramiyya*) but canceled the decisions that triggered it. He asked the commander-in-chief, Field Marshal Abd al-Ghani al-Jamasi—the famed chief of ground operations during the 1973 war—to deploy the army, declare a state of emergency, impose a curfew, and help put thousands of citizens in jail. The soldiers completed the task competently and returned back to their barracks after only three days.[133]

This dramatic era of liberalization and demilitarization ended with Sadat's assassination in 1981. The army did come back to public life in the next decade, but did so in order to embark on entirely different roles than those it had played in the previous thirty years. Under a new military president, the officers returned as business entrepreneurs, and to exercise novel forms of observing and disciplining the masses.

CHAPTER 2

The Good 1980s

Arms, Consumerism, and Scandals

> The thing that makes war both the starting point for an analysis of society and
> the deciding factor in social organization, is the problem of military organiza-
> tion or, quite simply, this: Who has the weapons?
> —Foucault, *Society Must Be Defended*

In his novel *Zaat*, Sonallah Ibrahim depicts the life of a female government employee who was born under Nasser's socialism, married under
Sadat's open market or infitah, and faced constant social pressure to
manage her family's needs in Mubarak's consumerist culture during the
1980s. Zaat's coworkers and neighbors bragged about owning imported
goods such as canned food, vacuum cleaners, washers, drinks, and clothes,
and she barely survived within this fierce competition of shopping with her
small income. She had a recurring dream about "destroying" her apartment's
old bathroom, as a TV commercial urged viewers to do, and renovating it
with trendy ceramics—which she eventually did when her husband got
a job in a rich, oil-producing Gulf country. Meanwhile, Zaat covered her
hair with a headscarf as the Gulf's conservative culture spread in Egypt.[1]
Fiction was not far from reality. In a 1984 book economist Ibrahim al-
'Isawi described how billboards advertising for luxury goods swept Cairo's
streets, and how making quick and big money through selling imported
goods, dealing in real estate, and smuggling foreign products afflicted society.
This gave birth to what he called a "parasitical" class of petite capitalists—
the infitah's nouveau riche—that mainly thrived on patron-client relations
with corrupt state officials.[2] Just out of long wars and facing the idleness
of peace, Egypt's charismatic and domineering minister of defense, Field
Marshal Abdel-Halim Abu Ghazala, decided that the army should join this
era of infitah.

Egypt fought the last war against and signed a peace treaty with its traditional enemy, Israel, in the 1970s. Throughout the 1980s the Egyptian Army almost lost its importance or relevance in society and was supposed to go back to its barracks. Nevertheless, it successfully managed to adapt to change and reposition itself within shifting domestic, regional, and global environments. Under Hosni Mubarak, the third military president of postcolonial Egypt, the army indeed enjoyed a good 1980s. It was an eventful decade of the military's infitah to U.S. arms, Arabian Gulf markets, and big profits from creating civilian enterprises that took advantage of a consumerist influx in Egyptian society. Although the military no longer controlled large numbers of citizens as drafted soldiers in camps and combat, it extended the methods of control that it inherited from the times of war to the entire society. The military was the most powerful state institution, with amassed weapons, strong external allies, and autonomous sources of wealth. Its gigantic business entities tapped into the expanding consumer market of all social classes, both to make a profit and to reinstate the military's close grip on everyday life. This was all devised by one empire-builder: Abu Ghazala. This almighty man eventually lost his career to the politics of scandal.

Abu Ghazala was minister of defense and military production for eight years, from 1981 to 1989. Anwar Sadat brought him from Washington, D.C, where he was serving as a military attaché, to appoint him first chief of staff and then defense minister. Mubarak kept him in the latter position and additionally named him deputy prime minister. Upon assuming power, Abu Ghazala expanded the defense industry to export an increasing amount of heavy and small armament to neighboring countries. Moreover, his military corps embarked on extensive economic activities in civilian sectors such as food production, building apartments, and car manufacturing. In his early career Abu Ghazala studied in the Soviet Union, but later he turned into a vocally anti-Soviet and pro-U.S. figure. Abu Ghazala visited Washington, D.C., on a regular basis and formed close ties with the U.S. Embassy in Cairo.[3] His relations with Washington remained good, until he tripped over a rocket technology smuggling attempt, which not only scandalously failed but also arguably led to his drastic demise shortly afterward. This was not the only scandal in the dramatic life of the field marshal. Abu Ghazala was known for being an observant and pious Muslim, with a wife who wore an Islamic veil, but stories of his alleged affairs with women filled the local press.

Generally, Abu Ghazala's years witnessed many crucial developments. They included improved U.S.-Egyptian relations, the Iran-Iraq War, the rising influence of Gulf states after an oil boom, and reluctant economic liberalization in Egypt. He sought to maximize the military institution's profits from the opportunities that these events opened. Abu Ghazala craftily repositioned the Egyptian military within three changing realms: international, regional, and domestic.

First, he reactivated the Egyptian military's role within a global Cold War that was approaching its end. Mubarak inherited from Sadat an Egypt that was already on the U.S. side of this war. Abu Ghazala's long reign exactly overlapped with the presidency of Ronald Reagan (1981–1989), who stabilized U.S. military aid to Egypt while preaching global neoliberalism as the Soviet Union was dissolving. There were many problems in the region, and the Reagan administration had certain expectations from the Egyptian Army pertaining to U.S. allies and foes in the Middle East. Iraq was fighting a war against Iran—a proxy war that Saddam Hussein entered on behalf of the United States against the nascent Islamic republic. Similarly, there was another proxy war in Afghanistan between local groups co-opted by the Soviet Union and the United States. In Libya, just to the west of Egypt, Qadhafi was a proclaimed Soviet ally, and to the east, the Palestinian resistance would not negotiate with Israel. The United States needed to provide protection to its oil-producing allies in the Arabian Gulf. Abu Ghazala posed as a close ally of Washington to help with its security concerns in the region. In return he enjoyed unprecedented access to U.S. arms. During his reign, this access turned into a fixed annual amount of $1.3 billion in military aid, which Egypt has continued to receive up to the present day.

Second, Abu Ghazala revived his military-industrial complex in a lucrative regional market thirsty for arms. During the Iran-Iraq War, his arms sales to Iraq reached a billion dollars in one year, and the Gulf states mostly footed Saddam's bill for being a U.S. ally. Abu Ghazala also sent weapons to the Afghan *mujahidin,* and the United States footed the bill this time. Abu Ghazala used the immense profits to further expand the defense industry and target other Middle Eastern and African markets. To satisfy both national needs and the infitah to the regional markets for weapons, the number of military factories under Abu Ghazala expanded to thirty plants, employing tens of thousands of workers. They manufactured and exported fighter jets, missiles, radar systems, armor, ammunition, and much more at hundreds of thousands of dollars every year. To fund such large ventures, the military budget reached 22 percent of government expenditure in FY 1982–83 and maintained almost the same figure until FY 1987–88 (see table 2). These years were the golden age for Egypt's arms industry.

Third, and most important, Abu Ghazala positioned the military in a domestic market of swelling consumerist needs of his officers and society as a whole. Having no more combat operations to busy themselves with, military corps switched their efforts to civilian economic activities that generated large profits and allowed the army a highly visible presence in social life. Upon signing the peace treaty, the Egyptian military created an economic entity called the National Service Projects Organization to establish business enterprises and assimilate the efforts of officers and conscripts alike in them. Although the size of the military was then reduced to between 300,000 and 450,000 personnel, this number was more than enough to expand a business empire. NSPO and other military corps acted as gigantic parastatal entities that took charge of government projects and embarked on their own enterprises as well.[4]

In this regard, the military took advantage of the ambiguous economic policies that Mubarak applied. Although Mubarak faced constant pressure from the United States and the IMF to fully liberalize the economy, which would entail full withdrawal of the state from the economy, he resented this for fear of bread riots similar to what his predecessor faced. The state continued to provide the masses with subsidized goods and services, and the military took advantage of the existence of such an "ambivalent market"— which was neither fully neoliberal nor socialist—by taking charge of many governmental duties for profit. Abu Ghazala's military parastatals constructed bakeries for subsidized bread, produced foodstuffs, built houses, renovated telephone lines, made cheap clothes, and so on for army and state needs alike. Moreover, they embarked on their own ventures of manufacturing cars and building luxury apartments, shopping malls, and lavish hospitals to cater to the infitah's nouveau riche.

From a Foucauldian perspective, there was nothing strange in such behavior of the Egyptian military. After all, Foucault views politics in the modern state as continuation of warfare, and Egypt's Abu Ghazala carried into post–peace accord politics what his army did during wartime: amassing resources and imposing omnipotent control over a disciplined population. Foucault explains: "It must not be forgotten that 'politics' has been conceived as a continuation, if not exactly and directly of war, at least of the military model as a fundamental means of preventing civil disorder. Politics, as a technique of internal peace and order, sought to implement the mechanism of the perfect army, of the disciplined mass, of the docile, useful troop, of the regiment in camp and in the field, on maneuvers and on exercise."[5] Foucault further elaborates in *Society Must Be Defended*, asserting:

> Power relations . . . are essentially anchored in a certain relationship of force that was established in and through war at a given historical moment. . . . While it is true that political power puts an end to war and establishes or attempts to establish the reign of peace and civil society, it certainly does not do so in order to suspend the effects of power or naturalize the disequilibrium revealed by the last battle of war. . . . [T]he role of political power is perpetually to use a sort of silent war to reinscribe that relationship of force, and to reinscribe it in institutions, economic inequalities, language, and even bodies of individuals. . . . We are always writing the history of the same war, even when are writing the history of peace and its institutions.[6]

Abu Ghazala pursued the typical military dream of an ideal society: placed under meticulous subordination and uninterrupted surveillance—just like a camp.[7] He made sure to make his army the most powerful institution in the state, and from that position he penetrated into the daily life of citizens targeted for urban observation and control. Interestingly, he did so through selling those citizens—whether rich, nouveau riche, middle class, or poor within a liberalized market—goods and providing them with services in the name of helping with economic development and the welfare of the nation. Thus Abu Ghazala reinstated the army's old role of ultimate domination over society, by forging novel methods and rhetoric of population control.

This chapter follows Abu Ghazala's good 1980s within his three global, regional, and domestic realms of action. The first section investigates how he built his institutional might through close ties with the United States and a flow of weapons. It also covers his defense industry and the related scandalous attempt at smuggling American rocket technology. The second section explores the process of turning military corps into parastatal enterprises, and the army's growing business empire that targeted markets of basic and luxury goods alike. Finally, the third section covers Abu Ghazala's elevated political influence and how he saved Mubarak's regime during the violent riots by repressed security forces. Moreover, it reveals how alleged affairs with women took down the religious field marshal.

U.S. Arms and Scandals

Abu Ghazala owed his successful military relationship with the United States to Sadat's persistent efforts to lay its foundations. After terminating Nasser's long-time military ties with the Soviet Union in the early 1970s, it took Sadat many years to persuade successive U.S. administrations that his Egypt was worthy of receiving American weapons. Sadat's attempt at showing loyalty to his new Western ally were met only by U.S. reluctance and insignificant shipments of arms. Only when Sadat visited Jerusalem and signed the peace agreement with Israel did U.S. reluctance end and the flow of military assistance to Egypt start. However, it came mostly in the form of debt and small grants. As the years passed, Egypt defaulted on paying back its accumulated debt, but its strategic importance to the United States grew essential. Finally, Abu Ghazala succeeded in turning U.S. arms shipments into an annual, fixed grant in 1986. In the following year the two countries also signed an agreement to coproduce M1A1 tanks. But the ambitious field marshal soon, and scandalously, damaged his relation with Washington for good.

Sadat decided to switch Cold War camps as early as mid-1972, when he terminated the service of about fifteen thousand Soviet military experts in Egypt and sent them home. In 1974, from Cairo, Secretary of State Henry Kissinger and Sadat announced a resumption of U.S.-Egyptian diplomatic relations, which were cut after the 1967 war. On the same occasion Sadat announced ending Egyptian dependence on Soviet arms, and this was followed by a U.S. military mission visiting Egypt for eight days even while assuring Israel that this mission was not tied to arms sales. In the following year Sadat went himself to Washington to request arms, and Kissinger supported such potential sales in Congress. In February 1976 President Gerald Ford agreed to sell Sadat a humble shipment of six C-130 transport aircraft along with spare parts and training at $65 million, to be paid immediately in cash. The sale faced heavy Israeli protestation and pressure on Congress to disapprove it.[8] As a U.S. Air Force official put it to justify the sale to seriously concerned members of Congress, it was only a tactical cargo plane for air logistics and "would not be of significance."[9] Not surprisingly, Sadat wanted much more. He asked the parliament to nullify the Egyptian-Soviet Friendship Treaty and then boldly demanded defense weapons from the United States. Meanwhile, Kissinger told Congress that the United States had "no commitment to rearm Egypt or to sell it any military supplies beyond a pending sale of six C-130." He added, "We certainly do not seek to become the major arms supplier of Egypt."[10] In the following year the United States again reluctantly sold Sadat another shipment of fourteen C-130 planes and a number of drones at the total cost of $250.9 million, and controversy erupted again in Congress.[11]

Things started to change after Sadat's 1977 historic visit to Jerusalem and his peace speech in the Knesset. In 1978 the Jimmy Carter administration announced a program of a "linked sale" of fighter jets to Egypt, Israel, and Saudi Arabia; that is, none of the three countries would receive its share without the others. Conspicuously favoring Israel and adding to military imbalances in the region, the sale was divided up as follows: 50 F-5 aircraft to Egypt, 60 F-5s to Saudi Arabia, and 75 F-16s and 15 F-15s to Israel.[12] Saudi Arabia promised to pay for Egypt's procurement, but it delayed the payment for many months and the United States postponed the sale for an indefinite period the following year amid Egyptian-Israeli peace negotiations that Saudi Arabia disapproved of.[13]

Finally, the Camp David peace accord with Israel radically altered things for Sadat in 1979. The Carter administration presented a military and economic aid package of $4.8 billion for Egypt and Israel together upon signing the agreement. The military aid was in the form of loans through the Foreign Military Sales (FMS) program to be received over the course of three years and paid back over a period of thirty years with a grace period of eleven years, whereas economic aid was all grants. Egypt's share was $1.5 billion of military loans and $300 million of economic aid, and Israel's significantly bigger share was $2.2 billion of military loans and $800 million of economic aid—when Egyptian population was around 41 million and that of Israel was 3.8.[14] U.S. security credit for Egypt aimed to replace obsolete Soviet equipment that lacked spare parts for upgrading. Congress raised questions about the ability of Egypt to repay the loans and discussed potential financial help to Egypt from other Arab countries. In this regard, Congress alluded to the fact that Saudi Arabia had refrained from funding the Egyptian purchase of F-5s the previous year and had now cut diplomatic relations with Egypt.[15]

The United States sought to maximize its benefits from such large sales through two main actions: gaining access to Egyptian officers and establishing a permanent military base in Egypt. While Sadat responded positively to the former, he strongly and repeatedly refused the latter. The sales included a number of 35 F-4 Phantom fighter-bombers and other equipment, followed after their arrival in Egypt by a U.S. Air Force unit with 450 military personnel to spend ninety days at an air base near Cairo for training with Egyptian military pilots.[16] As officials at the U.S. Embassy in Cairo noted then: "Training operations would give the U.S. greater access to Egyptian officers. The Egyptian government in the past has limited such contacts." Sadat did allow American soldiers to establish immediate relations with their Egyptian counterparts at all levels, and they could now "talk to any military personnel they wished to."[17] On the other hand, Sadat adamantly refused the American plan to construct an air and naval base in Ras Banas on the Red Sea. He turned down the Carter administration's request for a contractual agreement in this regard and only allowed U.S. units to use Egyptian facilities for temporary purposes and without any written obligations. U.S. troops did use Egyptian facilities in joint exercises to gain "desert experience," as the Afghan War was expanding, but this also benefited Egyptian officers acquiring more training on the new American weapons. The U.S. Air Force occasionally used an air base in Qina in Upper Egypt to stage operations, including one relevant to Iran. The United States sought to construct a marine laboratory for naval missions in Hurghada on the Red Sea, but nothing was built. Sadat also refused the U.S. request to take over two Israeli air bases in Sinai, which Israel was to evacuate upon its final withdrawal from the peninsula.[18]

As the new president Mubarak and his continuing minister of defense Abu Ghazala both affirmed adherence to the peace accord with Israel,[19] U.S. cash military sales to Egypt steadily increased in the immediately following years. Egypt received $550 million of military sales in 1981, and this increased to $900 million in 1982 and again to $1.325 billion in 1983—while Israel received $1.4 billion (1981 and 1982) and $1.7 billion (1983). Egypt's amount was fixed at $1.3 billion from 1984 onward, while Israel's was fixed at $1.8 billion.[20] In 1984 Abu Ghazala claimed that the Egyptian military budget was $1.8 billion dollars, or 15 percent of a total state budget of $15 billion.[21] This meant that procurement from the United States swallowed up more than 70 percent of Egypt's military budget and about 9 percent of the state budget. Egypt anyway did not pay the full amount as it bought things on credit and thus accumulated heavy debt to the United States.[22] In the meantime, the Reagan administration made another attempt to build the Ras Banas base on the Red Sea. In early 1982 U.S. defense officials were under the impression that Mubarak had consented to the idea, so Congress allocated initial funds to design it. Proposing an ambitious plan in the following year, the Department of Defense asked for about $99 million to construct this base in 1983. Sensing Egyptian hesitance in 1984, the Defense Department asked Congress to authorize the smaller amount of $55 million for the construction of the same base at a smaller scale. Egypt again turned down the project, allowing neither large nor small facilities.[23]

The most important shift in U.S.-Egyptian military relations took place when the Reagan administration decided to convert arms sales from loans to full grants and to do the same for Israel. In early 1985 Congress discussed the pressing dilemma of Egypt's inability to pay back its military debt accumulated since 1979, now reaching $4.55 billion, especially without any potential financial help from Saudi Arabia. In appreciation of Egypt's commitment to peace and as a reflection of U.S. desire to help modernize the country's armed forces, an assistant secretary in the Department of State stated before Congress: "We are requesting that the entire military assistance package [to Egypt] be provided in the form of forgiven credits. Between FY 79 and FY 84 we approved $4.55 billion in military assistance loans for Egypt. Payments on those loans now account for over ten percent of Egypt's annual debt service obligations. Continuing to support Egypt's military modernization program with loans would risk creating a situation where the modernization program would become an onerous burden on the Egyptian economy."[24]

Thus from FY 1986 onward, Egypt was to receive an annual 1.3 billion in military aid from the United States without interruption, an amount that continues today. In 1986 Egypt and Israel together received as grants two-thirds of U.S. military assistance worldwide.[25] In the same year Abu Ghazala complained that this amount was no longer enough to meet increasing regional security needs and pledged to ask U.S. officials for a raise of a several hundred million dollars.[26] But the amount has remained fixed ever since. At least one voice in Congress raised concerns about Israel's higher share, or "aid parity between Israel and Egypt," as he put it. After recognizing that this question was in the mind of many members of Congress, a State Department official responded: "Egypt should receive assistance comparable to that which Israel receives. But . . . comparability is not to be interpreted that the aid levels should be identical. We're dealing with two different economies, two different countries, and their specific needs differ."[27]

In return for this constantly flowing aid, the United States had specific, albeit unwritten, regional expectations of Egypt. The long list included assisting in the Persian Gulf security or protection of the oil-producing Arab states; containing the radical Palestinian front and persuading the Palestine Liberation Organization (PLO) to sit at the negotiating table for long-term Israeli security; targeting radical Muammar Qadhafi's Libya, an armed Soviet ally; watching Bashar al-Assad's Syria, a recipient of heavy Soviet military aid that regularly intervened in Lebanon; targeting the new Islamic republic in Iran, a prominent enemy of the United States since the hostage crisis of 1980; and maintaining good and militarily cooperative relations with Sudan to counter Qadhafi's influence. Throughout the 1980s Egypt fulfilled its duty against Iran when it provided Iraq with weapons during its war against Ayatollah Khomeini, and militarily threatened Libya and was a few times on the brink of war with Qadhafi. After receiving the aid package, Sadat showed willingness to help any Gulf country attacked by external forces. On the contrary, Mubarak was more cautious and expressed reluctance to make such risky commitments except on a case-by-case basis—depending on who asked for help in the region and the nature of the attack.[28] But Mubarak did deliver in this area momentously when Iraq invaded Kuwait in 1990, when the Egyptian Army took a pivotal part in the Western-Arab coalition to liberate this oil-rich state.

This takes us to the dilemma of accumulated military debt. It did not go away by converting sales to grants. But Mubarak met his greatest moment of luck by resolving the issue just at the right time at the turn of the decade when Iraq suddenly invaded Kuwait. At the tenth anniversary of the Camp David accord, in 1989, Egypt was to start paying back the United States its $4.5 billion of military debt with interest, at a time when Egypt's total foreign debt reached $44 billion. Facing the crisis, Egypt sought to conclude an agreement with the IMF to reschedule its debt, but the organization conditioned granting of the application on economic reform policies—which Mubarak resented for fear of public discontent.[29] In the summer of 1990 Iraq invaded Kuwait and the United States crucially needed the Egyptian Army's participation in the coalition to liberate the occupied Gulf country. A month after the invasion, President George H. W. Bush hurried to cancel the then $7.1 billion of Egypt's debt. He requested Congress's authorization to forgive the debt, but the Senate opposed the request and pressured him to withdraw it, citing issues of national budget deficit and domestic disapproval.[30] Two months later Bush's plan passed and the United States and other Gulf states canceled $14 billion of Egypt's military debt. Mubarak's armed forces played a vital role in the successful "Operation Desert Storm" to free Kuwait in January 1991. Bush again handsomely rewarded Mubarak by lobbying to make European allies forgive half of the $20.2 billion that Egypt owed them.[31]

As part of the military aid package, Abu Ghazala successfully pressed the United States to sign an agreement on coproduction of M1A1 tanks. In February 1987, a year after converting military assistance to a fixed annual grant, the ambitious Abu Ghazala requested coproduction of this advanced tank. Not welcoming the idea, the Defense Department suggested it might discuss the possibility "some years out in the future" but meanwhile sent a team to Egypt to inspect military production facilities that could be expanded and improved for new activities.[32] Two months later Abu Ghazala pressured the U.S. assistant secretary of defense for international security affairs, who was then attending the annual meeting of U.S.-Egyptian Cooperation Committee in Cairo, and even identified a location for manufacturing the tank in a factory under construction in Abu Za'bal, north of Cairo. Warming up to the potential profitable deal, General Dynamics planned to display this latest generation of American tanks in that year's summer joint U.S.-Egyptian military exercises, "Bright Star."[33]

In June the Reagan administration announced an agreement to coproduce the most advanced U.S. tank, the M1A1 Abrams, with Egypt without consulting Congress and only formally notified it in the following year. Prestigiously for Abu Ghazala, Egypt was the first country to build this machinery outside the United States, and he hoped to produce 1,000 to 1,500 tanks. Nonetheless, he needed U.S. permission for intended exportation, and it could veto any undesired resales. According to the *Washington Post*, Abu Ghazala "lobbied Washington for more than a year to get approval for the M1 . . . and has overcome U.S. Army opposition in Defense Department deliberations." However, the newspaper cited controversy in the capital about transferring sensitive military technology and critics of Egypt's ambition to become a military power, which they considered a threat to Israel.[34]

Immediately after receiving the good news, military factory 200 in Abu Za'bal collaborated with General Dynamics to modify the facility to adapt to producing the M1A1 Abrams on a massive scale. The M1A1 was the "best tank in the world," the U.S. defense secretary asserted after signing the deal with Abu Ghazala by end of 1988, authorizing Egypt to produce only 524 tanks.[35] Egypt was to make 40 percent of the tank, and the rest was to be manufactured in the United States and assembled in Factory 200, which also repaired M60 tanks and produced light armored vehicles. The factory opened for business in 1991, but trouble began even before that. After sacking Abu Ghazala, Mubarak had second thoughts about the extremely costly enterprise, and in fact to most of Abu Ghazala's ambitious defense industry ventures, in the shadow of the country's heavy debts and economic crisis. Furthermore, Iraq was trying to persuade Egypt to give up the venture and coproduce a less expensive, Soviet-model tank with it instead. But the production contract had cancellation penalties that Mubarak could not afford.[36]

The United States soon started to question, or rather regret, its decision. When the U.S. Government Accountability Office (GAO) assessed the project a few years later, it concluded that the United States should not have responded to Egypt's pressure to engage in this expensive partnership. It was a $3.2 billion project, where the United States carried $2.491 billion and Egypt $663 million of the cost. The GAO asserted that selling Egypt complete tanks was a much cheaper choice, costing only $1.9 billion. Its 1993 report on the matter stated:

> U.S.-paid costs include $1.881 million for the tanks and related support . . . , $150 to design and oversee the construction of the factory, and $460 million for coproduction support. Egyptian-paid costs include $605 million for factory construction and equipment, and $58 million for labor, supplies, cannon production, and other costs. . . . [State] Department officials, citing Egypt's insistence on coproduction and other factors, were convinced that Egypt would not accept complete U.S-built tanks as a substitute, so they never considered the option seriously. . . . Coproducing the tanks in Egypt, as opposed to providing complete U.S.-built tanks, increased program cost from about $1.9 to about $2.7 billion. . . . This $820 million added cost could have been used to provide support equipment for the new M1A1 tanks to fulfill other Egyptian military requirements.[37]

Moreover, this report revealed that Egypt would not achieve its hopes of technology transfer and self-sufficiency in tank production through this project. "Six increments of production were initially planned, with Egypt progressively completing more of the tank. However, the plans for Egypt completing more of the tank in each increment have been reduced, limiting the production technologies transferred to Egypt." The report affirmed that the Egyptian goal in the project conflicted with that of the United States. It stated, "From the program's inception Egyptian self-sufficiency was limited because, for security reasons, the United States retained control of key technology items needed to produce the tank," and added that financial constraints made technology transfer minimal.[38]

This takes us to a crucial dilemma in U.S.-Egyptian military relations: American refusal to transfer technology to Abu Ghazala's expanding defense industry. This led to a smuggling scandal that permanently damaged his friendship with Washington. When Abu Ghazala embarked on a highly ambitious plan for arms manufacturing, a good regional market had fortunately opened during the Iran-Iraq War. However, all the arms he received from the United States never gave him access to the know-how. When Abu Ghazala assumed his position in 1981, two main state bodies were engaged in arms production: the Ministry of Military Production, with fifteen factories, 70,000 employees, and $240 million worth of production; and the Arab Organization for Industrialization, with seven factories, 18,000 employees, and $100 million worth of production. The latter had an interesting story. Sadat created it in 1975 in collaboration with three Gulf countries, Saudi Arabia, UAE, and Qatar, providing capital to build a strong Arab defense industry, and it signed coproduction agreements with European firms. When Sadat signed the peace treaty with Israel, the three Gulf countries withdrew from the project and demanded their money back, and European partners were hesitant to continue. But Abu Ghazala carried on.[39] Expanded military plants reached thirty factories with about 100,000 employees and an average of $400 million worth of production. Exports jumped from $30 million in 1981 to $550 million in 1988.[40] These plants assembled French jets, Chinese fighters, Brazilian trainers, British helicopters, British missiles, aircraft engines, guns and ammunition, and much more. Arabian Gulf and African states placed orders.[41] Interestingly, the United States granted Egypt the right to export arms to the American market, but experts opined that this agreement—signed between Abu Ghazala and the U.S. defense secretary—was mainly symbolic.[42]

During these promising times, Egypt made considerable profits from arms sales to Iraq during its war against Iran, as well as to the Afghan *mujahidin* backed by the United States against the Soviets.[43] But it faced technological difficulties and issues of sustainability. Philip Stoddard of the Defense Intelligence College stated: "Military sales in 1982 reached $1 billion, making weapons Egypt's second largest source of export revenue after oil. Much of this trade was with Iraq, financed by subsidies from the Gulf states. . . . Whether Egypt will be able to maintain sales at these levels is open to question . . . much of Egypt's arms industry is in the developing stage."[44] Likewise, Lieutenant Colonel Stephen H. Gotowicki of the U.S. Army argued that Egypt's engagement in assembling advanced weaponry with Western producers did not render it technologically capable. "The Egyptians receive kits for assembly, but the technology involved is closely maintained by the Western partner."[45] Regarding U.S. technology in particular, Ralph Sanders, professor at the National Defense University, asserted that buyers of American arms generally enjoyed trivial access to the manufacturing technology:

> Through such [U.S. arms sales] transactions a buyer gains a minimum of manufacturing know-how but can learn about operating and maintaining new weapons. While securing this latter knowledge is indispensable for conducting military operations, it does little to help a country build a production base. In some cases, the buyer can reverse engineer the military item. Yet, this task proves formidable for many developing countries which lack the infrastructure and skilled talent to reverse engineer a complex end item.[46]

Anxious to get hold of technology, Abu Ghazala made an unsuccessful attempt at smuggling it. On June 24, 1988, the U.S. Justice Department charged two Egyptian military officers and two Americans for illegally shipping sensitive missile parts from the United States to Egypt. Assigned to the Egyptian Embassy in Washington, D.C., Lieutenant Colonel Mohammed Abdella and Rear Admiral Abdel-Rahim Elgohary plotted with an Egyptian American rocket scientist and an American representative of a military contractor to execute the secret mission. U.S. authorities had tapped their telephone conversations a month earlier and caught the defendants red-handed in Baltimore airport trying to load aboard an Egyptian military C-130 cargo plane a box of 430 pounds of carbon fiber material used in building advanced missiles. The tapped calls involved Abdelkader Helmy, a forty-one-year-old Egyptian-born rocket scientist in California; James Huffman, a marketing representative of Teledyne McCormick-Selph, a military contractor in California; and Admiral Elgohary, in the procurement office of the Egyptian Embassy in Washington. The three men discussed methods of transporting various substances out to Cairo. The court-authorized wiretapped conversations made references to the "minister," making Abu Ghazala a suspect. The Justice Department investigated his involvement but eventually decided not name him in the federal indictment after consulting with the State Department, which persuaded it to erase any mention of Abu Ghazala from the investigative summary. In October Helmy confessed that Abu Ghazala recruited him for the scheme and that he met him twice, once in Cairo and another time in Washington. He claimed that Abu Ghazala asked for his aid in buying material for an Egyptian military research and development program, after giving him the impression that the United States approved the plan. Helmy pleaded guilty.[47]

Abu Ghazal was never charged in the case, but this scandal allegedly was the main cause for sacking him in April 1989. Whereas Egyptian media mentioned nothing about the court case, U.S. and Western press drew direct ties between his ouster and his embarrassing involvement in the crime.[48] After the case became public in the U.S. press, Mubarak asserted that such a plot did not exist, the Egyptian military attaché in Washington refused to comment, and Abu Ghazala remained silent and did not step a foot in Washington again until his removal.[49] Allegedly the smuggled material was for a several-year-old joint program between Egypt and Argentina, financed by Iraq, to develop a medium-range missile named Condor II. Western intelligence reports claimed the program sought to manufacture a ballistics rocket that could deploy chemical or nuclear warheads, when Western allies worked on stopping the spread of this technology to Third World countries. They also claimed that Egypt had a secret facility, a plant under construction near Abu Za'bal, that imported chemical equipment from a Swiss company to manufacture pharmaceuticals but could be converted to make lethal gas. Egypt withdrew from the joint program after the sacking of Abu Ghazala, and Mubarak had to repeatedly vow that Egypt did not have or produce chemical weapons and should not be treated like Qadhafi's Libya through such accusations.[50] Meanwhile, Egyptian intelligence agents arrested two Egyptian-American brothers and a court sentenced one of them to ten years in jail for being a CIA spy. Their mother asserted that her imprisoned son was a hostage of "a high-stakes espionage showdown between Cairo and Washington"; a senior Egyptian military official told her that he could be swapped for the convicted rocket scientist, Helmy.[51]

Another incident placed an unpleasant shadow over U.S.-Egyptian military relations. The GAO documented and revealed many cases of corruption in arms sales pertaining to illicit commissions from American contractors to Egyptian ex-officers. It reported that U.S. military contractors misused Foreign Military Financing (FMF) program funds awarded to Egypt and Israel to cover large commissions, travel expenses for foreign officers, or non-American items. The Defense Security Assistance Agency (DSAA) responsible for FMF funds did permit contractors to pay commissions or contingent fees up to $50,000, but the contractors far exceeded this amount and submitted false documentation. In the Egyptian procurements case, Loral Aerospace International for missiles and related hardware paid commissions of over $1 million to UNITRA, an Egyptian firm that employed former Egyptian army officers, to conclude a $227 million contract. UNITRA represented other U.S. firms, including General Electric and Ford Aerospace. In another incident, Motorola, a subcontractor of Beech Aircraft for surveillance aircrafts, paid $417,000 to an Egyptian sales agent called Technical Aerospace Consultants. Furthermore, the Defense Criminal Investigative Service convicted the former president of Detroit Armor Corporation for paying a commission in an Egyptian contract and providing a falsified statement about it to DSAA. In another case that was investigated by a congressional committee, a former employee at Teledyne accused the firm of paying illegal commissions and overcharging the U.S. and Egyptian governments. In another area of auditing regulations, DSAA prohibited using FMF funds for any travel expenses for officials involved in the sales. Nevertheless, Westinghouse paid travel costs of Egyptian officials that reached $15,730 in a $189 million contract. The above-mentioned GAO report documents many cases of corruption and violations in Israeli transactions as well.[52]

Military Parastatals, Civilian Consumers

Although Egypt continued with the infitah policy during the 1980s, Mubarak resented the idea of a complete withdrawal of the state from the economy. He preferred for his government to continue to extend subsidized goods and services to the masses in order to appease the discontented lower classes. Meanwhile, he allowed the infitah's nouveau riche to multiply their fortunes through open trade and collected more remittances from migrant laborers in the Gulf. At any rate, all these social groups were fond of consumerism. Abu Ghazala's military took advantage of the existence of such an "ambiguous market." Military corps presented themselves as gigantic parastatal entities taking charge of many public services and construction projects. Abu Ghazala expanded the civilian activities of the MoD's newly created NSPO and deployed the military logistics sectors and the technical expertise of certain corps toward this goal. In addition, Abu Ghazala developed profitable business enterprises to compete in a thriving consumer market full of officers and civilian families from all social classes. In the process, he used conscripts as almost free labor, appropriated massive pieces of state land, and collaborated with local and foreign capital. Thus Abu Ghazala's army inserted itself practically everywhere in the urban milieu, and its projects visibly penetrated into the daily life of subordinated consumers. To justify such activities irrelevant to defense, Abu Ghazala perpetuated rhetoric about their dual goal of the army's self-sufficiency and assisting the state with its developmental plans.

From the onset of its creation, NSPO enjoyed exceptional access to government resources and the ability to collaborate with private capital by law. Presidential Decree no. 32 of 1979 established it as a corporation with its own legal personality, in order to undertake public projects requested by different ministries, authorities, local councils, and public-sector companies. According to its internal statutes, NSPO was to participate in building the national economy and achieve the state goals in this regard. Its budget was to be independent from that of the MoD, and it was entitled to open its own bank accounts in local or foreign currencies.[53] The organization's board of directors reflected its aim to tap into conscripts as a labor pool and the logistics sector as an existing infrastructural resource, as it included the head of the Armed Forces Logistics and Supply Authority and the head of the Armed Forces Organization and Administration Authority—responsible for conscription.[54] Allowing it to collaborate with foreign or local private capital, Presidential Decree no. 583 of 1980 authorized NSPO to "undertake all of its economic, industrial, agricultural, administrative, commercial, and financial services and activities inside and outside the country. . . . The organization can establish all kinds of companies, either individually or in collaboration with national or foreign capital."[55] Abu Ghazala revised the organization's internal statutes in a 1982 ministerial decree, authorizing it to establish all forms of companies either alone or in partnership with private capital, and adding the head of the military engineers to its board.[56]

Initially, NSPO focused heavily on food production, through widespread land reclamation of tens of thousands of acres near Cairo, Alexandria, Fayyum, and other areas. Its Food Security Division (FSD) grew into the "single largest agro-industrial organization in Egypt," Springborg asserts; "The LE488 million worth of food production by the FSD in 1985–1986 was some 18 percent of the total value of food produced in Egypt that year."[57]

Besides cultivating wheat for bread and other agricultural crops on its vast farms, NSPO built dairy plants, mechanical slaughterhouses, poultry farms, egg production units, fish farms, frozen vegetables factories, fodder mills, and so on. After supplying the army, it sold the remainder at almost half of the market price. In addition, NSPO built numerous automated bakery plants for subsidized bread along with sale outlets in order to help the state avoid bread shortage crises. In 1983 Abu Ghazala affirmed that the armed forces produced five million loaves of bread for civilians per day, constituting 25 percent of Cairo's daily consumption. By 1988 military factories assembled up to 2,600 automatic and half-automatic bakery plants for military and civilian consumption alike.[58]

Acting as superior parastatals, the Engineering Authority of the Armed Forces along with other corps constructed roads, bridges, and social housing for the Ministry of Housing and Urban Development. Furthermore, it constructed schools for the Ministry of Education; water desalination plants for the Ministry of Water and Sewerage; stadiums and sporting clubs with covered halls and swimming pools for big sports events; and the Nasr City international conference center. It also constructed airports for the Ministry of Civil Aviation, such as the West Alexandria airport, and manufactured optical equipment for the Ministry of Health. The signal corps renewed telephone infrastructure for the Ministry of Communication in various upper- and middle-class neighborhoods in Cairo. The military even constructed public "cultural palaces" for the Ministry of Culture across the country, and these premises included performance spaces, cinema screens, art exhibition halls, libraries, and women's and children's clubs—all designed after the taste of military engineers.[59] Interestingly, to make sure that these projects did not suffer from delays in receiving state funds, Presidential Decree no. 253 of 1985 allocated a monthly amount of $10 million from the country's oil production revenue to the MoD to finance its outstanding contracts.[60]

The military engineers of EAAF constructed whole new urban communities and suburbs in the outskirts of Cairo, extending over tens of thousands of acres—either on lands of evacuated camps or in desert areas. In 1981 Abu Ghazala announced the building of eleven thousand housing units in seven locations in Cairo and Alexandria. By the end of 1986 he announced the construction of twenty-three military suburbs containing tens of thousands of apartment buildings along with all needed services, such as schools, movie theaters, post offices, sporting spaces, and social clubs.[61] "In 1985–86, almost

5 percent of all housing constructed in the country was built by and for the military," Springborg asserted.[62] Officers and subofficers received these flats at affordable prices paid over the course of sometimes thirty years, in new, upper- or middle-class urban communities in accordance with their respective ranks. Many of them sold their apartments to civilians in the booming market of luxury and affordable housing in rapidly changing urban spaces on the outskirts of Cairo.

Whenever Abu Ghazala opened a new project the military executed, he reiterated the same rhetoric emphasizing that such economic activities were for the armed forces' self-sufficiency as well as to help the government with pressing economic problems. For instance, after inaugurating new phone cables in an upper-class Cairo neighborhood in 1983, he asserted, "The armed forces are ready to undertake any project to reduce the burden on citizens, within the boundaries of labor surplus and without affecting combat efficiency."[63] Having to hire the army to execute public projects, government officials maintained a discourse about the military's successful model of self-sufficiency and the importance of extending this model to civilian sectors. For instance, when the prime minister opened new bread bakeries with Abu Ghazala next to him in 1988, he affirmed that his cabinet meant to apply the military's efficient experience to other ministries and authorities.[64]

In the lucrative area of consumer goods and services, the military started with shopping malls. NSPO constructed and ran malls, including, for instance, a three-story department store near the ministry's headquarters in 'Abbasiyya. This mall sold home appliances, electronics, carpets, foodstuff, auto parts, refrigerators, garments, furniture, leather products, and other goods.[65] Moreover, the military also tried to fulfill the consumerist desires of the officers and upper-class civilians living in the up-and-coming suburbs through opening a chain of cooperatives, *jam'iyyat istihlakiyya*. Describing these "pleasant shops," Springborg indicated that they sold "a range of domestic and imported goods generally unavailable elsewhere in Egypt, or only to be had at much higher prices."[66]

In fact, military buildings contributed to the rise and spread of a unique and new phenomenon at the time: American-style shopping malls in Cairo. For instance, today's upper- to middle-class suburb of Nasr City was originally desert land that the state gave to the military to use for camps and bases. The military either constructed its own luxury apartments and shopping malls in Nasr City or sold out pieces of this land to private businesses to undertake similar enterprises. These building projects catered to the infi- tah's nouveau riche or migrant professionals in the oil-producing Gulf who sent remittances, and they sought to satisfy these social groups' desires for imported commodities. During the 1990s Nasr City alone had eight gigan- tic malls serving its new wealthy inhabitants. In her detailed description of how the military privatized its landholdings in this suburb for such purposes, Mona Abaza interestingly explains:

> The military gradually sold off its sizable camps and bases, located at the fringes of the desert, to civilians, until Nasr City became the quarter it is today. . . . The main road of Nasr City, which leads to the airport, has a large complex of high-rise buildings called al-'Ubur (the crossing), constructed after the 1973 victory to house army of- ficers. . . . These flats were then sold privately. . . . Al-'Aqqad Mall in Nasr City is a good example of how the army has managed to go civilian. This mall was constructed by the association of officers of the Republican Guards who sold it later to a group of individuals. The person who constructed it was a retired general. . . . Al-'Aqqad Mall is thirty thousand square meters in size and it includes 250 shops. . . . It was constructed after, and in reaction to, the entertainment-laden Tiba Mall. . . . The planners of this mall . . . were mainly targeting families attracted by the shopping.[67]

Meanwhile, the military did not forget to cater to less opulent consumer needs of the middle and lower classes, who enjoyed surplus income they made either through Cairo's infitah petty trading businesses or as migrant labor in the Gulf countries. In 1983 Abu Ghazala opened seven factories for garments, shoes, and wooden and metal goods. The Logistics and Supply Authority took lead of these large enterprises, and a furniture plant followed them later. To assert that their products were of high quality, he indicated that their manufacturing lines were built by newly imported technology from Germany and Japan. Abu Ghazala even hoped to export these goods to African and Arab markets.[68]

Abu Ghazala also attempted to tap into the upper and middle classes' rush to purchase cars in the ever-expanding city of Cairo. In the capital's infitah society, owning a private vehicle grew into another mark of social mobility and prestige. The car-manufacturing venture of Abu Ghazala incorporated an important aspect of military business: partnership with foreign capital. During these years social historian and economist Galal Amin was astounded by the immense number of private cars (*al-sayyarat al-khassa*) that suddenly flooded the already overcrowded streets of Cairo, rushing against cheap and decaying public transportation inherited from socialist times. The inhabitants of the new, up-and-coming suburbs needed to get downtown, and owning a private car became an "urgent" need for the affluent younger generations; subsequently public buses and trams were doomed as a low-class system for the poor. "Something happened that made private cars not only a means of transportation, but also a symbol of social mobility, and inability to buy one became a sign of failure and a source of great frustration. . . . It is hard to find a single commodity more expressing of social mobility than a private car," Amin noted. He added that the state now would rather invest in building new bridges and roads to accommodate the needs of these vehicles than spend on improving public transportation.[69] Young officers joined this wave, and the army accommodated their desires through a special plan for purchasing cars on credit.[70] In such a milieu, Arab American Vehicles (AAV)—owned by AOI—started to produce military and civilian cars alike in the late 1970s. It partnered with many Western corporations to produce Jeep and other brands. It assembled cars with the German Daimler Chrysler, the French Peugeot, the Japanese Suzuki, and others.[71]

Moreover, Abu Ghazala made an ambitious, yet scandalously corrupt, attempt to partner with a U.S. giant: General Motors (GM). He negotiated with GM, in his capacity as the head of the Supreme Committee of Egyptian Passenger Cars, for two years until the latter reluctantly signed a coproduction deal in 1986. GM was under pressure from the U.S. Embassy in Cairo to sign, and it finally accepted when USAID pledged to subsidize the project by up to $200 million through the economic aid package. Owning 30 percent of the joint venture, GM was to use the installations of a public-sector company, El-Nasr Automotive Manufacturing Company, to build two small Corsa and Ascona vehicles. Abu Ghazala allegedly aimed to use the project to develop an engine plant for the military. GM invited an Egyptian private business tycoon to act as its agent in the deal. The controversial deal raised objections by the Egyptian ministry of industry and oppositional press about turning the national automotive sector into a dependent of an American corporation. Moreover, some USAID staffers opposed it, causing a scandal.[72] Springborg relays that Abu Ghazala worked closely with the U.S. ambassador, Nicholas Veliotes, and commercial councilor, Ted Rosen, to conclude this tricky deal. "The redirection of the aid fund was forced on the USAID Cairo office by Rosen and Veliotes, Abu Ghazala's personal involvement and his commitment to GM being used to persuade reluctant USAID officials to take up an opportunity that they should not, out of obligation to U.S. national interests, allow to be passed up. Several USAID staffers objected strongly, arguing that this diversion made a mockery of the aid program. . . . These staffers were transferred to other duties."[73] The deal eventually fell through, and GM Egypt obtained a license to assemble its own passenger cars a few years later.[74]

At a time when private hospitals were rising to cater to local nouveau riche as well as Arabian Gulf medical tourists at high fees, Abu Ghazala invested in medical complexes, or semiprivate hospitals. Near the headquarters of the Defense Ministry in Cairo, the Kubri al-Qubba medical complex included not only subhospitals for all specialties but also a medical college, a nursing high school, a vocational school for medical equipment, and apartments for officers receiving treatment. Other large military hospitals were built across Cairo, Alexandria, Suez Canal cities, and so on, and they even brought in expensive Western physicians. Abu Ghazala announced that all military "specialized" hospitals, or *mutakhasissa*—a term that new, profit-oriented hospitals used to describe their expensive services—would offer civilians treatment at international high standards to save them the trip to seek medical care abroad.[75]

In all their activities, military businesses not only enjoyed exemptions from customs and tariffs on their imported and exported goods but also received millions of dollars every month from the state to finance the imports. The Egyptian parliament promulgated law no. 91 of 1983, of which article 6 exempted the MoD from all forms of customs and taxes on its imports intended for "armament purposes." Besides ammunitions and arms, the long list of waivers included machinery, transportation means, medical equipment, drugs, and other supplies that could pass as either military or civilian. The same article exempted the MoD's exports to other foreign governments or institutions also for armament purposes. A year later law no. 2 of 1984 extended the same exceptional privileges to the Ministry of Military Production and all its subsidiaries, from companies to units to authorities. When a presidential decree was on a new customs law some two years later, it maintained the same privileges for the MoD and MoMP intact and verbatim. The first article of law no. 186 of 1986 listed in detail the same waiver list in the two older laws.[76] Since all imports or exported goods by the two ministries were designated as secret shipments for national security purposes, it was hard to check on their contents to make sure such exemptions were for military rather than civilian economic activities.

This was all in unfair competition with the private sector, let alone the decaying public sector. While some infitah big or petty businessmen resented the army's economic activities, others saw them as an opportunity to profit by joining the military's patronage circle and becoming a part of its elect group of subcontractors. On the part of the army, since NSPO's laws allowed it to partner with local capital, it preferred collaboration with the private sector over the public sector in executing projects; "not only because it perceives it as more dynamic and possessing superior resources, but also because of its ability generously to reciprocate favors," Springborg explained.[77] This was the case in the agricultural sector. In public construction, the military engineers evidently had strong ties with the single contracting tycoon in the country then—Osman Ahmed Osman of Arab Contractors.[78] But many private businesses argued that military projects harmed them because they denied them fair competition over government contracts.[79] Expressing their discontent, some private voices pointed out the issue of taking advantage of poor conscripts in military projects, or, as they called them, "slave labor."[80]

Cheap or free labor was the most abundant resource in military projects, through a constant flow of conscripted soldiers. The year Abu Ghazala left his position, in 1989, around 550,000 of the male population between ages eighteen and thirty were drafted into the armed forces for a period of between one and three years, based on their level of education (see table 1). Abu Ghazala deployed conscripts who were not "medically, culturally, technically, or psychologically fit" in civilian projects.[81] For instance, bakeries used illiterate soldiers from the countryside, and Abu Ghazala asserted that such tasks suited them because they did not require experience or technological skills. While constructing one of the automatic bakery plants, EAAF attached a five-story barrack serving as a dormitory for the soldiers working in it.[82] Furthermore, he established several vocational schools per year across the country to train technicians to work for both military corps requiring specialized technical expertise and civilian projects. The young graduates of these schools were obliged to work for the military for five years, and after that they were given the choice to either leave or sign permanent contracts to be hired at low, noncommissioned ranks.[83]

In addition, in order to encourage conscripts who did not hold educational degrees but already owned technical expertise to use it while in military service, Decree no. 143 of 1980 reduced the period of military service for craftsmen and handymen under the condition that they practice their skills to benefit military departments till the end of their enlistment.[84] The situation was different for permanently hired labor at military factories. As Abu Ghazala expanded the MoMP's factories, he also expanded services for the around seventy thousand workers and employees in Abu Za'bal, Shubra, Helwan, and Maadi, including housing, health care, transportation, and day care for children of female employees. From the thousands of apartment buildings constructed for them, they could purchase flats on credit paid over the course of thirty years, and they received health care through numerous clinics attached to their factories or outside them.[85]

Land was certainly another overabundant resource used in military enterprises. Through controversial processes, the military seized hundreds of thousands of square meters of land that it appropriated during wartime inside the cities or in the desert to use as camps. The army either sold this land for profit or used it to erect projects. Only several weeks after Mubarak won a national referendum to become president in 1981, Abu Ghazala announced the demolition of military camps in main cities, especially Cairo and Alexandria, in order to sell the land or construct apartment buildings for officers on it. He asserted that those destroyed camps would be replaced by others away from urban areas. When EAAF announced the building of a new suburb near the Suez Canal for officers over the area of 12,000 acres, it did not explain how it obtained this land from the state but indicated that the cost of construction would be covered by the sale of the camps' lands "owned" by the armed forces.[86] Nonetheless, not all citizens agreed that the land of evacuated camps was the army's legitimate property. A prominent law professor, Muhammad Nur Farahat, argued that the military rights over this land was tied only to defense activities, and its authority over it should be terminated with the end of the wars. He also expressed concerns about the military entering one of the most lucrative areas of the infitah's quick profit—real estate—which would link the institution's interests to those of the period's tycoons.[87]

In fact, Sadat and Mubarak did enact a set of laws that established the army's property rights to lands of evacuated camps. A few days before his assassination, Sadat issued Presidential Decree no. 531 of 1981 creating an organization within the MoD to undertake the duty of selling "state-owned land and estates" that the armed forces evacuated in public auctions and at market price. Although this law stipulated that the revenue of the sales should go to creating alternative camps and procurement, the army officials often stated that it was spent on other things, such as housing for officers.[88] Mubarak decided to name the new organization the Armed Forces' Land Projects Organization (AFLPO) and expanded its duties to engaging in business ventures. Article 1 in Presidential Decree no. 224 of 1982 stated: "In addition to the specialties stipulated in . . . [the 1981 decree], the organization is to undertake all administrative, commercial, financial services and activities which could enable it to achieve its goals and develop its resources. For this goal, it is entitled to create all forms of companies and associations."[89] It is worth adding here that Presidential Decree no. 403 of 1990 authorized AFLPO to sell its claimed land occupied by civilians who did not hold legal titles (wadi'i al-yadd) through "negotiated sales"—that is, negotiating prices and concluding contracts outside of public tenders.[90]

Meanwhile, when the state revised its laws and regulations pertaining to its vast desert lands, it granted the military greater control over the land that fell outside AFLPO's jurisdiction—namely, land that had not been occupied by military camps. Sadat's parliament promulgated law no. 143 of 1981 in order to regulate desert land reclamation aimed at increasing the agricultural areas in the overpopulated country, but it stipulated that the minister of defense was to decide first on "strategic areas of military importance" that the government would not be allowed to dispose of without his "approval" and "according to his terms."[91] To consolidate his military grip over desert land, Abu Ghazala's ministerial decree no. 367 of 1986 classified desert land in the country under two categories: the first was strategic locations not to be sold to private holders without the approval of the minister of defense and under his terms and conditions, and the second was open areas where civilian projects could be built but after "notifying the armed forces," which reserved the right to impose certain requirements regarding the height of buildings. Government authorities in charge of planning agricultural and industrial projects should submit their plans to the armed forces first for examination and approval.[92]

After arbitrarily appropriating many kilometers of desert land by the north coast, AFLPO constructed a luxury sea resort on it. Reportedly the military evacuated the families that originally inhabited this area, and consequently they had to take refuge in a nearby monastery and were only allowed later to collect some of their personal belongings. While some of those families submitted complaints against the army at local administrative offices, others took the dispute to court, but in both cases they did not regain access to their land. AFLPO hired a public-sector contractor to construct the Sidi Krir resort, which initially included 40 villas, 55 buildings of 386 apartments, and swimming pools. Later on, these houses were sold to civilians at much higher prices. For instance, in 2014 a cabin was advertised at LE70,000, a villa at LE112,000, a spacious apartment at LE170,000. Construction of new units was continuous, and the public came to call it "the army's resort." The military repeatedly seized land to build other luxury accommodations on the shores of the Red Sea and Suez Canal as well.[93]

Oppositional press raised widespread controversy about military mass appropriation of land. Interestingly, among the critics of this practice on the leftist *al-Ahali* newspaper was a former minister of war and chief of intelligence under Nasser. With much outrage, Amin Huwaydi described how the army came to own most of Alexandria's shores and destroyed historic sites to build thousands of luxury residential towers instead in a very short period of time. He questioned the very legality of seizing this land: "Is the land on which military installations were constructed owned by the armed forces or the state? If it is owned by the state, has the cabinet agreed about this allotment to build residential flats on land whose price per meter is not less than thousands of pounds?"[94] In a liberal newspaper, *al-Wafd*, other writers voiced their absolute rejection of the practice. A former judge and law professor condemned damaging the distinct architectural style of monuments and green areas in Alexandria for the sake of quickly erected military buildings without proper planning. He indicated that the army inherited from the British colonial troops land they had occupied before 1952 and affirmed that it was illegal for the MoD now to keep this land. It was public property protected by the constitution. Moreover, the MoD and other state ministries in general were not valid legal entities eligible to hold ownership rights to land or real estate, he affirmed. He insisted that the revenue attained from these profitable uses should go into the state budget, not that of the MoD, and called on the parliament and other state auditing authorities to exercise their duties to monitor such income.[95]

This leads to another issue around which opposition press raised great controversy: the immense military budget, which was kept secret and outside the auditing jurisdiction of the Accountability State Authority.[96] When the parliament endorsed the state budget for FY 1986–87, it allocated

LE2.7 billion to the military in a total public budget of LE21.2 billion (thus 12.7 percent of public expenditure went to the military)—aside from the $1.3 billion (around LE1.69 billion) in military aid received from the United States.[97] Amid calls for budget cuts, Abu Ghazala proclaimed that the armed forces' budget "had no relation to" planned reductions in public spending—that is, it was immune. Condemning such a statement, a liberal political leader and later parliamentarian wrote that taxes on Egyptian citizens funded the budgets of the MoD and other civilian ministries so they all should be equally subjected to rationalization. He took the opportunity to express his rejection of the army's involvement in producing chicken and grains because it was not its original duty for the nation.[98] Many other leftist columnists demanded transparency and reductions in military expenditures. Meanwhile, regime supporters and officers or ex-officers wrote to state-owned newspapers, such as al-*Ahram*, to justify and defend the status quo.[99] Moreover, Abu Ghazala issued a ministerial decision designating NSPO as part of the "secret" military sites and exempting its financial accounts from inspection by the accountability authority. But he had to annul this decree shortly afterward,[100] probably owing to pressure from leftist newspapers.

The Pious Field Marshal and Politics of Scandal

Whether or not he was aware of it, Abu Ghazala's career replicated the model of Abd al-Hakim 'Amir, Nasser's infamous minister of war. Like 'Amir, Abu Ghazala showed religious piety, intervened in the economy, was a faithful football fan, and was occasional fodder for tabloid journalists over his affairs with women. Moreover, he enjoyed immense political power that was parallel to that of the president himself. Competing with Mubarak over realms of domination, Abu Ghazala was regularly visible in state-owned media, routinely met with foreign ambassadors, ceremonially opened public projects, traveled abroad on official visits, spoke at the annual convention of the ruling National Democratic Party, and much more. He gained even more political might when he handled well the violent riots of a division of security forces in 1986. For Mubarak, a former bomber pilot, Abu Ghazala, a former artillery officer, was an eminent threat that he could not remove. It was a cold war that finally ended when the latter's hegemonic persona surrendered to politics of scandal.

The field marshal's father was a government employee at the public telephone authority, and entering the military academy was his means for social mobility. Abu Ghazala alluded to the importance of religion in the army.[101] His one officially known wife, Ashjan, was an observant Muslim woman who covered her hair with a headscarf when it was a rare practice among elite women and almost nonexistent among wives of state officials. A biographer of Abu Ghazala described her as "quiet, humble, and religiously devout who performs all Islamic rituals along with her children."[102] Abu Ghazala's sister's daughter was married to a prominent leader in the Muslim Brothers and a parliament member, who was socially close to the field marshal and called him by his family nickname—"Uncle Tharwat." When the secular press confronted Abu Ghazala about the existence of Islamic fundamentalist officers in the army, he denied this but went on about the importance of religious doctrines for the soldiers and the efforts of the armed forces to foster devout orientations. He kept his connection to the village in the Delta where he descended from and built both a mosque and a complex of religious schools attached to al-Azhar grand mosque and university there.[103]

Generally during the 1980s Mubarak carried on Sadat's policy of demilitarizing the government. He hired a limited number of army officers into civilian positions, especially as governors. On the eve of Sadat's assassination, ten out of his twenty-six provincial governors were ex-generals. During his first two years as president, Mubarak slightly increased this number to twelve, probably to appease the military institution in this tough transitional time. Among the new appointees was the governor of Cairo, General Yusuf Sabri Abu Talib, who stayed in this civilian seat for six years. Alexandria, the second largest city after Cairo, was also assigned to an ex-general. However, Mubarak reduced the number of military governors to only eight in 1988, after consolidating his legitimacy in the previous year's presidential referendum. This number again shrank to only seven in 1989, when Abu Talib left Cairo to go back to the military as a temporary replacement for sacked Abu Ghazala and Mubarak appointed a civilian instead of him. It is worth mentioning that the generals never returned to this seat under Mubarak. However, Abu Ghazala single-handedly filled the rooms of political influence from which the army was pulled under both Sadat and Mubarak.

The religious field marshal emerged in an era of widespread social influence of political Islam linked to conservative Gulf capital. He successfully inserted himself into this scene. Mubarak left the door open, like Sadat did to certain Islamist actors, to move freely in both political and economic arenas. The Muslim Brothers, whom Sadat brought back from exile to eradicate remnants of Nasser's socialism, won a large number of seats in the 1987 parliamentary elections, owned publishing houses, built private schools for the new conservative wealthy classes, and established charitable institutions for medical services to win the poor's hearts and votes. This period also witnessed expansion of ideas of Islamic finance and the opening of Islamic banks and investment companies, targeting the remittances and savings of migrant labor in the Gulf and the Egyptian middle class that was rapidly turning to religiosity because of the influence of the Muslim Brothers and oil money. The owners of these projects constituted a new class of Islamist bourgeoisie, who led different lifestyles and adopted different, conservative clothes but still consumed in the same big American style of their secular counterparts in the larger infitah milieu. Although supported by the Muslim Brothers and state Islamic scholars, many of their investment companies turned out to be fraudulent, and migrant workers catastrophically lost their savings in them.[104]

Whereas Abu Ghazala received praise from some leading Islamists of the time, he faced harsh criticism from the leftists. For instance, Muhammad Abd al-Quddus, a Muslim Brothers member and prominent journalist, supported the field marshal when he was attacked by journalists of opposition parties. In a column highlighting the fact that Abu Ghazala's wife was veiled, Abd al-Quddus "saluted" him for refraining from attacking the Islamist movement as other secular officials did.[105] On the other side of the political spectrum, the leftist press criticized Abu Ghazala's relation to the ruling party and his dependence on the United States as an almost sole source of arms—besides the above-mentioned controversy over the military budget. Abu Ghazala was member of NDP's political bureau under Sadat and continued to be under Mubarak. Although Mubarak removed him from the party in 1984, Abu Ghazala insisted on participating in and giving speeches at its annual conventions. At the 1986 convention he delivered a statement that justified the large budget allocated to the armed forces and described their expansive duties. As Abu Ghazala never attended any other parties' meetings, a leader of the leftist al-Tajammu' Party rejected such behavior and questioned the relation between the military institution and the ruling party. Other members of the same party published against his strong pursuit of and nearly full reliance on U.S. weapons. This established a state of military dependency on the West, they said. Leftist economists linked his policy to the larger conditions of economic dependency imposed on Egypt because of its heavy unpaid foreign debt.[106]

In addition to his domineering role in domestic economy and politics, Abu Ghazala played an influential role in the country's foreign policy and strategic relations with the West and Arab states. He was a main figure in Egyptian negotiations about accumulated debt relief and visited foreign courtiers and received foreign officials, civilian and military alike, with noticeably high frequency. For instance, he traveled on official missions to lead talks on arms deals and financial dues with the most prominent global and Arab leaders of the 1980s. He went to Washington, D.C., numerous times to meet with Ronald Reagan and his administration; to Iraq to meet with Saddam Hussein; to France to meet with François Mitterrand; and to Kuwait to meet its emir. At home, among the civilian top officials he received were the German prime minister; the ambassadors of China, Japan, Turkey, the United States, Great Britain, Canada, France, Italy, Austria, Chile, Oman, Finland, Denmark, Norway, and others; a U.S. congressional delegation; a similar delegation from the Netherlands; the German foreign minister; and the Somali vice president. In the brief news published on both visits abroad and meetings in his office, it was unclear what exactly the minister discussed with civilian politicians. There were mostly vague and short statements about talks on "means of mutual collaboration" in a general sense. Meanwhile, he more justifiably received many military top visitors.[107]

Aside from serious politics, Abu Ghazala had other entertaining interests—or rather other unusual areas of penetrating into the lives of the civilian masses. The field marshal was a football fan. He was notably a follower of al-Ahli, the red-shirt team, as opposed to 'Amir, who was a fanatical fan of the rival team, Zamalik of the white shirt. Abu Ghazala attended important games and kept good personal relations with sports critics. When Mubarak stopped attending matches owing to some bad luck on his side, as he was present at too many defeats of al-Ahli, Abu Ghazala continued to go to matches. He even received his club's board of directors in his office at the Ministry of Defense, promising to immediately remove military equipment from a piece of land to allow the club to use the property to construct its own premises. After he left the army, he applied to be a member of the Zamalik club with an intention to run for its presidential seat, but the club's council declined his application for fear of his potential disloyalty.[108] In another area of activities, oddly enough, he once received a delegation from the Arab Society of Accountants to discuss their professional development and future across the region. He offered hosting their annual convention, in which the New York–based International Federation of Accountants was to participate, in Cairo.[109] Furthermore, he renovated and reopened the new military museum in Saladin's citadel twice, in 1982 and 1988; the facility included a pharaonic and an Islamic warfare section.[110]

The mighty Abu Ghazala saved Mubarak and the regime during the 1986 riots of the Central Security Forces. On February 25 of that year, a violent and widespread mutiny of the soldiers of this division, originally army conscripts of low educational levels assigned to serve at the Ministry of Interior as a paramilitary force, erupted from the Giza police barracks. For three long days, around ten thousand angry mutineers destroyed or set afire luxury hotels near the pyramids, stormed a prison and freed inmates near many military factories, burned cars, and caused great damage in the residential area of Maadi, where an American and a military high school existed. Dozens of civilians and soldiers were killed and hundreds were injured. The young conscripts were reacting to rumors about extending their period of military service from three to four years, but they also rioted against dreadfully inhumane living conditions within their barracks and brutally repressive treatment by police officers. They violently expressed their discontent during a time when shortages of food and other goods prevailed in the country. Army tanks quickly filled Greater Cairo's streets, and the troops clashed with the rioters in gun battles from atop armored vehicles and out of roaming helicopters, arresting many of them. The army enforced a curfew in Cairo for a full eleven days during and after the crisis. The government claimed that the munity was a conspiracy plotted and funded by communists and Islamic fundamentalists. The interior minister failed to quell the mutiny and was instantly sacked. Only the field marshal was able to rescue the president. In international media, Abu Ghazala then appeared as the most powerful figure in the regime, and observers wondered why he did not take advantage of the moment to move ahead with a coup overthrowing Mubarak.[111]

Rumors about Abu Ghazala's affairs with different women increased during his tenure and after he left office. While in power, he allegedly secretly married actress Safiyya al-'Imari.[112] Safiyya then was generally a second-tier actress in supporting roles, and she favored playing either an aristocratic woman or a seductive femme fatale—so she very much resembled Birlanti, whom 'Amir secretly took as a second wife. Safiyya starred in the most popular, longest-running drama in Egyptian TV history, *Layali al-Hilmiyya* (The Nights of al-Hilmiyya), whose first season aired in 1987. Ironically, this show depicted a gradually disgraced image of army officers. Among its many vivid characters that included pashas, workers, belly dancers, student activists, and communists in colonial and postcolonial Cairo, probably the dullest character was officer Mustafa Rif'at. He was originally a Free Officer who had led volunteer fighters during the Suez war in 1956 and later was appointed chairman of a complex of public-sector factories and companies. A failed manager who was removed from this position with the post-1967 economic reforms and was subsequently sent away to France, Rif'at had an affair with a belly dancer and married her to live off her fortune. In this show, Safiyya was an aristocratic villain, Nazik Hanim al-Silahdar, who left Egypt to escape her class's miserable life under the officers' socialism and took to Paris in self-exile, where she crossed paths with Rif'at during his years of shame and humiliation.[113] In real life, Safiyya denied the rumors about her marriage to the field marshal. Abu Ghazala died three decades later, but the story of his relationship with Safiyya is still alive.

On April 16, 1989, Mubarak informed the world that he had sacked his previously invincible minister of defense. Moreover, terminating any expectations of hiring him as vice president, Mubarak appointed the removed minster as presidential aid—an honorary position with little authority. The removal of Abu Ghazala shook international news, but local media quickly tried to soften the bold political move. For years Western newspapers had covered the endless news of a very active Abu Ghazala: stories of his arms deals, arms production, joint military training with U.S. troops, economic activities, and much more. A year before his removal, the *New York Times* noted how the audacious minister organized the first military parade celebrating the anniversary of the 1973 war victory in the country since the assassination of Sadat in a similar event, in which Abu Ghazala was sitting right next to the murdered president and survived the bloody assault. But the same newspaper also noted, in a rather sarcastic tone, the army's engagement in "milking cows," referring to the military economic activities in food production. Western newspapers also diligently covered the scandal of the rocket technology smuggling attempt and relevant investigations. Upon his removal, they immediately linked the decision to this scandal but also emphasized how he had been an impeccable political rival of Mubarak who had found it difficult to remove him. Some even alluded to his alleged affair with Safiyya al-'Imari.[114] Meanwhile, in the local press, pro-Mubarak op-ed writers quickly published articles about the normalcy of the decision in a state with well-established institutions like Egypt. They argued that the country had a democratic, stable regime whose legitimacy was respected by internal forces. They praised Mubarak as a wise leader whose policies served the national interest.[115]

To the shock of the military institution and observers alike, Mubarak appointed Abu Talib as the new minster of defense. Originally an artillery officer, Abu Talib had been outside the institution for the previous eleven years as he filled the civilian positions of governor of North Sinai, minister of public development, and finally governor of Cairo. Meanwhile, Mubarak assigned Abu Ghazala to a few seemingly important tasks in his new capacity as presidential assistant. He supervised a committee on privatizing the public sector in 1990. He played a role in negotiating with members of Congress in Washington, D.C., about waiving Egyptian military debt in 1991. He finally resigned and quit public life in 1993, without explanation.[116]

Immediately after his resignation, another scandal broke out, terminating any potential political career for the field marshal, or rather damaging his persona as a potential threat to Mubarak. Leaked audiotapes of Abu Ghazala's phone calls with Lucy Artin, a businesswoman and socialite in Cairo's power and business circles, were used to claim that he had an affair with her and to reveal his allegedly corrupt behavior in collaboration with other state officials. In a parliamentary session, a parliament member played aloud a segment of the tape of a phone conversation—legally recorded by an inspection office—between Abu Ghazala and Artin, and newspapers widely published its content. In the conversation Artin said: "You know the problem between me and my husband. I have won a court decision obliging his father to pay my alimony but he appealed the verdict as he is a well-connected man using his wealth." Abu Ghazala sympathetically asked her about the name of the judge hearing the appeal case and put her in contact with him. Later on, this judge and Lucy Artin were allegedly arrested together. The story had other interesting twists, as other top police officers tried to gain favors from the field marshal by making friends with Artin, presuming that she was close to him. She used to call him often during social gatherings to show her strong relations with him and collect advantages by relying on his power. During the investigation of the case, the general prosecutor issued a decision banning press from covering it. Abu Ghazala insisted that he never had an affair with this woman, and that certain regime figures had put her in his way to stage this defamation campaign.[117]

Abu Ghazala's replacement was only a temporary figure, filling the position until Mubarak identified the right person. Abu Talib served for a brief period and was quickly succeeded by the politically less charismatic Muhammad Husayn Tantawi in 1991. Tantawi stayed in his seat for full two decades. Abu Ghazala's model of a visibly dominant defense minister reached its demise by the politics of scandal. Two years later the era of the eventful 1980s ended when Egypt signed an agreement with the IMF to apply full-fledged neoliberalism. With this, the military institution shortly was transformed into an entirely different model of invisible hegemony. Tantawi's neoliberal officers were hence born.

CHAPTER 3

Neoliberal Officers Make Big Money
(1990s–2000s)

When there was a fear of that popular resistance movements, inertia, or rebellion might upset the entire capitalist order that was being born, every
individual had to be under a precise concrete surveillance.

—Foucault, *Society Must Be Defended*

A huge football fan, General Sayyid Mash'al—minister of military
production for more than a decade until the 2011 uprisings—
proudly opened an Olympic village and invited a FIFA official to
visit it. In a country where football is by far the most popular sport, Mash'al
used to thrill media by constant news of the victories of his ministry's rising team, his meetings with sports stars, and opening sporting spaces. He
welcomed civilian youth to play in the newly opened, extravagant facility.
It was a large investment that he was able to fund from the revenues of
the ministry's production of consumer goods. Almost half the manufactured
goods produced by the gigantic conglomerate of sixteen factories employing around forty thousand workers were for civilian use, such as TVs, refrigerators, home appliances, and pots and pans. Mash'al asserted that revenues
from the sales of this merchandise reached LE1.8 billion on the eve of 2011.
He was also a leading member in the ruling National Democratic Party and
occupied a seat in the parliament representing Helwan, a district in the south
of Cairo where many military factories are concentrated. He was often cap-
tured on camera dancing with constituents—mostly workers at his ministry's
factories—during his election campaigns, though his victories were later
disputed in court for suspected fraud. Mash'al repeatedly asserted on public
occasions how much he valued the workers at his plants and cared for their
families through extended services. At Factory 99, now producing butane
gas cylinders for home kitchens, the workers were sent to a military trial for

protesting against the killing of a coworker owing to an explosion of a gas canister resulting from what they claimed was an administrative mistake.[1]

A class of "neoliberal officers" was born in Egypt during the 1990s and expanded vastly through the 2000s. The Egyptian military converted large parts of its arms industry into civilian manufacturing and added new vast business enterprises to them. The birth of those neoliberal officers took place alongside Egypt's transformation into the market economy under Hosni Mubarak. Those officers did not necessarily believe in the dicta of the free market; in fact, they functioned against them and often distorted the market by enjoying privileges above those of private and public enterprises. But they took advantage of the open market to expand the military's business empire. Military entrepreneurs produced almost everything and presented services in almost every sector, from canned food to luxury cars, kitchen stoves, steel, and cement—to name just a few. They opened wedding halls and lavish hotels, and built ships and ran river transport firms. They grabbed immense pieces of land to construct toll highways and cultivate vast commercial farms. The neoliberal officers penetrated into the social realms and urban spaces of all social classes across the country, through activities that ranged from baking bread and building affordable flats or luxury summerhouses to selling medicine and sponsoring popular sports. They made big money but did not pay taxes or customs, were beyond public accountability, and outrageously violated labor rights.

The existence of a class of neoliberal officers is not exceptional or unique to the Egyptian military institution. In fact, it is a global phenomenon born in many other countries transforming to the market during the past three decades. The end of the Cold War rendered the American economic system a global model for all former socialist and postcommunist states to follow. Economic liberalization measures that regimes transitioning into the market economy applied required substantial cuts in public spending, including in military budgets. Many of these regimes allowed their military institutions to create business enterprises that compensated for their financial losses, most especially in order to avoid officers' mutinies or potential coups d'état.[2] The phenomenon of military business, or Milbus, as Jörn Brömmelhörster and Wolf-Christian Paes refer to it, emerged when the IMF and the World Bank pushed governments transforming to neoliberalism to adopt more conservative fiscal policies. To coup-proof their regimes, these governments hid military expenditures in "a complex web of budgetary and off-budgetary transactions, often incorporating elements of military business."[3] Kristina Mani argues that in developing countries at large, military entrepreneurs are capable of adapting to market shifts, yet they function above free-market rules and public accountability. Mani explains, "Military entrepreneurs are doubly powerful: not only do they have a near monopoly on the state's power of coercion, but they are also stakeholders in lucrative nonmarket enterprise run with minimum oversight from government officials or society at large."[4]

In Arab states in particular, Philippe Droz-Vincent explains that when armies in authoritarian regimes such as Egypt, Syria, and Iraq started to invest in the civilian sector, they maneuvered the market for their benefit and grew into "parasitic" and monopolistic tycoons. Droz-Vincent further indicates how embarking on civilian enterprises for these armies was initially "reminiscent of the 1950s and 1960s ideological fancy of the military modernizing the economic sector." The existing organizational assets and professional expertise of the Arab armies allowed them to transform into successful entrepreneurs under various degrees of economic liberalization within their states. However, he argues:

> Arab armies are not Weberian or Schumpeterian entrepreneurs in the strict sense but rather parasitic actors who know better than others how to play by or benefit from the rules of the game. In other words, the military knows how to make use of its comparative advantages, such as the cheap manpower of its conscripts, its access to technology and highly qualified civilian engineers, its heavy equipment infrastructure, its privileges (e.g., disguised subsidies, tax exemptions, and absolute financial autonomy), its monopolistic rights to produce goods of strategic interest, and its sheer size, which enables it to alter market conditions and circumvent regulations.[5]

Besides avoiding the officers' mutiny, authoritarian regimes transitioning to the market also fear public discontent resulting from the acute social disparities that economic liberalization usually generates. Arguably, they resort to entrenched securitization of urban milieus to contain potential social unrest. While making profits through widespread civilian enterprises in cities, ports, and small towns, army officers also fulfill a new security duty to their liberalizing regimes. They place those sites and the citizens consuming their goods and services under constant surveillance and diffused, invisible control. Stephen Graham defines such practices as "the new military urban-

ism" and describes "neoliberalism's relentless commodification, privatization, standardization and militarization of social life." Graham argues that
it is "no accident that the security-industrial complexes blossom in parallel
with the diffusion of market-fundamentalist notions of organizing social,
economic and political life. The hyperinequalities, the urban militarization
and the securitization sustained by neoliberalization are mutually reinforc-
ing." He cites Foucault's notion of population surveillance in this regard, and
indicates that "globally, the new military urbanism is being mobilized for
the securing of the strung-out commodity chains, logistics networks, and
corporate enclaves that constitute the neoliberal geo-economic architecture
of our planet."[6] Thus militarizing business and its urban locations are inseparable from neoliberalism.

In the 1980s Minister of Defense Abdel-Halim Abu Ghazala exercised
a highly visible form of militarizing urban life, by both creating a business
empire and exercising an audacious form of political hegemony. After his
eventful term, however, a different mode of almost invisible urban militarism
replaced his bold model. The new minister of defense, Muhammad Hussein
Tantawi, forged his own model where he continued to enormously extend
Abu Ghazala's business, but he abstained from conspicuous politicized public appearances—especially in order to submit to the military autocrat who
did not want another armed competitor for power. Instead, the officers
widely stretched into the consumerist markets of all social classes in order
to both accumulate profit and keep an invisible gaze over the docile and
discontented citizens alike. They securitized the liberalized economy for the
autocrat. Through such diffused presence everywhere, the army once more
converted the whole society into a de facto military camp, where all citizens
are watched by the invisible eye of profit-making officers.

Whether to contain potential coups or public rebellions, the process of
militarizing business took place gradually over the course of two decades.
In the early 1990s the Cold War came to an end at exactly the same time
as Egypt's participation in the second Gulf War, when a U.S.-led coalition
liberated Kuwait after Iraq invaded it. Rewarding its contribution to the
war, the United States assisted Egypt in canceling parts of its foreign debt to
Western countries and rescheduling other parts. This was still conditioned
on Mubarak applying economic reform policies following what is known as
the "Washington Consensus"—another term for neoliberalism. The reform
plans of the World Bank and the IMF in Egypt included cutting public
expenditure, a large chunk of which had gone to the sizable army with an

expansive defense industry in the previous decades. Around the same time, the George H. W. Bush administration launched an arms control initiative in the Middle East, which substantially limited technology transfer to Egypt's arms industry. Thus the Egyptian officers had no choice but to convert the military industrial complex into the production of civilian goods in order to secure revenue that would compensate for budgetary reductions.

During the 2000s the Egyptian military business embarked on a new stage of substantial expansion. This was when the ambitious elder son of Mubarak, Gamal, delved into the political and economic scene with an apparent scheme to inherit his father's presidential seat. A former banker and a believer in neoliberalism, Gamal accelerated the rate of transition to the market, which greatly benefited the military entrepreneurs. Gamal Mubarak took over the ruling party by forming the "Politics Committee," whose membership was composed of his close patronage circle of business tycoons and neoliberal minds in the country. From this very circle, a cabinet dominated by private business figures took form in 2004 and remained in office until the 2011 uprisings. This cabinet worked hard to privatize more public-sector enterprises, eliminate subsidies, liberalize agricultural land rents, reduce spending on public services, and so on. Similarly, the elected parliaments of 2005 and 2010 were dominated by Gamal's cronies and issued laws that contributed to the hastened market transformations. To appease the military institution as it watchfully witnessed a young civilian approaching the presidential seat—which had been occupied by only officers ever since 1952—Mubarak allowed the army to extensively expand its civilian enterprises.[7]

Therefore the rise of military entrepreneurs in Egypt went through two main phases. The first phase was in the 1990s, which was a troubled period of converting the defense industry into civilian production. The second was in the 2000s, which went much smoother and was marked by creating new lucrative projects and making big profits. In both phases, this growing class of neoliberal officers was far from being believers in the free market. Rather, the officers manipulated the new economy for their own interests. They exploited the market while being a privileged, nontransparent, and unaccountable player within it.

Generally, the list of military businesses that took form during these two decades fell under the umbrellas of eight different conglomerates and organizations, in addition to one kind of informal, illicit business: (1) the National Service Projects Organization, created with the peace treaty in 1979 and already engaging in civilian production during the 1980s, now owning eleven gigantic firms with subsidiaries; (2) the Ministry of Military Production, created in the 1950s and a conglomerate of sixteen factories involved in defense conversion; (3) the Arab Organization for Industrialization, created in 1978, with nine defense factories similarly converted to civilian production; (4) the Engineering Authority of the Armed Forces, functioning as a gigantic parastatal contractor for government and military construction projects; (5) the Maritime Industries and Services Organization, with four companies for shipbuilding and river transport; (6) the Department of Social Clubs and Hotels, which manages wedding halls, restaurants, cafes, and so forth; (7) the Department of Medical Services of the Armed Forces, which builds and manages military hospitals, admitting civilians for fees; and (8) the Armed Forces' Land Projects Organization, which uses military-owned land in construction projects. Finally, the military informally placed its hand over quarries.

This chapter follows the above-mentioned two phases of the evolution of military entrepreneurship in neoliberal Egypt. The first section investigates the 1990s era of "peculiar conversion," when the defense industry had to switch to civilian manufacturing under regional and global pressure yet with odd practices and dilemmas. The second section explores the 2000s period of establishing new lucrative businesses in almost all sectors of the economy to penetrate into the growing consumerist needs of every social class. The third section takes a closer look at the military's appropriation of hundreds of thousands of square meters of state land, mainly for commercial agriculture activities or to construct toll highways and collect their fees. The final section looks into how the generals further penetrated into the daily lives of citizens by strangely taking charge of activities that are rather inapt for professional armies, such as building and running football stadiums.

A Peculiar Conversion

In the early morning of Sinai Liberation Day in 1999, Mubarak visited a large exhibition of armed forces products. As he walked through the different halls and smiled and nodded with approval, he listened to the heads of each corps enthusiastically explaining their achievements in producing civilian goods. The camera followed him as he marveled at cans of processed food, boxes of drugs, sports equipment, and other such goods on display.

General Mash'al—still the head of NSPO then—once more stressed his organization's effort to achieve self-sufficiency for the army's needs and contribute to the country's economic development. The exhibition was organized by the headquarters of an NSPO firm, the chemicals complex near Giza, but numerous other corps and departments of the military came to proudly showcase their own commodities. The halls carried a wide range of goods that were mostly peculiar and irrelevant to the areas of expertise of the military bodies that manufactured them. More important, there was a conspicuous degree of duplication, as many military corps manufactured the exact same goods, evidently without any institutional coordination or sense of market competition.[8]

In the early 1990s Egypt officially stepped into the age of massive defense conversion, or transforming its military production lines to serve the civilian market. NSPO continued to rapidly expand its 1980s economic enterprises, but it was no longer the only military body doing so. Egypt's numerous military factories were busily manufacturing civilian goods hoping to sell them to local consumers in an open and globalized market, even aspiring to export them abroad. Military factories that used to produce serious ordnance such as ammunitions, missiles, aircrafts, rockets, explosives, pistols, and armor were now heavily utilizing their facilities and labor to produce consumer goods. Everything in these sites was now altered to adjust to such a major shift, from management and labor skills to sources of capital and technology. However, this process of conversion was a peculiar one: it was marked by inefficient management and lack of centralized planning, which resulted in producing oddly duplicated, futile, and sometimes even absurd commodities.

By 1991 defense conversion was inevitable in Egypt: the generals had no choice. This year marked the Gulf War and the end of the Cold War, which negatively affected the country's arms industry. Egypt's arms industrial complex had witnessed a golden age in 1980s, as it received enormous state support in terms of capital and labor; obtained technology from various advanced sources, including Britain, France, and China; and made great profits from exports on the regional market, especially to Iraq during its war against Iran. By the end of this decade, experts predicted that Egypt's arms production and exports would increase,[9] but unfortunately things went the opposite direction. At the regional level, Egypt's defense industry lost its existing and potential market in Iraq and the Arabian Gulf, and its arms sales in this area tremendously fell. This market was terminated not only because of the end of the Iraq-Iran War in 1988 [10] but also because of the sanctions imposed on Saddam Hussein during the 1990s after his invasion of Kuwait and defeat in the U.S.-led operation to liberate this small, oil-producing country. The end of another Cold War prolonged dispute, the Afghan War, also closed a considerable market for Egyptian arms sales to the jihadists.[11] Furthermore, other-oil producing Gulf states that were current or prospective customers of Egyptian arms sale now switched to the most advanced producer that helped them when in crisis, the United States, which sold those regional clients an ever-increasing amount of ordnance during the following two decades.

More important, right after the end of the Gulf War, the Bush administration took serious steps to restrict weapons production in the Middle East by introducing an "arms control initiative" restraining technology transfer of nonconventional and conventional weapons to the region. A May 1991 Congressional Research Service report titled "Middle East Arms Control and Related Issues" highlighted the expansion of the defense industry in Egypt. It stated:

> Egypt has a rapidly growing military industrial sector. It has cooperative ventures with several countries. . . . Egypt produces jet trainers of French design and Brazilian design and helicopters designed by French, British, and Italian firms. Small arms, machine-guns, motors, recoilless weapons, rocket launchers, artillery and electronic equipment produced by Egypt were designed in the Soviet Union, Sweden, Czechoslovakia, and Italy. Argentina and Italy cooperated on the development of the Condor II surface-to-surface missile until the project was terminated under U.S. pressure.[12]

At the end of the same month in which the report appeared, President Bush issued the "White House Fact Sheet on the Middle East Arms Control Initiative," which read: "The President announced today a series of proposals intended to curb the spread of nuclear, chemical, and biological weapons in the Middle East, as well as the missiles that can deliver them. The proposals also seek to restrain destabilizing conventional arms build-ups in the region. . . . The initiative calls on the five major suppliers of conventional arms to meet at senior levels in the near future."[13] The United States later even considered breaking already existing agreements of coproduction with Egypt. A 1993 GAO report questioned the value of U.S. coproduction of M1A1 tanks with Egypt—even though little technology transfer was involved.[14]

Now that Egypt's old dreams of building a large military industry targeting global markets were shattered, mass defense conversion began. Like the experiences of conversion in other states, Egypt applied this policy first to the traditional logistics sector before moving to new areas of civilian production and services. Military logistics industries are usually located in areas such as foodstuffs, apparel, transportation, telecommunication, construction, electronics, chemicals, petrochemicals, metalwork, and repair. Military departments involved in this sector were already engaged in civilian activities in the 1980s but now started to apply a systemic policy of widespread conversion.[15]

The hasty conversion process suffered from noticeable lack of institutional planning, so various corps duplicated producing the exact same goods without taking into consideration competing with one another over the same market. For instance, NSPO's vast farms yielded processed food, and so did the Third Army's farms. Several MoMP and AOI factories copied one another's work and also both copied NSPO's products. The most striking example is the number of factories that manufactured water and sewage sanitation plants. Military factories 10 and 270 and AOI's Engine Factory and Aircraft Factory all assembled similar systems, mainly to sell to government projects. Another example is in the chemicals sector. While NSPO had a large chemicals complex geared for civilian production, the MoMP had three chemicals factories (18, 81, and 270) that engaged in overlapping activities. Moreover, the Chemical Warfare Department produced pesticides, drugs, detergents, and vinegar—copying the goods of NSPO's chemicals complex. The Supply Authority also produced drugs, duplicating the work of the latter two. In addition, many converted industries produced vehicles and trucks of various forms, including Factory 200, Sakr Factory, and the Aircraft Factory. Both Banha for Electronic Industries, or Factory 144, and AOI's Electronics Factory produced TVs, personal computers, and satellite receivers. Many enterprises overlapped in manufacturing kitchenware, home appliances, furniture, irrigation equipment, sports equipment, and garbage recycling systems. The Department of Weapons and Ammunition produced sports equipment, which military Factories 54 and 999 already produced.[16]

Many odd incidents of conversion took place in these factories, but probably those of military Factories 99, 27, 360, and 81 were among the most interesting. For more than three decades since it was built in 1958, the Helwan

Company for Engineering Industries, also known as Factory 99, specialized in manufacturing casings for various sorts of ammunition, including anti-armor warheads, runaway bombs, and artillery rockets. It switched to producing completely different consumer and nonconsumer goods: stainless steel tableware and kitchenware, fire extinguishers, gas regulators, and auto parts such as engines and bumpers. Also for more than three decades since it was built in 1954, Shubra for Engineering Industries Company, known as Factory 27, produced small arms ammunition. It switched to manufacturing electric engines to use in assembling consumer goods such as electric fans and washing machines. Helwan Metal Devices Company, or Factory 360, built in 1964, used to produce sheet metal used in the construction of trenches and making mines sapper charges. It switched to also manufacturing washing machines and other home appliances, such as refrigerators, freezers, air conditioners, water heaters, and gas ovens. Furthermore, Heliopolis Chemical Industries Company, Factory 81, once manufactured ammunition for anti-aircraft guns and developed long-range bombardment rockets. It switched to irrelevant things such as paints and raw rubber for car tires.[17]

Other peculiar stories also took place in the plants of AOI. The Arab British Dynamics Company used to produce guided missiles with an English partner, British Aerospace Dynamics. In 1998 the company faced a crisis with the withdrawal of the British coproducer, leaving it with no sources of advanced technology. It reduced its activities to only installing missile launchers on jeep cars. In addition, it manufactured tobacco-producing machines, auto parts, gas stopcocks, medical equipment, industrial burners for bakeries, and furnaces. Sakr Factory, which originally produced artillery rockets, light guided missiles, and grenades, switched to manufacturing water storage plants, large electronic monitors for stadiums and advertisement boards, loaders, minibuses, agricultural and irrigation machines, and different sorts of trucks for sewer cleaning, water carrying, and postal services. The Aircraft Factory originally assembled and produced aircraft and had to diversify to produce ambulances, garbage recycling machines, and treatment plants for sewage, potable water, and industrial drainage. It also produced furnished trucks transporting vaccines and medical waste. The Electronics Factory that originally specialized in avionics, such as aircraft communications systems and radar, now shifted to producing TVs, personal computers, digital satellite receivers, telephone switching systems, photocopiers, and printers.[18]

However, this transition was partial, rather than being a complete overhaul. As in many other countries that engaged in defense conversion before or around the same time of Egypt, each military enterprise experienced only one degree or another of shifting to civilian goods, while maintaining its capability to increase its level of military production if the need for that occurred.[19] At this point in the early 1990s Egypt had around twenty-five overt military factories: sixteen functioned under the MoMP and nine under AOI. They were mostly built between the 1950s and 1970s and were geographically concentrated in limited areas—especially Helwan in the south of Cairo, Abu Za'bal north of Cairo, and on the Cairo-Suez road. That was besides a few of NSPO's companies partially engaged in military production. They all bought new machinery and trained their laborers, engineers, and managers to face the different era. Nevertheless, in a 2009 interview the head of AOI indicated that 70 percent of the conglomerate's production was civilian, and the remaining 30 percent was still military.[20] The shares differed in the much larger conglomerate of the MoMP. In a 2010 interview Mash'al stated that only 40 percent of his complex's outcomes were civilian, and the other 60 percent were still military.[21]

Switching from military to civilian production took place within a pervasive milieu of transforming into the market economy in Egypt. Upon the collapse of the Soviet Union, Egypt, among other previously socialist regimes, faced U.S. pressure to transform into neoliberalism. The IMF and World Bank's market reforms scheme in Egypt left a profound impact on the military budget and industry. In 1991, for example, the Egyptian Army's participation in the Gulf War with about thirty thousand soldiers resulted in many immediate financial rewards, starting by U.S. forgiveness of Egypt's $7.1 billion military debt and support of the Paris Club's decision to cut Egypt's $20.2 billion debt owed to European countries by 50 percent and reschedule the remainder. However, these rewards were conditioned on Egypt's transition to the market economy. In April of the same year Egypt negotiated and reached a U.S.-backed loan agreement with the IMF for $372 million in order to apply the World Bank's Economic Reform and Structural Adjustment program. In the following June the World Bank approved a structural adjustment loan of $300 million. One of the cornerstones of the stabilization program was the reduction of fiscal deficit through significant cuts in public spending, and this included eliminating subsidies, privatization of state-owned enterprises, foreign trade liberalization, and encouraging foreign investment.[22]

Amid the swift application of these market measures, the Egyptian defense industry was hurt on a few levels but benefited on many others.

Mending the budget deficit entailed cuts in military expenditures as a considerable part of public spending. The military budget drastically dropped in the early 1990s. In the mid-1980s the military received more than 20 percent of government expenditures, but this declined to less than 9 percent in FY 1992–93. It continued to drop during the 2000s with Gamal Mubarak's more radical neoliberal measures, until it drastically collapsed to 6 percent in FY 2010–11—the last public budget of Mubarak's regime (see table 2). Nevertheless, the regime compensated the military for these budget losses by allowing it to expand its civilian production activities, initially by converting large parts of the defense industry and later by creating new business ventures. Military factories not only weathered all waves of privatization and maintained their subsidies and privileges intact, but they also expanded further. By the end of the 1990s military industries employed about 200,000 workers.[23]

In addition, Egyptian defense conversion came with immediate legal advantages, particularly in tax breaks. In 1991 the state issued a new law authorizing the military to decide on its own tax exemptions. Article 29 of law no. 11 of 1991 exempted from the sales tax "all commodities, equipment, devices, and services . . . needed for armament for defense and national security purposes, as well as raw material, supplies, and internal parts involved in manufacturing them." With such vague wording, the military enjoyed the liberty to count any good it produced among those needed for "defense and national security."[24] The Ministry of Finance's statute attached to the law, issued as decree no. 161 of 1991, made this article applicable to the products of all MoD department and organizations, the MoMP, and AOI. It authorized the head of the MoD's Authority of Financial Affairs, or his assigned proxies, to issue their own certificates of sales tax exemption for any commodity labeled as needed for armament purposes, and it extended this to even imported goods, which were also exempt from customs and duties by other laws.[25] It is worth mentioning here that it is usually not permissible for civilian employees of customs to inspect the contents of containers owned by the military on grounds of keeping the secrecy of security-related items.

While Egypt undertook these transformations, namely, neoliberal transition moving hand in hand with defense conversion, there was an ongoing global wave of similar changes in many other states that once were on the Soviet side. In the 1980s and throughout the 1990s, numerous Latin American, eastern European, Asian, African, and Middle Eastern states likewise received conditional loans from international financial institutions and were required to liberalize their economies with measures including cuts in public spending. Defense budget cuts in these states similarly gave birth to military business, or generated the global phenomenon of Milbus, through which the transforming government extended economic privileges to its armed forces for fear of their discontent or mutiny after budget cuts. Brömmelhörster and Paes explain that in many places—from Russia, China, Indonesia, and Pakistan to Argentina, Guatemala, Costa Rica, and Panama—men in uniform turned to business.[26]

Evidently, undertaking defense conversion in a neoliberal milieu led to failure in achieving its manifest goal: to make armies help with national economic development. On the contrary, experiences of many states show that conversion while transitioning to the market economy made armies a burden on the economy rather than a fair competitor in and contributor to it. This is due to the extensive privileges they receive from their regimes at the expense of public and private businesses. According to free-market theoretical assumptions, defense conversion should take place smoothly and efficiently with little state intervention: the market should fix any problems that might occur during the process. Nevertheless, many theorists debunk this assumption and insist that centralized planning is essentially needed, at least because of the very nature of military business that resents abiding by the rules of a free market and superiorly acts above them.[27] Russia may present the most conspicuous example of defense conversion that went wrong because it took place while applying economic reform, whereas China presents an opposite case where the process succeeded because it took place under heavy government planning. Unfortunately, the 1990s Egyptian experience was closer to the Russian model and thus came out peculiar and inefficient.

In Russia, the perestroika reforms assigned extensive civilian tasks to the gigantic Soviet military during the 1980s and 1990s. The military then started producing everything from processed food and computers to civil aircraft and ships. However, as Julian Cooper noted, "[far] from diminishing that [military] sector in scope and influence, the state conversion program has expanded it, putting it in a position to determine the fate of the entire project of perestroika." He asserted that this was a direct result of the decentralized manner in which the process of conversion took place, embracing a misguided understanding of the free-market spirit, which ended up with the Soviet military having "a finger in every pie."[28] In 1993 the U.S. Defense

Department launched a program to help the post-Soviet regimes convert their huge defense industries, while the West also pressured these regimes to accelerate market reforms.[29] In this context, Russian military business further expanded, but it was "characterized by rather chaotic and arbitrary activities with minimal accountability. . . . Numerous scandals over corruption, revenue mismanagement and theft were reported."[30] In contrast, China managed a smooth and successful model for defense conversion during the 1980s and 1990s, which did contribute to economic development and growth. Under highly centralized state control, the People's Liberation Army (PLA) switched its main strategic industries—such as aviation, ordnance, aerospace, and shipbuilding—to competently manufacturing profitable and competitive civilian goods. By the late 1990s approximately 80–90 percent of Chinese military enterprises' production was civilian. The PLA produced taxicabs, cameras, motorcycles, pharmaceuticals, textiles, metals, electronics, machinery, and chemicals. Dongmin Lee argues that the Chinese case was successful precisely because the process was not left up to either the officers or market forces.[31]

The Egyptian case is obviously strongly similar to that of Russia, as well as those of many other eastern European states. Egypt shared with them the general characteristics of a peculiar conversion.[32] First of all, Egyptian defense conversion was inefficient and offered special privileges to military businesses that defied the very doctrines of a free market. In addition, it also became laughable by venturing into irrelevant sectors, which similarly happened in Russia when missile plants switched to manufacturing baby carriages or beer containers, or in Ukraine when other rocket factories moved to sausage making. Even U.S. defense conversion suffered from this when, for instance, aerospace companies moved into guitar making or serving mass transit. Furthermore, converted military factories in Egypt lacked commercial skills and civilian expertise in business administration and mass marketing, were alien to popular consumer tastes, and enjoyed limited access to capital and advanced technology. Thus they produced goods of lower quality with little market competitiveness yet sold them in the domestic market anyway, either to the government or to the middle and lower classes.[33]

This was the situation in the 1990s. In the following decade the military entrepreneurs left this confused experience of conversion and entered a completely different era: one of creating enormous new business ventures and amassing big profits.

Making Big Money

The year 2000 was another moment of great transformation in Egyptian military business, taking maximum advantage of the openness of the market. This was the year in which Mubarak's ambitious son Gamal joined the ruling NDP and repopulated it with his own patronage circle of business tycoons and market-oriented economists. Scheming to succeed his father as president of the country, Gamal adopted neoliberalism as his own ideology and decided to push forward the pace of market reforms in the country. Figures in Gamal's clientelist circle would soon form the cabinet in 2004, and his cronies would dominate the elected parliaments of 2005 and 2010. Polices of fast privatization of state-owned enterprises were quickly implemented, and laws to legitimize the process were hastily promulgated. Meanwhile, Hosni Mubarak granted the military a superior status within the liberalized economy. Apparently the autocrat then attempted to hit two birds with one stone. On the one hand, he aimed at coup-proofing his regime and his son's prospective one by appeasing the officers with civilian profits. On the other hand, as social disparities and relevant public discontent grew, the military's widely stretching businesses networks entered into almost every consumer market across the country in order to keep a close, securitizing eye for the autocrat on every citizen at the hearts of their daily life. The military conquered old and new markets targeting all socioeconomic groups in the nation, from the globalized bourgeois desiring luxury goods to the middle and lower classes in need of affordable supplies.

Audaciously using their membership in the privatization committee, the generals seized many public enterprises that were up for sale and transferred their ownership to the various military entities. Thus not only did they survive privatization, since all military enterprises that are theoretically state-owned remained intact, but they also took advantage of the process. Because advanced technology was indispensable in both old and new ventures, the officers partnered with American, German, Chinese, French, eastern European, Japanese, and more firms now entering the open market. With them, the military invested in new heavy industries, such as railway wagons, luxury cars, ships, steel, and cement. Military business continued to enjoy various forms of tax and customs breaks. When Gamal reactivated the country's stock market and both private and public enterprises were listed on it, none of the military companies registered themselves; the officers maintained full lack of transparency about their capital and annual revenue and sought to have no stockholders to share their firms with. While military entrepreneurs claimed to engage in these ventures to contribute to economic development and price control for the benefit of the masses, in fact they were just other profit-seeking market competitors, often hurting the very social groups they proclaimed to help with their welfare. Moreover, they reportedly treated their laborers through oppressive laws and sent them to military trials.

In his capacity as minister of defense, Tantawi was a member of the Supreme Privatization Committee along with other civilian ministers.[34] This apparently eased military appropriation of many public-sector projects that provided vital goods. AOI seized the only manufacturing plant of railway wagons in the country when it was privatized in 2004 and thus established a monopoly over this sector. For the lower- and middle-class inhabitants of southern and northern Egypt, as well as the inhabitants of the same social classes in Cairo, railways and the underground metro are essential parts of their daily lives. The affordable tickets of these trains carried provincial inhabitants to big Cairo to get their government papers signed or go to public hospitals for cheap treatment and allowed students to attend university. The metro carried millions of Cairo inhabitants daily to work. With a long career and good connections with global technology, SEMAF factory was quite influential in the daily lives of the Egyptian masses by being the sole producer of railway and metro coaches in the country. It was founded as a public-sector company in 1955, when Nasser celebrated its opening. In 1986 it entered into a joint venture with a French rail group to introduce the first fleet of underground metro cars to the long awaiting inhabitants of crowded Cairo.[35] Taking advantage of the big wave of privatization, AOI "annexed" SEMAF—located in Helwan near many other factories of AOI—with its more than 1,400 workers. The plant carried on with manufacturing train and underground wagons for its new military owner, which made deals worth billions of Egyptian pounds with and presented overhauling services to the government.[36]

In fact, AOI experimented for a few years with assembling rolling stock and selling it to the state, before it finally acquired the factory and monopolized this strategic sector. In 2002 AOI concluded an agreement with the National Authority for Railways to manufacture the internal components of three hundred wagons with the goal of substituting foreign imports.[37] A much larger and more crucial agreement took place between the same two parties in the following year, when AOI's Kader Factory—originally producing trainer planes and armor and now manufacturing vehicles, tractors, and furniture—engaged in modernizing the whole national railway fleet and produced new coaches in collaboration with Spanish, Romanian, and Hungarian companies. To accommodate this new business activity, Kader restructured its production lines in the Abu Za'bal workshop and intensely cooperated with SEMAF,[38] which led to the latter's seizure a year later. In 2005 the head of AOI, General Majdi Hatata, signed an agreement with the Japanese corporation Mitsubishi to cooperate in producing underground metro and tram wagons. The celebratory atmosphere of the contract-signing event made the deal appear as a semigovernmental one when three ministers attended—those of transport, finance, and local development. In 2008 General Hamdi Wahiba—the new head of AOI—announced the manufacturing of the third metro line trains.[39] In 2009 the sales manager of SEMAF made a trip to Japan to offer an advanced manufacturer, Kamioka, an invitation to enter the Egyptian market. An agreement was concluded and SEMAF became the representative of this company in the country.[40] The following year SEMAF concluded another agreement worth LE1.7 billion with another, larger Japanese partner, Mitsubishi, to expand metro lines in Greater Cairo.[41]

It is worth mentioning here that railway services in Egypt witnessed a drastic decline during the decade preceding the 2011 uprisings, as the number of train accidents per year increased catastrophically. Daily train crashes became the norm, and ministers of transport lost their jobs after nationally shocking incidents in which dozens of poor and rural passengers lost their lives.[42] According to an official state report, the average number of train accidents in 2008, 2009, and 2010 was 500, 550, and 623, respectively. The number of accidents per day reached 58 in 2010.[43] In Upper Egypt, middle- and lower-class passengers and students who mainly rely on trains to go to Greater Cairo assert that the quality of the wagons and the service inside them declined compared to those of the previous decade. The mid-1990s marked the introduction of the reputable Spanish rail company's coaches, which were particularly praised for their nicely designed interiors with portraits of the Nile and pharaohs and for their punctuality and cleanness. The 2000s, in contrast, were marked by the introduction of SEMAF's coaches, which lacked any artistic designs, efficiency, and cleanness, and the overall service considerably collapsed one year after the other till 2011.[44]

There were other incidents in which the military institution simply "annexed" a state-owned factory during the wave of privatization, without entering public tenders or fair competition with local or foreign bidders in a theoretically free market. For many decades after Nasser established it in Helwan in 1960, El Nasr Automotive Manufacturing Company (NASCO) had been a leading national manufacturer of affordable, small cars in the Soviet and eastern European socialist style. Like other public-sector companies, NASCO suffered from financial losses and the Accountability State Authority recommended its liquidation. However, the MoD blocked the process because of its interest in acquiring the company in 2010. The MoD sent a letter to the Holding Company of Metallic Industries, of which NASCO was a subsidiary, asking to halt the sale of the plant because the generals were studying its "annexation" to military conglomerates.[45] The situation of this car manufacturer would remain suspended and ambiguous until April 2013, when the MoMP officially appropriated it per the approval of the Islamist-dominated parliament assembled when the Muslim Brothers were in office.[46]

In the same area of car making, the military institution already owned another large assembly plant: AOI's Arab American Vehicles (AAV). Thanks to military collaboration with many multinational carmakers, especially Chrysler, Cairo's upper class now could afford to buy the huge luxury jeep cars that would further jam the congested streets and parking lots. Jeep Wrangler and Cherokee cars are seen in abundant numbers in the bourgeois neighborhoods of old Cairo and the gated suburbs of new Cairo. Thanks to the AOI's automotive factory, the globalized middle class of the city also gained affordable access to other new models of Hyundai, Peugeot, Toyota, Fiat, Suzuki, and many more. Located within the main complex of AOI's factories on the Cairo-Suez desert road, AAV was established in 1977 as an Egyptian-American venture to assemble military jeeps for Arab militaries. In a 2009 interview the chief executive officer of Chrysler Group Egypt excitingly indicated: "We came to Egypt in 1977 and started selling a year later. . . . What made Egypt unique was that we have an assembly plant here where we build Jeep products. . . . AAV is owned 49 percent by Chrysler LLC and 51 percent by AOI. . . . At the plant, we build Jeep Cherokee and two multifunctionals as well as military application Jeep Wrangler long-wheel bases. We also do some contract assembly for other companies. Most of the Jeep products we make today are used in Egypt."[47]

General Mustafa Husayn, the chairman of AAV through the 2011 uprisings, proudly explained the ability of his plant to produce up to seventeen thousand cars in each shift per year. The same general signed a deal with the Japanese Toyota to assemble several top-of-the-line models a year before the uprisings.[48] Meanwhile, discontented workers fighting what they claimed was corruption in the factory insisted on their Facebook page that the plant made an annual profit of billions of Egyptian pounds but refused to pay its laborers fair wages, and they accused Husayn of corrupt practices.[49] When Chrysler merged with Daimler—the German multinational automotive corporation that produces Mercedes Benz—between 1998 and 2007, DaimlerChrysler AG listed AAV as one of its joint venture partners. After the separation of the two parent corporations, Chrysler retained its old shares.[50] In 2008 Chrysler and AAV launched the manufacturing of Jeep J8 for both military and civilian use, and Chrysler celebrated a sales surge of 50 percent in Egypt during that year.[51]

In yet another incident of seizing vital state-owned enterprises that were supposed to be privatized, the military appropriated several maritime and river transport companies. In 2003 the MoD created a new organization called the Maritime Industries and Services Organization through Presidential Decree no. 204 of that year. With a headquarters in Alexandria and similar to NSPO, the organization was created as a corporation enjoying its own legal entity and immediately took possession of decades-old public enterprises. The organization took over three gigantic state-owned companies: the Egyptian Company for Ship Repairs and Building, Alexandria Shipyard, and the Nile Company for River Transport in 2003, 2007, and 2008, respectively. Moreover, it created another new venture, Triumph for Maritime Transport, in 2009. Needless to say, navy officers head the organization and its subsidiaries. The property rights of Alexandria Shipyard were "transferred" from the state to MISO, but the Ministry of Investment's decree to "sell" the company and the price paid for it were not published anywhere.[52] When the organization "purchased" the Nile Company for River Transport from its parent state-owned holding company, the head of the latter was a fellow former navy officer—General Muhammad Yusuf. Similarly, the price the military paid for the supposedly privatized company was not mentioned anywhere—even in the Ministry of Defense's decree no. 3 of 2010 that described the transaction and indicated that all facilities of the company now became the property of the military.[53]

MISO fostered good ties with Chinese, eastern European, French, and local firms. For instance, upon acquiring Alexandria Shipyard, the military hired a Chinese company to modernize its infrastructure and the technological capabilities of the company's huge shipbuilding facility that employed more than six thousand workers. The military claims that it invested LE1.5 billion in this modernization process, but without clarifying the source of this capital. The China Shipbuilding Trading Co. spent three years completing the project. When Field Marshal Tantawi and managing generals proudly celebrated the production of the first commercial ship, which they called *Freedom 3*, they declared that they had the help of a Ukrainian company that provided them with the designs and worked under the supervision of a French global company for inspection and testing.[54] In another instance, the Citadel Group, a local grand business close to the regime, purchased sixteen barges to be used for river transport from the same shipbuilding company at LE1 billion. These barges were to be employed in international trade between Egypt and the Sudan and in the Nile Basin countries.[55]

Amassing incredible plots across the country, the Nile Company for River Transport owned three separate ports specially allocated to its activities. The ports of Aswan, Tibbin in southern Cairo, and al-Nahda near Alexandria span tens of thousands of square meters. Presidential Decree no. 354 of 2009 allowed the company to appropriate all these areas of public land when it ruled to reallot the ownership rights of these previously state-owned facilities occupied by this river company to MISO. The company uses its three ports to ship petroleum, steel, fertilizers, cement, and many other commodities for private, state, and military businesses alike. The Aswan port has established a near monopoly over transporting international cargos between Egypt and Sudan. Interestingly, aside from river transport, the company provides many other services, including cinematic production. The company fuels touristic and commercial ships with solar power and repairs boats, as well as building and towing ships. For undefined reasons, it made about five popular films for famous drama and comedy stars such as Ahmad Makki and shot a video clip of one national song for the Egyptian pop star Muhammad Munir.[56]

Moreover, the military ventured into a crucial strategic sector: steelmaking. Therefore it entered into serious competition with the most politically influential business tycoon in Gamal Mubarak's clientelist circle, Ahmed 'Izz.[57] In 2005 Hosni Mubarak and a number of his minsters—in a cabinet dominated by Gamal's business elite—opened a large steel-rolling plant as part of military factory 100, probably to compete with 'Izz. It took the MoMP almost three and a half years to finish constructing the new plant with a total size of a million square meters, including buildings, storage places, gardens, and internal roads.[58] Also known as Abu Za'bal Company for Engineering Industries, Factory 100 was established in 1974 and originally produced ordnance such as anti-aircraft, tube artillery, and tank guns.[59] In fact, the MoMP initiated its experiments with steel rolling in a separate mill in the late 1990s and later moved the equipment of this mill to the new facility of Factory 100 in the north of Cairo.

This gigantic plant of steel needed large capital in order to acquire Western technology and expertise, which the regime made available to the military. Furthermore, the state extended tax advantages to the project. Before the parliament's Defense and National Security Committee, Mash'al revealed that the MoMP invested LE1.5 billion in this mill, in collaboration with a German company, SMS Siemag, and other global steelmakers.[60] As usual, this new venture enjoyed advantageous tax breaks: the minister of military production asserted that his projects in steel and other sectors are exempt from customs or pay very little duties.[61] The Chamber of Metallurgical Industries in Egypt lists the military steel plant among other "half-comprehensive" steelmakers in the country, as it only processes iron scrap and manufactures semifinished products, especially steel billets and sheets.[62] Another NSPO company benefited from the venture by feeding the mill with needed iron scrap, particularly NSPO's Queen Service Company, which was active in scrap trading.[63] There are many other public- and private-sector steel plants in Egypt that are all listed on Cairo's stock market, but military factory 100 is not.

Interestingly, the venture took place amid rapid social transformations that brought about a construction boom—both byproducts of Gamal's reforms. In the age of globalized business in Egypt, the ever-expanding bourgeois and upper- and middle-class professionals desired to buy new homes for marriage or to move into new luxury suburbs. The state supported this new real estate market by selling desert lands to real estate developers and increasing its spending on infrastructure in new suburbs. Apparently, the military sought to make a profit within this boom by selling steel to massive urban development projects on the outskirts of Cairo. Ironically, while the generals claimed that their factory would contribute to price controls and end monopolistic practices on the domestic market, the price of steel bars skyrocketed in the country and led to inflated home expenses, which grew into a profound source of national discontent a few weeks before the 2011 uprisings. Only cheaper Turkish steel bar imports, rather than military production, helped lower the swelling prices.[64] Thus the military mill delivered on few of its original promises to help national economy while collecting immense privileges from the state and taking advantage of emerging social needs to profit.

To take advantage of the same social transformations and the lucrative construction boom, the military ventured into another strategic industry: cement. NSPO created Arish Cement Factory in North Sinai in 2010, according to Tantawi's decree no. 42 of the same year, and opened it two years later when the army was in power after deposing Mubarak.[65] The brand new facility was erected on an appropriated piece of state land of around 210 acres, in addition to hundreds of other acres of surrounding quarries appropriated to feed it with raw material, and more land to construct roads connecting the plant to those quarries. This time, the military chose to collaborate with a non-Western partner to obtain technology and construct the facility—a Chinese state-owned company—and the MoD footed a bill of $370 million in total cost. According to a company statement, Sinoma Group was the first incidence of a Chinese contractor working in the construction sector Egypt. On behalf of his government, China's ambassador to Egypt himself cut the red ribbon opening the plant while standing next to Tantawi, thanking the Egyptian military for their good business. The plant has about eight hundred workers—all civilians except for the top managers, who are generals; many of them traveled to China to receive professional training.[66]

Once again, the generals managing the factory asserted that its main purpose is to establish self-sufficiency for the army, help with price control, and defy monopolistic practices on the domestic market—the exact same rhetoric iterated around the steel mill. This factory competes with many public- and private-sector cement producers in the country, again all listed in Cairo's stock market except for that of the military. One engineer officer claimed that the factory offers much lower prices for cement than other private and public ones do and already managed to lower the price by LE100 in the local market as soon as it opened.[67] However, similar to those of steel, cement prices skyrocketed shortly after the military factory was opened, which generated public discontent after the 2011 uprisings. The factory opened in April 2012, and cement prices immediately increased in the following few months, according to June and September monthly reports of the state's Central Agency for Public Mobilization and Statistics on construction material for the year.[68] Despite the extensive financial advantages it receives from the government, such as the usual tax breaks that NSPO's enterprises are entitled to, the prices of Arish cement are almost the same as other public- and private-sector products, or a few piasters cheaper per ton. Moreover, imported Turkish cement is usually significantly cheaper than that of the military.[69]

Egyptian culture also witnessed fundamental changes with the rise of neoliberal middle classes, as satellite TV channels proliferated and were filled with popular soap operas refining the lifestyle tastes of this class. Conquering this new territory, the military expanded its activities in manufacturing satellite receivers and home televisions. AOI had already been producing electronics since the 1990s in two of its factories.[70] To maximize its influence in this field, it purchased shares in Nile Sat, a joint-stock company controlled by the state-owned media apparatus hosting local and international channels. Later the generals decided to fully control Nile Sat, when a retired general occupied the seat of the company chairman. He was a former military intelligence officer whom the army later would appoint as minister of media after the uprisings.[71]

Meanwhile, workers at military enterprises were confused about their status: they were not sure whether they were just civilian skilled laborers at state-owned plants or military personnel. When they made mistakes or challenged their military administrators, they were shockingly sent to military trials. In August 2010, when workers at military factory 99 attempted to strike to protest poor safety measures in their work premises that killed at least one of them and injured many others, they were accused of exposing "military secrets" and sent to a military court. The director of the factory, an army general, had brought in a number of gas cylinders in order to test them out, even though the workers were not trained to use them. When several cylinders exploded, he allegedly told the workers that it would not matter if one or two of them died. When one of them did in fact die and others were wounded, they stormed his office, gave him a beating, and then staged a sit-in. Subsequently, eight of the workers' leaders were tried before a military tribunal on charges of attacking a public employee, refusing to work, and dispersing military secrets—as they spoke publicly about butane gas cylinders produced in the factory and used in home kitchens. The labor rights lawyer who defended them—Khaled Ali, who ran for the presidency after 2011—insisted that in accordance with military judiciary laws, these workers ought to be tried in regular civilian courts since they were non-combatant personnel and the factory was not a military site.[72]

Generally, as opposed to both public- and private-sector labor enjoying the right to unionize, workers at military enterprises could not create their own labor unions. Like their fellow workers in the MoMP's factories,[73] laborers at the Egyptian Company for Ship Repairs and Building were denied the right to organize themselves in unions. In 2008 in Alexandria, the nine hundred workers at this company, annexed to MISO in 2003, cried for help as the company used almost half of them as seasonal laborers and denied all of them the right to form unions or at least administrative committees to represent them and resolve their daily problems. They insisted that according to state laws, any business that has more than fifty employees must allow workers to create an administrative committee. They demanded equality with all other government employees who enjoy this right. A year later they organized a series of peaceful vigils to demand raises in their unfairly low wages, but instead the administration sent nine of them to a military tribunal because they protested on a "military site." The agony of those workers continued even after the 2011 uprisings, when they organized a strike to demand a minimum wage but their military administration rejected their requests.[74]

AOI's labor situation is even much more complicated. Created as an international entity by four Arabian Gulf states and based in Egypt in the mid-1970s, AOI is not subject to Egyptian laws—including labor laws. Although AOI ceased to be an international organization for the last three decades and a half, after the other three Arab states withdrew from it upon Egypt's signing of the peace treaty with Israel, the organization still enjoys an immune international status above state laws. The internal document titled "Laws, Decrees, and Statutes of AOI" stipulates that the organization answers only to its own bylaws in treating its laborers, and workers are not allowed to resort to state courts if a dispute arises between them and their administrators—who are mostly retired generals. Workers could address their grievances to a judicial committee with members from the Justice Ministry and the State Council's administrative courts. Article 14–5 of this statute stipulates that "the organization is exempt from being subject to the laws of the partner states and their internal legal systems, and from being subject to national judiciaries in resolving disputes between it and its producing units and also disputes that might erupt between the workers and the organization and its units, as they are to be heard before a judicial committee of the organization." While describing this as a "slavery statute," AOI's workers attempted to protest this oppressive situation in 2011, but nothing has changed.[75]

More tax breaks were legally extended to the expanding military enterprises during this period. Although these exemptions of various forms of fees should be applied only to goods used for production or sale of defense equipment, the army's civilian enterprises casually used them to avoid government charges. A series of laws already issued in the 1980s exempted the imports and exports of the MoD and MoMP and their projects from customs and all kinds of taxes and fees. In addition, the law creating AOI back in 1976 stipulated its exemption from all sorts of taxes, fees, or customs on all imports and exports.[76] In 2005 law no. 91, article 47, which regulated the income tax, exempted NSPO's annual profits from any dues to the state in this regard.[77] In the same year the Ministry of Finance's decree no. 861 pertaining to customs expanded the old military breaks. The first article of this executive statute stipulates that the minister of defense or an authorized proxy could now request an exemption for military shipments from the inspections that were the only way to ensure that they did contain commodities needed for armament rather than civilian material in order to qualify for duty breaks.[78] The modifications of the sales tax law issued in the same year maintained the breaks that AOI, MoD, and MoMP enjoyed in old laws. Article 29 of law no. 9 of 2005 stated that "all commodities, material, equipment, and services . . . required for armament purposes for defense and national security, as well as raw material and production necessities and the parts integrated into production, are exempt."[79]

It is documented that the MoD used the sales tax exemptions, for instance, to import and sell spare parts in the domestic market without paying legal charges to the government. In one case, the Cassation Court ruled for the Sales Tax Authority to collect about LE57,000 of accumulated dues from the MoD for this lucrative business activity for the five-year period between 1992 and 1997. The authority received certificates from a proxy of the MoD's head of financial affairs that alleged that these imported goods were needed for armament and therefore should be exempt from the sales tax according to law. Refusing to accept these certificates, the authority took the MoD to court and sued it to pay its dues on these nonarms sales. After many years of this running legal dispute, the Cassation Court finally ruled in favor of the authority in 2003.[80]

Grabbing Big Land

One woman in the Delta province of Sharqiyya took the head of the Air Force Academy to court. She sought to retrieve her piece of land, which the latter appropriated during wartime but never returned. The military destroyed all the buildings she had erected on this agricultural lot, which she had purchased from the government and reclaimed back in the 1950s, in order to construct an airstrip instead. Her case ran in civilian tribunals for many long years, until finally the Cassation Court ruled in her favor in 1993. In fact, her lawsuit was a rare incident, since many other inhabitants of her locality and other provinces across the country lost their lands to combatant activities—such as building camps or air force bases—during the years of conflict with Israel and failed to get them back. Those who dared to sue the army were faced by its claim that this was a sovereignty affair and thus fell outside of the jurisdiction of civilian courts. When the case of this woman reached the Cassation Court, the justices of the supreme tribunal established their authority over this kind of land dispute and ruled that the head of the Air Force Academy at Bilbis not only should return the land but also must pay her a financial compensation of LE55,000.[81] A few similar cases made it to this court, where the involved citizens succeeded in reclaiming their lost properties sometimes after more than two decades of legally challenging the military.[82] Nevertheless, numerous other citizens could not follow the same costly, risky path against the almighty institution.

In the age of making big money, military entrepreneurs grabbed large areas of state or previously private land. As a start, the lands that the military appropriated during wartime for "warfare necessities" were legalized and used for civilian enterprises in the 1980s.[83] In the following two decades the state issued new laws allowing the military to accumulate hundreds of thousands of square miles of desert land and hundreds of thousands of acres of other agricultural areas. The military not only continued to use them to build more apartment buildings for officers and civilians and create more commercial farms, as they had done in the past, but also began constructing new, lavish social clubs with wedding halls, restaurants, cafes, and other facilities open to civilians from all social groups at handsome charges. They also grabbed land to construct major toll highways across the country and monopolize their fee collection. Moreover, the military informally—or rather illicitly—controlled public quarries and made large profits from their rich mineral extractions, used, for example, in the production of building materials.

In 1991, the year military conversion to civilian production started, Mubarak's regime issued a new law to consolidate the army's absolute priority to state land over government authorities, one of whose duties is allocate land to private businesses. Law no. 7 of 1991 stipulates that state authorities responsible for developing or selling desert land should "coordinate" with the MoD first before making decisions and observe the rules and conditions that the latter sets. Only after the MoD decides on which areas are of "strategic importance" for potential military use can civilian governmental bodies assume control over their designated territories to develop them or allocate them to the private sector. This law created three official authorities for the purpose of developing desert land: tourism, agricultural development, and new urban community authorities.[84] In at least one instance, one of those bodies received land and the armed forces took it back. Presidential Decree no. 407 of 1994 ordered the tourism authority to return a piece of land to the military two years after obtaining it.[85] Furthermore, when Presidential Decree no. 153 of 2001 created a new authority, the National Center for Planning State Lands Uses, to act as a supreme organization for the centralization of state land allocations to different ministries and bodies, the decree again placed the military in a superior position above this authority by mandating its coordination with the MoD.[86] Interestingly, retired army officers would mostly be appointed to head these four authorities throughout the 2000s.[87] A prominent example among them was retired general 'Umar al-Shawadfi, who headed the last one from 2004 through the uprisings.

In 2002 the military issued a new decree in an attempt to renew and consolidate its control over desert land vis-à-vis civilian government authorities. The MoD's decree no. 146 of 2002 classifies desert land into two categories: areas of strategic importance and open areas where public and private projects could be erected—after consulting with the military and observing its conditions. It adds that the MoD might approve requests from state authorities to dispose of some land previously classified under the first category after modifying its categorization. The leaders of the field armies and military areas monitor business projects to make sure they abide by the terms and regulations of the military in using their land, and violating rules would allow the military to stop or demolish the erected facilities of these projects without prior warning. The officers are also entitled to cancel permission in case of transgressions violating "military requirements."[88]

Let us begin with the land that the military had already seized during wartime, which had been legalized by the 1980s codes. The military converted vast spaces of land that it had appropriated across the country into complexes of five- and four-star hotels, wedding halls, elite funeral homes in mosques, and social clubs with sporting areas for middle-class civilians to access with a fee. Furthermore, it constructed luxury sea resorts by the Mediterranean and the Red Sea shores. The Armed Forces' Department of Social Clubs and Hotels runs all these profitable facilities, and usually generals assume the high positions in this department. The military runs seventeen "houses" that function as wedding halls for middle-class families at affordable prices; the majority of them are in Nasr City and a few are in the elite and middle-class areas of Heliopolis, Zamalik, and 'Abasiyya. Each house carries the name of a military corps, such as House of Air Defense, House of Artillery, House of Infantry, and House of Electronic War. It also runs two mosques that function as funeral halls in Nasr City and Heliopolis. Funerals of famous state figures are usually held there, in addition to those of high-ranking military personnel. In terms of hotels, the military owns and runs fifteen five-star hotels in various places across the country, including Alexandria, Aswan, Marsa Matruh, and Fayyum. As for social clubs with sporting courts open for civilians by membership or day fees, there are at least eight of them in Cairo, Luxor, and Alexandria. Furthermore, the military owns and runs at least three sea resorts with luxury villas and apartments: Sidi Krayr and al-Fkhkhar Village near Alexandria, and al-Zuhur Village in al-'Ayn al-Sukha near Suez.

In Aswan, in the deep South of the country, the army seized a large piece of land from local inhabitants and first turned it into a military social club. In the past few years, the army dismantled this club and built a luxury four-star hotel overlooking the Nile Cornish in this touristic busy city and then leased it out first to a German company and then to a Danish one to administer. Although the official sign of the hotel first read Iberotel and then Helnan—the names of the Dutch and Danish tenants of the site, respectively—the inhabitants of the city informally call it "the army's hotel." The original owners of the land still keep legal documents that prove their property rights to it, but it seems impossible to them to retrieve it.[89]

Back in Cairo, middle-class citizens could pick from a wide variety of services at the military wedding halls at various prices. At the Electronic War House, they could rent the Cleopatra Hall at LE900 or the Louts Hall at only LE450, with added costs for a band, video recording, photographs, wedding cake, buffet, religious-official notary, hairdresser, balloons, and so on, bringing the average total to around LE10,000. Alternatively, they could pick a special offer worth LE6,500 for a hundred guests.[90] On the north coast, where the Sidi Krayr luxury resort is located, a bourgeois family could purchase a villa at about LE3.5 million. A smaller cabin in the same resort today costs LE1.5 million. Citizens often prefer buying summer houses in this military resort for guaranteed security and services.[91]

As luxury seaside resorts outside Cairo expanded, the growing upper and middle classes of the suffocated neoliberal city needed new roads to drive to their newly constructed summer homes. The military heavily weighed in by constructing toll roads and collecting their abundant daily revenue. In 2003 Mubarak issued Presidential Decree no. 330 of 2003 to allot expansive zones of desert land to the MoD, designating this land as areas of "strategic military importance" and prohibiting their sale to the public. The military seized about 1,286 square meters of land in the eastern desert.[92] Immediately afterward, the military used the very same area to construct two profitable toll roads: the Cairo-'Ayn Sukhna highway, connecting the new elite suburb of Qatamiyya in northeastern Cairo to the resorts of al-'Ayn al-Sukhna and Hurghada by the Red Sea; and the Helwan-Kuraymat road, a much needed shortcut between Cairo and Upper Egypt and also the Red Sea resorts. Whereas the Cairo-'Ayn Sukhna road opened in 2004, the Helwan-Kuraymat opened its second stage, reaching Beni Suef in Middle Egypt, in 2008.[93]

This was the first instance of building toll highways in Egypt, and the military has since established a monopoly over this realm, to the discontent of private business and citizens using those roads. NSPO created a new enterprise, a military contractor called Wataniyya Company for Construction, Development, and Management of Roads, initially to work on the two toll roads. The company's mission is to build new roads or develop existing ones and take charge of their maintenance, and it also enjoys the authority to rent or give usufruct rights to the lands bordering the roads and profit from this. In addition, the company collects daily fees for and monopolizes the high revenue of the advertising billboards lined along them. The company's statute enables it to collaborate with local or international capital as partners in business.[94] It hired a subcontractor from the public sector, a subsidiary of the Holding Company for the Projects of Roads, Bridges, and Land Transport, to help with the Cairo-Qattamiyya-'Ayn Sukhna road—which raises the question about why this state-owned enterprise did not take charge of the project to begin with.[95] With a sense of deep discontent, private businesses specializing in roads assert that this NSPO company came to monopolize 50 percent of the administration of the country's roads after 2011. At a press conference in the Federation of Egyptian Industries, these businesses also claimed that the military company engages in illegal practices in tenders that deprive many private businesses of rights and opportunities.[96] As for the users of the company's highways, truck drivers complained about high fees subject to arbitrary increases, which lead to inevitable increases in food and other commodity prices. When discontented truckers raised the issue to the government, the minister of transportation responded that these roads fell outside his authority.[97]

On January 23, 2011, two days before the mass uprisings, Presidential Decree no. 13 of 2011 designated new pieces of desert land in the eastern side of Upper Egypt's Nile as of "strategic military importance" and allotted them to the MoD. This time the military seized 1,908,215 square kilometers and immediately turned them into another toll road running through the southern part of the country.[98] The generals worked on it while in power amid continuous protests and instability in the months that followed the deposing of Mubarak and opened it before the end of the year, in October 2011. This road was the third stage of the above-mentioned Helwan-Kuraymat-Beni Suef road, extending it to reach Asyut province in Upper Egypt. The military engineers' authority took charge of constructing that extension.[99]

In the southwestern desert part of the country, the state granted the military 110,000 acres to create an export-oriented farm, where conscripts are used as cheap or nearly free labor along with local farmers hired through private contractors. It is located next to the vast farms in the area that are owned by other local, Saudi, and UAE investors and engaged in commercial farming mainly for exportation to the Gulf and other regions. NSPO created the Wataniyya Company for Land Reclamation and Agriculture of Desert Land in East 'Uwaynat to run this farm. This company started its activities in 1999 and had already cultivated 40,000 acres by the eve of the 2011 uprising. It harvested wheat, corn, vegetables, and fruits and ran vast barns for sheep and cattle. The provincial government constructed a local airport in the area to facilitate the exportation of the area's produce.[100] Interestingly, the proximity between the military and private investors in the area helped foster relations between the officers and a certain major business tycoon in Mubarak's regime. The military farm's immediate neighbor is Muhammad

Abu al-'Aynayn, a giant ceramic manufacturer who also owns 20,000 acres in the same area.[101] Such an important neighboring relationship helped Abu al-'Aynayn with workers' strikes in his plant in Suez after 2011, as he received the help of the military police in appeasing the laborers.[102]

The Nubariyya area, near Alexandria, took the form of desert tracts allocated to private investors and youth to reclaim, and the army obtained a large share of ten thousand acres in it for export-oriented agriculture. This is NSPO's October 6th farm, with attached barns and mills for dairy, poultry, beef, mash, and canned food, where female and male laborers were hired. The top administrators of the farm were army colonels, and they acted as large landowners in the area, in contrast to neighboring private and youth-owned small farms.[103] In an arbitrary move of the state granting conspicuous privileges to this military export-oriented agriculture project, Presidential Decree no. 403 of 2009 reallotted the land near the Nubariyya Canal, originally the property of the General Organization for of Nile Transit, to the MoD. Along with all the buildings and facilities on it, the land would be "used as a river port for the armed forces' shipments," the decree added.[104]

In addition to cultivating parts of this farm, NSPO leases other large plots in the area to private local and foreign agricultural companies, in addition to small peasants who sometimes had unpleasant experiences with their powerful landlords. By the time of the uprisings, NSPO collected rent that reached LE4,000 per acre annually. Military workshops manufactured cheap greenhouses and installed them in some areas, which raised this amount to more than LE12,000. Small peasants who tried to be direct tenants or indirect subletters of smaller parcels had to depend on credit to be able to afford such high rent. There were groups of local creditors who used to make a profit out of making loans to these peasants, and the military administration of the farm turned a blind eye to such exploitative practices so long as the peasants paid the rent regularly. Because of the unstable economic and security conditions that followed the 2011 events, many of these small peasants had difficulties selling their produce and failed to pay both rents and loans, and NSPO decided to terminate their leases and evacuate them.[105]

In 1997 the state declared Toshka territory, in the deep South of Egypt and close to the High Dam's rich water resources, a national project for land reclamation. Thus local and Arabian Gulf investors rushed to buy large pieces of land in this area for export-oriented agriculture. Next to the land of Saudi business tycoons, the military obtained 17,000 acres and embarked on cultivating them for profit.[106] Moreover, in 2003 the MoMP obtained the right to help the government in reclaiming 23,000 acres in the same area, as three different military factories were to manufacture and provide the project with necessary agricultural machinery such as tractors, plows, irrigation equipment, water pipes, electricity lines, and trucks. This deal amounted to roughly LE398 million.[107] Furthermore, different military corps obtained thousands of acres to create their own commercial agriculture projects in other areas of the country. The state granted the "Western Military Region"—by the Mediterranean near Marsa Matruh—100,000 acres for reclamation using the area's abundant rain. This farm spans a very long coastline that reaches 135 kilometers. The officers use some of the produce to feed the soldiers and sell the rest to civilians.[108] In addition, the military attempted to benefit from state activities relevant to land reclamation, even if the officers did not run the land themselves. Military factories made "surface water irrigation systems," with the World Bank's support, and sold them—directly or outside public tenders—to the Ministry of Irrigation and Water Resources. This civilian ministry then used them in the newly cultivated desert areas in Toshka.[109]

The military also used more of the land it appropriated during wartime to build numerous apartment buildings with attached shopping malls in different areas in Cairo and the provinces. The Armed Forces' Land Projects Organization constructed thousands of apartments, allocated some to the officers to share, and sold the rest to civilians. These lucrative constructions were erected in the upper- and middle-class areas of Nasr City, Zahra' Nasr City, Helwan, and October 6th in Greater Cairo, in addition to areas in the northern coast and Delta provinces. In one incident, the military illegally annexed a large piece of 30,000 square meters in the nouveau riche neighborhood of Nasr City to use for one of its many housing projects in the area, but the Syndicate of Engineers—which was the original owner of this land—managed to retrieve it through civilian courts.[110] Since the military mainly targets the upper and middle classes as its potential clientele of upscale homebuyers, the designs of these apartments match these social groups' taste and lifestyle, with regard to the large number of rooms, fashionable interior division, luxury finishing, and classy building gates. It usually made sure these newly constructed urban spaces would include at least one mosque, a mall, many grocery stores, and an exclusive social club for families. The price of a luxury military apartment of about 120 square meters in Nasr City area after the uprisings was around LE400,000 per unit, and the price for an apartment of 86 square meters in the same area was around LE250,000. In the October 6th area, the price of a 100 square meter unit was LE135,000.[111]

For a civilian, buying a military-built apartment might not be the safest decision to make in life: the new owner could end up in military jail at any moment for any minor dispute with the mighty landlords. In one incident, a civilian inhabitant bought an apartment, including a share in the land, in an AFLPO building in Nasr City. The contract indicated that AFLPO had no authority over the apartment after its sale, and the owner should consult with his fellow civilians' "union of building owners" regarding future decisions about it. Many years later he wanted to convert it from residential to commercial use, along with another piece of land that was part of the building, which he leased from the union. For unclear reasons, AFLPO was not happy with this act, so it sued him in the military court of eastern Cairo for "trespassing on military property." In 2009 the court ruled in favor of AFLPO, sentencing the owner to prison, forcing him to evacuate the rented area, and making him pay more than LE2 million as a fine. Luckily, the Supreme Constitutional Court annulled the military's court verdict on grounds of "lack of jurisdiction."[112]

The military formally and informally, or rather illicitly, controlled quarries in many areas of the country—especially in the South—and limited private businesses' access to them. The army had its own extended quarries to use or lease out. In many incidents, tenants of the army's mines complained about arbitrary and oppressive practices against them. In one incident, NSPO canceled a contract granting usufruct rights to its quarry in Aswan to a public-sector company because the latter exported part of the produce to China before obtaining NSPO's approval. NSPO insisted that it had officially registered its property rights to this mine in 2009 and faxed the company to immediately evacuate the mining site—amid great discontent among hundreds of laborers who lost their jobs because of the dispute. The fax indicated that the company had no right to claim compensation or sue NSPO for the sudden termination of the contract because the lease stipulated that the latter had the power to keep the security deposit and demand immediate evacuation if the company violated it. The company's workers insisted that such an oppressive decision not only left them jobless but also wasted tons of material that was ready for exportation and would generate much needed income for the country.[113]

More important, local government officials enjoyed full authority over quarries in their provinces, and they were mostly retired officers.[114] In Fayyum province in 2000, retired general Salah Hilmi—the general secretary of the province and the head of its quarries department—succeeded in lobbying allies in the parliament to block a law that aimed at placing mines under closer control of the Ministry of Oil and Mineral Resources. He managed to collect the signatures of 140 parliament members to force the Committee of Local Administration to turn down the law. [115] In 2008 the neoliberal government attempted to revive the law but again failed. Appointed officers in local departments of quarries then generally gave random licenses to local businesses, which extracted low-quality construction material without proper inspections. Serious investors suffered from these practices and insisted that the usufruct leases they had to sign to use the mines were written in oppressive language and violated their legal rights. When central government experts in Cairo tried to revive the law and increase state control over quality and prices in 2008, they recalled how General Hilmi had blocked the proposal many years earlier.[116] To their frustration, they faced the same situation again as co-opted parliamentarians turned down the new law proposal. The absence of such necessary legislation continued after the 2011 uprisings.[117]

In Aswan, the most southern province in the country, whose appointed governor was always a retired general, the mining sector is a realm of corrupt gains for retired colonels. Before the 2011 uprisings, Colonel 'Ala' Muhammad Isma'il—appointed as the head of the quarries, the industrial zone, and the investment authority in the province—allegedly split large public mines into smaller units and leased each of them at a conspicuously high rent. He recorded only a portion of this rent on official papers and submitted little of what he collected to the provincial treasury. Local victims of his practices reported that in one year he collected a total of LE277,000 in rent but actually submitted only LE25,125 of it to the state. In addition, he gave arbitrary perks to the board of directors of a particular large quarry—apparently to co-opt them for complicity in corruption. He appointed many other retired colonels in official positions in the department of local quarries.[118]

Moreover, the military dominated state mines indirectly. Small private businesses could only enjoy usufruct rights over public quarries and had to obtain security licenses to run them. Miners had to apply to the armed forces to acquire these licenses and use explosives, and in this way the military controlled hundreds of thousands of square meters of quarries across the country, used to extract construction material, limestone, marble, granite, and much more. Such licenses were valid for limited periods, and miners had to go back to the military to renew them regularly. In addition, military factories monopolized the provision of explosives, such as dynamite, necessary to use in quarries and sold them at arbitrarily high prices. Before 2011 military factory 81 used to provide the Cairo Chamber of Commerce's quarries department with the explosives it needed, and the factory raised its prices threefold, in addition to multiplying truck fees on military-controlled toll roads, under the Supreme Council of Armed Forces' government. Consequently, many companies faced great losses and had to close down.[119]

Bread, Homes, and Football

While military enterprises made big money and grabbed big land, they continued to act as gigantic parastatal entities that took charge of extending social services on behalf of the government to the citizens. They possessed a dominant status by providing public supplies and services and undertaking government construction projects. Although Mubarak now officially applied full-fledged liberalization of the economy, as opposed to wrestling with limited openness in the 1980s, he still kept an expansive social role for the state, or he still maintained an "ambiguous economy" that was neither fully neoliberal nor socialist. Functioning with parastatal privileges within such an ambivalent economic milieu, military enterprises took charge of baking subsidized bread, constructing social housing, collecting garbage, opening clinics, making medicine, delivering home electricity meters, and supporting championships of popular sports to appease the Egyptian masses. Thus their profit-seeking, pervasive presence cast its invisible shadow over every possible locality and social stratum.

In spite of persistent pressure by the IMF and World Bank on Mubarak's liberalizing regime to eliminate subsidies, they continued. To make subsidized bread available in abundance, the army's numerous giant bakeries made bread daily, and conscripts both baked and distributed loaves through their units' outlets. Moreover, the MoMP's factories manufactured automated bread bakeries for the government. For example, in Qina in the South, the army operated eight gigantic complexes to make bread for the Ministry of Supply, producing about 700 million loaves every year for civilian consumption. In Cairo, NSPO built ten complexes for bread for the Ministry of Social Solidarity, and their products covered Greater Cairo, including Giza and Qalyubiyya. Furthermore, military factories manufactured thousands of kiosks for bread sales.[120] These kiosks also exist by the walls of many military camps, where conscripted soldiers sell cheap loaves to long lines of low-income civilians living in surrounding neighborhoods.[121] When a bread shortage crisis swept the country in 2008, Mubarak officially delegated NSPO to take charge of resolving it. Subsidized bread was infamous for its poor quality, as citizens complained about misshapen loaves and often reported having found odd objects such as dead insects, pieces of wood, thread, or even tiny screws in them. The 2011 uprisings were preceded by severe bread crises and limited riots, which the military obviously contributed to.[122]

The Engineering Authority of the Armed Forces, commonly known as al-Hay'a al-Handasiyya, was a dominant contractor for state projects in the country, functioning above and in collaboration with the private sector. It constructed bridges, roads, stadiums, airports, hospitals, schools, water sanitation plants, governmental premises, factories, and houses for crisis relief in remote areas, and it generally took charge of national crisis relief efforts. More important, military engineers dominated the field of building affordable apartments for low- and middle-income civilians, funded by either the government or professional syndicates and trade unions, including the large Mubarak's Project for Youth Housing.[123] Interestingly, during the 2000s the army annually held an "Engineering Authority Day" (*yawm tafawwuq al-hay'a al-handasiyya*) to celebrate its excellence. On this day, Tantawi used to watch a documentary on the fundamental role that military engineers played in designing the historic bridge used to cross the Suez Canal in the 1973 war and then praise their contribution to national economic development and the welfare of the lower classes.[124]

EAAF always won government contracts to build tens of thousands of apartments in social housing projects—without entering into free and fair tenders in competition with private businesses. Military engineers usually concluded direct agreements with the government (*bi-l-ittifaq* or *bi-l-isnad al-mubashir*), which article 1 of the public tenders law no. 89 of 1998 permitted—albeit only as an exceptional measure in hiring contractors; the rule was supposed to be the holding of open tenders. EAAF charged the government arbitrary prices beyond market rates and used subcontractors from the private or public sector to execute assigned projects, with the government eventually footing the bill.[125] The field of building social housing—such as *masakin al-shabab* for youth and *al-iskan al-'a'ili* for low-income youth and families—was generally under the control of three main entities:

the Ministry of Housing, its New Urban Communities Authority, and the military engineers of EAAF. Interestingly, retired army generals and colonels dominate the high administrative positions in the ministry and its authority. The two of them directly granted EAAF contracts to contribute to building middle- to low-income suburbs in the outskirts of Cairo, in areas such as October 6th and May 15th City. To justify its close relation with the government, EAAF usually asserted that it was the most efficient and fastest builder in the country for the state to rely on. Evidently, the work of EAAF was not the most competent: many citizens complained about extensive delays and corruption in the projects where they had paid deposits and reserved units. Moreover, some employees inside the ministry and the authority campaigned for the firing of the corrupt retired officers appointed there.[126]

In the realm of medical services, military corps established an ever-increasing number of hospitals or medical complexes that extended services to civilians at high fees. They were either affordable or luxury hospitals catering to the rich and the middle class alike. Extremely well funded, military hospitals enjoy the reputation of introducing such high-quality services that famous movie starts and singers seek treatment there. Military corps built around forty-four advanced medical facilities spread across twenty out of the country's twenty-seven provinces, of course including Cairo and Alexandria. They are all placed under the Department of Medical Services of the Armed Forces, headed by generals rather than physicians. Military doctors and nurses who serve in the facilities are trained at the Military Medical Academy and attached specialized institutes as well as military nursing schools for female and male nurses.[127] One of the largest and most luxurious military hospitals is the International Medical Center, located on the desert road between Cairo and the Suez Canal city of Ismailiyya. Its story is rather interesting. Mubarak opened it in 2004 with lavish suites to cater to wealthy Egyptians and Arabs. Originally funded by U.S. military aid and constructed in collaboration with the Pentagon, the facility was supposed to receive wounded American soldiers in the region—especially after the U.S occupation of Iraq. But the Pentagon eventually found it too commercial, catering more to "medical tourism" and not abiding by its standards of proper military medical facilities. No American soldiers go to receive treatment there.[128]

Moreover, the military produced medications and sold them to public hospitals. The medical department at the army's Authority of Supply owned a drug factory and a "pharmaceutical city" in northern Cairo, at the industrial area of al-'Ashir min Ramdan. It also produced prosthetic devices for artificial limb replacement services. The Ministry of Health ordered these goods for its state-run hospitals, and they also fed military hospitals.[129] Interestingly, AOI's Arab British Dynamics Company ventured into making infant incubators, along with hospital beds, also for the Ministry of Health. Moreover, the ministry ordered mobile clinics from AOI to use in remote areas, which manufactured highly equipped ambulances and trucks at its Aircraft Factory in Helwan. The same factory took charge of outfitting trucks to be used in transporting vaccines and medical waste.[130]

Likewise, military enterprises manufactured and directly sold commodities and equipment to the Ministries of Electricity, Irrigation and Water Resources, Education, Oil, and more—again without competing with the private sector in open tenders. AOI signed a cooperation agreement with the Ministry of Investment to provide it with various kinds of equipment and spare parts for state-owned factories and agricultural businesses, after a visit that the neoliberal minister Mahmoud Muhi al-Din had with the organization. Muhi al-Din also made an agreement with AOI's Engines Factory to provide Alexandria port with gigantic grain conveyers at a cost of 45 million pounds.[131] The same factory built industrial water sanitation plants for the local office of the Ministry of Irrigation and Water Resources in Gharbiyya province in the Delta.[132] Moreover, AOI concluded an agreement with the Ministry of Communication to develop new electronic devices and control systems for it. AOI's Electronics Factory and its engineers were to take charge of this collaborative venture.[133] Interestingly, on the eve of the 2011 uprisings, the Cairo Cleaning and Beautification Authority concluded a LE70 million deal with AOI to buy needed equipment manufactured at the latter's factories.[134]

In the same realm of garbage collection, the Ministry of Local Development hired the MoMP to manufacture recycling and fertilizer production plants to be used in rural areas. At the end of 2007 officials announced that this project's total spending had reached more than LE300 million. The same ministry hired the MoMP to manufacture fire trucks.[135] For the Ministry of Health and the Ministry of Environment, the MoMP manufactured hundreds of incinerators for medical waste.[136] The Ministry of Environment hired both the MoMP and AOI to manufacture plants to treat agricultural solid waste into organic fertilizers and to modernize traditional brick kilns that caused air pollution.[137] For the Ministry of Electricity and Power, the MoMP manufactured modernized electronic meters to be installed in every home and business across the country, and it also made energy-saving lightbulbs.[138] For the Ministry of Irrigation and Water Resources, it embarked on a project to modernize irrigation systems to use surface irrigation for 3.7 million acres across the country, at a cost of LE1 billion.[139] For the Ministry of Higher Education responsible for public universities and institutes, the MoMP and AOI assembled hundreds of thousands of computers for students and faculty to buy on credit.[140] The MoMP similarly assembled computers and built a factory for student food in Aswan for the Ministry of Education.[141] Even when the state was contemplating its dubious project of the unification of the call to prayer, or *adhan*, whereby mosques would be obliged to play the same recording of the call on loudspeakers, the MoMP entered into the heated religious controversy erupted around this widely rejected attempt. It made an offer to the Ministry of Religious Endowments to install four thousand devices for this purpose in Greater Cairo's mosques.[142]

Football was always, and still is, the most popular sport in Egypt, and it mattered significantly to Minister of Military Production Mash'al. The news of his ministry's football team constantly thrilled media—even though it never won any national or international cups. Mash'al granted this team so much attention and funds that its stories in national press surpassed those of the actual manufacturing activities of military factories. Mash'al himself was far from being a typical military entrepreneur: he was socially a highly active figure who penetrated into the lives of tens of thousands of workers employed by the ministry, the larger local communities around its factories, and beyond to the whole nation. Besides serving as head of NSPO and then minister for more than a decade, Mash'al was a leading member of Mubarak's ruling party and occupied a seat in the parliament on its ticket for three consecutive terms—in notorious elections marked by fraud—representing the inhabitants of a Helwan district where most military plants are located. He extended medical care in his electoral district and led "health caravans" to provide free health services and medications to his constituents right before elections. Mash'al did not miss a national or social celebration in his district. On Mother's Day, he held big ceremonies to honor exemplary mothers among his constituents and distributed awards to them, but he also used this occasion to support the regime by making political speeches. On Labor Day, he greeted the workers of his factories for their great efforts and honored many of them, and he urged the workers of the nation to rally behind and support President Mubarak to ensure stability in the country.[143]

Back to football, Mash'al built a great stadium in the ministry's Olympic city for his team as well as to national and international games. He invited the prime minister, one of Gamal's close business clients, to cut the ribbon and FIFA's vice president to visit the venue. Allegedly, the latter admired the stadium for following the highest global standards in its construction and services. On his side, Mash'al proudly asserted that this stadium was the only one of its kind in the country that applied the most advanced technology and had large screens, a hotel, and big garages.[144] Catering to the extremely popular sport nationwide, this was but one of many other colossal stadiums that the military institution owned and ran to accommodate important matches and conspicuously make considerable profits. The armed forces owned at least seven gigantic facilities that hosted numerous national matches, including the stadiums of Burg al-'Arab near Alexandria and of the Air Defense in the outskirts of Cairo. In addition, military contractors constructed many other football stadiums for the Ministry of Youth and Sports in southern and northern Egypt.

Military business was everywhere: it is virtually impossible for any civilian individual to escape its omnipotent presence in and its watchful eye over everyday life. The military business indeed made big money through numerous and expansive enterprise, while penetrating into the urban spaces and social realms of every citizen in the nation. But this did not happen only by providing these often odd and inapt goods and services to the subjected masses. It also took place through retired officers occupying a large number of top administrative positions in the state bureaucracy. Retired generals appeared in every locality as governors of provinces, heads of ports, chairmen of public companies, administrators of government authorities, and much more. They industriously took part in mismanaging Mubarak's inefficient neoliberal economy and controlling the discontented population—a dilemma that the following chapter will explore.

CHAPTER 4

The Republic of Retired Generals
(1990s–2000s)

In the perfect [military] camp, all power would be exercised solely through exact observation; each gaze form a part of the overall functioning of power. . . . [T]his model of the camp or at least its underlying principle was found in urban development, in the construction of working-class housing estates, hospitals, asylums, prisons, schools: the spatial "nesting" of hierarchized surveillance.
—Foucault, *Discipline and Punish*

In the summer of 2014 more than three years had passed since the military deposed Mubarak in response to mass uprisings, and another holy month of Ramadan had just ended. Ex-general 'Umar al-Shawadfi—then governor of the Delta province of Daqahliyya—was celebrating the Eid by attending the early morning prayer in a crowded local mosque. Upon the end of the prayer, a group of citizens aggressively stopped al-Shawadfi to complain about the dire conditions of potable water and sewerage services in their village, located only a few meters away from the governor's office. One of the complainers shouted, "We drink sewage water, your excellency." Infuriated by such criticism, al-Shawadfi impatiently said, "We cannot fix thirty years of corruption in a single day and night," and he stormed out of the mosque surrounded by his provincial officials. Ironically, al-Shawadfi was himself an integral part of those three decades of malgovernance in Egypt: he was Hosni Mubarak's head of the main agency controlling state land, the National Center for Planning State Land Uses, from 2004 and remained in this crucial position until he was appointed governor in 2013. Corruption in land sales was a visibly notorious component of Mubarak's neoliberal bad practices. Officer engineer al-Shawadfi had been tagged as "the black box" of Egypt's land sale deals, and the parliament questioned him a year before the uprisings about at least one publically known case of corruption pertaining to the sale of thousands of acres of public land to a Kuwaiti-Egyptian real estate firm.[1]

Al-Shawadfi was one of many heroes of the 1973 war who retired from service only to collect more rewards from the nation in return of fighting this war. Throughout the 1990s and 2000s Mubarak appointed a large number of ex-generals in top bureaucratic positions in his successive neoliberal cabinets. For a short period after fighting this war, which restored Sinai from Israeli occupation, those heroes, or *abtal harb uktubar*, mainly kept to their barracks and were marginalized in politics under Anwar Sadat's scheme of demilitarization. But Mubarak brought them back to public life, first by allowing them to initiate a business empire, as indicated in the previous chapter, and then by assigning them an ever-increasing number of key posts in the state bureaucracy. Remilitarizing the Egyptian state went hand in hand with economic liberalization, and with this Egypt steadily grew into becoming a republic of retired generals.

While Mubarak maintained a civilian face for the state in Cairo by forming cabinets of civilian technocrats, retired generals were the invisible, de facto rulers of the country. They occupied pivotal positions under Cairo's civilian ministers and controlled citizens' everyday lives in almost every locality. Retired generals were the actual rulers of most of provincial Egypt, occupying seats of local governors, heads of towns, heads of neighborhoods, and so forth. They also managed every sea, river, and land port and dominated public transportation as a whole from buses and ferryboats to airlines. Moreover, they took charge of government authorities that provided basic public services to the citizens, from water and sewerage and affordable housing to garbage collection and urban beautification. More important, ex-officers were hired heads of numerous government authorities responsible for the main economic activities of the liberalized state. They managed public authorities allocating state land to public projects or private business, along with the authorities of investment, import and export, tourism, and much more.

Arguably, Mubarak embarked on such a strategy of hiring retired generals in bureaucratic positions in order to coup-proof his regime. To avoid officer mutiny, the military president of the country sought to appease his home institution and co-opt as many as possible of its older leaders by extending such political privileges to them. This strategy became particularly important in the 2000s, when Mubarak was grooming his civilian son, Gamal, to inherit his presidential seat. This plan of political succession was fundamentally problematic to the officers, who had been commanded only by military presidents ever since the 1952 revolution. In other words, the military institution had monopolized the presidential seat since Gamal Abdel Nasser, and it was hard to see it lost to a young civilian. Gamal Mubarak took over his father's ruling party, the NDP, and appointed his business cronies to its high committee on devising the country's politics in 2000. By 2004 major tycoons in Gamal's clientelist circle formed the cabinet, which the public sarcastically called the "government of businessmen" (*hukumat rijal al-a'mal*), who rapidly applied extreme neoliberal measures. Amid Gamal's imposed changes, appeasing the old war heroes was necessary for the Mubaraks.

On the eve of the Arab Spring uprisings, Egypt was not the only Arab authoritarian regime that adopted one or another coup-proofing strategy. Many other countries, such as Syria, Libya, Iraq, Yemen, and Saudi Arabia, followed various means of appeasing their officers and reducing the potential for military coups. Holger Albrecht asserts that before the Arab Spring, coup-proofing was an important survival tool for authoritarian regimes in the region. Albrecht investigates the Syrian and Egyptian cases to argue that both Bashar al-Assad and Mubarak kept professional armies that enjoyed a degree of political influence, and "civilianized former officers" were involved in day-to-day politics. Both regimes bought the loyalty of the officers by extending to them economic advantages and opportunities for personal gains. In the Syrian case, fostering religious and ethnic bonds with select officers was an essential coup-proofing tool. Nevertheless, he adds, the armies of the two states reacted in entirely different ways to the 2011 uprisings against their respective autocrats. Whereas in Syria the army intervened in support of the regime, though with a large number of defectors, in Egypt it abandoned the regime and intervened to take over. Thus coup-proofing does not always work, Albrecht asserts.[2]

Arguable as well, even if it was peacetime, the military autocrat and his old war heroes still treated society as if there was an imminent war that required permanent guarding of civilian localities. In a conversation with a young Egyptian military intelligence officer who was studying in the United States at the Marine Corps University, I asked him why the military today controls civilian positions in charge of public transportation and keeps its own firm for constructing roads. His simple answer was, "So if the enemy invades, the army knows the entrances and exits of the country." He did not indicate exactly who the enemy was, though.[3] The perceived need to watch out for an imaginary invader of the country's urban localities was translated into retired officers practically occupying and controlling those localities. It also translated into controlling the provision of public services that cut through urban vicinities and run through the lives of the citizens inhabiting them. It rendered the whole urban landscape as a potential battlefield, and every city as a huge camp whose inhabitants must be kept under surveillance. "The apparatuses of the security work, fabricate, organize, and plan the milieu. . . . The milieu is a set of natural givens—rivers, marshes, hills— and a set of artificial givens—an agglomeration of individuals, of houses, etcetera," Foucault states about experiences of other modern states. The Egyptian regime probably followed their example.[4]

Another interpretation of such militarization has to do with the fear of internal rather than external enemies of the regime. This was presented in the previous chapter on the military business empire. As neoliberal policies generate acute social disparities and increase the level of public discontent, the securitization of urban realms becomes a necessity to contain potential public unrest. Neoliberalism brings an urgent need to keep an uninterrupted gaze over the potentially rebellious masses. Stephen Graham's definition of the notion of "new military urbanism" asserts that it is a phenomenon inseparable from neoliberalism. "I define [new military urbanism] as the emerging constellation of military and security doctrine and practice which posits that the 'key' security challenges of our age now center on the everyday sites, spaces and circulation of cities," Graham explains.[5] Such a notion is applied by the U.S. Army in its global war on terror in cities such as Baghdad, where it fights not simply through asymmetric combat but mainly by laying down the infrastructure, planning for urban development, and using technology of daily surveillance. In Mubarak's Egypt, officers and ex-officers were happy to provide the regime with such securitization services to contain lower-class potential unrest, and also in some sites to manage local terrorism. They did so when officers created expansive civilian businesses spread across urban vicinities to both make profits and keep an eye on the consuming masses. They also did so when ex-officers occupied civilian public offices in almost every locality and engaged in daily interaction with the subordinated population. Their invisible gaze cast its shadow over every individual, outside or even inside the home, in the entire nation.

This chapter investigates how Mubarak remilitarized the Egyptian state by appointing war heroes in the second stratum of top state positions. It argues that ex-generals were major participants in running Mubarak's dysfunctional market and were evidently integral contributors to the fallacies of the autocrat's neoliberalism that eventually collapsed under public rage in 2011. Such infamous fallacies included clientelism, conspicuous cronyism, inefficiency, severe decline of public services, entrenched social disparities, and widespread corruption. Ex-generals were the very government officials who ushered in the swift transition to the market by running critical administrative posts in control of provincial development, foreign investment, allotment of state land, export and import activities, holding companies, maritime transport, civil aviation, and much more. The economically inexperienced retired generals attempted to attract foreign capital to invest in some of the areas they controlled, but they were not always very successful and added to the stagnation of the public sector they ran. Meanwhile, many of them distorted the liberalized market by preventing the privatization of public enterprises for the interest of the military institution, or through favoritism toward business tycoons. Dramatically, retired officers took control of certain public services that noticeably decayed on the eve of the 2011 uprisings, from water and sewerage systems to public buses and boats.

Generally, each corps in the armed forces dominated high appointments in a certain sector of civil service that did or did not match its expertise. Generals originally coming from the ground forces in the army, such as infantry, artillery, and air defense corps, were mostly appointed as governors. Meanwhile, ex-navy rear admirals and admirals swept positions as heads of ports, as well as government authorities of maritime navigation and safety, and chaired relevant state-owned companies. Military engineers flooded the Ministry of Housing and its various authorities responsible for distributing state land or building affordable housing. Finally, ex–air force pilots controlled the sector of civil aviation, all the way from the seat of the minister to heads of relevant authorities and holding companies.

Mubarak was able to hire retired generals in these positions based on the legal codes of civil service, which granted the president arbitrary powers to hire and fire incumbents in high government ranks. Sadat promulgated law no. 47 of 1978 to reduce the military presence in the cabinet, and Mubarak used the same law to bring them back. Article 16 of this law authorized the president to issue decisions to appoint employees in senior positions. While the law stipulated that a medical council should check the health suitability of the candidate, article 20 exempted those hired by the president—convenient enough to the elderly retired officers. Other articles exempted these presidential appointees from any tests to prove their qualifications for the job and gave only the president the authority to fire them. In 1992 Mubarak amended this law to authorize the president to renew the terms of service for high-level incumbents indefinitely. The armed forces' laws, on the other hand, did not mention anything pertained to allocating civilian jobs to re-tired officers. That process took place informally and was highly selective. The military retirement law, no. 90 of 1975, regulated issues of financial compensation at the end of service and assigned pensions based on rank but did not include provisions pertaining to new jobs of personnel after the end of their service. Pensions were relatively low, the equivalent of monthly salaries without the extra perks the officers enjoyed while in service. Thus civilian posts were a good means for a significant increase in postretirement income for those who were lucky enough to receive them. Retired officers in civil service received both military pensions along with civilian salaries.

A considerable number of personnel retire from the military every year, but only a select group of high-ranking officers received prestigious ap-pointments in the bureaucracy. To keep the hierarchical structure of the Egyptian military, the institution dismisses a significant number of officers at the ranks of colonel and brigadier general in their early forties. It promotes only a small number into the ranks of major general, lieutenant general, and chief of staff, who in turn usually retire in their early fifties. Depending on the rank at which they left service and the degree of loyalty to the lead-ership, officers could receive anything from a governorship to a middling bureaucratic position like a public relations employee in a state organization. Officers who desired civilian jobs received crash courses in management and business administration in state preparation centers. For example, at the Leadership and Management Development Center (LMDC) they attended short courses of between a few days and several weeks on topics such as strategic management, communication with workers, and charismatic lead-ership or "personal attractiveness."[6]

This chapter traces selected profiles of interesting retired generals who assumed civilian positions in the two decades that preceded the 2011 upris-ings. Most information cited in this chapter was published in newspapers after the onset of the uprisings, specifically under transitional governments when state-owned and private newspapers enjoyed an unprecedented, al-beit fleeting, historical moment of freedom of the press. Although names of military bureaucrats under Mubarak were publicly known before the upris-ings, there was little information about how they managed their duties and their relation to local citizens or government workers. Immense knowledge about them was finally and widely revealed in the press in 2011, as local citizens filed a plethora of lawsuits or sent complaints to the public pros-ecutor against some of the retired generals who misgoverned them. More information was also unearthed as employees and workers in government offices protested against their military administrators and the press openly reported their narratives and demands in the midst of the revolutionary fervor. This chapter relies on what citizens and civilian workers alleged about their military administrators and cites their stories as told primarily through published sources.

Governing Provincial Egypt

A provincial governor in Egypt is a high position at the same civil rank as a minister. He enjoys extensive executive powers coordinating the work of local offices of the central government, along with the high salary and perks of a cabinet member. During his first decade in power, Mubarak appointed almost the same limited number of officers in positions of governors as Sadat did. Thus he maintained a demilitarized provincial Egypt. However, this number gradually increased until it reached its peak in the 2000s. Mubarak selected most military governors from the ground forces, such as the artillery, infantry, and air defense, and a few came from other areas such as national intelligence, which is populated by army officers. This section begins with a general overview tracing the gradual increase in their numbers over the course of three decades. Then it zooms in on salient profiles of prominent military governors, the urban and rural areas they presided over, and the impact of their governance on local communities and the services they received from the liberalized state.

Egypt has twenty-six provinces, or governorates. They are conventionally divided into two categories: border governorates, which always received military governors because of their strategic locations, and nonborder governorates by the Nile or the Mediterranean, which rotated between civilian and military governors. There is a fixed number of nine border governorates, close to Israel-Palestine in the Northeast, Libya in the West, Sudan in the South, and Saudi Arabia in the Southeast: two in Sinai (North and South Sinai in the Northeast); three in the Suez Canal area (Suez, Ismailiyya, and Port Said, also in the Northeast); Matruh in the Northwest; al-Wadi al-Jadid in the East; Aswan in the South; and Red Sea in the Southeast. While Sadat often hired civilians in border provinces, Mubarak hired military in all nine. Moreover, he gradually increased the number of military governors in nonborder provinces. For instance, retired commanders of the Second and

Third Field Armies, based in Ismailiyya and Suez, respectively, were often appointed in border provinces. Ex-generals with backgrounds in the infantry, armored, artillery, signal, air defense, frontier guard, special forces (sa'qa), or military police corps were appointed in other areas across the country. A few from the Republican Guard and the General Intelligence Service, which is mainly staffed by army officers, were placed in this position after leaving service.

In 1981, the year of his assassination, Sadat left behind ten retired generals appointed as governors—which amounted to 34 percent of the total number of twenty-six governors. Six of them were in border provinces, and Cairo had had a military governor since the 1977 bread riots. In 1982 Mubarak slightly increased this number to twelve, adding Alexandria and Suez. Mubarak largely kept the same personnel that Sadat had hired in their positions, replacing only two with other fellow officers, in Aswan and Cairo. In 1983 he replaced the military governor of Cairo with General Abu Talib, who stayed for six years in this crucial position before being appointed minister of defense. After winning the 1987 referendum that renewed his presidency, Mubarak reduced the number to only eight: six in border provinces, one in Middle Egypt, and Cairo's General Abu Talib. After Abu Talib left his seat, Cairo never received other military governors under Mubarak.

The 1990s witnessed a gradual increase in their numbers. In 1997 eleven retired generals were governors: the nine border provinces in full, besides Alexandria and the City of Luxor. Mubarak made Luxor—a center of pharaonic relics and international tourism—a city of special status in 1989 after separating it from Qina province, to be governed by a retired general ever since. He then made Luxor an independent governorate in 2009 and appointed retired generals as its governors. Thus Mubarak granted a fixed status to Luxor similar to that of border governorates. He also appointed a considerable number of police officers as governors in the 1990s because of the wave of Islamic fundamentalism and terrorist attacks. In 1999 he increased the number of military governors to twelve, in addition to hiring five police generals to the post.

During the 2000s and after Gamal Mubarak's strong appearance on the political scene, Hosni Mubarak changed governors three times. With the pressure of fresh oppositional movements, especially Kifaya and the spread of youth protests, Mubarak held the first presidential elections in the country in 2005. Instead of running and winning alone in a referendum, as had been the case since Nasser, he competed with other candidates and still won.

Immediately afterward he hired fourteen military governors: nine in border governorates, a fixed one in Luxor, three in Middle Egypt, and one in the Delta. Between 2008 and the 2011 uprisings, he introduced two new governorates, making a total of twenty-eight, and maintained the same number of fourteen military governors: one in Giza for the first time, one in Upper Egypt, two in the Delta, the fixed one in Luxor, and the regular nine in border governorates. Interestingly, police generals occupied seven governorates on the eve of the uprisings. One of them, al-Gharbiyya in the Delta, where a huge textile workers' strike took place in 2008, was in the hands of an army general, but he lost it to a police officer after the violent turmoil in the city of Mahalla, where the public textile plant was located. Similarly, Alexandria was assigned to a police general in 2006 but was returned to army generals after the uprisings.

One of the most interesting military governors was General Muhammad Abd al-Salam al-Mahjub, who had a long career of ruling two provinces before serving as minister from the early 1990s to the 2011 uprisings. He was also an active member in the ruling National Democratic Party. A graduate of the military academy who used to work for the General Intelligence, al-Mahjub ruled Ismailiyya from 1994 until 1996 and became governor of Alexandria—the vital Mediterranean port and second largest city in Egypt after Cairo—for almost a decade from 1997 to 2006. After leaving Alexandria he became responsible for the administration of all Egyptian provinces, as he was appointed minister of local development from 2006 to the 2011 uprisings. While minister, he won a seat in the parliamentary elections in Alexandria on the NDP's list and used the help of a famous religious preacher to reach victory. This was Mubarak's last outrageous parliamentary election of 2010, when candidates from oppositional parties did not win any seats.

While ruling Alexandria, al-Mahjub changed the face of urban life in this historic metropolis. He started out as an enthusiastic and popular administrator who busied himself with the restructuring and beautification of the populous city. He constructed a new sea corniche road, reorganized the train station, built new public transportation stands, and hired a French cleaning company to handle the city's garbage collection. His support of private businessmen, especially contractors, resulted in a construction boom, and he granted many of them the right to administer the public beaches and collect admission fees. In return, he asked them to contribute to his beautification efforts in cash and kind. As the years passed without actual improvement in people's standard of living beyond removing garbage and relocating microbus stops, public discontent against al-Mahjub grew. On the one hand, his encouragement of real estate investment that was intended to generate economic activities in fact crowded the city with high, ugly cement buildings containing many vacant luxury apartments of absentee landlords. After the 2011 uprisings a large number of Alexandria inhabitants submitted legal complaints to the public prosecutor about al-Mahjub grant-ing illegal licenses for businessmen to construct over-height buildings.[7] On the other hand, the local government constructed extremely low-funded public houses with poor infrastructure and no basic services, especially sani-tation provisions. Those flats quickly struggled with collapses in their walls because of sewage leaks in lower-class areas such as New Nasiriyya.[8] The same lower classes grew nostalgic about the good old days when they had free admission to their city's long public beaches without newly imposed fees of private companies that took over the sea corniche.

More important, al-Mahjub faced local citizens' accusations of favoring a number of businessmen by granting them large pieces of state land at conspicuously low prices along with licenses for illegal construction. Alleg-edly among his cronies was Mohammad Abu al-'Aynayn—a tycoon owning ceramic plants and a vast farm that neighbors a military one in the western desert—who obtained land downtown and by the coast at only 5 percent of its market price.[9] Al-Mahjub's administration also granted him permission to build a commercial mall whose height exceeded the legally authorized measures in the historic city. In March 2011, in response to local protests, an Alexandrian court issued a decision to temporarily seize the properties of al-Mahjub and his wife and impose a travel ban on the couple, on grounds of wasting tens of millions in state funds. However, three months later, under the Supreme Council of Armed Forces regime, al-Mahjub's family recov-ered their fortunes and the travel ban was lifted. The case disappeared from media and nobody heard of it again.[10] As a minister of local development, al-Mahjub also faced accusations of squandering UNDP aid funds by distrib-uting around LE3 billion as bonuses for his favorite circle of top employees and recording it otherwise in official documents and financial reports sub-mitted to the donor. This case likewise disappeared, and the former officer enjoyed lasting impunity.[11]

Another interesting, or rather legendary, figure is General Samir Faraj, who had a peculiar career before he was hired as governor of Luxor from 2004 to 2011. Originally an infantry officer who studied and taught in Brit-ain, he kept a top position in military intelligence before being hired as director of the Department of Morale Affairs—responsible for military propaganda in and outside the armed forces. He also studied art, history, media, and business administration in Egypt and the United States and obtained a PhD; he wrote a dissertation on "the role of media in preparing the state for defense to reach Egyptian national security" in a high military academy.[12] This motivated Mubarak to hire him as the director of the Cairo Opera House, the highest cultural place for classical and modern music and art in the country, between 2000 and 2004. He had a short experience as a first undersecretary to the Minister of Tourism that he came to use in governing Luxor, a major pharaonic attraction for international tourism. Mubarak first hired Faraj as the head of this important city's high council, and then he turned the city into its own governorate in 2009.[13] Upon the arrival of Faraj, Luxor was already full of problems and deeply rooted discontent caused by policies of the preceding fellow officers who governed it. For instance, his predecessor General Silmi Salim destroyed thousands of houses and bazaars and displaced families in order to reconstruct an ancient pathway connecting two pharaonic temples—a UNESCO-funded project that was never completed and later led to huge protests.[14] Salim was also in charge of the city when the massacre of fifty-eight tourists took place at the hands of Islamic fundamentalists in 1997.

The angry youth protesting against Faraj in 2011 claimed that he collaborated with local business tycoons in land sales, violated the law of public tenders, destroyed more houses and bazaars, and confiscated more land for the sake of that never-completed pharaonic pathway. After he was sacked in April 2011, citizens filed lawsuits against him regarding land corruption. Two litigations accused him of manipulating public tenders for the interest of favored investors in tourism, to whom he was claimed to have sold land at less than the market price—resulting in wasting hundreds of millions of Egyptian pounds from public funds. He was also accused of directly assigning projects to certain private contractors outside the scope of fair and competitive tenders. The public prosecutor received these accusations but could not investigate them because they were beyond his civilian jurisdiction—an existing law entailed that army officers in or out of service should be tried only in military courts[15]—and had to send them to the military prosecutor in Cairo, who allegedly ordered the imprisonment of Faraj. However, the case disappeared and the public never heard about it again [16]

After serving as the commander of the Third Field Army, Mubarak's senior chamberlain, General Muhammad Sayf al-Din Galal, ruled the Suez governorate for more than a decade, from 1999 until the uprisings. Known for his close ties with the NDP's business tycoons, Galal faced massive protests by local inhabitants who targeted him personally in his province, and allegedly he had to hide for months from angry crowds.[17] In fact, the bloodiest events of January 2011 were first ignited in the city of Suez, as protesters there burned down police stations in lower-class neighborhoods and clashed in street battles with security forces. Under the long reign of Galal, this city suffered from high unemployment rates and poverty due to its economic marginalization in the national economy, coupled with bread shortage crises, frequent labor strikes, and lack of affordable housing for youth. Galal evidently paid less attention to these problems and put more effort into urban beautification projects, which further angered the citizens, according to a local blogger. For instance, he demolished slums and removed the railways from downtown Suez, besides restructuring main streets, squares, and the market area regardless of the inhabitants' opposition to such disarray in their spaces.[18]

Galal was particularly infamous for accusations of land corruption. For example, to encourage investments in this vital governorate overlooking the Suez Canal, the cabinet in Cairo issued law no. 83 of 2002 that created the economic area northwest of the Gulf of Suez, which allowed businesspeople to obtain usufruct rights to use pieces of land for fifty years at LE25 per square meter. Galal favorably granted certain businesspeople the right to fully purchase this land at only LE5 per square meter. Four bought all 90 square kilometers of the area: Ahmed 'Izz, the steel and iron tycoon; Abu al-'Aynayn, a ceramic tycoon; Naguib Sawiris, a telecom tycoon; and an Egyptian Chinese company. By law they were exempt from taxes on bank loans, sales taxes, and all other kinds of fees.[19] On another note, the commander of the military police himself intervened to settle workers' aggressive protests against Abu al-'Aynayn at his Suez plant to demand fair financial rights after the 2011 uprisings.[20]

Originally a military engineer, General Ahmed Zaki 'Abdin had a long career in the Egyptian bureaucracy that enabled him to survive the 2011 events and maintain a prolonged power status. He was the governor of Beni Suef in Middle Egypt from 2006 to 2008 and then moved to rule the northern province of Kafr al-Shaykh in the Delta from 2008 to 2011. Right before that he was the head of the Engineering Authority of the Armed Forces (EAAF), which is one of the largest contractors for public construction in the country.[21] Prior to that he had served as the head of the Central

Agency for Construction, taking charge of building infrastructure, services, and housing in desert and less inhabited areas, and the head of the Cooperatives and Construction Authority. Although mass protests against him led to his removal from his position as governor of Kafr al-Shaykh,[22] the Muslim Brothers regime appointed him minister in 2012.

As the governor of Kafr al-Shaykh, a large province overlooking the Mediterranean with rich fishing and agricultural resources, 'Abdin once officially announced that he had fully resolved the crisis of potable water shortage by finishing relevant public works, and only a few lines in the water supply system were yet to be completed—including those in Mutubas. Six years later, however, a succeeding governor formed a special committee to study the severe problems with the water system in all the villages of Mutubas and commissioned the holding company responsible for the water systems to urgently find remedies to similar problems spreading across the whole governorate.[23] 'Abdin also officially initiated the construction of affordable youth housing, about 100,000 apartments, with services provided.[24] Youth in Kafr al-Shaykh rushed to apply and submitted required down payments and kept the receipts. Two years after his public appearance to announce this project, a dozen of those who had applied sued him for never receiving their apartments and accused him of planning to sell their flats in a public auction at high prices. Plaintiffs insisted that they had paid thousands of pounds to reserve apartments and kept official documents proving their claims. They argued that 'Abdin violated these contracts, denying them their legal rights, because of the good location of these subsidized apartments, which encouraged him to turn them into a profit-generating project. Although the public prosecutor in Cairo issued a decision to stop the sale of these apartments in auctions, 'Abdin refused to abide by the decision, claiming that he would invest the income in building more affordable houses for youth.[25]

During the reign of 'Abdin, the governorate was medically ranked number one in the country in terms of the spread of hepatitis C and its extremely poor health services at large.[26] When 'Abdin decided to move the wholesale local market of vegetables and fruit to a new area outside of the capital city of the province, he forced the merchants to pay excessively high monetary installments to acquire merely usufruct rights to the new stores there. In an outraged response, local merchants organized a large strike and refused to sell food to the public, demanding to be charged an affordable rent instead. 'Abdin never responded to their demands, which resulted in accumulated debt on the sellers, who feared imprisonment, and caused consequent increases in food prices.[27] Furthermore, many citizens accused him of nepotism and corruption, especially in land allocations. One lawsuit accused him of seizing thousands of acres originally allotted to a local association for agricultural reclamation and selling them to Cairo's elite officials, their families, and relatives of the Mubaraks.[28] Challenging continuous mass protests against him and protected by army soldiers and armored vehicles, 'Abdin managed to stay in office for a year and a half after 2011, until the brotherhood's premier appointed him minister of local development responsible for all provinces across the country.[29]

After finishing his service as the commander of the Second Field Army in Ismailiyya by the Suez Canal, General Fu'ad Sa'd al-Din ruled three key governorates consecutively in different areas in the country. He was first appointed governor of Ismailiyya from 1999 to 2004. He was then moved to the large Delta province of Munufiyya—the home province of Mubarak—which heavily supported the ruling NDP. Finally, he moved on to rule Minya in Middle Egypt—a governorate with a strong presence of Islamic fundamentalists and reoccurring sectarian strife between Muslims and Christian Copts. Sa'd al-Din resurfaced on the political scene in 2013, when he served in Abdel Fattah al-Sisi's presidential election campaign and advocated for the new constitution.[30] Upon his arrival in Minya, Sa'd al-Din vowed to resolve the water and sewage problems by raising funds to complete the long suspended projects and promised to finish large parts of the system by the end of his first year. Minya continued to suffer from lack of sewerage lines, regular water cuts, severe wastewater flooding in the streets, and collapses of houses due to immense leaks until 2011.[31]

When tens of people died in a ferryboat accident while celebrating holidays in a Minya village in 2007, this catastrophe revealed entrenched negligence by the governorate's local councils under Sa'd al-Din.[32] Minya is a large province split between eastern and western areas by the Nile, and its inhabitants heavily rely on public and private boats to move from one side of the river to the other. The local councils officially oversaw most of these ferryboats and were responsible for ensuring safety measures onboard both public and private ones. However, most of them were decades old, without basic maintenance, dangerous, and simply unfit for human use. In the above-mentioned accident, the scaffold that the villagers used to cross to the boat was decaying, so it broke off abruptly and whole families drowned. This particular ferryboat used to serve about thirty thousand inhabitants in three villages, and similar boats served other areas in the governorate. Furthermore, emergency forces always arrived too late to the areas where boat accidents took place, which increased the number of deaths. Sa'd al-Din never fixed the problem, as more accidents with a high death toll occurred in the area.[33] Completing the ongoing construction of a high bridge could have solved the problem, but Sa'd al-Din also never finished building this vital overpass.[34]

Among border governorates, South Sinai was the share of the favorite, lucky officers, while North Sinai was assigned to the less favored, probably unfortunate ones. On the one hand, the former is far enough from the troubled frontiers with Gaza and Israel and enjoys the fruits of investments in the Red Sea elite resorts such as those of Sharm al-Shaykh—where the Mubaraks built their holiday palaces. On the other hand, the latter is economically underdeveloped, constantly affected by eruptions of conflicts in Gaza by the border town of Rafah, and occupied by militant Islamists as a nest to easily hide in in its mountainous areas. Three fortunate governors of South Sinai served as commanders of the Republican Guard, that is, Mubarak's personal protectors, before he hired them to control South Sinai: General Mamduh al-Zuhayri (1993–1997), who also governed Suez (1997–1999); General Mustafa 'Afifi (1997–2005); and General Muhammad Hani Mutawalli Jad al-Rabb (2006–2010).

The first, General al-Zuhayri, was involved in many absurd cases of land sales. For instance, he helped at least one business tycoon obtain a valuable piece of land on a hill to construct a luxury hotel—violating the original military designation of this land as a "strategic area and natural reserve" prohibited from sale for security and environmental reasons. Allegedly when the minister of defense refused al-Zuhayri's request to sell this land to private business, al-Zuhayri used his personal connection with Mubarak to obtain the permit for the 52,000 square meters with attached coast and anchorage after removing the security unit stationed there. This area later became Lido Hotel of Sharm al-Shaykh.[35] After moving to govern Suez, he quickly became involved with other business tycoons in similar obscure cases of land sales. An official report of the Accountability State Authority (ASA) indicated that he granted 'Izz, the steel tycoon and top leader of Gamal's patronage circle, 21 million square meters west of the Gulf of Suez at the trivial price of LE5 per meter. According to an ASA official report, 'Izz not only never paid the full amount, as he paid just the first of four installments, but also resold part of this land at LE5,000 per meter to a foreign company under the reign of al-Zuhayri and his successor military governors of Suez.[36]

The second South Sinai governor, General 'Afifi, claimed after 2011 that he was surprised to learn about the degree of corruption that had spread in the country and that Mubarak's regime took advantage of his innocence.[37] Meanwhile, one citizen insists that "crony capitalism" (*ra'smaliyyat al-mahasib*) was the norm in the governorate during the reign of 'Afifi. He governed South Sinai during the crucial years when infamous business tycoons, especially billionaire Husayn Salim, who fled the country upon the 2011 uprisings, accumulated millions of square meters of coastal land to construct elite resorts on them, and when Mubarak himself built his family's five palaces in the same area.[38] In one incident, a member of the local council in South Sinai submitted a legal complaint to the public prosecutor accusing 'Afifi of wasting public funds by allowing another business tycoon in tourism to seize more than 2 million square meters of land in an area of hotel concentrations through direct allotment and without public tenders, at only LE100 per meter when the original price was LE7,000. Neither the ASA nor the public prosecutor took action regarding this case. Being "more occupied with business than security"—as one local citizen asserts—it was during 'Afifi's reign that the disastrous terrorists attacks by al-Qaeda took place in Sharm al-Shaykh in 2005. Eighty-eight people were killed and another two hundred injured.[39]

As soon as he left office, news about claimed corruption of General Sa'd Abu Rida, who ruled the Red Sea governorate from 1997 to 2006, became widespread. This governorate is very similar to South Sinai in terms of its rich investments in luxury resorts and tourism in areas such as Hurghada, which grew to become a gold mine for illicit profit. Abu Rida's name was implicated in cases of land corruption in collaboration with private business. For instance, it is claimed that he directly and outside of competitive public tenders sold to a local contractor large pieces of coastal land that the government originally allotted to affordable housing for youth and low-income citizens in the governorate. The contractor then built luxury villas, apartment buildings, and resorts. Abu Rida assigned this contractor the land at only LE20 per square meter, whereas he sold similar pieces to the general public at LE300. Top government officials in Cairo, including the prime minister, owned holiday homes in this illicitly built urban area. Abu Rida's family allegedly created private businesses benefiting from his position, as indicated in reports of the Bureau of Illegal Profiting, which banned the family from travel; the Cairo airport authorities denied his daughter boarding on international flights in 2013.[40]

The famous workers' strike of April 6, 2008, in the Delta province of Gharbiyya led to the demise of its military governor, engineer General Shafi'i al-Dakruri. The large town of Mahalla in this governorate is home to the largest, decades-old, state-owned textile plant in the country, Egypt Company for Spinning and Weaving in Greater Mahalla, where tens of thousands of workers are employed. Al-Dakruri arrived in this governorate in 2004, at the height of the privatization scheme, and faced many workers' protests during his term; they fiercely resented privatization and asked for a minimum wage. If their plant were to be sold to private investors, thousands of them would have been laid off—as was the case in many other, similar public-sector plants. Al-Dakruri survived a large labor protest in 2006 demanding salary increases and a strike in 2007 to raise the minimum wage, but he fell after the most famous strike of 2008. The strike turned into a violent protest, and media circulated an image of protesters taking down a giant photograph of Mubarak installed in a local square. Al-Dakruri's local security apparatus notoriously used excessive force against the angry protesters. As the incompetent general failed to appease the workers, the situation escalated into an international scandal for the Egyptian regime and inspired endless other uprisings.[41] Only eleven days after these bloody events, on April 17, Mubarak sacked al-Dakruri and replaced him with a police general.

The Upper Egyptian governorate of Sohag was traditionally assigned to police generals—especially during the 1990s when fundamental Islamism nested in southern areas—until an intelligence general took it over in 2006. Like many of the above-mentioned fellow officers, General Muhsin al-Nu'mani was accused of land corruption in Sohag, and the public prosecutor officially received cases filed against him in this regard. In addition to directly allotting pieces of state land to certain businessmen outside competitive tenders and at much lower rates than the market price, he gave members of the local council of the province for free the land that the government originally designated for building affordable youth housing. The ASA's local office in Sohag estimated the value of only one of these pieces at LE104 million. Furthermore, many local citizens insist on his involvement in rigging the results of the 2010 parliamentary elections for the interest of an NDP member from Gamal's close circle.[42] Although al-Nu'mani was removed from this governorate after the 2011 uprisings owing to youth protests against him, he survived the wave of change as the SCAF appointed him minister of local development for a few months. While in this important position, he refused to dissolve existing local councils still dominated by NDP figures nationwide—until a court decision mandated that he do so.[43]

Moving further south to Aswan, a border governorate endowed with touristic, industrial, fishing, mining, agricultural, and commercial resources, we find ex-officers continuously running it. While the citizens of Aswan remember the many good deeds of General Samir Yusuf, the former commander of the Border Guard and governor of Matruh before ruling Aswan from 2001 to 2008, they fiercely criticize his successor General Mustafa al-Sayyid, former commander of the Second Field Army, who ruled them from 2008 and stayed in office until 2013 despite protests against him. Yusuf reconstructed many main roads, painted houses, and renovated the old bazaar in the city of Aswan. As a rare exception, Aswan was clean, beautiful, and well organized. When al-Sayyid followed him, public services collapsed, leaving Aswan's urban and rural localities, for instance, drowning in sewer water. When heavy rain flooded the mountainous villages of the governorate in 2010, more than a thousand houses of poor families were destroyed and their agricultural land and livestock drowned, because the local government did not construct properly functioning diversion canals to protect these frequently affected areas.[44] Furthermore, al-Sayyid hired a fellow retired general, Kamal Maghrabi, as the manager of the High Dam Port Authority in control of commercial transportation with Sudan, during whose term Lake Nasser was hazardously polluted because of inefficient safety inspection services over passing shipments of chemicals.[45] Al-Sayyid also placed the profitable quarries of Aswan under the control of many retired colonels, hired at high salaries.[46]

Mismanaging Public Authorities

Although Mubarak never hired ex-officers as ministers in civilian sectors, they constituted a large portion of the second stratum of government incumbents who managed public authorities—especially those responsible for liberalizing the economy and providing public services. Evidently, they were mostly not very successful in luring private investments to the liberalized sectors they led. Moreover, a drastic decline in public services in the areas that they controlled was conspicuous. According to their previous expertise in their respective corps, ex-officers were appointed to control certain sectors. It is not feasible to calculate the exact number of retired officers appointed in administrative government positions, which could be anywhere in the bureaucratic hierarchy, since the government does not make information about its employees available. However, one can trace their presence in some exemplary areas that they intensively occupied and investigate key figures who played decisive roles in a highly fraudulent neoliberal economy.

A key player in privatization and opening the market for foreign capital, engineer officer Muhammad al-Ghamrawi was the head of the General Authority for Investment and Free Zones (GAFI) from 1999 to 2004. Before that, al-Ghamrawi held the important position of the minister of military production from 1993 to 1999. Moreover, he was the secretary general of NDP's Cairo office from 2001 onward, rendering him responsible for selecting candidates for parliamentary elections.[47] While minister of military production, he showed strong support for the ongoing economic liberalization in the country, praising its success and contribution to growth.[48] Later, as the head of GAFI, he put out great effort to attract Arab and foreign investors to buy the public-sector enterprises put up for sale.[49] Apparently, al-Ghamrawi did not meet with much luck in this mission. He always gave media official statements about upcoming joint ventures between Egypt and the Arabian Gulf, European, or American businesses, but in many cases these projects never materialized. For instance, in 2000 he announced that Intel Corporation would open an electronic chip manufacturing plant in Egypt with $1 billion in investments, and that the project would create 1,500 jobs.[50] In reality, Intel only kept a small office for sales and marketing in Cairo, and there were no material traces of its expansion on the ground. In another instance, in 2003, al-Ghamrawi announced creating the Alexandria Fertilizer Company (AlexFert) as a shareholding chemicals plant, with dense Arabian Gulf capital. He indicated that the cost of the "new" enterprise was $330 million, 31 percent of which came from Arabian Gulf partners as follows: $33 million from an Emirates company (20 percent), $18.5 million from a Bahraini company (11 percent), and $33 million from an Egyptian-Kuwaiti joint company.[51] Nonetheless, this project was an expansion to an already existing company, Abu Qir Fertilizers and Chemical Industries in Alexandria, established in 1976. He carved a new shareholding enterprise from the old company, and the new one was located at the exact same address as the old. More important, the new company's list of shareholders had no Arabian Gulf partners, except for the Egypt-Kuwait Holding Company dominated by al-Kharafi group and owning 38 percent of AlexFert's shares—all other investors are Egyptian banks and companies.[52]

Al-Ghamrawi created many free zones across Egypt, where industrial, import, export, and service businesses enjoy tax and tariff exemptions, hoping for foreign direct investment (FDI) to increase in Egypt. Consequently, he announced official numbers regarding foreign capital flow that differed substantially from those presented by the United Nations Conference for Trade and Development (UNCTAD). For instance, in February 2004 he announced that FDI in 2001–02 rose to $2.7 billion and again increased to $3 billion in 2002–03.[53] In reality, in 1998, a year before al-Ghamrawi assumed the position, FDI flows in Egypt were a little above $1 billon, and they tremendously declined in 2002 to $646.9 million and again in 2003 to only $237.4 million—all according to an UNCTAD report.[54] He indicated that Italian FDI in Egypt was around $330 million, when its total during three years from 2001 to 2003 was less than $4 million. In 2002 he stated that Japanese investments in Egypt also reached more than $300 million, when Egypt received no FDI from Japan in 2001, only $1 million in 2002, and $2.2 million in 2003.[55] Apparently al-Ghamrawi met success mainly with Chinese investors. The year he left office, he estimated the value of the Chinese investments in Egypt at $147 million.[56]

Moreover, al-Ghamrawi was unsuccessful on the legal terrain. He relentlessly sought to issue a new investment law placing all powers of dealing with investors in the hands of his own authority, claiming that this would ease the flow of capital into the country. Nevertheless, he failed to pass such a law in the parliament, while economic experts and investors insisted that it would hinder rather than stimulate local and foreign capital. All he could do was to modify the existing investment codes, in law no. 162 of 2000.[57] No wonder that when Gamal Mubarak's new cabinet took power in 2004, al-Ghamrawi stayed in his seat for only a few months before Gamal's new minister of investment decided to replace him. The country's FDI tremendously increased immediately after al-Ghamrawi was sacked, reaching more than $5 billion in 2005.[58] However, this did not leave this field without military influence. For example, General Majdi Amin assumed the position of the first undersecretary of the Ministry of Investment in 2010. As for al-Ghamrawi's fate after the 2011 uprisings, a lawsuit filed by a human rights organization accused him, among many other state officials, of corruption in implementing privatization policies.[59] Furthermore, he was accused, among other NDP leaders, of staging the "camel battle" by thugs against protesters in February 2011. Nonetheless, he has since enjoyed impunity.

From 2006 onward Mubarak placed control over state land in the hands of General 'Umar al-Shawadfi—who survived the uprisings and expanded his power after 2011. Generally, three main authorities managed state land, as specified by law no. 7 of 1991: the New Urban Communities Authority, the Tourism Development Authority, and the Agricultural Development Authority. They were responsible for land allocation for investments in their fields. Presidential Decree no. 153 of 2001 created a new organization to coordinate the work of all state authorities dealing with land and called it the National Center for Planning State Land Uses (NCPSLU). Its main goals are to maximize the use of public land toward large national projects and "to attract local and foreign capital to invest and create developmental projects in all realms on state land."[60] In the 2000s only the tourism authority was in the hands of retired generals, while the ministers in Gamal's government of businessmen were in control of the three authorities. Thus Mubarak probably felt the need to balance this by putting an ex-officer above all of them through creating NCPSLU and appointing al-Shawadfi to head it. After 2011 SCAF kept al-Shawadfi in this crucial position and additionally appointed other retired generals as heads of the other three authorities mentioned above—making state land fully under military control.[61]

Al-Shawadfi's name was implicated in at least one known major case of land corruption, where Gulf capital was involved. In 2002 a Kuwaiti-Egyptian company purchased 26,000 acres in a rural area near Giza at a reduced price of only LE200 per acre; the documented purpose was agricultural reclamation. But the company cultivated only a part of the land and resold other tracts at multiplied prices. Moreover, it reportedly exploited parts as profitable quarries, excavated others for ancient monuments illicitly traded, and illegally sized an additional 11,000 acres in the same area.[62] Al-Shawadfi actively assisted this company in changing the land's original arena of business from agriculture to the much more lucrative urban construction so it could avoid penalties for violating the original terms of the contract. The company later applied to build its own airport in the area—all with the approval of other supporting generals in different positions. The public prosecutor received a legal complaint from angry local inhabitants who insisted that al-Shawadfi facilitated the transgressions of the company.[63] After remaining in his seat under both SCAF and the brotherhood until

2013, al-Shawadfi was appointed governor of the large Delta governorate of Daqahliyya.[64]

Several generals succeeded one another in heading the Tourism Development Authority, which controlled thousands of kilometers of coastal land designated for touristic enterprises.[65] After a presidential decree created this authority in 1991, General Husayn Badran served as chairman for five years. Badran survived the uprisings and was appointed advisor to the minister of tourism in 2014. Similarly, his successor, Majdi Qubaysi, head of the authority from 2002 to 2005, ascended from there to two other prestigious positions, becoming governor of Fayyum and the Red Sea governorates consecutively. By the time Qubaysi left it, the authority had randomly allocated a total of 180 million square meters of coastal land—without environmental or economic planning—to a few favorite businessmen who claimed they would construct luxury resorts on them. In reality, they used only about 10 percent of the area they bought toward the declared purpose and resold large parts at inflated prices.[66] The generals kept control of this authority after the uprisings, as General Tariq Sa'd al-Din headed it from 2011 until he was appointed governor of Luxor at the end of 2013.

In the same realm of state land, former intelligence officer General Muhammad al-Misiri was head of the Union of Cooperative Housing for seven years, from 2007 to 2014. Although the union is theoretically a nongovernmental organization that serves as an umbrella for civil associations building affordable apartments in new urban areas, the government hires its leaders. Meanwhile, the state assigns it some social housing projects in developing areas. Al-Misiri was appointed by Gamal's minister of housing and remained in office until he was sacked because of mass complaints against his mismanagement of poorly constructed units. Under al-Misiri's leadership, the union was infected by widespread bribes of employees and direct commissioning of select contractors outside of public tenders to work on state or affiliated associations' construction projects. Those contractors in turn extensively delayed deliverances for long years, asked individuals who reserved flats for additional payments, and laid poor infrastructure in completed buildings. The union never imposed proper penalties on them for such behavior. Prices of public affordable apartments constructed by the union doubled partially because of the corrupt administration of the organization, and affiliated associations insisted that the union hindered their work rather than facilitating it. Overall, cooperative housing declined under al-Misiri's leadership.[67] Another general, engineering officer Adil Nushi, immediately succeeded him.

For almost a decade, from 1999 to 2008, mechanical engineer General Sami 'Imara served as deputy head and then head of the National Authority of Potable Water and Sewage. Before that, he served as the head of the Red Sea Urban Development Bureau, and after leaving the authority he was appointed governor of the Delta province of Munufiyya until 2011. The main tasks of this vital authority are to design state policies to develop water and sanitation services across the country and to supervise the implementation of large national projects in this regard.[68] Noticeably, the country suffered from a severe decline in the infrastructure of sanitation services, pollution of potable water, incomplete lines across the North and South of the country, and wasted public funds during the final decade of Mubarak's reign. Other generals succeeded 'Imara in controlling this authority.[69] Two years after he left the authority, while serving as governor of Munufiyya, many water and sewage pipes broke in this governorate, leaving it in hazardous sanitary and environmental conditions. Overall, citizens complained that public services at large drastically collapsed in Munufiyya during his reign and accused him of colluding in corruption with NDP figures, so mass protests targeted his office, asking for his removal during the 2011 uprisings.[70]

On the same note of failed sewerage systems, engineer officer Sayyid 'Abd al-'Aziz al-Sayyid Shihata was promoted from the head of the Cairo Agency for Sewage Projects to the head of the Central Agency for Urban Development. His agency has ten subagencies under it, responsible for developing new and old remote areas in Sinai, Upper Egypt, and the northern coast; constructing roads, developing slums, contributing to water and sewage projects, and constructing new urban communities in desert areas are among its tasks.[71] General Shihata was promoted to governor of Giza in 2008 and stayed in office until 2011, when he faced mass protests against him because of collapsed public services. He also faced strikes organized by workers and employees in many sectors against his alleged administrative incompetence and injustice—including about three thousand workers at the Giza water and sewerage company who were asking for fair wages.[72]

Another important service body that the generals dominate is the Cleaning and Beautification Authority. While General Majdi Basyuni was heading this authority in 1999, the famous environmental crisis of Cairo's black smog broke out: skies covered by dangerous black clouds, resulting from burned waste, left residents short of breath.[73] After him, taking charge of Cairo's infamously dirty streets, General Muhammad Laban privatized garbage collection services by hiring foreign cleaning companies (Italian and Spanish in particular) in 2003, and he added their fees to the public electricity bill. Citizens were shocked that these fees were sometimes higher than the bill itself, and local garbage collectors who lost their source of income loudly protested. Interestingly, he signed contracts with terms unfavorable to the authority, which allowed the foreign companies to get away with delivering poor services and avoid penalties. The authority could not terminate the binding contracts, and citizens became furious about accumulated garbage, unswept streets, and paying for a service they did not receive; they soon resorted back to their local garbage collectors. Many citizens sued the authority, and a court of appeals verdict ordered the removal of the garbage fees from electricity bills a year later. General Nabil Badawi, who succeeded Laban until 2009, tried to amend the unfair terms of the foreign companies' contracts but failed to resolve the matter or break them. Cairo streets grew even dirtier, littered with huge, always full trash containers that stray cats and dogs roamed around.[74]

The Land Survey Authority, which is traditionally headed by geologists, also fell into the hands of retired generals.[75] In 2001 it was turned into a profit-making organization that provides mapping, meteorological, astronomical, and other services for Egyptian and foreign clients and in 2004 was placed under the Ministry of Oil. General Muhammad Abd al-Latif headed the authority and survived the uprisings. He came from the armored vehicles corps and served as the commander of Public Defense Forces, then was appointed head of the authority. Accusing him of entrenched corruption, angry workers of the authority forced Abd al-Latif to leave office with the protection of military police after the 2011 uprisings. However, he challenged them and returned to office, until he was promoted to governor of the Mediterranean province of Damietta by the military-led interim government in 2013.[76] But when he arrived at his new office, local citizens in the province voiced their concerns about his alleged history of corruption and complained about the government's wrong choice in their opinion.[77]

Between 2002 and 2006 military chemist Muhammad Hilal, commander of the chemical war corps, was appointed head of the Department of Production Sufficiency and Vocational Training.[78] Created in the 1950s during the industrialization developments to be responsible for training skilled workers for the public sector, this department was historically led by civilian engineers. In his testimony about Hilal, engineer Sayyid Abd al-Qadir Sayyid, who headed this department in the 1990s, indicates that he was appointed to this position with no relevant experience. Lacking necessary technical expertise to run it, he focused on disciplinary issues, such as strictly watching timesheets. Moreover, he hired a large number of fellow officers in the department. Sayyid asserts that Hilal brought his military "tribe" with him and changed the whole office structure in order to replace the top administrators with ex-officers. Sayyid adds that this was frustrating for the department's staff who were waiting for their turn for promotion to leadership positions, as installing army officers blocked their legitimate ambitions. He also asserts that the services of the department declined under these officers.[79]

As ports and trade is an area mainly dominated by officers, many ex-generals headed the General Organization for Export and Import Control. It is an authority that controls international commerce by taking charge of keeping official registers, inspecting shipments, and issuing licenses through offices in all key airports and sea and river ports in collaboration with the customs and duties offices.[80] General Muhammad al-Banna managed this authority from 2005 to 2009, and he was accused of profiteering from his public office after the 2011 uprisings. The Customer Protection Agency revealed that the authority licensed imported U.S. food products that were unfit for human consumption and potentially contaminated, and economic experts suggested that corrupt officials at the authority were behind such incidents. Al-Banna refused to provide the agency with a list of these products or information on the importing company without stating valid reasons. Allegedly, he obtained tens of thousands of pounds additional to his salary every month for "attending committee meetings" and hired a large number of needless "advisors" who gained exaggeratedly high salaries—many of whom resigned upon the uprisings to avoid prosecution.[81]

Militarizing Sea, River, and Air Transport

Egyptian transport is one of the sectors in which ex-generals established a near monopoly over its top posts. Mubarak placed sea, river, land, and air transportation services, whether for local public or for international commercial purposes, in the hegemonic hands of ex-officers. They controlled the Suez Canal as well as the public authorities of all forms of ports across the country. Interestingly, chairing state-owned holding companies in this sector, the officers managed to stop their privatization for the interest of the military institution. Nevertheless, they did not have much luck in drawing private investments to these companies to meet the original state plan.

Navy officers established a monopoly over top positions controlling port authorities—from the Suez Canal Authority to all seaport authorities throughout the 2000s. Ever since it was nationalized in 1956, the Suez Canal Authority's chairman was always a military engineer,[82] until Mubarak changed this tradition and appointed the former commander of the navy, Vice Admiral Ahmad Fadil, in 1996. Keeping this position for sixteen continuous years, until 2012, Fadil presided over annual revenue worth billions of dollars, for instance reaching $5.4 billion in 2009. He ordered occasional increases in toll fees,[83] yet without giving the canal employees the fair wages that they expected. In June 2011 about ten thousand workers in the canal's subsidiary companies protested, demanding the resignation and trial of Fadil as a key member of Mubarak's corrupt regime, and also asked for a legitimate raise of 40 percent in their wages in accordance with a recent decision issued by the postuprising minister of labor, and another increase in their trivial meal allowances. Many of the angry protesters hung an effigy of Fadil during protests against him.[84]

Besides the vital Suez Canal, navy generals headed the Maritime Transport Sector (MTS), under which the numerous authorities of seaports of the Mediterranean, Red Sea, and Port Said are grouped. They also headed MTS's Authority of Maritime Safety, monitoring these commercial and touristic harbors.[85] In addition, navy officers controlled the River Transport Authority along with the High Dam's Port Authority.[86] Interestingly, a number of specific names of navy officers rotated in heading the above-mentioned authorities managing maritime and river transport throughout the 2000s. Apparently Mubarak trusted these particular people and reshuffled them from one authority to another, promoting many of them to manage MTS as a whole (see table 3). Moreover, in 2002 the prime minister issued a decree that allowed the MoD to create its own agency to supervise all Egyptian ports and inspect foreign ships. During the final decade of Mubarak's regime, the maritime sector evidently witnessed a decline in its services and suffered catastrophic incidents of sinking of passenger ferries, with death tolls reaching the thousands.[87]

Egyptian MTS's international ranking drastically collapsed during the 2000s. In 2000 Egypt was on the International Maritime Organization's (IMO) "white list" of safe navigation and port control, but it moved to the "grey list" after five years and was finally blacklisted after another five years. A 2010 report issued by the IMO ranked Egypt one of the most dangerous countries for maritime transport and placed it on the same blacklist that included North Korea, Libya, and Syria. An internal official attributed this to widespread corruption in safety inspection of ferries and cargo ships, poor maintenance of facilities, and violations of international laws regulating ship quality and operation.[88] After the 2011 uprisings, young workers at the maritime sector created a Facebook page advocating for the demilitarization of their workspaces and criticizing the inefficiency and corruption, in their opinion, of their managing ex-admirals.[89]

Among the chairmen of the MTS, who were in charge when the decline took place, was former commander of the naval operations Rear Admiral Shirin Hasan, appointed from 2004 to early 2006. Apparently, Shirin did not believe in the importance of foreign capital and private business in the sector; on the contrary, he was suspicious of them. While head of the MTS, Shirin made statements about the necessity of stimulating more Arab and foreign investments in operating ports, but later, after he left this position, he warned against foreign monopolies over that sector and advocated that public-sector companies should crowd out private businesses by seizing the new investment opportunities.[90] Shirin headed the Port Said Ports Authority for about a year after leaving the sector. Later he assumed an honorary position as an undersecretary of the Ministry of Transportation but then moved on to serve as a board member or consultant to several private companies—local and foreign. The internationally shocking and catastrophic incident of a Red Sea passenger ferry, *al-Salam 98*, sinking on its way back from Saudi Arabia with a death toll of more than 1,300 lower-class travelers, mostly migrant laborers and pilgrims, took place under Shirin's leadership in 2006. Questions about favoritism toward the business tycoon owning the ferry—who was also an NDP member—were raised in the media, and a disciplinary court charged Shirin for not applying safety rules to the company owned by this local capitalist. Moreover, workers in the sector and in the East Port Said ports claimed that he allowed foreign investors and local business in Gamal's patronage circle to establish monopolies over container-handling activities.[91]

Another figure was Rear Admiral Mukhtar 'Ammar, who chaired all MTS ports together with supervising the Maritime Safety Authority from 2006 to 2008. Before that, 'Ammar was chairman of the Damietta Port Authority and vice chairman of Port Said ports. Ironically, Rear Admiral

Hisham al-Sirsawi, managing the Red Sea Ports Authority when the *al-Salam 98* ferry catastrophe took place in his area of jurisdiction in 2006, was promoted to succeed Mukhtar as chairman of the MTS. As head of the Red Sea ports, Sirsawi controlled the pilgrimage sea route between Egypt and Saudi Arabia, which travelers from low-income groups who are unable to afford to fly to Mecca and Medina, and many of them complained during Sirsawi's term about the extremely poor and unsafe quality of the ferries and expressed their fear of becoming victims of other deadly incidents like that of *al-Salam 98*.[92] Later, as head of MTS, Sirsawi, like his predecessor, allegedly allowed monopolistic activities of foreign companies in many ports—according to the angry employees rejecting his nomination for minister of transportation in 2011.[93] Rear Admiral Husayn al-Harmil, in charge of the Maritime Safety Authority when the *al-Salam 98* sank, was similarly promoted rather than punished. After being referred to a disciplinary court for granting a license to the ferry despite inspection reports deeming much of its equipment hazardously out of order, al-Harmil moved upward to manage the Damietta Port Authority from 2007 to 2009.[94]

Another interesting figure in this realm was Rear Admiral Ibrahim Yusuf, who chaired both the ports of Damietta and Alexandria between 2002 and 2007. While chairman of the Alexandria Port Authority in 2005, Yusuf signed a contract with a Chinese container handling company granting it usufruct, licensing, and operation rights over 250,000 square meters in three platforms under his jurisdiction at a significantly low price—only $3 per meter. A high court verdict annulled this contract in 2012, uncovering that the authority allowed the company to enjoy monopolistic concessions in return for only 10 percent of their revenue and without any obligations to provide maintenance services or compensation for damages in platforms and premises. The 2011 uprisings did not terminate Yusuf's career: he was appointed minister of the business sector (in control of public-sector companies) in 2011 and advisor to the minister of transportation by the end of 2013.[95] Similarly, Rear Admiral Abd al-Hamid Tawfiq Abu Jundiyya managed both the Alexandria and the Damietta ports consecutively for a few years before being promoted to chairman of the MTS from 2009 to early 2011. He was appointed advisor to the minister of transportation after the uprisings, and chairman of the Egyptian Navigation Company. A British court proved Jundiyya's implication in a case of corruption and ruled that the Egyptian government must pay large compensation to a Dutch transportation company that was hurt by his policies and was asked to pay extensive bribes by employees under his jurisdiction. Moreover, the same court ordered to seize the accounts of Egyptian government's Banque Misr in Paris.[96]

Moving from sea to river ports, identical stories exist. For six continuous years, from 2006 to 2012, General Karim Abu al-Khayr chaired the River Transport Authority. Presidential Decree No. 117 of 2008 allowed this authority to create its own companies or partner with the private sector to build new commercial harbors.[97] The authority is also responsible for the public system of river ferryboats in the country, which lower- and middle-class passengers rely on as a basic means of transportation in Upper and Lower Egypt. Abu al-Khayr introduced the Build-Operate-Transfer (BOT) system to river ports, through which private investors were to sign concession contracts with the state to construct or renovate a port in return for operating it for a long period. Many state authorities transitioning to the market granted such concessions in various sectors, but Abu al-Khayr did not meet much success in applying them as most of his public tenders targeting investors failed. For instance, businesses abstained from participating in the tender to construct and operate Qina's port in Upper Egypt, which was planned to serve a commercially busy area with agricultural and heavy industrial produce, because of lack of transparency in and autocratic behavior of the authority. Only a state-owned company decided to invest in the port, and shortly afterward a legal dispute erupted between this company and the authority, preventing completion of the project.[98] Surprisingly, Abu al-Khayr was appointed advisor to the privatized EgyTrans, a giant shareholding transport services company, in 2013.[99]

Like in sea boats, the river ferryboat system notoriously declined under Abu Khayr and other navy officers during the 2000s. Many deadly incidents of sinking boats took place in various provinces with tens of victims each time—mostly poor passengers. The U.S. Trade and Development Agency granted the Egyptian River Transport Authority $257,000 to conduct a feasibility study to develop passenger and commercial activities in this sector in 2003, when Rear Admiral Samir Tawifq Ibrahim was in charge of this authority and signed the funding agreement.[100] Between this date and 2011, the sector suffered neglect and old ferries turned into junk, with a significantly high frequency of drowning. For instance, in the Middle Egypt governorate of Minya, where villages rely on ferryboats as the only means to travel between the eastern and western sides of the Nile, one local inhabitant described them as "swimming coffins." Hundreds died in the authority's sunken boats in numerous incidents—especially on crowded holidays—to the extent that after the 2011 uprisings the new governor of Minya had to make a promise to stop this particular problem in order to appease public anger.[101]

The considerably underdeveloped High Dam Port, in the South of the country, came under the control of General Kamal Maghrabi in 2010, and he continued to chair it until 2013. This is the port that serves commercial activities between Egypt and the Sudan, but its ship movement was considerably slow. In this vital port, big ferries ran only once a week, on Mondays, from Aswan to Wadi Halfa, and passengers and cargos had to reach their final destination in Khartoum by train.[102] It is worth mentioning here that the inland port leading from Aswan to Sudan, the Qastal-Halfa port, was also under the control of generals heading the Inland and Dry Ports Authority. The same authority controls the Libya-Egypt western desert port of Sallum, where smuggling of goods and weapons is common, and the troubled Rafah border crossing leading to Gaza, which is occasionally closed for political reasons.[103]

Finally, air force generals populated the civil aviation sector. Between 2002 and 2011 the minister of civil aviation was the well-known former commander of the air force Lieutenant General Ahmad Shafiq—later prime minster during the 2011 uprisings and presidential candidate in 2012. Accusations of corruption, including favoring certain contractors in Gamal's circle of cronies in the construction of the new Cairo airport outside of public tenders, were pressed against him and widely circulated in media after the uprisings, but no court convicted Shifiq of any of them.[104] General Abd al-Fattah Katu of the air force served as chairman of the Civil Aviation Authority in the late 1990s and in 2001 moved on to chair the Egypt Air Holding Company with its nine subsidiaries, from which he mysteriously resigned two years later. At least two court cases accusing him of corruption and incompetent management of both the authority and the holding company were heard before and after the uprisings. Criminal accusations included colluding with a British-Egyptian contractor in his capacity as the head of the authority to help win the public tender to build a local airport in the Gulf of Suez, along with wasting public funds in his capacity as chairman of the holding company. But the courts cleared him of all charges.[105] Similarly, General Samih Hifni managed the Authority of Civil Aviation in 2009 and later moved to head the gigantic holding company. Originally the presidential pilot, Hifni enjoyed a strong relation with the Mubaraks and was an NDP member. He was accused of providing illicit licenses and privileges to foreign companies and individuals.[106]

This takes us to other holding companies controlled by retired officers in the transport sector. Through such control, the officers managed to prevent the privatization of these companies for the interest of the military institution, yet they were not very successful in attracting private capital to develop them. With Gamal's accelerated wave of privatization, many state-owned enterprises created in the 1950s–60s were grouped under holding companies, each owned tens of subsidiaries involved in similar economic activities, and all were placed under the Ministry of Investment. These holding companies were listed in the stock market and went through a process of development in preparation for their sale to the private sector. The army tried to exert a degree of influence over the Ministry of Investment, the territory of Gamal's close client Mahmud Muhi al-Din, but could not go far in this regard. The officers were only able to get hold of some positions within the ministry as assistants of and advisors to the minister or managers of his office and chaired a limited number of holding companies.[107] Nevertheless, the military was able to establish control over the holding companies in public transport and related commercial activities in sea, river, land, and air, grouped under the Holding Company for Maritime and Land Transport (HCMLT), besides the Egypt Air Holding Company. Moreover, these two giants successfully survived the sweeping tide of privatization under their military chairmen. It is worth mentioning here that immediately after taking over power in 2011, the ruling generals established immediate control over all the holding companies in all sectors.

Rear Admiral Muhammad Yusuf has chaired the HCMLT continuously from 2006 to the present. Created in 2000, the HCMLT's sixteen subsidiaries include the cargo and container handling companies of Alexandria, Port Said, and Damietta ports; the national Upper Egypt and Delta bus companies; a warehouses company; car manufacturing and repair plants; import-export companies; and a wood trading firm.[108] Furthermore, it owns shares in many other commercial and passenger transport enterprises across the country. Gamal's minster of transportation, Muhammad Mansur, who was a prominent business tycoon in this sector himself, attempted to privatize public transportation enterprises, including those grouped under the HCMLT. In 2008, while Yusuf was in office, Mansur stated that "Egypt should garner $8.9 billion of private investment in ports, roads and other transport over next three years" and that he expected "$16.3 billion to come into the sector over the next five years."[109] Yusuf did seek to modernize the sector through the Public-Private-Partnership (PPP) system meant to attract local and foreign capital to invest and share profit in the process, and other generals managing subsidiaries attempted to achieve the same goal.[110] But they did not meet much luck.

The year he became chairman, Yusuf announced great plans for partnership with investors in light of state support of the private sector. He opened a public tender to modernize a subsidiary originally established in 1960, the Engineering Automotive Manufacturing Company (EAMCO), which has three plants producing buses, tractors, and engines, all chaired by a retired general. He announced that four global companies expressed interest in competing to win the bid. Eventually, though, nobody applied and the company received no investments, and Yusuf went silent about the incident for the following years. In late 2013, still under the leadership of Yusuf, EAMCO's chair, engineer General Ra'fat Masruja, announced in a press conference that the company had signed a contract with an international firm, the Chinese FAW, to coproduce various vehicles. Yusuf attended the ceremonial event of the claimed signing of the deal. Masruja asserted in this conference that it took his company more than a year of negotiations to reach the deal, and EAMCO was going to produce FAW vehicles by Egyptian hands. Nonetheless, in late 2014 the same Chinese firm announced another deal with the MoMP to coproduce commercial cars and asserted that its negotiations with EAMCO were still ongoing.[111] Similarly, aside from state budget allocations, trivial amounts of domestic and foreign money arrived to other subsidiaries of the holding company. For instance, under rear admirals serving as chairmen, the private sector and individuals bought only 3 percent of the shares of the Damietta for Container and Cargo Handling Company in the stock market, and only 4.28 percent in its Alexandria counterpart.[112] To help with lack of capital in the former, the military-run Damietta Port Authority signed a concession agreement with a Kuwaiti firm, including Chinese and U.S. shareholders, to build and operate a deeper container terminal for oversized ships in the port in 2006, but the contract was marred by corruption and the firm never fulfilled it.[113]

There are two cases of privatization that took place during Yusuf's term and mysteriously went in favor of the military that fully seized the public enterprises that were up for sale. The first case is that of the Alexandria Shipyard, which was up for privatization in 2002 after going through five years of reconstruction, reforms, paying debts, and so on.[114] Upon assuming power in the holding company, Yusuf decided to "transfer" the assets of this shipyard to the MoD's Maritime Industries and Services Organization in 2007 and asked the Ministry of Finance to reschedule its dues.[115] The second is the Nile Company for River Transport, which was lined up for privatization when its chairman was General Ali Hasan Imam. Likewise, it was "sold" to MISO in 2008, and it changed its name to Wataniyya River Transport.[116]

The national bus companies across the country, serving millions of lower- and middle-class provincial passengers, including conscripts, are located under the HCMLT. Their service notoriously declined in the 2000s. For instance, the Upper Egypt Transport and Tourism Company, with a large fleet of hundreds of buses that also targets tourists, never kept a punctual travel schedule and experienced extensive delays; had broken seats; often had insufficient availability of already overpriced tickets; and made unannounced fare increases. Moreover, its vehicles often broke down and stopped for hours on desert roads. Tourists rarely took them.[117] The West Delta Bus Company was in no better condition: its passengers suffered from frequent road accidents partially due to lack of maintenance of vehicles, and its drivers were paid extremely low wages, mostly employed on temporary contracts and once had to strike in the face of a sudden 30 percent cut in wages.[118] The Holding Company for Roads, Bridge, and Land Transportation Projects, responsible for the construction of the routes on which these buses operated, was chaired by a retired general in the late 2000s, and he supposedly spent about LE1.8 billion on relevant public projects annually. He blamed the numerous traffic accidents that took place in Egypt on a regular basis primarily on drivers, when citizens across the country constantly complained about poorly paved and barely repaired roads.[119]

Air navigation and services holding companies chaired by generals were relatively more successful in connecting to foreign capital—albeit with the indispensable help of the World Bank through its big loans. These companies were placed under the Ministry of Civil Aviation, managed by former commander of the air force Shafiq. Vice Air Marshal Ibrahim Manna' chaired the Holding Company for Airports and Air Navigation from 2003 until he was appointed minister of civil aviation in 2011. The World Bank granted his company a loan of $335 million in 2004 in order to construct Cairo airport's third terminal and other projects. Vice Air Marshal Fathi Fath Allah chaired Cairo Airport Company, the holding company's subsidiary. The World Bank made sure that the private sector took part in this large project through assigning it management contracts. Thus, at the end of the same year as receiving the loan, a Turkish company won the bid to build the new terminal, and a German company acquired a contract to manage the airport as a whole. The holding company received another World Bank loan of $280 million in 2010 to renovate terminal two.[120] Meanwhile, Egypt Air Holding Company did not receive similar capital and its service suffered. In 2002 its chairman was Vice Marshal Abd Al-Fattah Katu of the air force, who moved there after heading the Authority of Civil Aviation for a few years. In 2004 Egypt Air announced financial losses and closed down a dozen of its offices abroad.[121]

To sum up, retired generals were the invisible de facto rulers of Mubarak's Egypt and exercised entrenched militarization of civilian workplaces and the nation's life as a whole. It is a life that was deeply afflicted by corruption, cronyism, inefficiency, infrastructural decay, and overall social disparities. They were an integral part of Mubarak's authoritarian government and failed neoliberal economy. Such suffocating military penetration into everyday life was felt by the repressed and impoverished masses. Thus, when the 2011 uprisings erupted, they did not only call for the fall of the dictator but also demanded ousting the ruling ex-officers. Workers, government employees, and revolutionary youth all cried out for the demilitarization of their civilian work sites, as well as the entire state and society. It was a unique yet short-lived moment that the following chapter will investigate.

CHAPTER 5

Angry Workers, Islamic Grocers, and Revolutionary Generals (2011–2014)

The social order is a war, and rebellion is the last episode that will put an end
to it. . . . War [is] a permanent feature of social relations. . . . War is both the
web and the secret of institutions and systems of power.
　　　—Foucault, *Society Must Be Defended*

As soon as the ruling Supreme Council of Armed Forces assumed power in February 2011, all hell broke loose. A widespread wave of labor protests erupted throughout the country upon overthrowing Mubarak and terminating his neoliberal regime. The ruling officers strongly condemned the strikes and sit-ins and described them as selfish acts seeking merely "sectorial" benefits, or *matalib fi'awiyya*, rather than national demands for the entire struggling society. They accused the protesters of "stalling the wheel of production" at a time when the country was in dire need of building its postrevolutionary economy. In fact, the largest of these labor demonstrations emerged from government authorities controlled by retired generals or economic enterprises owned by the military. Moreover, many protesters in these places created pages on social media calling for the demilitarization of their workspaces. Such pages became platforms for steering a public controversy about claimed corruption of military administrators and vociferously pressing demands to recivilianize public offices. In firm reaction, military police intervened to disperse workers' sit-ins, and SCAF issued a law that prohibited labor strikes and sent violators to civilian and military trials. In solidarity, revolutionary youth launched a campaign for demilitarizing all state civilian positions, calling it NoMilCivilPositions or li-'Askarat al-Waza'if al-Madaniyya. The campaign diligently compiled lists and drew electronic maps locating ex-officers in such posts in Cairo and every province across the country.[1]

Between 2011 and 2013 the Egyptian generals turned revolutionary. They supported mass uprisings against two regimes, those of Hosni Mubarak and the Muslim Brothers, and deposed both of them. On January 25, 2011, protests erupted in Cairo's Tahrir Square to demand that Mubarak step down. Army tanks surrounding the square claimed to back the eighteen-day sit-in until the autocrat was eventually ousted. Immediately afterward SCAF offered its help to run the country for a short transitional period of six months. Grateful for such favors, the Egyptian masses chanted "the army and the people are one hand," while state-owned media played the 1960s national songs of Gamal Abdel Nasser's other revolutionary era. The army revived its historical image as the guardian of the nation and the savior of the country in times of distress. SCAF stayed in power for a full year and a half, until it delivered the authority to an elected president from the Muslim Brothers in June 2012. Exactly one year later, as this president drastically failed in running the country's crumpling economy and public discontent escalated again, the military decided to overthrow him. Cheerfully expressing their appreciation, the celebrating masses filled Tahrir Square in the lead-up to the ouster of the brotherhood, and they carried posters of Nasser and General Abd Fattah al-Sisi, the new minister of defense. The army's public relations department funded the production of a song, titled "Tisalm al-Ayadi," greeting the soldiers' hands that saved the nation, invoking the aura of the 1973 war victory. It quickly became the most popular song among Egyptians across social classes and was played at weddings and birthday parties.

There is a big mystery in the unfolding of these events. The Egyptian generals were an integral part of Mubarak's regime and intimate allies of the Muslim Brothers' short-lived government. The military built an economic business empire and occupied top state positions under Mubarak, and the brotherhood's civilian president happily and extensively added to these supreme privileges of the generals—as this chapter will detail. Nevertheless, the military institution successfully managed to separate itself from both collapsed systems, dust itself off from their failures, and emerge as the patriotic savior of the nation twice in the course of three years. Not only did the generals weather difficult waves of change in a short period of time, they also victoriously came out of them with maximized gains in business and politics. They even managed to gain back the presidential seat after losing it to a civilian for one brief year in the six decades since the first military president took office in 1952. While doing so, the generals swiftly switched socioeconomic alliances from one group to another. In 2011 they severed their ties with many of Mubarak's neoliberal cronies and allied themselves with the wealthy Islamists. In 2013 they formed relations with various leftist and liberal icons to overthrow the brotherhood. The generals' success in adapting to fundamental transformations, their ability to restore the image of the fair guardian of the nation, and the tactics they deployed to retain absolute control are a mystery that this chapter attempts to decipher.

The chapter begins by tracing the immediate threats the military institution's privileges faced upon the fall of Mubarak, and SCAF's long battle to eliminate such threats, discipline dissent, and further diffuse surveillance. While in power, SCAF faced a sweeping wave of labor discontent particularly targeting generals who were managing business enterprises or were in civilian offices. Furthermore, SCAF faced heavy media criticism and political activism amid the revolutionary fervor calling for the demilitarization of the state and transparency of the military budget. The ruling officers resorted to various tactics to handle this internal combat, ranging from unleashing military police and using military trials to promulgating new laws. The chapter then moves in its second section to the marriage of convenience struck between the military and Muslim Brothers between mid-2012 and mid-2013. Such a deal enabled the brotherhood to sweep parliamentary and presidential elections, and the generals to keep and even expand their business and political superiority. The final section explores the events ending this short marriage and taking down the brotherhood's regime in mid-2013 at the hands of Minister of Defense al-Sisi. Mobilizing old methods of war propaganda to manipulate the nation was an indispensable weapon used to reach victory and to repossess complete power in this last battle against rebellion.

It is important to note here the significance of social media and newspapers as main primary sources utilized in this chapter. Social media platforms, especially Facebook and YouTube, were essential in documenting the crucial revolutionary moments, as activists from all backgrounds used them to register their grievances against government incumbents. The chapter uses such sources to collect narratives of discontent against ex-officers and officers. Moreover, traditional newspapers during this period enjoyed an unprecedented degree of freedom of expression, taking advantage of the revolutionary influx and publishing endless stories of rebellion even against the military institution, which had remained a forbidden territory to investigate for decades. This honeymoon of press freedom was unfortunately short-lived.

The chapter, however, capitalizes on the brief period of fluidity in informal and formal publishing on causes of unrest to depict a highly blurred political scene and locate where the military institution stood within it.

Strikes, Strikes Everywhere

The long-established system of military privileges almost fell apart with the fall of its thirty-year patron, Mubarak. After abandoning his aging president and imprisoning many of his cronies, Hussein Tantawi had to exert immense effort to face public unrest against the generals themselves and salvage them from tumbling with the regime. Immediately after taking over power, SCAF had to face three forms of instant challenges to its inherited almighty status. The first was a massive wave of labor strikes, coupled with peaceful or violent protests, against military public administrators and business managers mostly to demand fair wages. This was accompanied by bold calls for demilitarizing the state pressed by public employees and revolutionary youth. Finally, to make things worse, newspapers opened the Pandora's Box of questioning the military's unaudited budget and untaxed civilian business profits for the first time in decades. While the military institution seized the state apparatus for about seventeen months, it took measures that successfully saved its system of privileges from falling apart. It reinstated its omnipotent surveillance and full control over the civilian battlespace.

Because the maritime sector was entirely dominated by retired navy officers under Mubarak, it became a visible focal point of widespread workers' unrest. For instance, sit-ins and hunger strikes erupted at the various locations and companies of the Suez Canal Authority, whose head for the previous fifteen years was the former commander of the navy, Vice Admiral Ahmad Fadil. At the navigation office of the port of Ismailiyya, employees organized a hunger strike demanding the right to fair wages and benefits for around 12,000 workers at the canal. Fadil ignored the strikers for long days, until many of them had to be hospitalized. Meanwhile, around 150 seasonal laborers also went on a hunger strike demanding permanent contracts after serving at the canal for more than ten years through private contractors who paid them trivial wages. Similarly, workers at all seven companies affiliated with, but not owned by, the canal authority embarked on an open strike against broken promises of wage increases and lack of basic health insurance. Fadil persistently rejected their demands or allegedly made more broken promises, and negotiations with him repeatedly failed.[2] Thus thousands of workers in all three ports of the canal carried on with strikes and sit-ins for months and resorted a few times to more aggressive methods of rebellion, such as blocking roads and burning tires around the canal's administrative premises. Fadil deployed military police to deal with the protesters, and the military prosecutor summoned many demonstrators for investigations and consequently imprisoned them.[3]

Labor rioters forced out retired rear admirals who controlled the Mediterranean port of Damietta. Although he had just been appointed head of the port to replace another ex–rear admiral who was reshuffled to another port, Ibrahim Fulayfil lost his position owing to fierce labor pressure for his expulsion. Posting scandalous videos of him on YouTube, surrounded and verbally attacked by angry workers, protesters accused him of favoritism and corruption.[4] He was purged but later appointed head of the Maritime Safety Authority instead. In fact, protests in that authority had already forced out another former rear admiral, Mustafa Wahba, whom ASA's official reports accused of embezzlement and granting illicit bonuses and allowances.[5] As around 1,300 workers at the Damietta Container and Cargo Handling Company insisted on firing their chairman and vice-chairman, who were both ex–rear admirals, they held a sit-in that interrupted ship movements. The Damietta's governor mediated an agreement between the angry workers and the chairman and he was saved from being sacked, but protests were renewed months later against inefficient management. Workers carried their banners against the chairman to Cairo for an open-ended sit-in in front of the cabinet near Tahrir Square.[6]

On their Facebook page, the Youth Coalition of the New Urban Communities Authority demanded purging all military administrators from this important public organization, which implements state plans of building affordable housing. "Military leaders failed to manage national projects [of social housing] . . . , did not stop the wasting of public funds, and did not achieve social justice," the group posted.[7] As they sarcastically described their workplace as "the estate of retired officers of the armed forces," around 1,500 workers went on strike at the public authority of the Red Sea ports to demand termination of all contracts of military managers and advisors.[8] At another public authority, that of land survey, employees were scandalized by what they saw as unjust policies of their manager, ex-general Muhammad Abd al-Latif. They claimed that he hired them at a salary less than LE200 per month (around $35), without benefits or allowances. Accusing him of corruption, furious workers forced Abd al-Latif to leave his office and never return. The workers caught this event on a YouTube video, where he was seen being escorted out of the authority's premises by the military police amid female workers' ululation and chanting of a folk song alluding to deposed rulers that went "goodbye, oh you with a tipped turban" (*ma'sa el-salama ya abu 'imma mayla*).[9]

Against the militarization of civil aviation and unfair wages, employees and laborers at the airports of Luxor, Aswan, Sharm el-Sheikh, Hurghada, and Sinai embarked on widespread strikes, later joined by fellow employees at Cairo airport. They were particularly ignited when SCAF's prime minister broke his promise to appoint a civilian minister to succeed Lieutenant General Ahmad Shafiq, minister for almost ten years before 2011, and hired another retired air force commander instead—now a businessman and agent of an international jet manufacturing company. Moreover, the commander of military police and SCAF member, Hamdi Badin, and the commander of the air force had to negotiate with employees who organized a large sit-in at the Egyptian Holding Company for Airports and Air Aviation to protest against the ex–air marshal who chaired it. They agreed to disperse only after this chairman resigned, but another air force officer already heading Cairo airport soon came to replace him. Under the new air marshal's control, all former officers in top positions at the Egyptian Company for Airports—a subsidiary of the above holding company—were granted permanent contracts, consequently depriving qualified and experienced civilians of the chance to reach high administrative positions in the company for years to come. Meanwhile, Cairo airport—another subsidiary of the same holding company chaired by successive air marshals—witnessed its own wave of labor protests pressing for demilitarization as well as fair wages.[10]

Things turned chaotic at military factories, run by Sayyid Mash'al, who was minister of military production for more than a decade and a parliament member on the NDP's list. Around five thousand workers at Factories 99 and 45 went on strike, pressing multiple demands, at the top of which was "no military trials for civilian labor." They also asked for a doubling of their significantly low bonuses.[11] Similarly, around a thousand workers at Factory 63 launched a sit-in inside their facility demanding an increase in bonuses, insisting that Mash'al promised them such a raise during his parliamentary election campaign and never fulfilled his promise. Unable to contain such unrest, the factory's manager was fired, but protests continued.[12] Meanwhile, about three thousand workers at Factory 200 requested the prosecution of

Mash'al and the chairman of the plant, accusing them of financial abuses and wasting public resources. In reaction, the administration closed the factory altogether and its buses stopped running in order to abort the protesters' sit-in. Thus a few hundred of those workers decided to hold a vigil in front of the cabinet near Tahrir Square.[13] Around 150 workers at Factory 9 who were hired for years on temporary contracts organized a sit-in demanding a more secure form of employment with fair wages.[14] At the military-owned apparel factory in Tanta in the Delta, workers organized a vigil followed by an open-ended sit-in after they asked for financial equality with the low-ranking officers serving at the plant along with access to health care at military hospitals. "They earn millions and we earn pennies," they insisted while repeating famous Tahrir Square's slogans on social justice and freedom. The military managers of the plant reacted by simply closing its doors and suspending its activities until dissidents abandoned their demands.[15] Young workers at these plants created a Facebook page called "Coalition of Military Factories' Youth" and used it to mobilize for more protests.[16]

Technicians and engineers suffered from hazardous conditions that left many of them sick without health insurance at El Nasr Company for Intermediate Chemicals—a complex of seven factories owned by NSPO in Fayyum. Tantawi had just opened three new plants that were added to this complex, but its employees now listed alleged cases of corruption of managing officers and complained about the oppressive and humiliating treatment they received. Thus they organized a sit-in demanding not only proper health care and safety measures—such as being supplied with protective masks—but also fair wages and a just bonus percentage of the annual profit. Direct confrontations erupted between the military and the protesters, and some employees escalated the situation by blocking part of the Cairo-Fayyum road. They insisted that the military environmentally harms surrounding vicinities through this industrial complex's use of poisonous material.[17] In other cases, protests broke out even at toll highways constructed and operated by NSPO. Truck drivers hired by quarries blocked the Qatamiyya-al-'Ayn al-Sukhna road to protest toll increases. They also protested lack of security on this road, which rendered them victims of robbery and car thefts under the blind eye of army and police forces.[18] After the military administration broke its promises to provide them fair wages, the workers of the Nile Wataniyya Company for River Transport—owned by the military's MISO—threatened to escalate their actions by blocking waterways leading to the company's headquarters until their demands were fulfilled.[19]

After assuming power, SCAF placed the state-run holding companies and their numerous subsidiaries under the control of ex-generals, who faced intense labor protests.[20] Mubarak's privatization scheme grouped state-owned enterprises under the control of holding companies, each owning many subsidiaries in the same sector, to be developed and later put up for sale to local or foreign investors.[21] SCAF placed all these enterprises under the control of ex-general 'Adil al-Muzi followed by ex–vice admiral Muhammad Yusuf. They both chaired holding companies for years before 2011 and were appointed ministers of the Public Business Sector in control of holding companies after the uprisings. Around 1,500 workers at the National Cement Company near Helwan, headed by an ex-general and a subsidiary of the holding company for chemicals, organized a sit-in to demand an increase in wages. Al-Muzi endorsed a raise, but SCAF canceled it a few months later and subsequently workers renewed their protests.[22] The company of grain silos and storage—a subsidiary of a holding company of food industries—had many ex-generals on its board of directors, and its employees cried about corruption and violations of labor rights in it. Suffering from poor safety measures and lack of insurance while working at underground storage, laborers at the company's office at Damietta Port went on strike. The "military governor" of the city—who functioned as a shadow governor next to the appointed civilian or ex-military one after the uprisings—negotiated with them to suspend the strike and promised to carry their requests to higher authorities in Cairo. Although the laborers did collaborate, the company later reduced their percentage in annual profit and they in turn expressed their discontent on their union's Facebook page.[23]

To contain such a gushing flow of dissent, SCAF hastily issued a new legislation to prohibit all forms of labor protests. Law no. 34 of 2011, signed by Tantawi in April, stated that SCAF recognized the "sectorial" needs of all social groups and their right to peaceful demonstrations to pursue them. But it placed the state under emergency law and banned any protests that might affect the country's stability or national production. The new law stipulated: "During the status of emergency, whoever organizes a vigil or any activity that leads to preventing, delaying, or hindering work at any state institution, a public authority, or a public or private work organization will be penalized by imprisonment and paying a fine between LE20,000 and LE50,000 or either form of punishment. Whoever incites or calls or advertises by oral or written or any other public means . . . for any of the aforementioned acts should receive the same punishment, even if they do not reach their goal."[24]

Because they were the first group to be sent to a military trial and jail based on this antistrike law, the workers of Petrojet—an oil and gas company—drew the attention of human and labor rights organizations. Officers dominated the petroleum and natural gas sector, and thousands of employees at state-owned oil companies protested their poor conditions as well as the militarization of their workspaces. A group of two thousand from different companies organized a vigil in front of the Ministry of Petroleum demanding a minimum wage and "removing all officers from the oil sector's companies." They insisted, "It is meaningless that a retired general occupies the place of civilians and earns thousands of pounds, when the sons of the place are paid dimes and nickels."[25] Employees in companies such as Petrotrade, whose chairman was ex-general Muhammad Mustafa Darwish, organized an open sit-in in front of the parliament, but the Islamist-dominated legislature ignored their chants and banners.[26] The workers at the Qina Gas factory of the Petrogas company, whose chairman was ex-general Yasir Zakariyya al-Niklawi, were fired after accusing the administration of selling subsidized produce on the black market.[27] Their fellow workers at Petrojet first organized a large sit-in in front of their company's headquarters to protest the firing of hundreds of them, and when the administration did not listen, they took it all the way to the doors of the Ministry of Petroleum and camped there. In violent reaction, military police arrested and detained many of them at military prison, where they claimed receiving inhumane treatment for weeks. They were sent to a military court where five of them were sentenced to a one-year jail term. Since this group was the first to be punished by the SCAF's new law and in a military rather than a civilian tribunal, their case raised profound resentment among human rights activists. The Egyptian Center for Social and Economic Rights hosted a press conference for them to speak and condemn military trials at large.[28]

Amid the revolutionary fervor of early 2011, the phenomenon of creating "independent labor unions"—separate from the old regime-controlled unions—became widespread. Independent labor unions were banned or constrained for years under Mubarak, but a leftist minister in the first postrevolutionary cabinet legalized them.[29] They took form in public-sector enterprises and holding companies. The independent union of Alexandria Container and Cargo Holding Company submitted a legal complaint to the public prosecutor to request an investigation of cronyism and illegal financial transactions in the firm, which was chaired by ex–rear admiral Ahmad Mansur al-'Arabi. Not only did the public prosecutor ignore their complaints, but also Mansur accused the union's leaders of inciting the workers to strike and subsequently a civilian court sentenced five of them to three years in jail—again applying Tantawi's antistrike law.[30]

Many of the problematic ex-officers who served Mubarak shortly had to go—or were sometimes reshuffled to other places—to appease angry dissidents across the country. For instance, Mash'al finally left his ministerial seat after occupying it for twelve years. He also lost the parliamentary seat that he had repeatedly won as an NDP member in notoriously fraudulent elections. Muhammad Darwish, chairman of the oil company Petrotrade, lost his position but moved to head a mineral water company, where he still faced other labor protests.[31] 'Abd al-Salam al-Mahjub also had to go. An ex–intelligence general, al-Mahjub was minister of provincial development from 2006 until the uprisings and served as governor of Alexandria for nine years prior to that, in addition to being an active NDP member for almost two decades. Muhsin al-Nu'mani, another ex–intelligence general, who was appointed as minister of provincial development during the uprisings after serving as governor of Sohag, also had to go. As minister, he faced national anger when he refused to dissolve local councils dominated by corrupt NDP members. There were also protests emerging from Sohag calling for his removal. Meanwhile, an ASA report revealed that he had violated laws while governor of Sohag by depositing millions of pounds of collected fines into a local fund rather than sending them to the national treasury.[32]

At the level of provincial governors, SCAF also had to get rid of some under immense pressure from local protesters. When Mubarak quit power, he left behind fourteen governors from a military background, many of whom faced violent protests demanding their removal during or after the uprisings. SCAF sacked eleven of them by the end of 2011 but replaced them with other generals. Overall, SCAF changed governors twice during 2011, once in April and another time in August. The first time, fifteen out of twenty-seven newly appointed governors were ex-generals, and the second time, this number was slightly reduced to fourteen—in both cases exceeding 50 percent of appointed provincial rulers.

Angry rioters forced out the military governor of Suez, who had ruled the province for more than a decade with a long record of accusations of corruption. With its high rate of unemployment, Suez witnessed some of the most violent demonstrations in the country that were met by bloody police backlash during the uprisings. General Sayf al-Din Jalal—former commander of the Third Field Army—allegedly hid in a state cabin surrounded by strong security guards to avoid attacks of local angry mobs. Not only was he removed right away from his position after the events settled down, but he was also banned from entering Suez ever again by a government decree.[33] The former head of the Cairo Opera House and governor of Luxor for seven years, General Samir Faraj faced large local protests insisting on his removal during and after the uprisings. Angry youth who protested in Luxor's squares, in parallel to Tahrir's national protests, pressed accusations of cronyism, corruption, and unjust enrichment against him until he was removed.[34] During the uprisings, Red Sea province's local protesters carried their banners against their governor all the way to Tahrir Square in Cairo to make their demands to depose their military governor more visible. Having a long career in Mubarak's neoliberal system, military engineer Muhammad Majdi al-Qubaysi was governing Red Sea province after occupying the same seat in Fayyum and serving as chairman of the public authority for tourism development. When SCAF did not depose him right away after Mubarak left, continuous local protests citing his links to the NDP's cronies took place for months, until he was finally sacked in August 2011.[35]

Those sacked ex-generals enjoyed lasting impunity. Immediately after they were gone, local citizens submitted a flood of legal complaints against them to either the Administrative Control Authority (ACA) or the public prosecutor, especially with accusations of illicit enrichment. There is no published evidence that ACA carried out investigations and issued reports about these cases. Moreover, military intelligence officer General Muhammad Farid al-Tuhami headed the authority from 2004 to 2012. Like other fellow officers, he faced angry demonstrations, organized by civilian employees at the authority, accusing him of covering up the crimes of Mubarak's clients. For instance, the case of General Sa'd Abu Rida, governor of Red Sea province from 1997 to 2006, who was accused of cronyism along with NDP business tycoons in Hurghada, disappeared at al-Tuhami's office. The same thing happened to the cases of General Abd al-Jalil al-Fakharani, governor of Ismailiyya from 2006 until he was removed in 2011, and General Mustafa al-Sayyid, governor of Aswan between 2008 and 2013, whose investigation results were never made public. Nobody heard about either their conviction or acquittal.[36]

As a matter of fact, Tantawi modified the law of military courts in a way that raised controversy within and outside the parliament. The new law granted officers immunity from being tried in civil courts for crimes of corruption committed while in service, even after their retirement. Law no. 45 of 2011 stated in article 2 that "only military courts, excluding any other court, enjoy jurisdiction over crimes . . . of illegal profiting committed by officers of the armed forces . . . even if investigation start after their retirement."[37] This law was sometimes casually extended to ex-generals in civilian positions whose names were implicated in corruption cases years after taking off their uniform. Some citizens' legal complaints against them were sent to the military prosecutor for investigation, and nobody heard about the cases again. This is true in the case of Faraj: not only did his case disappear at the office of the military persecutor without declared results, but he was reportedly appointed chairman of the Holding Company for Energy and Gas soon after being sacked from the governorship of Luxor.[38] It is also true in the case of Mash'al, whose alleged crimes as an NDP key member and minister of military production were silenced at the same office.[39]

Meanwhile, national media opened a Pandora's Box questioning military business enterprises and their unaudited profits. For almost three decades, opposition press abstained from raising any discussions about military spending and earning, ever since the campaign they launched against Abu Ghazala in the mid-1980s. The press kept silent about such information classified as "national security secrets"—even those relevant to civilian production of the army. SCAF had to intervene to prevent publication of an issue of *Egypt Independent*, the English edition of *al-Masry al-Youm*, when political scientist Robert Springborg—who famously wrote about Abu Ghazala's commercial enterprises back in the 1980s—published an op-ed criticizing Tantawi at the end of 2011.[40] Incapable, however, of repressing all critical voices in many other newspapers capitalizing on postrevolutionary fervor, the military had to develop passive means to tame them. I myself had an interesting experience in this regard, which earned me an unprecedented visit to military factories and a six-hour interview with the chairman of AOI in early 2012. Shortly after this encounter, the military held its first press conference to share information about its business profits with journalists and economists.

Under a pseudonym, I published my first Arabic article on the Egyptian military and economy at end of 2011 outside Egypt.[41] Soon afterward, former blogger and then editor-in-chief of *al-Masry al-Youm*'s online edition, Nora

Younis, invited me to write a series of articles on the same matter, which I did this time using my real name. One of them mentioned widespread strikes in the factories of AOI, headed then by retired chief of staff Lieutenant General Hamdi Wahiba. At car, aircraft, engine, and other plants of the organization's twelve factories, thousands of workers protested to demand a fair share in annual profits. They diligently posted news of their activities on their many Facebook pages and blogs—such as "Against the Corruption of AOI" (*Didd Fasad al-Hay'a al-'Arabiyya li-l-Tansi'*) of laborers at the Arab American Vehicles plant. Military police dispersed one strike, the military managers suspended labor leaders, and several workers were persecuted for using social networks to criticize the administration.[42] Wahiba sent me a rare, and probably unprecedented, invitation from a military official to a civilian to visit AOI and learn about the rights that its laborers enjoy in March 2012. The leaders of the above-mentioned demilitarization youth campaign, a human rights lawyer, leftist journalists, and a video cameraman accompanied me on this historic visit—for both documentation and solidarity purposes. Wahiba was respectful and good-humored. He spoke for several hours about his employees' fair wages that already exceeded the national minimum; their unique perks and benefits in transportation and health care; and how annual profit was distributed between reinvestment and perks. Wahiba asserted that labor strikes at AOI were limited and that the press exaggerated their size. But he also confirmed that he terminated one of them by contacting SCAF, which dispatched twenty soldiers from the military police to disperse it. On the second day of this visit, Wahiba allowed me access to two factories to interview workers and administrators there.[43]

On the other side of the bench, I interviewed labor activists who played leading parts in the strikes at AOI's plants. "AOI's problem is its administration," one angry middle-aged worker stated. "It is a bunch of retired army generals who came to AOI to get both a pension from the army and a salary from AOI. The problem with AOI's bylaws is that they vest all powers to the lieutenant general, as though it was the word of God," he added. When asked why ex-generals occupied so many civilian positions in the organization's factories, Wahiba asserted that it was because "the military produces the best managers." The interviewed workers also bitterly complained that AOI was run by a set of obsolete laws issued back in 1978, which deny the workers the rights to unionize or receive just trials in civilian courts. AOI is not subject to national Egyptian laws; it only answers to its own internal bylaws. Workers at AOI are not allowed to unionize or resort to a state court if a dispute arises between them and the administration. They address their legal issues to a judicial committee made up of members of the Justice Ministry and the State Council. Because AOI was originally created as an international organization that had other Arab state members and was meant only for military production, subjugating its workers solely under its bylaws was initially justified. Nevertheless, the organization has been owned solely by Egypt for the past three decades, after other Arab countries withdrew from it, and 70 percent of its production is already civilian and only 30 percent military—according to Wahiba's statement.[44] One worker described the internal statute they were subjected to as "a law of enslavement."

The vice minister of defense for financial affairs and SCAF member General Mahmud Nasr held a press conference where he delivered a presentation on the army's contribution to the national economy. He also pledged to "fight" in order to protect the armed forces' businesses and profits. It was an unprecedented conference to which journalists and economists were invited in March 2012. Nasr asserted that the military institution supported the government after the uprisings by depositing $2 billion into the central bank. When economists who were present the press conference referred to lack of transparency in the military budget and inquired about the sources of the large sum deposited at the central bank, Nasr replied, "Our money does not belong to the state; it is the sweat of the Ministry of Defense ['araq wazarat al-difa'] from the revenue of its enterprises. . . . We will not allow the state to intervene in it." Not only did the SCAF member separate military finances from the national budget, he also openly refused any public oversight. Wael Gamal, prominent economic journalist who attended the conference, cited Nasr's words in more detail: "We will fight for our economic enterprises and we will not quit this battle. We will not leave our thirty-year sweat for somebody else to ravage, and we will not allow anybody to come near the armed forces' projects." Gamal asserted that Nasr tacitly "threatened" those who wanted the parliament to scrutinize the military budget.[45]

In reaction to this unreserved attitude, a youth campaign emerged to call for boycotting the civilian products of the military. On its Facebook page, "Boycott SCAF Products," it posted images of various brands of cars, canned food, pesticides, home appliances, pasta, and so forth and urged citizens not to buy them.[46] Another popular street campaign titled "The Military Are Liars" ('Askar Kadhibun), which screened videos of the army's brutal practices against protesters, also incorporated data on the military's civilian products in their footage, which was then played in the streets for the public to see.[47]

Under such constant socioeconomic pressure, SCAF opted for vague economic policies in order to avoid more unrest. On the one hand, SCAF's two appointed prime ministers and their ministers of finance repeatedly promised that Egypt would maintain its market economy and apply the reform program that Mubarak agreed on with the IMF, which included privatization of the public sector and reducing subsidies.[48] A renowned labor rights organization, the Egyptian Center for Social and Economic Rights, won major court cases to annul the sales agreements of many privatized state-owned companies and order their return to the state on grounds of corruption and unfair treatment of workers.[49] However, SCAF's minister of international cooperation challenged these verdicts and reassured the new private owners that their contracts were binding; meanwhile, SCAF asserted that workers' disputes would be settled through other reconciliatory means outside court. Khalid Ali, the rights lawyer who led this legal campaign, carried on with more lawsuits questioning the legality of the entire process of privatization. This put SCAF in a difficult situation with foreign investors, especially Arabian Gulf capital, who had to face great financial losses by returning the public enterprises they had purchased and considered internationally suing the Egyptian government to demand compensation. As a result, SCAF amended the investment law to authorize the government to negotiate and settle such disputes outside of court, even if lawsuits were already filed but no verdicts were reached yet. Prime Minister Decree no. 32 of 2012 formed a committee, with the membership of relevant ministers, to oversee investors' disputes with state bodies. The recommendations of this committee were to be legally enforceable.[50]

On the other hand, SCAF's cabinets terminated the privatization program entirely and even closed down the Ministry of Investment, which was responsible for the public sector under the auspices of Gamal's neoliberal economists.[51] The ministry's holding companies that were lined up to be sold to local or foreign capital were all placed under the control of two ex-generals—the above-mentioned al-Muzi and Yusuf subsequently—who were appointed heads of the Public Business Sector, which was shortly turned into its own ministry. In addition, SCAF turned down an IMF loan worth $3 billion with relaxed terms, offered right after the uprisings to help the postrevolutionary economy. IMF delegations visited Egypt at least twice in 2011 to evaluate Egyptian economic needs and offered to lend the country a few billion dollars to assist with the budget deficit. Although the cabinet seriously pursued and negotiated this loan, SCAF was reluctant to conclude it. It would have entailed measures affecting the lower classes, especially cuts in food and gas subsidies. The generals hesitated to bear the social consequences of such a loan amid endless unrest and under the pressure of the public opinion that historically viewed the IMF as an arm of Western domination.[52] A group of leftist economists and journalists led an antidebt campaign because the IMF's loan conditions ignored social justice needs.[53] Eventually, SCAF did not take it.

In the meantime, SCAF not only saved but also further expanded the military business empire—invading into new territories of the citizens' consumer markets and everyday life. In collaboration with a Chinese firm, Tantawi opened al-'Arish cement factory in April 2012. The value of the contract was about $370 million, through which the firm provided the plant with designs and machinery. It was originally concluded in 2007, but the military completed construction after taking power.[54] At the inauguration ceremony attended by the Chinese ambassador to Egypt, Tantawi asserted that the factory was part of NSPO's efforts to develop Sinai through military investments without burdening the state budget. He also asserted that the factory would fulfill military and civilian needs alike toward self-sufficiency and contribute to price control.[55] Nonetheless, cement prices skyrocketed within a few months of the opening of this factory, which appeared to be just another competitor in the domestic market with many other public and private sector producers. It even competed with holding companies placed under the control of ex-generals. Moreover, the prices of the products of the military factory are the same as and sometimes higher than those of private- and public-sector companies. All these companies are listed on the stock market and pay customs and taxes, while NSPO's factory is not listed and is exempt from dues to the state. This exemption did not, however, reflect in its prices, which are almost the same as those of the private sector. In July 2012 the state's Central Agency of Public Mobilization and Statistics issued a report indicating a considerable increase in cement prices in the domestic market, which means that the military factory played no role in price control.[56]

Similarly, Tantawi expanded the military's chemicals complex in Fayyum in October 2011, by adding three new plants. At the value of LE500 million, he opened factories of fertilizer, alum, and phosphoric acid used in agricultural and industrial activities. Thus NSPO's El-Nasr Company for

Intermediate Chemicals now owned seven factories. After again asserting that these new projects would contribute to national economic development and create jobs, Tantawi added that the fertilizer factory aimed at ending monopolies in the domestic market, making this commodity abundantly available across the country. Three months later, prices of fertilizers skyrocketed amid a shortage crisis—market supply was 50 percent less than the previous year, and the head of peasants' informal union complained about monopolies and the black market.[57] Tantawi also asserted that these plants were environmentally friendly. Nonetheless, farmers residing and working around them complained that they were causing an environmental disaster only two months after they were opened. The pollution they emitted damaged agricultural produce and killed livestock on about 15,000 acres of surrounding land.[58]

Furthermore, AOI expanded the activities of its existing enterprises. Its Arab American Vehicles began to assemble a new Toyota luxury car—the Fortuner SUV. The Japanese giant was to produce three thousand units of this vehicle per year using AAV's plant as an assembly subcontractor.[59] AOI's train wagon company, Semaf, won a government contract to produce more than two hundred coaches for the national railways. It was a LE3.6 billion contract, signed by Hamdi Wahiba, and included delivery of these wagons in thirty months, an overhaul of other coaches and locomotives, development of hundreds of railway trails, and renovation of twenty train stations and their signal systems. The Ministry of Finance paid a LE100 million deposit to initiate the project.[60] Semaf signed another contract with Mitsubishi to assemble underground metro coaches for the Ministry of Transport. It was a LE21 million deal that included making three coaches without engines.[61] The AOI's Sakr Factory built two seawater sanitation plants for the Mediterranean province of Matruh—whose governor then was an ex-general.[62]

This is while Tantawi opened a toll highway in Upper Egypt and called it the "Army Road." The military engineers at EAAF constructed this road extending over 309 kilometers from Helwan to Asyut at the cost of LE4.2 billion. Mubarak allocated its land to the army on January 23, only two days before the uprisings. Presidential Decree No. 13 of 2011 designated this huge piece of land as part of "strategic areas of military importance" and allotted it to the MoD, yet the ministry used it immediately afterward in a profitable civilian enterprise. This was the third and final phase of two other Upper Egyptian toll roads that the military had constructed east of the Nile.[63] Overall, military engineers continued to be the largest contractors for public construction projects. For the ministry of housing and its central development authority, EAAF embarked on a gigantic social housing project to build thousands of apartments for low-income families. General Tahir Abd Allah, a SCAF member and head of EAAF, asserted that the army "donated" the land for this project and announced that two new urban settlements would be called the cities of "the Army and the People."[64] Military engineers also built bridges and developed many existing roads and squares for the Ministries of Transportation and Housing in Cairo and beyond. Meanwhile, the wedding halls of the military engineers' social club continued to offer its luxury and affordable services to the middle classes.[65]

Likewise, SCAF salvaged and further enhanced its political privileges within the bureaucratic apparatus—toward more encompassing hegemony and surveillance over the urban spaces of the rebellious population. Using the presidential authorities it amassed upon replacing Mubarak, SCAF appointed a huge number of retired generals in civilian posts, in either old spots that used to be occupied by ex-officers or new key places. A group of young revolutionaries created a Google Map locating geographical areas and workplaces where officers occupied civilian or business positions in the country up until June 2012—when SCAF handed over power to an elected president. They called this electronic map Kharitat Hukm al-'Askar and managed to identify on it 447 locations at top and medium administrative levels in the offices of ministries and state authorities in Cairo and all provincial areas.[66] A few examples are listed below.

Ex-generals took great interest in controlling the water and sewerage holding company, which naturally has subsidiaries in all cities in the country as the only national provider for potable water and sanitation systems. The chairman of the parent holding company was ex-general al-Sayyid Nasr 'Arafat, and numerous other retired generals chaired the company's offices in governorates as such Giza, Sharqiyya, Luxor, and Asyut. Within the same realm retired generals headed the Holding Company of Land and Maritime Transport, the Food Industries Holding Company, the National Cement Company, the Egyptian General Company for Tourism and Hotels (Egoth), Egypt Company for Real Estate Asset Management, Egypt's stock market, and more. In the realm of public authorities, ex-generals headed the General Organization for Export and Import Control and the Administrative Control Authority, Industrial Development Authority, the New Urban Communities Authority, and the General Authority for Agricultural Development Projects, Authority of Tourism Development, and many more. The

Suez Canal Authority remained in the hands of Ahmad Fadil, and the heads of the Red Sea port cities remained under the control of retired admirals. The state-owned oil sector remained highly militarized, as retired generals run many natural gas and oil companies.

The list did not end there. The minister of local development and fourteen of the twenty-seven provincial governors were retired generals. Ex-generals were also appointed as heads of districts in large cities, such as 'Umraniyya, 'Agouza, and Dokki in Cairo, or of small towns such as Armant in Luxor. In the Ministry of Health, the minister's assistant for financial and administrative affairs was a retired general, among many other generals in the bureaucratic offices of the ministry. There were dozens of retired officers in the Ministry of Environment. Interestingly, even the head of the Supreme Constitutional Court now was originally an army officer who previously served as a judge in military tribunals. This justice, Faruq Sultan, also served as the head of the Supreme Presidential Elections Commission, which finalized the list of presidential candidates and oversaw elections in mid-2012.

Islamic Grocers and Democratic Generals

Once SCAF released him from Mubarak's military prison, Khayrat al-Shatir—the deputy supreme guide of the Muslim Brothers and supposedly the most powerful man in the organization—fully resumed his business activities as well as political life. A military court had charged him with crimes such as money laundering, and his multimillion-dollar companies were confiscated four years earlier. As the Muslim Brothers enjoyed immense political influence and their newly created political party was sweeping various kinds of elections after the 2011 uprisings, al-Shatir seized this rare historical moment for his religious fraternity and revived his economic enterprises in large festivities. Thus he opened a gigantic grocery store in a Cairo upper-class neighborhood and granted it a religious name, Zad—a Qur'anic term meaning food provisions. Originally an engineer, al-Shatir proudly walked around the branches of this chain and posed for media photos near imported consumer goods such as canned foodstuff, detergents, sweets, meats, and kitchen tools. Moreover, he submitted papers required to run for presidential elections and launched a well-funded campaign using his photo with a slightly shaved beard and a platform promising an ambitious "economic renaissance project" for Egypt.

After deposing Mubarak, SCAF had a conspicuous marriage of convenience with the Muslim Brothers based on power-sharing arrangements. After decades of persecuting the brotherhood and allying itself with the lower and middle classes in Nasser's times, followed by alliances with the business elite in Mubarak's era, the Egyptian Army now decided to fully reconcile with the brothers and divide the postrevolutionary realms of influence with them. The Egyptian people went to the ballot boxes to vote four times under SCAF: in a referendum for a constitutional declaration, two parliamentary elections, and one presidential election. At every election, the ballot boxes' results were in favor of the Islamists—particularly the Muslim Brothers. When a member of the brotherhood won the presidential seat and SCAF handed him the post, the military maintained and further expanded its economic and political privileges under his regime.

A month after deposing Mubarak, SCAF formed a legal committee to amend some articles of the 1971 constitution and use it temporarily to run the country. SCAF appointed an Islamist judge who was a Muslim Brothers sympathizer to head this small committee of only seven members and put on it a leading member of the brotherhood who had just gotten out of jail. No other political stances were represented in this committee. It drafted a constitutional declaration consisting of eight articles and called for public endorsement through a referendum. Islamists of all affiliations aggressively mobilized the masses to vote for these articles, and a Salafi preacher even called the whole event *ghazwat al-sanadiq*, or the conquest of the ballot boxes.[67] Islamists carried religious slogans and distributed religious pamphlets outside polls. Leftists and liberals opposed the declaration and mobilized for a no vote. Eventually, 77 percent of the population voted in favor of the eight articles, but SCAF issued a constitutional declaration consisting of sixty-three articles instead. Article 2 stated that Islam was the official religion of the state and that the principles of shari'a were the "main" source of legislation. Islamists considered the passing of this article a great victory against a secular campaign to either eliminate it or at least retain the original wording of the 1971 constitution to stipulate that shari'a was but one source of legislation. Article 56 stipulated that SCAF would enjoy the following list of powers: legislative authority; appointing the cabinet and state officials, ratifying state budget, and monitoring its implementation; appointing a number of parliament members; representing the state in foreign relations and concluding international treaties; pardoning or reducing legal penalties; and all other authorities established for the president in laws and decrees.[68]

The Muslim Brothers pushed for hastily holding parliamentary elections, which took place in November 2011. That November witnessed the bloody events of Muahmmad Mahmud Street—off Tahrir Square leading toward the Ministry of Interior's headquarters—where violent clashes between protesters, the police, and the army lasted for four continuous days. An official report issued by a state human rights investigative committee recorded that about sixty protesters were killed, mostly by intense teargas, thousands were severely injured, and some lost their eyes to police rubber bullets.[69] During the battles, the brothers and the Salafis accused the slain dissidents of trying to delay what they called the postrevolutionary "wedding of democracy" ('urs al-dimuqratiyya), that is, elections. The elections eventually did take place, and army soldiers secured the voting sites. Violating electoral rules, Islamists heavily used religious slogans and distributed publications with religious signs inside and at the doors of electoral commissions. In addition, civil society organizations that monitored the voting process recorded cases of electoral bribes, or buying votes from rural and urban poor citizens by distributing food items to them.[70] The Muslim Brothers, or their Freedom and Justice Party (FJP), won 43 percent of the seats in this parliament, and their Salafi allies won 22 percent. The elections of the upper house, the Shura Council, followed in January and February 2012, with very low turnout and resulted in FJP winning 58 percent of the seats and the Salafis 25 percent.

The testimonies of some ministers who served in SCAF's cabinets during these crucial months speak of frustration about undeclared arrangements concluded between the brotherhood and the ruling officers. Ahmad al-Bur'i, minister of labor force and a law professor, asserted, "We felt great repression imposed on us by SCAF in many subjects, in which it was evident that there was [previous] agreement or semi-agreement between them and Muslim Brothers."[71] Similarly, Juda Abd al-Khaliq, minister of social solidarity and leftist professor of economics, asserted that SCAF in fact delivered power to the Muslim Brothers from the moment it formed the constitutional declaration committee and appointed an Islamist to head it. He added that the fact that other political forces, liberals and leftists, were highly fragmented helped SCAF to make arrangements with the brothers. "The end result was that SCAF gave power to only one political faction, the Muslim Brothers, and the other political forces realized their mistake of fragmentation and began to rearrange their papers when it was already a bit late," Abd al-Khaliq opined.[72] Prominent intellectual and old Nasser confidant Mohammad Hassanein Heiakl, who regularly met with Tantawi and SCAF members, asserted that they were under U.S. pressure to allow the Muslim Brothers to play a greater role in shaping post-Mubarak politics.[73]

Finally, when the presidential elections started in mid-2012, the Islamists felt so empowered that a large number of them from various ideological shades submitted applications to the Supreme Presidential Elections Commission for candidacy approval. The Muslim Brothers alone had two official candidates and a third nonofficial one: al-Shatir, engineer and deputy supreme guide of the brothers; Mohamed Morsi, another engineer and head of the brothers' political party; and Abd al-Mun'im Abu al-Futuh, a physician and a forty-year key member of the brotherhood who had just been dismissed by his leadership who disapproved of his desire to run for the presidency.[74] Al-Shatir, famously the most powerful and richest man in the organization, was the principal candidate of the brotherhood, but the organization feared that his application would be declined on the pretext that he had served jail time. Thus they had the much less charismatic and subordinate Morsi place another spare application. Media described Morsi as "the spare tire" (el-istibn), and he had to defend himself against such widely circulated stigmatization.[75] Another two Islamists with strong ties to the brotherhood also ran: the Salafi preacher Hazim Salah Abu Isma'il, whose father was a Muslim Brothers parliament member, and lawyer Muhammad Salim al-'Awwa, a Muslim Brothers legal supporter. The electoral commission did after all decline the application of al-Shatir, and the brotherhood's spare candidate ran.

Three Islamist candidates were accepted to run for the first round, against prominent leftist figures such as Nasserite Hamdeen Sabbahi and labor rights lawyer Khalid Ali. Some ancien régime figures competed with them, especially Lieutenant General Ahmad Shafiq of the air force—Mubarak's prime minister during the uprisings in 2011 and former minister of civil aviation. It is important to note here that the platforms of the all Islamist candidates refrained from addressing the issue of demilitarizing civilian positions in the Egyptian state and monitoring the military budget. Only leftist candidate Khalid Ali openly discussed this issue in his published platform. The first round of elections concluded in May 2012, and resulted in Morsi, Shafiq, and Sabbahi winning 5.7, 5.5, and 4.8 million votes, respectively.[76]

The tense runoff took place in June 2012 between Morsi and Shafiq. The electoral violations committed more prominently by Morsi supporters were evident, but the army seems to have turned a blind eye. A coalition of civil society organizations that monitored elections reported that the brotherhood's party carried religious banners and chanted slogans about shari'a, campaigned during the silence period, and bribed voters by distributing food provisions such as meat, sugar, lentils, oil, and fava beans in poor areas. Morsi supporters also transported voters en masse to electoral sites in free microbuses in Cairo and violated electoral rules by standing in front of voting commissions to direct citizens to vote for their candidate.[77] The brotherhood announced the victory of Morsi on TV at four o'clock in the morning; he received 51.7 percent of the votes and his opponent got 48.3 percent. On the day SCAF handed him power, June 30, 2012, Morsi began his first national address by deeply thanking the armed forces. He saluted the Egyptian military and added, "Only God knows how much love I have in my heart [for it]."[78]

By the end of the elections, the relationship between SCAF and the brothers witnessed some tension but soon went back to normal. Immediately after polls closed and in order to secure its hegemonic position against the newly elected president, SCAF issued an addendum to the previous year's constitutional declaration. It granted the armed forces full autonomy over military affairs, reserved many traditionally presidential authorities to SCAF, and granted SCAF supreme power over the process of drafting a full new constitution—which was to take place soon after the presidential elections. Furthermore, as the Islamist-dominated lower house of the parliament—the People's Assembly—was just dissolved by a Constitutional Court verdict, SCAF granted itself legislative powers.[79] In August 2012 Morsi sacked Tantawi and replaced him with General Abd al-Fattah al-Sisi as new minister of defense, after a grave incident in Sinai where terrorist groups killed a large number of conscripts. He also sacked most members of SCAF and replaced them with newly promoted commanders of the corps of the armed forces. Morsi sacked Hamdi Wahiba of AOI and replaced him with the removed chief of staff, and the retired commander of the navy replaced Ahmad Fadil in heading the Suez Canal Authority. After fully restructuring SCAF, Morsi issued his own controversial constitutional declaration, granting himself ultimate authority over the process of drafting a new constitution. After the dust settled, al-Sisi engaged in full cooperation with Morsi's government, and the military collected more old and new economic and political privileges.

First of all, the brotherhood's new constitution granted the military institution a semiautonomous status within the state. The Muslim Brothers–

dominated upper house of the parliament formed a committee to draft the constitution. Not only were the majority of members of this committee brothers followed by Salafis, but also many liberal and leftist public figures, revolutionary youth movements, and representatives of churches withdrew from it to protest the despotic practices of its Islamist members. Despite the withdrawal of 15 of its 100 members, the committee carried on with finalizing the draft, and most hastily passed its 236 articles in one night in a single session aired on public TV. A public referendum followed to promulgate it in December 2012. Article 197 of this constitution kept the military budget above state oversight and public scrutiny. It placed the authority to oversee military spending and earning in the hands of the National Defense Council, a governmental body consisting mainly of military officers internally nominated. The parliament was obliged to consult the same council about any future laws relevant to the armed forced before they were issued. "The Council is responsible for matters pertaining to the methods of ensuring the safety and security of the country and to the budget of the Armed Forces. It shall be consulted about draft laws related to the Armed Forces. Other competencies are to be defined by law," the article stated. Article 195 stipulated that the minister of defense should always be chosen from ranking officers, that is, no civilian could be appointed minister of defense. Article 198 allowed military trials of civilians if they commit crimes that "harm the armed forces," without defining such crimes.[80]

Second, the brotherhood's upper house assisted the military in expanding its business enterprises and seizing additional economic advantages. This legislature, called the Shura Council, was elected in early 2012 with a low turnout of only 7 percent, to mainly function as a consultative body to the lower house and with limited legislative powers. After the Constitutional Court dissolved the lower house before the presidential elections, the Muslim Brothers converted the Shura Council into a full-fledged parliament. This was when its spokesman was a leader in the Muslim Brothers' political party, members of this party occupied 58 percent of its seats, and 25 percent were occupied by their Salafi allies. Morsi later appointed 90 of this council's 270 members, including four army officers. The council decided to "annex" a state-owned car factory to the Ministry of Military Production. Established in the 1960s, Al-Nasr Automotive Manufacturing Company was about to be liquidated after accumulating financial losses over the years, but the minister of military production agreed with the Shura Council's Committee of Human Development to obtain and operate it. Thus this plant joined other previously state-owned enterprises that the military seized during the wave of privatization. The Muslim Brothers and the military both celebrated the event as a hopeful benchmark for reviving the Egyptian car industry. Headed by a general, the company desperately negotiated with foreign manufactures to collaborate in assembling or trading activities. But as of the writing of this chapter, the plant has not operated.[81]

Furthermore, the Shura Council agreed to issue a law to increase military retirement pensions by 15–20 percent annually. While discussing this increase, prominent members of the brotherhood's party, such as 'Isam al-'Iryan, praised the great efforts that the armed forces exerted to keep the nation secure. This was the second raise in two years, as SCAF had already used its legislative authority to increase military pensions by 15 percent in early 2011. The Shura Council's committee that made the decision this time was the National Security and Arab and Foreign Affairs, whose key member was Muslim Brothers' leader and lawyer Subhi Saleh. He was also on SCAF's constitutional declaration drafting committee back in 2011.[82] The same committee authorized the armed forces to establish a medical school and other public health colleges to train staff for its hospitals that admit civilians for profit; the head of the civilian physicians' syndicate rejected this act.[83] In addition, the council unanimously agreed to issue a law to create a credit fund to extend loans to officers and considered making them Islamic "good credit" exempt from paying interest. The photos of the council's bearded members raising their hands high to universally vote yes for this law filled newspapers, and long-term SCAF member General Mamduh Shahin appeared delighted and enjoying friendly chats with Muslim Brothers' parliamentarians inside a council hall in these images.[84] Moreover, the Housing and Urban Communities Committee at the council commended the role the armed forces played in public construction projects.[85]

This takes us to the parastatal role that Morsi granted to military organizations—in keeping with Mubarak's policy. At the event opening a number of roads that EAAF constructed, Morsi praised the armed forces for both contributing to the state plans of economic development and enhancing its professionalism. Speaking of al-Sisi, Morsi asserted at the same event that, "in addition to his exceptional military training, he enjoys an exceptional engineering mind."[86] In a joking tone, Morsi asked the head of the military engineers to salute the civilian prime minister—who was handpicked by the brotherhood—so he would facilitate their business.[87] Outside of competitive public tenders, Morsi's cabinet directly granted EAAF contracts for numerous public construction projects. According to General Tahir Aballah, head of the military engineers, Morsi asked his authority to take charge of developing roads between Cairo and major ports and constructing new toll highways. He also asked the authority to build bridges, public clinics and hospitals, water sanitation plants, electric power stations, schools, museums, youth sporting clubs, an airport in Sohag in Upper Egypt, houses for the Nubian community in Aswan, and much more. When hundreds of college students at al-Azhar University faced food poisoning in their dorms' dining halls, the armed forces immediately stepped in and took charge of renovating this public university's kitchens by supplying new stoves, pots, pans, and other material from the fine production of military factories.[88]

Other military enterprises equally benefited under Morsi. The MoMP invested in assembling tablets in its Banha for Electronics Company, naming them Inar. Different ministries in the brothers' cabinet placed orders to buy thousands of this item outside competitive public tenders, including the Ministries of Communication and Higher Education.[89] Interestingly, shortly afterward AOI started assembling its own tablet, in collaboration with Intel Corporation, and named it Pluto. AOI negotiated with the Ministry of Education to sell its Pluto tablets to public schools. Colonel Ibrahim al-Sa'id, the MoMP's marketing manager, insisted that his ministry's Inar was of much higher quality than AOI's Pluto.[90] Meanwhile, AOI signed a protocol of collaboration in the field of renewable energy with Morsi's minister of electricity.[91] After it completed the construction of the Upper Egypt toll road from Helwan to Asyut, NSPO's company for roads obtained the right to operate and collect its revenues for a period of fifty years. The concession contract granted by Morsi's cabinet included NSPO's right to control billboards and lease their licenses to private advertisement companies.[92] Morsi himself went to Upper Egypt to open a new production line in an NSPO pasta factory. Ironically, to pacify the angry lower classes, and only a few days before the protests that deposed Morsi, his cabinet concluded a deal with NSPO to charitably distribute bags of pasta to the poor during the holy month of Ramadan.[93]

Moreover, the military was allowed to acquire more land to use in commercial activities. The brotherhood's civilian governor of the Delta province of Sharqiyya issued decision no. 3141 of 2013 to allot 500 square meters to NSPO in order to build a large mall. A Muslim Brothers' local leader, also a member of the Shura Council, posed for pictures with an army colonel while receiving the land deed. This particular tract already had a hall erected on it for medical functions, such as a parking lot for ambulances and a first aid unit, and the colonel was to demolish them but promised to build another one instead.[94] In the neighboring province of Daqahliyya, the military entered into bloody clashes with the inhabitants of eighteen houses in a small village because the latter claimed ownership rights to the land the houses were built on; some had been there for thirty years. The local police forces assisted in the evacuation and demolishing process and burned down three of the homes, killing the livestock inside, under the watch of the ex-military governor of the province. In a YouTube video recording of the incident, one impoverished inhabitant said in deep distress, "The army is supposed to build us lodging places in cases of crises, such as earthquakes and the likes, rather than being the one that destroys our homes." When the inhabitants resisted by burning tires and clashing with soldiers, the police used tear gas to disperse the crowd, leaving tens of villagers injured and suffocated.[95]

In a much more outrageous case of land grab, the army violently seized a whole island inhabited by farmers and fishers south of Cairo, Qurasaya located between Giza and Maadi. Enjoying a unique location, this land had been on the radar of business tycoons for years, hoping to get their hands on it to construct profitable touristic attractions. Qurasaya's residents filed a lawsuit against the army's transgressions back in 2007, with the help of the Egyptian Center for Social and Economic Rights, and won a verdict in 2010 that proved their legal rights as tenants of the island's state-owned land. The same verdict confirmed their right to renew their leases with the government.[96] A few months later the military registered the land of the island for itself at the public notary in order to establish property rights over it, claiming that it had already used the island as a strategic point to secure the capital. By the end of 2012 army soldiers invaded the island, but its impoverished people fiercely resisted in bloody clashes. The battle left one resident dead; twenty-five others were sent to military trials. A prisoners' rights organization asserted that the arrested were brutally tortured by electric shocks and heavy sticks. The military spokesperson officially stated that army would "firmly stop aggressors at any cost and sacrifices."[97] It is worth mentioning here that large areas of the Maadi Nile corniche, overlooking this island, are owned by the military and used for profitable projects, such as wedding halls, a partially for-profit gigantic hospital, and military factory 54.

Morsi made no attempt at scrutinizing military budget. On the contrary, in response to rumors that had circulated in the media about reducing this budget, he addressed the officers, stating, "Your rights, money, and properties are preserved. I assure you that your spending has increased during the last period . . . with the approval of the president [i.e., himself]. . . . The armed forces' money, savings, and allocations are not affected."[98] The independent head of the state's ASA, which audits governmental spending, complained that he had no access to the accounts of military-owned civilian businesses. "This is not acceptable that the authority cannot even monitor the wedding halls of the armed forces. What is the relation between the armed forces' wedding halls and national security?" he exclaimed.[99] When he later mistakenly announced that Minister of Defense al-Sisi agreed that the authority should monitor the army's commercial activities, the military spokesperson denied the news.[100] Meanwhile, in early 2013 Transparency International published a long report about corruption in the Egyptian military. Compiled by the organization's Defense and Security Program, the report classified the Egyptian Army at the lowest category on its anticorruption index, "Band F," with a "critical level of corruption," next to four African countries and four other Arab countries—including Syria, Libya, and Yemen.[101]

To continue Mubarak's coup-proofing strategy during his final decade in power, Morsi appointed or maintained a large number of retired generals in top bureaucratic positions. When he hired provincial governors, ten out of twenty-seven were ex-officers; seven were Muslim Brothers. Furthermore, Morsi appointed an ancien régime figure as the minister of local development, ex-general Ahmad Zaki 'Abdin, who served as governor of two provinces under Mubarak. Other ex-generals occupied positions that they long held in public authorities, such as heads of maritime safety and the New Urban Communities Authority, and the chairman of Port Said Container and Cargo Handling Company. Less than two weeks before Morsi was overthrown, however, the brotherhood panicked about the approaching uprisings and sought to appease the masses and expand their own power against other forces, so they reshuffled a large number of governors. They reduced the number of ex-generals to only seven and increased the Muslim Brothers to thirteen and appointed one Salafi figure.[102]

While securing this front, or in other words attempting to co-opt the military and coup-proof their nascent regime, the Muslim Brothers exercised parallel efforts to expand their originally "secret" business empire and establish their own clientelistic network. Generally, the Muslim Brothers' emerging patronage order mustered the same qualities as Mubarak's authoritarianism: one ruling party, a neoliberal economy, and patron-client relations with a select business elite. The term "brotherhooding" (*akhwana*) of both the state apparatus and private business was widely used in media to describe their policies.[103] Luckily, the brothers' economic enterprises expanded without being serious rivals to those of the military. While the military focused on heavy industry and construction, the brothers were most experienced in retail activities, such as establishing gigantic groceries, clothes retailers, or furniture stores for imported consumer goods. The brotherhood lacked needed business skills and technical experience in the heavy industrial sectors that would qualify them to pose any significant threat to the military on the domestic market.

The brotherhood's political party, FJP, came to replace Mubarak's NDP as the single ruling party. Although mostly unqualified and without previous experience, FJP's top members replaced NDP's officials in key government posts such as ministers, governors, and heads of governmental organizations. For instance, the ministers of media, justice, interior, finance, labor forces, and youth were either FJP leading figures or loyal to the party. FJP's minister of labor forces modified the trade union law in order to place the Egyptian Federation of Trade Unions under his party's control—replacing previous NDP domination. Law no. 79 of 2012 promulgated that trade unions' council members who reached retirement age should be dismissed and replaced—most probably by FJP affiliates. The law affected around 170 labor union leaders, who argued that it violated the treaties that Egypt had signed with the International Labor Organization entailing that the government should not intervene in the internal affairs of unions. A prominent leftist leader of a labor rights organization, Kamal Abbas of Dar al-Khadamat al-Naqabiyya, asserted that such legal modifications were part of Morsi's scheme of "brotherhooding" unions and considered it an act of "thuggery."[104]

The FJP's economic policies kept Gamal Mubarak's neoliberalism intact. This included extending reforms toward eliminating subsidies and increasing the role of private businesses. Along these lines, the brothers negotiated a $4.8 billion loan with the IMF—the same loan that SCAF had hesitated to accept—which would have entailed implementing more of Gamal's reforms if obtained. Interestingly, the brothers made sure to advocate that this loan did not violate shari'a law, which prohibits paying interest on debt. Their negotiations eventually fell through.[105] The FJP's platform called for the withdrawal of the state from providing subsidized services to the masses and expanding the role of business in managing state affairs. Accordingly, safeguarding the rights of the poor was considered an act of social solidarity delivered through charities rather than a state obligation. This package of essentially American market principles was then dubbed "Islamic" by the brotherhood's ruling party. In its fourth chapter, the platform read: "Economic activity is to be conducted in conformity with Islamic market mechanisms, which depend on fair competition and restrict free economy [without manipulation or monopoly]. Economic activity will also rely on Islamic investment and funding methods. There will be multiple forms of ownership rights, with regard to public and private property, on the condition that property is used to carry out their social function to achieve fair expenditure and establish social solidarity. The state will have a decentralized role."[106]

Like the NDP under Gamal, FJP fostered a patron-client network with business tycoons allowing them to benefit from the openness of the market —with added privileges for the Muslim Brothers' businessmen. As was the practice in most of their affairs, the brothers concealed their vast economic enterprises and kept them secret. It was impossible to determine the number of companies the religious fraternity owned or how much revenue they received every year. We at least know, however, that when al-Shatir stood military trial in 2006, more than seventy companies owned by the brotherhood were confiscated. We also know through the records of this trial that these businesses were mainly trading companies that primarily sold imported goods targeting upper- and middle-class consumers. The brotherhood's businessmen registered their projects under the names of their wives or sons-in-law so they would be hard to track down and avoid the watchful eye of the security apparatus. Al-Shatir was but one example. The branches of al-Shatir's shops were located in the upscale, luxury shopping malls in Cairo. For instance, his Rawaj Company, founded in 2002 and in which he owned 75 percent of its shares, had five subsidiaries for importing foreign brands of clothes and furniture—including Istiqbal and Sarar for luxury Turkish furniture and apparel, respectively, with branches in City Stars mall in Nasr City.[107]

As a matter of fact, Mubarak had imposed significant restraints on the Muslim Brothers businesses before 2011: he placed a ceiling on where they could invest as well as their profit margins. This explains why they were largely confined to selling imported goods and running giant supermarket franchises. Nevertheless, as Mubarak's regime fell and the Muslim Brothers seized power, it was expected that they would take such historic opportunity and invest in serious industries. But they continued to be stuck in what they knew best. After all, the commercial activities they invested in could be easily justified as shari'a friendly; Prophet Muhammad had a famous saying that "nine-tenths of livelihood is in trade" (*tis'at a'shar al-rizq fi al-tijara*). After being released from military prison in 2011, engineer al-Shatir launched a new giant enterprise. It was a grocery franchise, Zad, in Cairo's affluent neighborhood of Nasr City.[108] He thus added another grocery retailer to those that key Muslim Brothers owned, such as the Seoudi Market chain located in many upper-class areas of Cairo such as Zamalek and New Cairo, besides the al-Mahmal, Awlad Rajab, and Radwan chains located in middle- and upper-class areas across the country. Their fast food and department store chains, such as Mu'min and al-Tawhid wa-l-Nur, similarly flourished after the brothers assumed power.[109] Hasan Malik was a key businessman among the brothers. He created a new business association and invited Muslim Brothers entrepreneurs as well as Mubarak's cronies to join it and called it IBDA', or "Start."[110] Adopting a policy of favoritism, Morsi held regular meetings with Malik and a selected group of businessmen—a bearded entourage that accompanied the president when he traveled on official international trips to places such as China and Brazil. Malik was quite influential and rumors spread that he schemed to establish monopolies.[111]

Since the brothers had no experience with manufacturing or heavy industries, business territories were conveniently demarcated between them and the military. The brothers were mostly content with their realm of retail, and the generals carried on with their industrial and contracting activities. At least one short-lived conflict took place between the two groups over these divisions, but it was quickly resolved. A leading FJP member accused the former head of AOI, ex–chief of staff Wahiba, of corruption. Shortly after Morsi dismissed Wahiba from his position, Hasan al-Brins, the brotherhood's governor of the Delta province of Kafr al-Shaykh, claimed that he kept 5 percent of AOI's annual profit for himself and used to give 10 percent to Mubarak. Al-Brins asserted that Morsi had fired him for this reason and pledged to assist his president in purging other corrupt figures in the state. Outraged by what he affirmed to be false allegations, Wahiba threatened to take al-Brins to court for slander. The issue came to a swift end with Morsi's spokesperson officially denying these claims and asserting that "the president appreciates the role that . . . the former chair of AOI . . . played," and al-Brins himself apologized for spreading misinformation.[112]

Around the same time, young members of the brotherhood were, for the first time in decades, admitted into military colleges, including Morsi's nephew. Ever since the 1950s and through Mubarak's years, sons of Muslim Brothers or Islamist families at large were denied access to military academies—especially after jihadist cadets from the military technical college assassinated Sadat in a military parade in 1981. The head of the war academy under Morsi expressed the change in policy, saying, "We do not look at the political affiliations of the applicant's family. If we are in front of a student with excellent educational and physical qualifications, why should not we admit him?" He added that the war academy did admit cadets from the brotherhood as well as the Salafis in the 2012–13 entering class. He asserted that Morsi's nephew was admitted to the technical college because he reached high grades in physical fitness, not because of his familial relation to the president. He also denied that military colleges faced pressure from the FJP's leaders to admit their sons.[113]

Mysteries of Saving the Nation

When the mass protests erupted against the Muslim Brothers on June 30, 2013, the military once more presented itself as the savior of the nation. Moreover, it proclaimed to be the only remaining corruption-free, efficient institution capable of alleviating old and recent predicaments in the country. It is a big mystery: despite being an integral part of Mubarak's authoritarianism and a supremely privileged ally of the Islamist brothers, the military institution still managed to wipe off and reinvent its image anew as the fair guardian of the nation. It took down the brotherhood's president and short-lived regime amid unprecedented and largely unconditional public support for the officers.

The military institution's sweeping success in resurrecting its good image could be interpreted by a number of complex reasons. Above all is the sheer persona of the minister of defense, al-Sisi. Economic failure of the brothers, public fear of the return of fundamental Islamism, the support of Gulf states, and well-crafted propaganda campaigns all played central roles in overthrowing Morsi, but al-Sisi's ability to capitalize on discontent and forge "national consensus" around his personal character in a short period of time was a decisive factor in tying this net. While doing so, al-Sisi molded other mysteries: he formed alliances with domestic and regional forces that seemed fundamentally at odds with each other and yet happily collaborated around his pragmatic persona. Al-Sisi incarnated Nasser's spirit and fostered strong ties with leftist actors, but he also created connections with the rigid Salafis and similarly garnered the support of liberal groups. He made strong alliances with highly conservative regional polities, especially Saudi Arabia, that ironically extended immense funds to his left-oriented interim government.

The Muslim Brothers' regime collapsed on the very first anniversary of the inauguration of its president. The Egyptian people take pride in being a "religious nation by nature," or *sha'b mutadaiyyn bi-tab'u*—as the recent generations that worked in conservative oil-rich Gulf countries called themselves. Thus they enthusiastically voted for Islamists in both parliamentary and presidential elections after deposing Mubarak. Apparently this religious nation turned out to be not very pious after all, or at least it did not want to be ruled by an Islamic government shortly after voting one into incumbency. It was easy for many social classes and political stances in the country to subscribe to a youth campaign to overthrow Morsi because of the failure of the brothers at various levels and the discontent their behavior generated. The Muslim Brothers failed to deliver basic public services and run the economy, attempted to conservatively restrain social life, integrated fundamental Islamists into Egyptian politics, deployed police brutality against dissidents, and renewed authoritarian practices. In terms of public services, a website called MorsiMeter.com traced the list of basic needs that the president pledged to instantly fix during his first one hundred days in power in five primary areas: garbage collection, traffic, bread supply, gas supply, and internal security. After the end of those hundred days, out of a list of sixty-four promises, only ten were delivered, and only 39 percent of the population was satisfied with the president's performance in those ten.[114]

Lacking sophisticated business experience beyond retail, the brotherhood struggled with running Egypt's complex economic map with many sectors in dire crises after the 2011 uprisings. Their grand "economic recovery program," which they dubbed the Renaissance Project, failed to deliver its declared promises. As Alison Pargeter, expert on political Islam, puts it, this project was a "vague and generalized wish list that bears little relation to the reality on the ground . . . Brotherhood's political naïveté, with their seemingly believing that promises alone will be sufficient to bring people over to their side."[115] Since the uprisings against Mubarak targeted social disparities resulting from neoliberal policies, observers argue that discontent quickly rose against the brothers because they followed the same market model. Bearded business cronies controlled the economy, while the brothers extended some services in the form of charities in the fields of health care, food, clothes, and so on to alleviate poverty in some rural and lower-class urban areas as they used to do before coming to power.[116] Furthermore, Morsi attempted to alter the lifestyle and morality of the Egyptian people in accordance with the brothers' dogma. For instance, he tried to impose a 10:00 pm curfew on cafes, restaurants, shopping malls, and other locations, with the hope that the masses would go to bed early and wake up early to catch the dawn prayer and fulfill their national duties as productive citizens afterward. Morsi's decision was mocked and met with rejection across the country. Nobody abided by this curfew or others that the feeble president unsuccessfully attempted to impose on other occasions.[117]

When Morsi celebrated the 1973 war victory two months after his inauguration, he invited the very jihadists who were convicted of assassinating Sadat, the hero of this war, to attend.[118] Two weeks before his ousting, Morsi gathered tens of thousands of Islamists from different factions at Cairo Stadium in order to declare international jihad in Syria. Without military pre-approval, Morsi announced that the "Egyptian people and army" together were going to help free Syria from its tyrannical regime by supporting the militant rebels there.[119] In this mega stadium Islamist assembly, many extremist Sunni clerics made hard-core sectarian statements with Morsi's consent, and this was followed a few days later by massacring eight Shi'is in a village near Cairo.[120] Three weeks before that stadium incident, terrorist cells in the Sinai Peninsula kidnapped seven army soldiers. An army operation freed the soldiers, but the kidnappers escaped without being identified. After the end of this crisis, some former officers asserted that the Muslim Brothers facilitated the criminals' escape and claimed that the brotherhood and Hamas sponsored jihadists and other incidents of kidnapping soldiers in the troubled peninsula.[121] For many Egyptians from different generations, the dark memories of the 1970s and the 1990s widespread terrorism in the country are still vividly alive in their minds, and such actions by Morsi instilled great fear and generated profound disdain among them.

Morsi decreed a despotic constitutional declaration by the end of 2012. In reaction, prominent liberal and leftist leaders along with revolutionary youth formed the National Salvation Front (NSF, Jabhat al-Inqadh al-Watani), to save the country from the growing authoritarianism of the brothers. Led by Mohamed ElBaradei—the great inspiration for Egyptian youth in initiating the 2011 protests, former director of the UN's International Atomic Energy Agency, and Nobel Peace Prize laureate—joined forces with leaders from the most active political parties, socialists, social democrats, liberals, and communists along with leaders of trade unions, professional syndicates, and youth revolutionary movements to form a high-profile front. Among the key figures in NSF was Hamdeen Sabahi, the Nasserite presidential candidate who came in third in the 2012 race. As Morsi's declaration granted him supra powers to protect the Islamist-dominated constitution-writing committee, ElBaradei said that it created a "new pharaoh" and vowed to continue escalating peaceful resistance.[122] In the meantime, Morsi's state security apparatus, joined by volunteer fighters from young members of the brotherhood, clashed with and killed young protesters to defend the authority of the brothers. On the second anniversary of the uprisings on January 25, 2013, it was reported that forty protesters were killed, and ElBaradei's front rejected an invitation to hold a dialogue with the president a few days after these bloody events.[123] Morsi's police brutality continued for months afterward, and unarmed protesters were shot by security forces or attacked and tortured by the brotherhood's young volunteer fighters while, for example, protecting the presidential palace. A human rights organization, Nadim Center for the Rehabilitation of Torture Victims, documented two hundred cases of torture, kidnapping, and killing committed by Morsi's police during his first one hundred days in power.[124] ElBaradei's front tirelessly carried on with mobilizing the masses against the new oppressive regime.

Presiding over the simmering political scene and observing how resentment unfolded, al-Sisi asserted that the military was not loyal to one political faction or another and was there only to protect national security.[125] When appointed minister of defense by Morsi, al-Sisi was a barely known character among the members of the then sacked SCAF. Nonetheless, his persona began to be revealed, or rather take shape, as events progressed. Originally an infantry officer, al-Sisi studied for a year in the U.S. Army War College, served as a military attaché in Saudi Arabia, was the commander of the northern military region based in Alexandria, and finally served as the head of military intelligence before he was promoted to minister of defense. Al-Sisi revived Nasser's image and deployed it to build his own popularity among the older generations and the lower classes. However, he was a typical Egyptian citizen of his time and place in terms of being a devout Muslim using common pious rhetoric. The brotherhood and Salafis both perceived him as a highly religious figure and admired his diligent observance of praying and fasting beyond compulsory Islamic duties.[126] Meanwhile, al-Sisi visited Nasser's shrine on the anniversary of his death and met with members of the late leader's family. After deposing Morsi, al-Sisi again did the same thing, this time accompanied by Nasser's aging officials, Nasserite political figures and labor leaders, and Nasser's family, who all extended unconditional support to him.[127]

For many months al-Sisi seemed to be content with the privileges that the brotherhood's government granted to the army and invited Morsi to many ceremonies where the president watched the graduation of new cadets and the opening of new military projects.[128] Nonetheless, al-Sisi apparently still perceived the brothers as an international organization whose historically entrenched foreign connections and open relations with jihadists posed a threat to Egyptian national security. In a lengthy interview, al-Sisi indicated that he had studied the Muslim Brotherhood's major goals and structure and the place of the president in it through a systematic collection of intelligence. He asserted that the brothers and Morsi had put the interest of their international organization above that of the Egyptian nation-state and fueled society with a violent version of Islam. "The intellectual and doctrinal structure of this group . . . affects their efforts to run any state. There is a large difference between the doctrinal and intellectual frameworks of a group and those of a state, and the two must work together in harmony. When the two clash, a dilemma emerges. . . . The image of Islam now in the world is harmed by those who call themselves Islamists. . . . Islam became the equivalent of killing, blood, destruction, and ruin," he said.[129]

In a short period of time, al-Sisi attempted to build "national consensus" around his hitherto obscure persona to confront the brothers. Oddly, he pragmatically crafted alliances that incorporated all shades of political stances, from leftists to liberals and even Islamist Salafis. He added to them the Coptic Church to represent the nation's Christian minority and al-Azhar Islamic institution as a representative of nonpoliticized Islam. Since youth movements were essentially needed to translate this consensus into dynamic activism on the ground, the military covertly backed a Nasserite group of youth who launched a campaign called Tamarrud (Rebellion) to collect signatures to impeach Morsi.[130] A week before the protests, al-Sisi issued an ultimatum asking the brothers to reconcile their political differences with other political parties and groups, but the brothers did not take action. After tens of millions joined protests against Morsi across the country, al-Sisi issued another forty-eight-hour ultimatum calling on the Muslim Brothers to respond to the masses' demands for Morsi's resignation and holding early presidential elections, but again the brotherhood did not respond. Al-Sisi's arrangement to forge a consensus was finally put into effect. In a televised speech on July 3, al-Sisi stood alongside ElBaradei representing all oppositional stances in NSF, the head of the Salafi political party, the patriarch of the Coptic Church, the Grand Shaykh of al-Azhar, two youth members from Tamarrud, a prominent female journalist representing women, and other commanders in the armed forces to announce the ousting of Morsi and delivering power to the head of the Supreme Constitutional Court.

Cheerfully expressing their appreciation of the army's decision, celebrating women and men filled Tahrir Square with posters of Nasser next to those of al-Sisi. The military's public relations sector, the Department of Morale Affairs, funded the production of a song titled "Tisalm al-Ayadi" honoring the hands of the soldiers who rescued the nation, invoking memories of old war victories. The song quickly became so popular among Egyptians of all social classes that it was played at weddings and used as background for belly dancing on family occasions. As a matter of fact, the Morale Affairs Department had an indispensable role in mending the army's public image in the months that followed overthrowing the brothers. It is after all a typical modern army's propaganda apparatus that deploys media to disseminate messages for mass mobilization purposes. With the aid of military helicopters flying across the country, this department filmed panoramic footage of the millions protesting against Morsi in Cairo and the provinces on June 30 in order to provide visual evidence that the event was in fact an actual mass revolution rather than a military coup. It produced a short documentary based on these scenes called *The Army of the People*.[131] Furthermore, the department filled the country's streets with gigantic billboards displaying kind-looking yet strong officers, made videos to encourage citizens to vote for a new constitution, and produced several other songs. As a byproduct of these well-funded efforts, a cult of personality grew around al-Sisi. Female and male fans from all social classes alike printed his photos and name on T-shirts, birthday cakes, chocolate bars, golden necklaces, and more.[132]

The military also managed to restore its image by presenting material "gifts" to the middle and lower classes, distributing charitable items to the poor, and delivering immediate crisis relief services to hurting localities. During organized national festivities, military helicopters threw "gift coupons" over enchanted masses in public squares, which they could use to claim military-produced consumer goods at the army's commercial outlets.[133] In the Delta province of Kafr al-Shaykh, the armed forced distributed twenty thousand large boxes of food items to poor families, and it did the same thing in Cairo's poor neighborhood of Imbaba. At the large premises of the Mahalla textile plant, where widespread labor protests used to erupt, the military sent the same number of food boxes especially for this company's workers. These boxes carried the colored logo of the MoD on them, and women from low-income households were seen happily carrying them atop their heads.[134] The army's charities significantly increased during the holy month of Ramadan. In a village in the southern province of Sohag, as tens of thousands of impoverished masses crowded in front of a local government office distributing MoD food boxes, two women were killed. The number of available boxes, around forty thousand, was rumored to be too small compared to the number of needy families, so fighting over receiving shares led to injuries and deaths.[135] In other news, military engineers rushed to rescue the town of al-Saff in Giza when a local bridge over its canal suddenly collapsed. Army bulldozers and advanced water suction machines contained the crisis and repaired the bridge in no time, according to the proud statements of the military spokesperson.[136]

Interestingly, al-Sisi chose to lean toward his leftist allies—especially social democrats and Nasserites—in forming the interim government after deposing Morsi. Besides, he received immense support from old communists and socialists following the ousting. Apparently opting for a left-oriented cabinet was meant to appease the working classes and reduce labor strikes that had erupted from 2011 onward. The first appointed interim premier was Hazim al-Biblawi, economist and leading member of the Egyptian Social Democratic Party, and he hired a number of ministers who had the same political stance in his cabinet. The minister of labor, Kamal Abu 'Ita, was a Nasserite leader of independent labor unions. The minister of social solidarity, Ahmad al-Bur'i, was also a strong supporter of independent labor unions besides being a leading member in ElBaradei's al-Dustur Party and NSF. A social democrat and a Nasserite were appointed ministers of international cooperation and education, respectively. However, this predominantly leftist cabinet that embraced polices of social justice noticeably failed in calming workers' protests, especially when it stood incapable of responding to their long-standing demand of raising the minimum wage. When thousands of workers renewed their strikes and sit-ins across the country, this cabinet had to resign, and many observers attributed its decision largely to its incompetence in containing labor discontent.[137]

Similarly, the al-Sisi-led interim regime gave more influence to leftist forces in drafting a new constitution. Although they resented preserving military privileges and attempted to prevent writing them into the new text, they eventually gave in to the army's pressure. The interim president appointed a committee of fifty public figures, many of whom were Nasserites, communists, human rights activist, and so on, along with representatives of labor unions, peasants, professional syndicates, liberal political parties, the Coptic Church, women, Salafis, and more. The draft did introduce many progressive articles serving the rights of workers, women, youth, religious minorities, ethnic groups, and others. Nonetheless, to please the Salafis, article 2 maintained the wording inherited from the brothers' abolished constitution, which read, "The principles of Islamic shari'a are the main source of legislation." Leftist and liberal members of the committee led a fierce battle to eliminate other inherited articles on the military budget, economic enterprises, and trials of civilians in military courts, among others, and the two representatives of the armed forces on the committee adamantly insisted on keeping them.[138]

In the promulgated constitution, article 203 states that the military budget should be listed as only one figure in the state budget to keep it classified and should be discussed only by the National Defense Council—whose members are mostly officers. The same council should be consulted on the drafting of any future laws related to the armed forces. Article 201 states that the minister of defense must be an officer, that is, no civilians could occupy this position. Article 204 says that civilians who attack military enterprises should be tried in military courts. In one incident after this constitution passed, one young citizen had a fight with a colonel running a military gas station, and the army subsequently sent him to a military prosecutor.[139]

At the opposite end of the political spectrum, al-Sisi fostered regional alliances with conservative Gulf states that feared the ideological expansion of the brothers. Ironically, they supported his left-oriented interim government with abundant funds, but these funds eventually worked for the interest of the military institution. Saudi Arabia and the United Arab Emirates in particular granted billions of dollars to Egypt to help stabilize the country and assist with infrastructure projects after ousting the brotherhood, but the military monopolized the implementation of these projects. The head of the military engineers, General Tahir Abd Allah, indicated that UAE donated $4.9 billion to building schools, hospitals, bridges, sewerage systems, affordable housing, wheat silos, and other facilities but stipulated that the military should take charge of these public works. Abd Allah claimed that the Emiratis said, "We will support the Egyptian people but through the army. If the people want a hospital, the armed forces will build it."[140] Thus EAAF and other military contractors visibly embarked on numerous construction projects for the civilian Ministries of Health, Education, Housing, and so forth, yet without having to go through competitive public tenders. To ease the process, the interim president issued Decree no. 82 of 2013 to amend the public bids and tenders law, allowing the government to conclude agreements with contractors through "direct allotment" in "urgent" matters for construction projects worth up to LE10 million. Presidential Decree no. 48 of 2014 decided to count AOI among "government authorities," that is, military bodies, eligible to benefit from this law and receive direct government contracts—although it is legally still an "international" organization.[141] Mohamed al-Dahshan, an economist and blogger, traced and calculated the number and value of the publicly announced government contracts that the military won between September and November 2013: they reached LE7 billion during the course of only two months.[142]

Despite his success in forging domestic and regional alliances with all these contradictory political forces, al-Sisi encountered difficulties in winning Western support. The oldest Western friend of the Egyptian Army, the United States, informally viewed the deposing of the brotherhood as a coup and consequently suspended military aid to Egypt. The Obama administration had fostered close relations with the Muslim Brothers since early 2011,[143] based on the latter's willingness to maintain the peace accord with Israel and contain Hamas—officially the Palestinian branch of the brotherhood—next door in Gaza. While Morsi was cultivating oppressive policies at home, Secretary of State Hillary Clinton and President Barack Obama showered him with praise for mediating a ceasefire between Israel and Hamas.[144] Moreover, considering the success of the Turkish model of neoliberal Islamists in power and the brothers' desire to work with the IMF to continue with the market economy policies, the brothers posed no threat to the American economic model.[145] Three weeks after al-Sisi-led coalition deposed Morsi, the Pentagon suspended the shipment of twelve Lockheed Martin F-16 fighter jets to Egypt, probably for the first time ever since Egypt started to receive an annually fixed military aid package of $1.3 billion after signing the peace treaty with Israel in 1979. This was followed by freezing the shipment of twenty Boeing Harpoon missiles and around 125 M1A1 Abrams tank kits. They were only released about two years later, after al-Sisi was already elected president and had spent many months in office.[146] During this difficult period, al-Sisi sought procurement elsewhere, especially in Russia. Field Marshal al-Sisi visited Vladimir Putin near Moscow to negotiate a $2 billion arms deal. On the same visit, Putin supported al-Sisi's candidacy for president.[147]

Business as usual, the military added more to its already inflated economic privileges during the interim period, sometimes through outrageous presidential decisions. For instance, the interim president, Adli Mansur, who was the head of the Supreme Constitutional Court, decided to increase the military budget by around LE700 million when the cabinet failed to raise the minimum wage for workers owing to a long-standing deficit. The military Organization of Public Services, responsible for building commercial malls, was allocated an additional LE500 billion, and the Authority of Military Production received more than 180 million. The president had to issue decrees amending the already authorized budget of FY2012–13 to put these new raises into effect.[148] In another, more shocking decision, the interim president decreed the "transfer" of all the assets and facilities of al-'Arish Port in Sinai to the armed forces. The port spans around 50,000 square meters overlooking the Mediterranean Sea, houses three platforms of around 400 meters, and includes administrative buildings. The decision was based on the army's legal authority to designate areas as having strategic importance and place them under military control.[149] In the same realm, the cabinet granted NSPO's road development company a ninety-nine-year concession contract to run the toll highway of Shubra-Banha, connecting Cairo to the Delta, and another fifty-year concession to finish and operate the Cairo-Alexandria desert highway.[150]

Unsurprisingly, the interim government carried on the custom of appointing a large number of retired officers to top bureaucratic positions, many of whom were not exactly successful at restoring the army's good image and in fact achieved the opposite. Out of twenty-seven appointed governors, sixteen were ex-generals, which was the highest number in four decades. As a new governor of al-Daqahliyya, ex-general 'Umar al-Shawadfi faced occasional verbal attacks by angry local citizens about lack of public services in the province. Al-Shawadfi headed Mubarak's center for state land uses for more than seven years, which did not help him in dealing with discontented citizens. In one incident, a female student asked him in public to clean the dirty city instead of wasting his time only attending useless meetings. In another incident in a mosque, a few angry citizens confronted him about a hazardous situation with sanitation services in their village. In both cases, the publicly irritated al-Shawadfi responded by reciprocating slander.[151]

The governor of Port Said, ex-general Samah Qandil, had to physically place his hands on the mouth of an angry local merchant to stop him from screaming against expanded corruption in the vegetables wholesale market. General Qandil said, "Stop . . . enough . . . we know," while the muzzled merchant waved his hand with a zucchini—which alludes to corruption in the Egyptian popular culture. The incident embarrassed the general, as he was touring the market with the civilian minister of supply, while the media took and posted photos of his unprofessional behavior.[152] The former head of the Damietta Port, ex-general Fulayfil, who was forced out of his office by protests back in 2011, was now running the Maritime Public Authority—a crucial organization inspecting navigation safety. A newspaper op-ed harshly criticized Fulayfil for traveling abroad frequently at government expense on the pretext of attending business meetings, while leaving the technical structure of the authority to decay. After he returned from a London trip, he was spotted using a state-owned ship to travel for free to the holy lands in Saudi Arabia to perform pilgrimage, the same op-ed claimed.[153]

After all is said and done, al-Sisi not only won the hard battle of restoring the military's good image as the sole guardian of the nation but also brought back another important item to his institution: the presidential seat. Lost to a civilian for only one brief year in six decades, the presidency returned to the army through elections that scored al-Sisi sweeping public support in summer 2014. After Nasser, Sadat, and Mubarak, al-Sisi has become the fourth officer to take off his uniform, put on a civilian suit, and rule the subordinated nation.

Conclusion

Demilitarizing the Nation?

In today's Egypt you cannot miss it: the omnipotent presence of the military institution everywhere across the country. The Egyptian military intensively occupies the economic realms and social spaces of citizens from all social classes in every urban locality. It owns business enterprises that invest in almost everything and produce almost anything. It owns factories for pasta, home appliances, cement, steel, jeep cars, fertilizers, and much more. It bakes subsidized bread, produces foodstuffs in vast farms, builds bridges and roads, constructs social housing, erects football stadiums, and so on. It runs hotels with lucrative wedding halls, sea resorts with luxury summerhouses, and apartment buildings along with lavish villas. It runs gas stations, shipping firms, domestic cleaning companies, and spacious parking lots. It constructs toll highways to collect their daily fees. Above all this, ex-generals control the state's bureaucratic apparatus in charge of managing the population's everyday life. They seize the top government positions in control of public transportation, water and sewerage services, land allocation, Internet lines, housing projects, and much more. They administer sea, river, air, and land ports and oversee foreign trade activities. By tapping into domestic consumer markets and managing every urban vicinity, the military keeps constant surveillance over and penetrates into the everyday life of docile or discontented individuals in the nation. Meanwhile, it perpetuates a nationalistic discourse about saving the nation from and securing it against internal and external threats alike. This situation is far from being a new phenomenon that emerged with the recent ascent of a new military president, Abdel Fattah al-Sisi; its deep roots are entrenched in the past sixty years of the country's history.

Is it possible to demilitarize the Egyptian state, economy, and whole society in the foreseeable future, after full six decades of hardly interrupted militarism?

In Egypt's postcolonial history, al-Sisi is the fourth officer since 1952 to take off his uniform and govern the country. Before him, Gamal Abdel Nasser, Anwar Sadat, and Hosni Mubarak all formed authoritarian regimes where fellow officers enjoyed superior political and economic privileges. While Egypt weathered many fundamental moments of transformation during the past few decades, including mass uprisings in 2011, the country's semiautonomous military institution managed to adapt to these changes and survive. At crucial moments of socialist, neoliberal, or revolutionary transition, the Egyptian military managed to maintain a hegemonic position within the state structure and maximize its economic profits. Evidently, the officers have successfully weathered the latest shaking wave of revolutionary unrest and come out of it with full retention of dominance. During the past three decades in particular and within a neoliberal economy, the domineering officers created a gigantic business empire and occupied pivotal bureaucratic positions in the state, which allowed them visible or mostly invisible penetration into the consumer markets and urban spaces of all social classes of the subordinated masses. Such heavy securitization of everyday life granted the officers an uninterrupted gaze and continuous control over manipulated citizens, in times of both civil peace and unexpected turmoil.

Militarizing Egypt precisely began on July 23, 1952, when a group of young officers deposed the monarch, kicked out the British occupation, and created a postcolonial republic. The officers were the self-appointed saviors of the nation and guardians of its progress. Their charismatic leader and the first military president of the country, Nasser, soon embarked on a "revolution from above" as he transformed Egypt into socialism. Army officers and "military technocrats" occupied top government positions in this socialist state, installed themselves as the managers of its public-sector factories and companies, and became the leaders of its single ruling party, the Arab Socialist Union. While Nasser fought wars carrying the banner of Arab nationalism, the military institution enjoyed a bloated budget and a superior status over the country's political affairs and industrial sector. Nonetheless, Nasser's system was socialism without socialists: the very officers, bureaucrats, and social groups that applied socialism did not believe in it and were never the faithful ideologues he envisioned. It was a heavily securitizing form of state capitalism, where the single ruling party imposed entrenched surveillance over its managers and submissive workforce alike. As soon as Nasser abruptly died, fake socialists hurried to break loose from the entangled circuits of securitization by fleeing the one ruling party, dismembering it, and dismantling state capitalism as whole.

After the 1967 defeat by Israel, the army politically and economically fell from grace. Demilitarizing the nation then seemed possible. Nasser's successor and the second military president of the country, Sadat, took radical steps to reprofessionalize the army, marginalize the officers in politics, and reduce their economic influence. He redirected them to focus on war efforts in order to retain the land that was lost in the defeat. Every time an officer retired from civil service, Sadat appointed a civilian instead of him. Moreover, the army's economic control over the public sector declined when Sadat fully and swiftly reversed Nasser's socialism and liberalized the economy by applying the "open door" (*infitah*) policy. He privatized parts of the state-owned enterprises that officers had managed, and the army now had to share influence with a rising community of crony capitalists. Overall, after Egypt fought its last war against Israel in 1973 and signed a peace treaty with it in 1979, the army almost lost its importance and relevance in society.

Nonetheless, the army quickly managed to overcome these hard times, return to its hegemonic place within the state, and resume its efforts of militarizing the country under the third military president of the country, Mubarak. It successfully managed to reposition itself within a partially liberalized economy to invade old and new spaces of influence. Field Marshal Abdel-Halim Abu Ghazala, Mubarak's first defense minister and charismatic politician, made the military the most powerful institution in the state through U.S. arms, ties with oil-producing Arabian Gulf states, and, more importantly, civilian businesses. Throughout the 1980s Abu Ghazala entered the domestic consumerist markets of all social classes to sell civilian goods for profit. His economic enterprises enjoyed a parastatal, superior status within these open markets, and he used conscripts as cheap or free labor. Thus Abu Ghazala's army invented new tactics of penetrating into the daily life of citizens and restoring urban surveillance and control. It did so through selling those citizens—whether rich, nouveau riche, middle class, or poor in a liberalized economy—goods and providing them with necessary services. It asserted that its primary goal was helping with economic development and the welfare of the nation. During the time of peace, Abu Ghazala turned the whole society into a large military camp, subjected to the army's constant watch and hegemony. This was only a starting point for a practice that continues until the present day.

This novel mode of postwar or peacetime militarization fundamentally expanded in the 1990s and 2000s, when the age of full-fledged neoliberalism arrived in Egypt. Mubarak had to cut public spending, but he allowed the army to expand its business empire in order to appease the officers and "coup-proof" his regime. The military did so first by embarking on a process of defense conversion, namely, converting major parts of the defense industry to target the civilian market. After that, the military embarked on new lucrative ventures, such as opening new factories for consumer or capital goods, reclaiming more commercial farms, and constructing toll highways. This was the time in which Mubarak was grooming his son Gamal to succeed him as president, and he needed to further appease the officers. For instance, within an accelerated wave of privatization, the military "seized" many of the privatized state-owned enterprises. Meanwhile, military entrepreneurs forged new alliances with the local business elite and foreign capital. When Mubarak's authoritarian regime was infamous for clientelism, the military entrepreneurs formed their own patron-client relations with favored private businesses. Thus a class of "neoliberal officers" was born to invade more consumer markets for legal or illicit profit and extend their invisible daily gaze over more urban vicinities.

Furthermore, Mubarak appointed retired generals in numerous bureaucratic positions in control of the regime's liberalized economy. While former army officers occupied high positions in almost every part of the country, they preferred certain locations where influence and wealth were concentrated. Generals coming from the ground forces were mostly appointed as governors of provinces, directors of small towns, or heads of both the wealthy and the poor but highly populated districts in Cairo. Military engineers dominated the ministry of housing and its various authorities, mainly responsible for allocating state land and construction of social housing. And ex-air force pilots controlled the sector of civil aviation, from the position of minister to chairman of affiliated holding companies. Ex-navy rear admirals and admirals controlled the maritime transport sector as they were appointed heads of all the country's sea and Nile ports, as well as chairmen of government authorities of the Suez Canal, maritime navigation and safety and relevant state-owned holding companies. These officers securitized the public sphere in a troubled neoliberal milieu. They kept a close eye over a society marred by social disparities and simmering with discontent. Most of these retired officers were evidently contributors to the fallacies of Mubarak's neoliberalism and autocratic regime that eventually collapsed under public rage in 2011.

When the 2011 uprisings broke out, a public attempt at demilitarizing the nation shortly failed. The same protests that took down Mubarak's regime targeted the militarization of civilian spaces in the country. The long-entrenched system of military privileges almost fell apart. The Supreme Council of Armed Forces assumed power and disseminated self-congratulatory propaganda about saving the nation from Mubarak. But it soon found itself in a difficult position where it faced numerous labor strikes and sit-ins in military enterprises as well as government offices that ex-generals controlled to demand long-denied rights or call for general demilitarization. Nevertheless, the officers once more quickly weathered this challenging wave of change. They switched alliances to the wealthy Islamists and delivered power to a Muslim Brothers president. Shortly afterward, the newly appointed minister of defense, al-Sisi, decided to capitalize on the mass protests that erupted against the economically failed and politically repressive government of the brothers in the summer of 2013 to overthrow their president. The army produced more propaganda about saving the nation again from another autocratic regime, and a year later al-Sisi swept presidential elections. During these eventful three years, the military managed to further expand its business enterprises and appropriate more bureaucratic positions, and hence optimized its uninterrupted urban surveillance and subsequent control over the manipulated and quelled masses.

When the Egyptian Army succeeded in fully retaining power after the "Arab Spring" uprisings that spread across the region in 2011, it stood among a few Arab militaries that managed to remain intact and keep its hegemonic status within the postrevolutionary state. In other neighboring states that witnessed mass unrest, especially Libya, Syria, and Yemen, military institutions not only lost their command over the political and economic affairs of their authoritarian regime but also faced severe factionalism or full dismantling. In Egypt, on the contrary, the aging military autocrat was overthrown, but his army stayed fully intact and shortly reinstated the ancien régime.

In fact, the military regime since then has deployed a novel form of militarization, by using counterterrorism rhetoric toward the population's consented control. Upon the overthrow of the Muslim Brothers president, an unprecedented wave of terrorist operations plagued the country, especially in Sinai to target military units and kill dozens of soldiers. The Egyptian military has adopted the tactics of the war on terror that were already used by the U.S. and Israeli armies to control cities such as Baghdad or Gaza. Stephen Graham asserts that with the global war on terror, Western armies introduced new mechanisms of urban militarism in which warfare is no longer limited to symmetric battles but includes the securitization of life as a whole. Graham explains:

> The current "transformation" in the military thinking and practice is the shift from the "battlefield" to "battlespace." . . . The concept of battlespace encompasses everything from the molecular scales of genetic engineering . . . through the everyday sites, spaces, and experiences of city life, to the planetary spheres inner and outer space or the internet's globe-straddling "cyberspace." . . . U.S. commanders in Baghdad have emphasized the need to coordinate the entire "battle-space" of the city, addressing civilian infrastructure, the shattered economy and cultural awareness, as well as "the controlled application of violence," in order to try and secure the city.[1]

In Egypt's war on terror, the army that already had securitized the country in the past few decades now has new justifications to turn the entirety of the Egyptian citizens' lives into a "battlespace." In the name of fighting domestic terrorism, the army accumulated more profit and repressive power.

Less than a month after electing a new military president in the summer of 2014, the Egyptian middle and lower classes woke up to the dreadful news of sudden increases in the prices of basic goods. On a hot Ramadan day, the government significantly reduced food and gas subsidies and followed this by raising electricity bills. To make things worse, al-Sisi refused to respond to ongoing labor strikes demanding a minimum wage because of the acute budget deficit, and a court verdict later decided to send striking employees to early retirement for violating shari'a law, which entails obedience to the authorities. Meanwhile, al-Sisi approved an increase of LE8.3 billion to the military's budget in fiscal year 2014–15 and another increase of LE4 billion in the following year, and raised military pensions by 25 percent. Furthermore, new laws granted additional tax breaks to hundreds of military commercial properties, such as hotels, sea resorts, and shopping malls, and the new president hired more retired generals in top civilian positions across the offices of his government. Economic conditions in the country grew much worse than they were after the 2011 uprisings. Thus, in a charitable move to alleviate the sufferings of the needy citizens, the military sold cheap foodstuffs from the produce of its expansive farms and distributed tens of thousands of free food boxes in villages and Cairo's slums.[2]

In 2015, ex-generals headed the public authorities of industrial development, agricultural development, import and export control, maritime transport, railways, sea and Nile ports, and the Suez Canal, to name only a few. The crucial positions of minister of transportation, chair of the national Telecommunication Holding Company, and chair of the Maritime and Land Transport Holding Company were all occupied by other ex-generals. When a new cabinet was hired later in the year, the new civilian premier inherited an ex-military top official from his two predecessors to help pick the new ministers of his government.[3] Meanwhile, military contractors continued to function as gigantic parastatal entities that took charge of executing public construction projects of bridges, roads, hospitals, schools, affordable housing, sporting clubs, and so forth. Around the same time, the military obtained about 4,000 square meters for land reclamation and commercial farming in the western desert, and another 40,000 square meters to build four gas stations in Upper Egypt.[4] Al-Sisi issued a law to exempt a list of 574 military premises from the real estate tax, including supermarkets, hotels, sea resorts, movie theaters, and apartment buildings. He issued another law to authorize the Ministry of Defense to establish private security firms, and a third law authorizing the Ministry of Military Production to open its own contracting firm.[5]

The military institution's urban control brought about reoccurring maladministration crises. When the second largest city in the country, Alexandria, was disastrously flooded by heavy rain in the autumn of 2015, al-Sisi immediately sacked its newly appointed civilian governor upon receiving a military intelligence report evaluating the situation from the Northern Command based in the city.[6] However, the seven ex-generals and colonels heading Alexandria's populous districts went untouched. In fact, the previous governor of the city was another ex-general who once claimed that he spent around LE9 billion to develop the sewerage and rainwater drainage systems in the city. But the regime had to sack the ex-general chairing the public water and sewerage holding company in the city and replaced him with yet another retired general.[7] While planning a protest against these ex-officers, Alexandrian youth openly discussed on Facebook their fear of being arrested and jailed under the antiprotest law and eventually had to cancel the protest.[8]

Under such militarism, the country's existing economic crisis is growing acutely worse. The ruling officers have so far adopted ambivalent policies regarding which economic model to follow. On the one hand, al-Sisi imposes a state and military upper hand in running the economy by initiating grand national projects and maintaining traditional government support for the lower classes, à la Nasser's socialist model. On the other hand, he pursues the IMF's market reforms by gradually eliminating subsidies and stimulating local and foreign private capital, following Mubarak's neoliberal footsteps. Deploying an ultranationalistic discourse, al-Sisi aspires to revive Nasser's socialist state under military control, and yet he is in dire need of local and foreign capital that only thrives in a liberalized market. On the side of leading an interventionist state, al-Sisi has invested in mega national projects that consume the country's limited resources and are unlikely to generate substantial income in return, such as digging an extension of the Suez Canal or building a new administrative capital outside Cairo. On the other side of running a laissez passé state, al-Sisi's laws on private investments meant to stimulate foreign capital are still uncrystallized and controversial. The Egyptian pound has been drastically devalued, prices of basic goods have skyrocketed, unemployment rates have further increased, and foreign investors have not yet arrived in the country.[9] Meanwhile, the military continues to distribute tens of thousands of charitable food boxes to the needy and hold soup kitchens to feed the poor from its own products during religious occasions.[10]

Contemporary Egyptian intellectuals and economists criticize this unclear situation. For example, Galal Amin highlights the lack of social justice in the regime's policies, by commenting on the kind of investments that al-Sisi drew during the festivities of the above-mentioned economic conference. Amin points out that they were mostly projects in real estate, such as building new, upscale suburbs around Cairo that are funded by Arabian Gulf capital. Amin asserts that economic development in a "hungry country" is far from being the same as real estate development for the consumption of the country's upper class.[11] Mahmoud Abd al-Fadil inquires about whether al-Sisi could be another "modified version" of Nasser, as many lower classes initially assumed or hoped before electing him president. Abd al-Fadil asserts that al-Sisi's government's focus on mega projects is a part of adopting neoliberal visions about how wealth would trickle down from rich investors to poor consumers, and he debunks these visions. He explains that al-Sisi's state ignores other crucial areas of investment that Nasser gave most of his attention to, especially fostering the public sector. Al-Sisi also does not apply centralized planning in the agricultural sector, which suffers from severe dilemmas, as Abd al-Fadil asserts.[12]

As soon as he assumed office, al-Sisi called on the Egyptian masses to contribute to an ambitious project of digging a "New Suez Canal." National banks issued investment certificates to sell to thousands of patriotic citizens standing in long lines and succeeded in collecting LE64 billion (around $9 billion) to fund the project. Ex–vice admiral Muhab Mamish, head of the Suez Canal Authority, enthusiastically asserted in various media that the project should increase the canal's annual revenue to LE200 billion in five years ($28 billion), by LE40 billion per year ($5.5 billion).[13] Al-Sisi ordered completion of the project within only one year, rather than five years according to the original plan, which required tapping into the country's limited reserves of foreign currency to pay the international contractors executing it. In the following year, only two months after opening its new extension in lavish festivities, Mamish announced that the canal's revenue declined due to the slower traffic in international trade.[14] The canal's revenue declined from $5.4 billion in 2014 to $5.1 billion in 2015.[15] Meanwhile, the Egyptian central bank revealed its crisis of dollar shortage and had to drastically devalue the Egyptian pound. Prices of food and basic goods immediately soared, outraging the middle and lower classes. The head of the central bank was sacked after he stated that the new canal project had consumed huge quantities of his bank's foreign currency to be accomplished at such high speed.[16]

Public discontent about soaring prices along with the government's policy of gradual elimination of subsidies was instantly reflected in the ongoing parliamentary elections. Al-Sisi had been ruling without an elected parliament for almost two years, and these long-awaited elections should have formed a council to review the hundreds of laws that he issued using his temporary legislative authority.[17] In spite of al-Sisi's televised speech stimulating them to cast their votes, Egyptian voters across social classes and geographical areas showed considerable apathy toward these elections and the turnout was shockingly low. Many liberal and leftist political parties that struggled with legal constraints had withdrawn from the elections, leaving it to the pro-Sisi candidates, who included many ex-generals, business cronies, and wealthy rural notables. An ex-general led the well-funded electoral list

"For the Love of Egypt," which swept the polls,[18] and more than fifty ex-officers from both the army and police won seats.[19]

Al-Sisi held an international economic conference in order to declare the country open again for foreign investment. It was a big party to which he invited important world leaders, including the IMF's director Christine Lagarde. At a packed hall, Lagarde delivered an uplifting speech in which she praised the reform process that al-Sisi had initiated immediately after coming to the presidency, which included reducing energy and food subsidies and raising taxes. She enthusiastically declared that Egypt's "journey to higher growth started."[20] Secretary of State John Kerry of the United States also attended the party and delivered a small speech asserting that America was committed to supporting these reforms. As soon as Kerry returned to Washington, D.C., the United States shipped the military equipment that was long due to Egypt and was suspended for almost two years after al-Sisi overthrew the brotherhood.[21] At the same economic conference, Arabian Gulf states showered the country with a total of $12 billion to be deposited in the Egyptian central bank and invested in large projects. Among the generous donors were Saudi Arabia and the United Arab Emirates, and the latter effortlessly assisted Cairo in undertaking market reforms following Dubai's model.[22] What Lagarde, Kerry, and the oil-rich attendees of the conference did not notice, or chose to ignore, was the overwhelming militarization of the Egyptian economy and society.

Evidently, there is a pressing need to demilitarize Egypt. But is this a feasible process within the current domestic milieu?

Scholars who have discussed the possibility of taking the Egyptian military out of politics mainly emphasize the necessity of altering the very nature of the existing political system in order to guarantee civilian, democratic control over the army. For example, Philippe Droz-Vincent indicates that the current system is highly dependent on the military as a supposedly neutral actor and the only legitimate arbiter to mediate civilian differences and enable ruling coalitions. Thus he asserts that "civilianizing" the state in Egypt requires security sector reforms that should be strongly intertwined with political reforms to change the regime's character as a whole. "Security sector reforms have to be related to the political processes needed to put them into effect. . . . True civilianization will begin when ruling Egypt is no longer conditional on the military's acquiescence or convening a ruling coalition, or on ideas related to the role of the military as the savior of Egypt, but on such civilian political processes as elections, parties, and coalitions," Droz-Vincent affirms.[23]

Robert Springborg suggests three potential scenarios to demilitarize the Egyptian state. He argues that Egypt now has a system of "delegative authoritarianism" similar to what existed in many Latin American states in the past. Al-Sisi did enjoy a substantial degree of popularity, and a considerable segment of the citizens unconditionally delegated their authority to him on various occasions. For example, when he appealed to the masses to "delegate" him to fight a wave of terrorism resulting from deposing the brotherhood in 2013, tens of millions positively responded through demonstrations across the country. When he ran for president a year later, he swept the election. Springborg explains that al-Sisi practices decision-making with autonomy because he perceives himself as the "embodiment of the nation and the main custodian and definer of its interests."[24] Al-Sisi prefers to address the masses personally by using emotional and religious speeches and shows disinterest in state institutions, political parties, or NGOs. Springborg asserts that the international system prefers to sustain al-Sisi's regime to other, more chaotic options. Springborg envisions three different scenarios to terminate such a situation. The first is another coup by displeased officers. The second is another "coup-volution," or events similar to those of 2011 that would urge the military to save the nation again and form new political alliances with civilian forces. The third is a real revolution.[25]

I argue here that in order to demilitarize Egypt, three main steps need to be considered. First, divesting the Egyptian military of its business enterprises is an essential requirement for civilianizing the state—albeit this might not be a near possibility. The entrenched economic interests of the military institution provide it with both incentives and resources to uphold political hegemony. As this book has explained, not only did the military own a business empire under Mubarak, but also ex-officers occupied key civilian positions in control of the economy in the state apparatus and ran them in a way that facilitated and enhanced military economic interests. During the few years that followed the deposing of Mubarak, the military forged variant political alliances toward imposing an upper hand on the political system, which guaranteed protecting and further expanding its economic interests. The autonomous profit that the army makes away from public accountability has enabled it to co-opt media, political parties, and nongovernmental organizations and devise costly propaganda campaigns to resume full power.

Divestiture is undoubtedly required to reduce the military's domination over the economically subordinate civilian forces.

If the Egyptian military is divested of commercial activities, it will follow a global trend that many other militaries have lately adopted. When the Egyptian military decided to invest in for-profit economic enterprises three decades ago, it followed an already spreading global trend in which the militaries of states such as Russia, China, Brazil, Pakistan, and many others in eastern European, Latin America, and Asia developed business interests. The end of the Cold War rendered the market economy a global model for all former socialist and postcommunist states to follow, and economic liberalization measures required substantial cuts in public spending—including in military budgets. Many transforming regimes allowed their military institutions to create business enterprises that compensated for their financial losses and helped avoid officers' mutinies. Thus the phenomenon of military business, or Milbus, was born as a means to appease the military and coup-proof liberalizing governments. The Egyptian military joined this trend from the 1990s onward, when it converted large segments of its defense industry to civilian production and ventured into new commercial projects. However, as military business distorted market reforms, turned into burdens on economic development, and increased the political influence of the officers in many areas, another trend toward divestiture soon emerged—but Egypt has not joined it yet.

An early and prominent example of a state that succeeded in divesting its military of business is China. The People's Liberation Army created commercial enterprises during the economic reform period in the 1980s, and the civilian leadership already ordered it out of business by the end of the 1990s. The PLA's business conglomerates took part in almost every sector of the Chinese economy, but they enjoyed tax breaks and other perks and were marred by corruption, smuggling, and profiteering problems. The ruling Communist Party launched a divestiture campaign in 1998, and the PLA immediately responded and gave up its enterprises except for some that it kept for national security or social reasons.[26] Another successful example in Latin America is Argentina, where its military liquidated its business in the mid-1990s. Under the last military dictatorship in Argentina (1976–1983), military businesses in civilian strategic sectors reached their peak, but they were similarly suffering from corruption and inefficacy. The state privatized military business after transitioning to democracy and neoliberalism.[27]

Other, less successful examples exist, such as Indonesia. The military in Indonesia has been heavily involved in commercial activities for long decades, also with deep problems of corruption, mismanagement, and lack of transparency. Government measures for divestiture in the 2000s failed to dismantle the military business empire, along with a failed attempt at civilian control of the armed forces.[28]

It seems highly unlikely that the Egyptian officers today would respond to calls for divestiture, especially under a president who is placing no pressure on them to do so. Recently, the Egyptian military has viciously rejected public criticism of its economic activities. In a press conference in 2012, the vice minister of defense for financial affairs and SCAF member General Mahmud Nasr pledged to "fight" to protect the armed forces' business. Nasr asserted: "Our money does not belong to the state; it is the sweat of the ministry of defense from the revenue of its enterprises. . . . We will not allow the state to intervene in it. . . . We will fight for our economic enterprises and we will not quit this battle. We will not leave our thirty-year sweat for somebody else to ravage it, and we will not allow anybody to come near the armed forces' projects."[29]

The second step is curbing the financial support that the military regime receives from conservative Arab Gulf states to sustain itself. Fearing the ideological expansion of the Muslim Brotherhood into the Gulf states after it took power in Egypt and other post–Arab Spring states, oil-producing UAE and Saudi Arabia generously funded the Egyptian military's efforts to overthrow the brothers and rebuild a new military regime. For instance, UAE donated $4.9 billion to the al-Sisi-led interim government between mid-2013 and mid-2014 but stipulated that the military should take charge of managing these funds to cover the needs of the Egyptian people. Thus military contractors used them in new public construction projects such as building public schools, hospitals, and social housing. The head of the military engineers, General Tahir Abd Allah, indicated that the Emiratis said, "We will support the Egyptian people but through the army. If the people want a hospital, the armed forces will build it."[30] In al-Sisi's international economic development conference of early 2015, UAE, Saudi Arabia, and Kuwait each pledged $4 billion to support the Egyptian economy. Moreover, UAE hired private consultants to help Egypt develop its private sector.[31] Civilianizing the Egyptian state requires eliminating the influence of these conservative rich states over the country's domestic politics.

Finally, the military regime counts on the support of foreign states and international organizations for sustenance, and it is necessary to limit such support. The most important foreign backer of al-Sisi's regime now is Russia, which recently concluded arms deals worth billions of dollars with Egypt. The regime is in dire need of such ties with Russia in order to overcome tense relations with the United States and delays in American military aid. France similarly supports the regime with costly procurement. Another crucial international backer is the IMF. An IMF mission visited Egypt in September 2015 and praised the applied economic reforms, including cutting subsidies, but pointed out high unemployment, fiscal deficit, and shortage in foreign currency reserves that would last the country for only three months of imports. The mission concluded its visit by stating that the IMF "will be ready to support Egypt and its people in any way that is useful," [32] and soon afterward the regime initiated negotiations with the fund over a package of financial aid.[33] Such aid will only prolong the military regime's ability to endure simmering discontent and evolving unrest.

As Egypt today faces one acute crisis after the other, demilitarizing the nation seems more necessary than ever. Taking the Egyptian military out of the economy and recivilianizing the state is an indispensable part of a postrevolutionary transition to actual democracy that goes beyond manipulated ballot boxes. Whereas the hegemonic privileges that the army currently enjoys render any attempt at demilitarization an impossible process, simmering public discontent and unfolding unrest might push for military concessions in the future.

Appendix

TABLE I

Size of the Egyptian Armed Forces, 1965–2015

Year	Active						Reserves					Population
	Total	Army	Navy	Air Force	Air Defense command	Para-military*	Total	Army	Navy	Air Force	Air Defense command	
1965–66	180,000	150,000	11,000	10,000–15,000					5,000			29,000,000
1966–67	190,000	160,000	11,000	15,000				120,000	5,000	3,000–4,000		30,000,000
1967–68	180,000	140,000	11,000	15,000				60,000	5,000	4,000		31,000,000
1968–69	211,000	180,000	12,000	15,000		90,000 national guard only		100,000	5,000	4,000		31,500,000
1969–70	207,000	180,000	12,000	15,000		90,000 national guard only		100,000	5,000	4,000		32,100,000
1970–71	288,000	250,000	14,000	20,000		90,000 national guard only						33,000,000
1971–72	318,000	275,000	14,000	25,000		120,000 national guard only						34,150,000

Year										Total
1972–73	325,000	285,000	15,000	25,000		100,000				34,900,000
1973–74	298,000	260,000	15,000	23,000		100,000	500,000	14,000	20,000	35,700,000
1974–75	323,000	280,000	15,000	28,000		100,000	500,000	14,000	20,000	36,000,000
1975–76	322,500	275,000	17,500	30,000			500,000	15,000	20,000	37,520,000
1976–77	342,000	295,000	17,500	30,000		120,000	500,000	15,000		38,040,000
1977–78	345,000	300,000	20,000	25,000		50,000	500,000	15,000		38,880,000
1978–79	395,000	350,000	20,000	25,000		50,000	500,000			39,760,000
1979–80	395,000	350,000	20,000	25,000		50,000	500,000	15,000		40,460,000
1980–81	367,000	320,000	20,000	27,000		49,000	500,000	15,000		44,465,918
1981–82	367,000	235,000	20,000	27,000	85,000	139,000	300,000	15,000	20,000	45,610,430
	180,000	180,000	15,000	10,000	50,000					
	con	con**	con	con	con					
1982–83	452,000	320,000	20,000	27,000	85,000	139,000	300,000	15,000	20,000	46,807,221
	255,000	180,000	15,000	10,000	50,000					
	con	con	con	con	con					
1983–84	447,000	315,000	20,000	27,000	85,000	139,000	300,000	15,000	20,000	48,061,546
	255,000	180,000	15,000	10,000	50,000					
	con	con	con	con	con					
1985–86	445,000	320,000	20,000	25,000	80,000	139,000	323,000	15,000	12,000	50,748,187
	250,000	180,000	10,000	10,000	50,000		380,000		30,000	
	con	con	con	con	con					
1986–87	445,000	320,000	20,000	25,000	80,000	439,000	500,000	14,000	20,000	52,173,840
	250,000	180,000	10,000	10,000	50,000	300,000	604,000		70,000	
	con	con	con	con	con	CSF				

(continued)

TABLE I (*continued*)

Year	Active						Reserves					Population
	Total	Army	Navy	Air Force	Air Defense command	Para-military*	Total	Army	Navy	Air Force	Air Defense command	
1987–88	445,000	320,000	20,000	25,000	80,000	439,000	604,000	500,000	14,000	20,000	70,000	53,617,678
	250,000	180,000	10,000	10,000	50,000	300,000						
	con	con	con	con	con	CSF						
1988–89	445,000	320,000	20,000	25,000	80,000	379,000	604,000	500,000	14,000	20,000	70,000	55,035,937
	250,000	180,000	10,000	10,000	50,000	300,000						
	con	con	con	con	con	CSF						
1989–90	448,000	320,000	18,000	30,000	80,000	374,000	604,000	500,000	14,000	20,000	70,000	56,397,273
	250,000	180,000	10,000	10,000	50,000	300,000						
	con	con	con	con	con	CSF						
1991–92	420,000	290,000	20,000	30,000	80,000	374,000	604,000	500,000	14,000	20,000	70,000	58,922,018
	252,000	180,000	12,000	10,000	50,000	300,000						
	con	con	con	con	con	CSF						
1992–93	410,000	290,000	20,000	30,000	70,000	374,000	604,000	500,000	14,000	20,000	70,000	60,108,373
	252,000	180,000	12,000	10,000	50,000	300,000						
	con	con	con	con	con	CSF						
1993–94	430,000	310,000	20,000	30,000	70,000	374,000	304,000	200,000	14,000	20,000	70,000	61,272,847
	272,000	200,000	12,000	10,000	50,000	300,000						
	con	con	con	con	con	CSF						

Year											
1994–95	440,000	310,000	20,000	30,000	80,000	374,000	254,000	150,000	14,000	20,000	70,000	62,434,527
	272,000	200,000	12,000	10,000	50,000	300,000					
	con	con	con	con	con	CSF					
1995–96	436,000	310,000	16,000	30,000	80,000	174,000	254,000	150,000	14,000	20,000	70,000	63,595,629
	222,000	200,000	12,000	10,000	50,000	100,000					
	con	con	con	con	con	CSF					
1996–97	440,000	310,000	20,000	30,000	80,000	232,000	254,000	150,000	14,000	20,000	70,000	64,754,566
	272,000	200,000	12,000	10,000	50,000	150,000					
	con	con	con	con	con	CCFS					
1997–98	450,000	320,000	20,000	30,000	80,000	230,000	254,000	150,000	14,000	20,000	70,000	65,922,626
	320,000	250,000	10,000	10,000	50,000	150,000					
	con	con	con	con	con	CSF					
1998–99	450,000	320,000	20,000	30,000	80,000	230,000	254,000	150,000	14,000	20,000	70,000	67,112,877
	320,000	250,000	10,000	10,000	50,000	150,000					
	con	con	con	con	con	CSF					
1999–00	450,000	320,000	20,000	30,000	80,000	230,000	254,000	150,000	14,000	20,000	70,000	68,334,905
	320,000	250,000	10,000	10,000	50,000	150,000					
	con	con	con	con	con	CSF					
2000–2001	448,500	320,000	18,500	30,000	80,000	230,000	254,000	150,000	14,000	20,000	70,000	69,599,945
	322,000	250,000	12,000	10,000	50,000	150,000					
	con	con	con	con	con	CSF					
2001–02	443,000	320,000	19,000	29,000	75,000	325,000	254,000	150,000	14,000	20,000	70,000	70,908,710
	322,000	250,000	12,000	10,000	50,000	250,000					
	con	con	con	con	con	CSF					

(continued)

TABLE I (continued)

	Active						Reserves					
Year	Total	Army	Navy	Air Force	Air Defense command	Para-military*	Total	Army	Navy	Air Force	Air Defense command	Population
2002–03	443,000	320,000	19,000	29,000	75,000	330,000	254,000	150,000	14,000	20,000	70,000	72,247,626
	322,000	250,000	12,000	10,000	50,000	250,000						
	con	con	con	con	con	CSF						
2003–04	450,000	320,000	20,000	30,000	80,000	330,000	410,000	300,000	20,000	20,000	70,000	73,596,068
	322,000	250,000	12,000	10,000	50,000	250,000						
	con	con	con	con	con	CSF						
2004–05	450,000	320,000	20,000	30,000	80,000	330,000	410,000	300,000	20,000	20,000	70,000	74,942,115
	322,000	250,000	12,000	10,000	50,000	250,000						
	con	con	con	con	con	CSF						
2005–06	468,500	340,000	18,500	30,000	80,000	330,000	479,000	375,000	14,000	20,000	70,000	76,274,285
		190,000–	10,000	10,000	50,000	325,000						
		220,000	con	con	con	CSF						
		con										
2006	468,500	340,000	18,500	30,000	80,000	397,000	479,000	375,000	14,000	20,000	70,000	76,274,285
		190,000–	10,000	10,000	50,000	325,000						
		220,000	con	con	con	CSF						
		con										
2007	468,500	340,000	18,500	30,000	80,000	397,000	479,000	375,000	14,000	20,000	70,000	77,605,327
		190,000–	10,000	10,000	50,000	325,000						
		220,000	con	con	con	CSF						
		con										

2008	468,500	340,000 190,000–220,000 con	18,500 10,000 con	30,000 10,000 con	80,000 50,000 con	397,000 325,000 CSF	479,000	375,000	14,000	20,000	70,000	78,976,122
2009	468,500	340,000 190,000–220,000 con	18,500 10,000 con	30,000 10,000 con	80,000 50,000 con	397,000 325,000 CSF	479,000	375,000	14,000	20,000	70,000	80,442,443
2010	468,500	340,000 190,000–220,000 con	18,500 10,000 con	30,000 10,000 con	80,000 50,000 con	397,000 325,000 CSF	479,000	375,000	14,000	20,000	70,000	82,040,994
2011	468,500	340,000 190,000–220,000 con	18,500 10,000 con	30,000 10,000 con	80,000 80,000 con	397,000 325,000 CSF	479,000	375,000	14,000	20,000	70,000	83,787,634
2012	438,500	310,000 190,000–220,000 con	18,500 10,000 con	30,000 10,000 con	80,000 80,000 con	397,000 325,000 CSF	479,000	375,000	14,000	20,000	70,000	85,660,902
2013	438,500	310,000 190,000–220,000 con	18,500 10,000 con	30,000 10,000 con	80,000 80,000 con	397,000 325,000 CSF	479,000	375,000	14,000	20,000	70,000	87,613,909

(continued)

TABLE I (*continued*)

	Active						Reserves					Population
Year	Total	Army	Navy	Air Force	Air Defense command	Para-military*	Total	Army	Navy	Air Force	Air Defense command	
2014	438,500	310,000 190,000–220,000 con	18,500 10,000 con	30,000 10,000 con	80,000 80,000 con	397,000 325,000 CSF	479,000	375,000	14,000	20,000	70,000	89,579,670
2015	438,500	310,000 190,000–220,000 con	18,500 10,000 con	30,000 10,000 con	80,000 80,000 con	397,000 325,000 CSF	479,000	375,000	14,000	20,000	70,000	90,000,000 (estimate)

*Paramilitary includes Central Security Forces (CSF), National Guard, Frontier Corps, and Coast Guard.

**con = conscripts

Sources: The Military Balance (London: International Institute for Strategic Studies, 1965–2015); World Bank, Population Index 1981–2014, http://data.worldbank.org/indicator/SP.POP.TOTL.

TABLE 2

Egyptian Military Expenditure, 1950–2015

Fiscal Year	Amount in LE Million	Amount in USD Million	Percentage of GNP	Percentage of Government Budget
1950–51	108.9		3.9	
1951–52	132.1		4.7	
1952–53	126.6		4.9	
1953–54	166.3		5.7	
1955–56	258.2		8.4	
1957–58	189.8		5.5	
1959–60	220.5		6.1	
1960–61	294.3		7.6	
1961–62	315.3		7.1	
1963–64	324.4		8.5	
1965–66	475.5		11.0	
1967	645.0		12.7	
1968	690.0		12.5	
1969	805.0		13.0	
1970	1,262.0		19.0	
1971	1,495.0		21.7	
1972	1,510.0	1,245		
1973	4,071.0	2,270	31.0	
1974	6,103.0	2,716	22.8	
1975	4,859.0	2,864		
1976	4,365.0		37.0	
1976–77		2,579	22.8	38
1977–78		2,927		40.4
1978–79		2,305		29.6
1979–80		2,044		22.5
1980–81		2,279		19.7
1981–82		3,673		14
1982–83		2,321		22
1983–84		2,281		22
1984–85		2,589		23
1985–86		2,583		22
1986–87		2,462		19.5
1987–88		2,539		22
1988–89	3,873	2,129		16.9
1989–90	3,926	1,335		10.7
1990–91	5,042	1,468		10

(continued)

TABLE 2 (*continued*)

Fiscal Year	Amount in LE Million	Amount in USD Million	Percentage of GNP	Percentage of Government Budget
1991–92	5,766	1,599		10
1992–93	6,624	1,710		8.5
1993–94	6,982	1,816		9
1994–95	7,621	2,243		9
1995–96	8,267	2,442		13.5
1996–97	7,765	2,280		
1997–98	9,240	2,717		
1998–99	9,638	2,818		10.5
1999–2000	10,124	2,955		10.1
2000–01	11,569	3,324		10.5
2001–02	12,148	3,116		9.8
2002–03	13,333	2,842		9.3
2003–04	14,563	2,389		9.0
2004–05	14,804	2,380		8.3
2005–06	15,621	2,678		8.3
2006–07	17,330	2,993		7.9
2007–08	19,197	3,317		6.9
2008–09	21,718	4,048		6.0
2009–10	22,831	4,053		6.8
2010–11	25,397	4,425		6.1
2011–12	25,480	4,259		5.9
2012–13	27,592	4,525		4.5
2013–14	30,947	4,320		4.5
2014–15	39,276	5,478		4.8
2015–16	43,205	5,645		4.9

Sources: Stockholm International Peace Research Institute (SIPRI), *SIPRI Military Expenditure Database* (1988–2005), http://www.sipri.org/databases; *The Military Balance* (London: International Institute for Strategic Studies, 1965–2015); Egyptian Ministry of Finance (2006–2016), http://www.mof.gov.eg/; U.S. Department of State, *World Military Expenditures and Arms Transfers 1972–1982, 1985, 1989, 1990, 1991–1992, 1996*, http://www.state.gov/t/avc/rls/rpt/wmeat/; Samer Soliman, *The Autumn of Dictatorship: Fiscal Crisis and Political Change in Egypt Under Mubarak* (Stanford: Stanford University Press, 2011), 62; currency exchange calculator, http://www.oanda.com/.

TABLE 3

Maritime Transport Sector

Port(s)	Years	Chairman
Suez Canal Authority	1996–2012	Ahmad Fadil (vice admiral, former commander of navy)
	2012–14	Muhab Mimmish (vice admiral, former commander of navy)
Maritime Transport Sector— umbrella for all seaports below	2001	Muhammad Muhsin al-Masri (rear admiral)
	2002–04	'Isam Badawi (rear admiral)
	2004–06	Shirin Hasan (rear admiral)
	2006–08	Mukhtar 'Ammar (rear admiral)
	2008–09	Hisham al-Sirsawi (rear admiral)
	2009–11	Abd al-Hamid Tawfiq Abu Jundiyya (rear admiral)
	2011	'Isam Abd al-Mun'im (rear admiral)
	2012	al-Sayyid Hamid Hidaya (rear admiral)
	2013	Muhammad Abd al-Qadir Jab Allah (rear admiral)
Alexandria Ports Authority (2 ports)	2001–03	Muhammad Faraj Lutfi (rear admiral)
	2004–07	Ibrahim Yusuf (rear admiral)
	2007–09	Abd al-Hamid Tawfiq Abu Jundiyya (rear admiral)
	2009–10	Nabil Hilmi (rear admiral)
	2008–11	'Isam Abd al-Mun'im (rear admiral)
	2011	al-Sayyid Hamid Hidaya (rear admiral)
Damietta Port Authority	2002–05	Ibrahim Yusuf (rear admiral)
	2005–06	Mukhtar 'Ammar (rear admiral)
	2006–07	Abd al-Hamid Tawfiq Abu Jundiyya (rear admiral)
	2007–09	Husayn Harmil (rear admiral)
	2009–11	al-Sayyid Hamid Hidaya (rear admiral)
	2011–12	Ibrahim Fulayfil (rear admiral)
	2013	Musta 'Amir (rear admiral)
	2014	Abd al-Qadir Darwish (rear admiral)
Port Said Ports Authority (3 ports)	2004	Mukhtar 'Ammar (vice chairman)
	2006	Shirin Hasan (rear admiral)
	2008	Hisham al-Sirsawi (rear admiral)
	2008–12	Ibrahim Siddiq (rear admiral)
	2012–14	Ahmad Najib Sharaf (rear admiral)

(continued)

TABLE 3 *(continued)*

Port(s)	Years	Chairman
Red Sea Ports Authority (ports of 3 governorates, including Hurghada)	2003–04	Muhammad Salah al-Walili (rear admiral)
	2005–06	Mahfuz Taha (rear admiral)
	2006–08	Hishal al-Sirsawi (rear admiral)
	2008–11	Mamduh Daraz (rear admiral)
	2011–13	Muhammad Abd al-Qadir Jab Allah (rear admiral)
	2013–14	Hasan Falah (rear admiral)
Authority for Maritime Safety	1999–2002	Fu'ad Shirin Abd al-Halim (rear admiral)
	2002–05	Mustafa Tawfiq Khattab (rear admiral)
	2005–06	Husayn Jamil al-Harmil (rear admiral)
	2006–08	Mukhtar 'Ammar (supervisor while chairman of MTS)
	2008–10	Muammad 'Isam Abd al-Mun'im (rear admiral)
	2010–12	Mustafa Muhhamd 'Izz al-Din Wahba (rear admiral)
	2012–14	Ibrahim Fulayfil (rear admiral)
	2014	Tariq Ghannam (rear admiral)
River Transport Authority	2003 (or before)–2006	Samir Tawfiq (rear admiral)
	2006–12	Karim Abu al-Khayr (rear admiral)
	2013	Abd al-Qadir Darwish (rear admiral)
	2014	Mustafa 'Amir (rear admiral)
High Dam Port Authority	2010–13	Kamal al-Maghrabi (general)
	2014	As'ad Abd al-Majid (rear admiral)
Nile Valley Transport Authority (joint Egyptian-Sudanese)	2010–14	Jamal Abd Allah (civilian engineer)
	2014	Mustafa Bahri (general)

Notes

Introduction

1. Dalia 'Uthman, "al-Liwa' 'Ismat Mudir al-Kuliyya al-Harbiyya: Khirriji al-Kuliyya hum Qadat al-Mustaqbal," *al-Masry al-Youm*, 31 July 2015.

2. Nur Rashwan, "Video: Ra'is Hay'at al-Naql al-Nahri al-Muqal Bakiyan," *al-Shorouk*, 29 July 2015; 'Umar Abd al-Azizi, "al-Liwa' Isma'il Najdi Ra'is al-Hay'a al-Qawmiyya li-l-Anfaq . . . ," *al-Masry al-Youm*, 1 June 2015.

3. Sada El-balad, "Liqa' ma'a al-Liwa' Naji Fu'ad Ra'is Sharikat Queen li-Sina'at al-Makaruna," 8 January 2015, https://www.youtube.com/watch?v=lmvQ EdTEwrc; Islam Aba Zayd, "Iqbal Kabir 'ala Janah al-Intaj al-Harbi fi Awwal Ayyam Ma'rad al-Qahira li-l-Muntajat," *al-Bawaba News*, 19 March 2015.

4. Michel Foucault, *Discipline and Punish*, trans. Alan Sheridan (New York: Vintage Books, 1979), 168–72.

5. Michel Foucault, *Security, Territory, and Population*, trans. Graham Burchell (Basingstoke: Palgrave, Macmillan, 2007), 94.

6. Robert Springborg and Clement Henry, "Army Guys," *American Interest* (May/June 2011). After the uprisings its global rank fell to number 16 in 2011 and to 18 in 2015. See http://www.globalfirepower.com/countries-listing.asp, accessed 1 October 2015.

7. Nazli Madkour, "Egyptian Defense Programmes and Their Impact on Social and Economic Development of Egypt" (M.A. thesis, American University in Cairo, 1980), 192.

8. Ministry of Defense, http://www.mod.gov.eg/mod/Mod_CMC01.aspx, accessed 1 September 2015.

9. Muhammad Ahmad Tantawi, "Mudir al-Kuliyya al-Harbiyya: Ijmali al-Mutaqaddimin li-l-Kuliyyat al-'Askariyya 92 Alf Talib," *al-Youm al-Sabi'*, 26 November 2014.

10. Sali al-Kahkawi, "al-Wasta wa-Marakiz al-Ta'hil wa-l-Rashawa al-Abwab al-Maftuha li-Dukhul al-Kuliyyat al-'Askariyya Qabl al-Thawra," *al-Ahali*, 17 August 2011.

11. Walid Darwish, "al-Kuliyyat al-'Askariyya Taqbal 25 min Abna' Sina'," *al-Dustur al-Asli*, 15 November 2012.

12. "Li-l-Marra al-Thalitha fi 'Ahdih . . . al-Sisi Yuqarrir Ziyadat al-Ma'ashat al-'Askariyya bi-Nisbat 10%," *CNN Arabic*, 29 June 2015.

13. Law no. 505 of 1955 and Law no. 127 of 1980, respectively.

14. Ahmad Abd Allah, *al-Jaysh wa-l-Dimuqratiyya fi Misr* (Cairo: Dar Sina li-l-Nashr, 1990), 96–99; Judith Miller, "Cairo's Army Has a New Job: Milk the Cow," *New York Times*, 29 November 1985.

15. See, for example, Muhsin al-Bidiwi, "Ra'is al-Hay'a al-Handasiyya: Natawalla Insha' 1361 Kilo min Ijmali 3200 Kilu Turuq Jadida . . . ," *al-Youm al-Sabi'*, 22 August 2014; Mada Misr, "Imbraturiyyat al-Jaysh al-Iqtisadiyya: Da'm al-Sulta al-Hakima Yuhaddid Nufudh al-Qita' al-Khass," *Mada Masr*, 24 December 2014; Dalia 'Uthman, "Mudir Jihaz al-Khidma al-Wataniyya Yatahaddath 'an Mashru'at al-Jaysh al-Iqtisadiyya . . . ," *al-Masry al-Youm*, 6 February 2015.

16. Marwa Awad, "In Egypt's Military, a March for Change," *Reuters*, 12 April 2012.

17. Rajab Jalal, "al-Ra'is al-Mu'aqqat Yusdir Qararn Jumhuriyyan bi-Raf' Rawatib al-Mujanaddin bi-l-Jaysh," *al-Masry al-Youm*, 20 August 2013.

18. See, for instance, Jihad Abd al-Mun'im, "al-Hamla al-Sha'biyya li-l-Taw'iya bi-l-Dustur Tarfud al-Tajnid al-Ijbari," *al-Wafd*, 15 November 2014; Ahmad Muhammad Muntasir, "al-Tajnid al-Ijbari al-Misri . . . Ra's Mal al-Quwwat al-Musallaha," *al-Hiwar al-Mutamaddin*, no. 4724, 18 February 2015.

19. See Paul Amar, "Egypt as a Globalist Power: Mapping Military Participation in Decolonizing Internationalism, Repressive Entrepreneurialism, and Humanitarian Globalization Between the Revolutions of 1952 and 2011," *Globalizations* 9 (2012): 179–94.

20. Muhammad Abd al-Halim Abu Ghazala, *Al-Mushir Abu Ghazala wa-l-Sahafa* (Interviews with Minister of Defense and Military Production Abu Ghazala) (Cairo, 1996), 5–6, 13; *Al-Malaff al-Watha'iqi li-l-Mushir Muhammad 'Abd al-Halim Abu Ghazala* (Cairo: Markaz al-Ahram li-l-Tanzim wa-l-Microfilm, 1981–1989), part 1, 30–47.

21. *Al-Malaff al-Watha'iqi li-l-Mushir Muhammad 'Abd al-Halim Abu Ghazala*, part 2, 431, 426.

22. Ahmad Abd al-Khaliq, "al-Qwwuat al-Musallaha Tahtafil bi-Tafawwuq al-Hay'a al-Handasiyya," *al-Ahram al-Masa'i*, 31 October 2010.

23. Abu Zayd Kamal al-Din, "Wazir al-Difa': al-Quwwat al-Musallaha Milk al-Sha'b wa-Sanad li-l-Umma al-'Arabiyya wa-l-Islamiyya," *al-Wafd*, 15 June 2015.

24. See Muhammad al-Minshawi, "al-'Aqida al-Qitaliyya li-l-Jaysh wa-Tanaqudat al-Qahira wa-Washington," *al-Shorouk*, 28 August 2015; Muhammad al-Minshawi, "Amrika Hawalt Taghir al-'Aqida al-Qitaliyya li-l-Jaysh al-Misri Lakin al-Mushir Tantawi Rafad," *al-Shorouk*, 7 July 2015.

25. Joe Stork, "Arms Industries of the Middle East," *MERIP* 17, no. 144 (January/February 1987); Yezid Sayigh, *Arab Military Industry: Capability, Performance, and Impact* (London: Brassey's Putnam Aeronautical 1992).

26. Ahmad Abd al-'Azim, "al-Fariq Hamdi Wahiba- Ra'is al-Hay'a al-'Arabiyya li-l-Tasni' fi Hiwar li-Roz al-Yusuf," *Roz al-Yusuf*, 3 November 2009; Ibtisam Ta'lab, "Dr. Sayyid Mash'al Wazir al-Intaj al-Harbi li-l-Masry al-Youm (2–2) . . . ," *al-Masry al-Youm*, 15 September 2010.

27. Jeremy Sharp, "Egypt: Background and U.S. Relations," Congressional Research Service, 24 July 2015, 18, https://www.fas.org/sgp/crs/mideast/RL33003.pdf.

28. Alex Blumberg, "Why Egypt's Military Cares About Home Appliances," *NPR*, 4 February 2011.

29. Reuters, "Nass Muqabalat Reuters ma'a al-Sisi," *Reuters*, 15 May 2014.

30. See http://el3askarmap.kazeboon.com/ and https://www.facebook.com/el3askar Map, both accessed 1 May 2013.

31. See General Samir Faraj's website, http://samirfarag.com/index_ar.html, accessed 7 September 2015.

32. Wala' Ni'mat Allah, "al-Mahdi Ra'isan li-Ittihad al-Idha'a wa-l-Tilifizyun," *al-Wafd*, 26 February 2011.

33. See, for instance, films on the Ministry of Defense's website, http://www.mod.gov.eg/mod/MoreVideos.aspx, accessed 7 September 2015.

34. James T. Quinlivan, "Coup-Proofing: Its Practice and Consequences in the Middle East," *International* Security 24, no. 2 (Fall 1999): 131. The list of important coups in the region included Turkey in 1923, 1960, 1971, 1980, and 1997; Iraq in 1936, 1941, 1963, and 1968; Syria in 1949, 1954, 1961, 1963, and 1970; Egypt in 1952; Yemen in 1962; Algeria in 1965 and 1991; Libya in 1969; Sudan in 1958, 1969, 1971, and 1989.

35. See Uri Ben-Eliezer, "A Nation-in-Arms: State, Nation, and Militarism in Israel's First Years," *Comparative Studies in Society and History* 37 (April 1995): 264–85.

36. Nazih Ayubi, *Over-Stating the Arab State* (London: I. B. Tauris, 1996), 260; Elizabeth Picard, "Arab Militaries in Politics," in *The Arab State*, ed. Giacomo Luciani (Berkeley: University of California Press, 1990), 193.

37. See, for example, Majid Khadduri, "The Role of the Military in Middle East Politics," *American Political Science Review* 47 (June 1953): 511–24; George Haddad, *Revolution and Military Rule in the Middle East* (New York: Robert Speller & Sons, 1973), vols. 1–3; Ayubi, *Over-Stating the Arab State*, 259–60.

38. See Ellen Kay Trimberger, *Revolution from Above: Military Bureaucrats and Development in Japan, Turkey, Egypt, and Peru* (New Brunswick, N.J.: Transaction Books, 1978), 41–43.

39. Ayubi, *Over-Stating the Arab State*, 258.

40. A recent research project compares civil-military relations in Latin American and Middle Eastern armies through historical and contemporary perspectives. See Nefissa Naguib (project director), "Everyday Maneuvers: Military-Civilian Relations in Latin America and the Middle East," Chr. Michelson Institute, Bergen, Norway, http://www.cmi.no/research/project/?1713=everyday-maneuvers, accessed 1 August 2015.

41. David Pion-Berlin, "Turkish Civil-Military Relations: A Latin American Comparison," *Turkish Studies* 12 (June 2011): 293, 300–303.

42. Samuel Huntington, *The Soldier and the State: the Theory and Politics of Civil-Military Relations* (Cambridge, Mass.: Harvard University Press, 1957), 7–17, 79, 83.

43. Rebecca Schiff, *Military and Domestic Politics: A Concordance Theory of Civil-Military Relations* (London: Routledge, 2009), 111, 114–20.

44. Ayşe Gül Altınay, *The Myth of the Military-Nation: Militarism, Gender, and Education in Turkey* (New York: Palgrave Macmillan, 2004), 2–3.

45. Ibid., 6–9.

46. For the early period from 1936 to 1956, see Uri Ben-Elizer, *The Making of Israeli Militarism* (Bloomington: Indiana University Press, 1998).

47. Baruch Kimmerling, "Patterns of Militarism in Israel," *European Journal of Sociology* 34 (1993): 199, 200–206.

48. See, for example, Yagil Levy, Edna Lomsky-Feder, and Noa Harel, "From 'Obligatory Militarism' to 'Contractual Militarism'—Competing Models of Citizenship," *Israel Studies* 12 (Spring 2007): 127–48.

49. Chalmers Johnson, "American Militarism and Blowback," in *Masters of War: Militarism and the Blowback in the Ear of American Empire*, ed. Carl Bogg (London: Routledge, 2003), 119–22.

50. Andrew J. Bacevich, *The New American Militarism: How Americans Are Seduced by War* (Oxford: Oxford University Press, 2013), 2.

51. Jörn Brömmelhörster and Wolf-Christian Paes, eds., *The Military as an Economic Actor: Soldiers in Business* (Basingstoke: Palgrave Macmillan, 2003), quote on 9.

52. Ayesha Siddiqa, *Military Inc.: Inside Pakistan's Military Economy* (London: Pluto Press, 2007), 1–25, quote on 1.

53. Kristina Mani, "Militaries in Business: State-Making and Entrepreneurship in the Developing Countries," *Armed Forces and Society* 33 (July 2007): 592, 606–7.

54. Philippe Droz-Vincent, "From Political to Economic Actors: The Changing Role of Middle Eastern Armies," in *Debating Arab Authoritarianism: Dynamics and Durability in Non-Democratic Regimes*, ed. Oliver Schlumberger (Stanford: Stanford University Press, 2008), 202.

55. Ibid., 203.

56. See Frank A. Mora and Quintan Wiktorowicz, "Economic Reform and the Military: China, Cuba, and Syria in Comparative Perspective," *International Journal of Comparative Sociology* 44 (April 2003): 87–91, 108–16; Droz-Vincent, "From Political to Economic Actors," 202.

57. Mora and Wiktorowicz, "Economic Reform and the Military," 109. Emphasis is mine.

58. Adam Seitz, "Patronage Politics in Transition: Political and Economic Interests of the Yemeni Armed Forces," in *Businessmen in Arms: How the Military and Other Armed Groups Profit in the MENA Region*, ed. Zeinab Abul-Magd and Elke Grawert (New York: Rowman & Littlefield, 2016).

59. İsmet Akça, "Military-Economic Structure in Turkey: Present Situation, Problems, and Solutions," in TESEV Democratization Program, *Policy Report Series*, Security Sector 2, Istanbul, July 2010, quote on 10.

60. Kevan Harris, "The Rise of the Subcontractor State: Politics of Pseudo-Privatization in the Islamic Republic of Iran," *International Journal of Middle East Studies* 45, no. 1 (2013): 45–70; Harris, "All the Sipah's Men: Iran's Revolutionary Guards in Theory and in Practice," in Abul-Magd and Grawert, *Businessmen in Arms*.

61. Ali Alfoneh, *Iran Unveiled: How the Revolutionary Guards Is Transforming Iran from Theocracy Into Military Dictatorship* (Washington, D.C.: AEI Press, 2013).

62. Saeid Golkar, "Paramilitarization of the Economy: The Case of Iran's Basij," *Armed Forces and Society* 38 (April 2009): 625–48.

63. Joe Stork, "Arms Industries of the Middle East," *MERIP* 17 (January/February 1987), http://www.merip.org/mer/mer144/arms-industries-middle-east.

64. Alex Mintz, "The Military-Industrial Complex: American Concepts and Israeli Realities," *Journal of Conflict Resolution* 29 (December 1985): 628–29.

65. Stockholm International Peace Research Institute (SIPRI), http://www.sipri.org/research/armaments/milex/milex_database, accessed 4 August 2015; Arie Egozi and Dennis-R Merklinghaus, "The Israeli Defense Industry," *Military Technology* (October 2010): 109–25.

66. Egozi and Merklinghaus, "The Israeli Defense Industry," 125; "How Israel High-Tech Happened," *Globes Israel's Business Arena*, 15 August 2000, http://www.globes.co.il/en/article-258771.

67. Barbara Opall-Rome, "'No Turning Back' for IMI Sale," *Defense News*, 21 March 2015; Sarah Toth Stub, "Israel Moves to Sell Weapons Factory That Developed Uzi," *Wall Street Journal*, 13 July 2015.

68. Mehran Kamrava, "Military Professionalization and Civil-Military Relations in the Middle East," *Political Science Quarterly* 115 (2000): 67–92.

69. Risa Brooks discussed the subject of coup-proofing as early as 1998 in her *Political-Military Relations and the Stability of Arab Regimes* (New York: Routledge,

1998); James Quinlivan analyzed it in 1999 in "Coup-Proofing: Its Practices and Consequences in the Middle East," *International Security* 24 (Fall 1999): 131–65.

70. Holger Albrecht, "Does Coup-Proofing Work? Political-Military Relations in Authoritarian Regimes Amid the Arab Uprisings," *Mediterranean Politics* 20 (2015): 39.

71. See Quinlivan, "Coup-Proofing," 131–65.

72. Albrecht, "Does Coup-Proofing Work?," 39.

73. See Holger Albrecht, "The Myth of Coup-Proofing: Risk and Instances of Military Coups d'Etat in the Middle East and North Africa, 1950–2013," *Armed Forces and Society* (August 2014): 1–29, doi: 10.1177/0095327X14544518.

74. Zoltan Barany, "Armies and Revolutions," *Journal of Democracy* 24 (April 2013): 63–64.

75. See Hicham Bou Nassif, "A Military Besieged: The Armed Forces, the Police, and the Party in Bin 'Ali's Tunisia, 1987–2011," *International Journal of Middle Eastern Studies* 47 (2015): 65–87.

76. Derek Lutterbeck, "Arab Uprisings, Armed Forces, and Civil-Military Relations," *Armed Forces and Society* 39 (2013): 39–42.

77. See Philippe Droz-Vincent, "Prospects for 'Democratic Control of the Armed Forces'? Comparative Insights and Lessons for the Arab World in Transition," *Armed Forces and Society* 40 (2014): 696–723.

78. Ibid.

79. Lutterbeck, "Arab Uprisings, Armed Forces, and Civil-Military Relations," 42–44.

80. See Lahcen Achy, "Algeria Avoids the Arab Spring?," *Carnegie Middle East Center*, 31 May 2012, http://carnegie-mec.org/publications/?fa=48277#immune.

81. Robert Springborg, *Mubarak's Egypt: Fragmentation of the Political Order* (London: Westview Press, 1989); Ahmad Abd Allah, ed., *al-Jaysh wa-l-Dimuqraitiyya fi Misr* (Cairo: Sina li-l-Nashr, 1990).

82. Steven A. Cook, *Ruling but Not Governing: The Military and Political Development in Egypt, Algeria, and Turkey* (Baltimore: Johns Hopkins University Press, 2007).

83. Hazem Kandil, *Soldiers, Spies, and Statesmen: Egypt's Road to Revolt* (London: Verso, 2012).

84. My report on this visit and other articles on AOI appeared in Arabic at *al-Masry al-Youm*. Examples of translations of them are Zeinab Abul-Magd, "Time for Civilian Handover," *Egypt Independent*, 1 April 2012; and Abul-Magd, "Stalin's Moustache and the Military's Wheel of Production," *Egypt Independent*, 29 March 2012.

1. Socialism Without Socialists (1950s–1970s)

1. The novelist was Yusuf al-Siba'i, former officer in the cavalry corps and professor at the military academy, and the filmmaker was 'Izz al-Din Dhu al-Fuqqar, who was a colonel when he quit the military.

2. Michel Foucault, *Society Must Be Defended*, trans. David Macey (New York: Picador, 2003), 277.

3. Michel Foucault, *Discipline and Punish*, trans. Alan Sheridan (New York: Vintage Books, 1979), 221.

4. On these security apparatuses, see Hazem Kandil, *Soldiers, Spies, and Statesmen: Egypt's Road to Revolt* (London: Verso, 2012).

5. Ellen Kay Trimberger, *Revolution from Above: Military Bureaucrats and Development in Japan, Turkey, Egypt, and Peru* (New Brunswick, N.J.: Transaction Books, 1978).

6. Nazih Ayubi, *Over-Stating the Arab State* (London: I. B. Tauris, 1996), 259, 258.

7. Trimberger, *Revolution from Above*, 147.

8. Anouar Abdel-Malek, *Egypt: Military Society; the Army Regime, the Left, and Social Change Under Nasser* (New York: Random House, 1986), 44–45.

9. Ibid.

10. Ibid., 94; Kandil, *Soldiers, Spies, and Statesmen*, 37.

11. Morroe Berger, *Military Elite and Social Change: Egypt Since Napoleon* (Princeton, N.J.: Princeton University Press, 1966), 21.

12. The Ahmed 'Urabi revolt.

13. Majid Khadduri, "The Role of the Military in Middle East Politics," *American Political Science Review* 47 (June 1953): 520–23. Muhammad Naguib's memoirs state that many dreamed of an Egyptian Ataturk and thought Nasser could play this role. Muhammad Naguib, *Kuntu Ra'isan li-Misr: Mudhakkirat Muhammad Najib* (Cairo: al-Maktab al-Masri al-Hadith, 1984), 181. Nasser refers to the 1948 war as a reason for Egypt's coup in *Falsafat al-Thawra* (Cairo: Bayt al-'Arab li-l-Tawthiq al-'Asri, 1996), 106–11.

14. Khadduri, "The Role of the Military in Middle East Politics," 521.

15. Ibid., 518.

16. Berger, *Military Elite and Social Change*, 21.

17. Birlanti Abd al-Hamid, *al-Mushir wa-Ana* (Cairo: Maktabat Madbuli, 1992). A photo from his office is published in Rashad Kamil, *Hayat al-Mushir 'Abd al-Hakim 'Amir* (Cairo: Dar al-Khayal, 2002), 16; the same book refers to his opinion on women (139).

18. Naguib, *Kuntu Ra'isan li-Misr*, 156, 201–7; Berger, *Military Elite and Social Change*, 21.

19. Keith Wheelock, *Nasser's New Egypt: A Critical Analysis* (New York: Frederick and Praeger, 1960), 47–48.

20. Ahmad Abd Allah, ed., *al-Jaysh wa-l-Dimuqraitiyya fi Misr* (Cairo: Sina li-l-Nashr, 1990), 35. For tables of all names of military officials and ministers, see 40–50. At the level of minister, Mark Cooper notes that "of 131 ministers who served under Nasser, 20.6 percent were officers and 13.9 percent were officer technocrats." Mark Cooper, "The Demilitarization of Egyptian Cabinet," *International Journal of Middle Eastern Studies* 14 (May 1982): 208.

21. Khalid Muhi al-Din, *al-An Atakallam* (Cairo: Markaz al-Ahram li-l-Tarjama wa-l-Nashr, 1992), 41–48, 131–40, 191; Naguib, *Kuntu Ra'isan li-Misr*, 202.

22. Tawfiq al-Hakim, *'Awdat al-Wa'i* (Beirut: Dar al-Shuruk, 1974), 39–40.

23. Nasser, *Falsafat al-Thawra*, 106–11.

24. Naguib, *Kuntu Ra'isan li-Misr*, 166–69.

25. Aziz Sidqi interview, EBHRC, AUC, Cairo, March and April 2004.

26. Wheelock, *Nasser's New Egypt*, 38–50; Khalid Muhi al-Din, *al-An Atakallam* (Cairo: Markaz al-Ahram li-l-Tarjama wa-l-Nashr, 1992), 87–100. Also see Naguib, *Kuntu Ra'isan li-Misr*, 185.

27. The strike was in Kafr al-Dawwar and the two laborers were Mustafa Khamis and Muhammad al-Baqari. Muhi al-Din, *al-An Atakallam*, 182–84.

28. See Isma'il Sabri 'Abdullah interview, EBHRC, AUC, Cairo, November–December 2004. Similarly, Fu'ad Mursi, a Marxist friend of Abdullah's who served in the Ministry of Industry, was put in jail but after being released was hired as head of a public-sector company and won a seat in the parliament in the late 1960s.

29. See full texts of early laws in Rashad El-Badrawy, *The Military Coup in Egypt: An Analytical Study* (Cairo: Renaissance Bookshop, 1952), 225–57; Abdel-Malek, *Egypt: Military Society*, 89–102.

30. Laura James, *Nasser at War: Arab Images of the Enemy* (New York: Palgrave Macmillan, 2006), 3–4.

31. Muhi al-Din, *al-An Atakallam*, 191–92; Abdel-Malek, *Egypt: Military Society*, 101–2.

32. Sami Moubayed, *Syria and the USA: Washington's Relations with Damascus from Wilson to Eisenhower* (London: I. B. Tauris, 2012), 85–108.

33. Abdel-Malek, *Egypt: Military Society*, 99–100.

34. Ibid., 99–104.

35. The full text of the 1956 constitution is published in *al-Qarart al-Kubra li-Thawrat 23 Yuliu. Al-Juz' al-Awwal- Qararat Siyasiyya* (Cairo: Wazarat al-I'lam, al-Hay'a al-'Amma li-l-Isti'lamat, 1985), 23–37.

36. Abdel-Malek, *Egypt: Military Society*, 106–8. For a detailed account of the Suez Crisis, see James, *Nasser at War*, chap. 2.

37. See Salim Yaqub, *Containing Arab Nationalism: The Eisenhower Doctrine and the Middle East* (Chapel Hill: University of North Carolina Press, 2004).

38. Abdel-Malek, *Egypt: Military Society*, 89–117, 145–72.

39. Michel Aflaq, *Fi Sabil al-Ba'th* (Baghdad: Hizb al-Ba'th al-'Arabi al-Ishtiraki, al-Qiyada al-Qawmiyya, Maktab al-Thaqafa wa-l-I'lam al-Qawmi, 1987), 282–89.

This foundational book was originally published in Beirut by Dar al-Tali‘a in 1974.

40. On details of the creation of the United Arab Republic, see: P. J. Vatikiotis, *The Egyptian Army in Politics: Pattern for New Nations?* (Bloomington: Indiana University Press, 1961), 140–86. Despite the declared animosity, ‘Aflaq described Nasser as a historic Arab leader and nationalist fighter later in his life.

41. Abdel-Malek, *Egypt: Military Society*, 76–78, 129–30, 151–57.

42. My emphasis. For the full text of the 1962 National Charter and ASU's law, see *al-Qarart al-Kubra li-Thawrat 23 Yuliu.* For an analysis of the charter, see Robert Stephens, *Nasser: A Political Biography* (New York: Simon and Schuster, 1971), 344–55.

43. ‘Abd al-Latif al-Baghdadi, *Mudhakkirat ‘Abd al-Latif al-Baghdadi* (Cairo: al-Maktab al-Misri al-Hadith, 1977), part 2, 148, 226.

44. Ilya Harik, "The Single Party as a Subordinate Movement: The Case of Egypt," *World Politics* 26 (October 1973): 87–88.

45. Ali Ed-Dean Hillal Dessouki, "The Party as a Mass Political Organization in Egypt, 1952–1967" (PhD diss., McGill University, 1968), 152.

46. Anwar al-Sadat, *Al-Bahth ‘an al-Dhat* (Cairo: al-Maktab al-Misri al-Hadith, 1978), 227.

47. Dessouki, "The Party as a Mass Political Organization," 151.

48. Samir Amin interview, EBHRC, AUC, Cairo, 20 April 2004. For a full list of prime ministers and ministers during this period, see Mahmud Zuhdi, *al-Wuzarat al-Misriyya* (Cairo: Markaz Watha'iq wa-Tarikh Misr al-Mu‘asir, 2008).

49. About *ahl a-thiqa* and *ahl al-khibra* rule, see Aziz Sidqi interview.

50. al-Baghdadi, *Mudhakkirat*, part 2, 155, 228–29; Ahmad Hamrush, "Wada‘an Kamal al-Din Husayn," *al-Ahram*, 22 June 1999; Ahmad Salama, "Kamal al-Din Husayn wa-‘Alaqatuh bi-l-Ikhwan al-Muslimin," *IkhwanWiki*, http://www.ikhwanwiki .com/index.php?title=%D9%83%D9%85%D8%A7%D9%84_%D8%A7%D9%8 4%D8%AF%D9%8A%D9%86_%D8%AD%D8%B3%D9%8A%D9%86, accessed 15 June 2016.

51. Abd Allah Imam, *Ali Sabri Yatadhakkar* (Cairo: Roza al-Yusuf, 1987), 6–11.

52. Ibid., 52–55.

53. al-Baghdadi, *Mudhakkirat*, part 2, 155.

54. Rania Badawi, "‘Aziz Sidqi fi al-Hiwar al-Akhir Qabl Rahilih ‘1–2,'" *al-Masry al-Youm*, 4 March 2008.

55. Raymond Hinnebusch, *Egyptian Politics Under Sadat: The Post-Populist Development of an Authoritarian-Modernizing State* (Cambridge: Cambridge University Press, 1985), 131–32.

56. For a full biography of Sayed Marei, see Robert Springborg, *Family, Power, and Politics: Sayed Bey Marei—His Clan, Clients, and Cohorts* (Philadelphia: University of Pennsylvania Press, 1982).

57. Mahmoud Abdel-Fadil, *al-Tahawwulat al-Iqtisadiyya fi al-Rif al-Misri (1952–1970)* (Cairo: al-Hay'a al-Misriyya al-'Amma li-l-Kitab, 1978), 51–92.

58. Arthur Goldsmith, *Biographical Dictionary of Modern Egypt* (Boulder, Colo.: Lynne Rienner, 2000), 160. Samir Amin emphasized Qaysuni's liberal stance in the interview with EBHRC.

59. Nashwa al-Hufi, "Wazir al-Iqtisad wa-Munafidh al-Ta'mim fi 'Ahd Abd al-Nasir Hasan 'Abbas Zaki," *al-Masry al-Youm*, 24 July 2009.

60. "Hiwar Hasan 'Abbas Zaki (2)," *al-Ahram*, 1 January 2005; Yusuf Ibrahim, "Rahil Hasan 'Abbas Zaki Muhandis Tanfidh al-Ta'mim fi 'Ahd Abd al-Nassir," *Masr Alarabia*, 29 November 2014.

61. Aziz Sidqi interview EBHRC, AUC, March and April 2004.

62. Ranya Badawi, "'Aziz Sidqi fi al-Hiwar al-Akhir: Qabla Rahilih '2–2,'" *al-Masry al-Youm*, 5 March 2008.

63. Nazih Ayubi, *al-Dawla al-Markaziyya fi Misr* (Beirut: Markaz Dirasat al-Wahda al-'Arabiyya, 1989), 101. See also Ayubi, *Bureaucracy and Politics in Contemporary Egypt* (London: Ithaca Press, 1980).

64. See Mark Cooper, "State Capitalism, Class Structure, and Social Transformation in the Third World: The Case of Egypt," *International Journal of Middle East Studies* 15 (November 1983): 451–69.

65. For instance, Abd al-Halim Hafiz's song "Hikayat Sha'b." In his visit to Aswan to report as a journalist on the High Dam, novelist Sonallah Ibrahim dashed the rosy image that singer Abd al-Halim Hafiz and poet Abd al-Rahman al-Abnudi depicted of the dam's workers. He documented the miserable life of laborers who died in great numbers from disease, accidents, or simply strong heat. He also documented how Egyptian workers, in contrast to Russian laborers, were not as hardworking or skilled and resented doing lowly tasks. Sonallah Ibrahim, *Najmat Aghustus* (Cairo: Dar al-Thaqafa al-Jadida, 1974).

66. Dessouki, "The Party as a Mass Political Organization," 157.

67. Imam, *Ali Sabri*, 76–77.

68. Ayubi, *al-Dawla al-Markaziyya fi Misr*, 109–10.

69. Adil Jazarin interview, EBHRC, AUC, Cairo, 22 March, 31 March, and 6 April 2004.

70. Ayubi, *al-Dawla al-Markaziyya fi Misr*, 109–10.

71. Samir Amin interview, EBHRC, AUC, April 2004.

72. *Usama Anwar 'Ukasha, Layali al-Hilmiyya*, 1987 (first season), 1988 (second season), 1989 (third season), 1992 (fourth season), and 1995 (fifth season). Produced by state-owned Egyptian TV.

73. For details about the Vanguard Organization, see Ayubi, *al-Dawla al-Markaziyya fi Misr*, 118–24.

74. Fathi Ghanim, *Zaynab wa-l-'Arsh* (Cairo: Rosa al-Yusuf, 1988), part 2, 214–18. The novel was originally written in 1972–73.

75. Abdel-Fadil, *al-Tahawwualt al-Iqtisadiyya wa-l-Ijtima'iyya fi al-Rif al-Misri*, 22–29, 46–47, 53–57. Also see Alan Richards, *Egypt's Agricultural Development, 1800–1980: Technical and Social Change* (Boulder, Colo.: Westview Press, 1982), chap. 6. Richards states: "The consolidation of the rich peasants' position in the countryside was perhaps the most important aspect of the reform. . . . The Nasser regime continued to rely on the well-to-do peasants as a 'mediator' between the government and the mass of the peasantry. . . . Government regulations certainly did little to weaken the strength of the rural middle-class" (178).

76. al-Hakim, *'Awdat al-Wa'i*, 48–49.

77. Article No. 1 in Presidential Decree No. 87 of 1964 stated that board members of cooperatives had to be members of ASU. See *al-Jarida al-Rasmiyya*, no. 68, 23 March 1964.

78. Ihsan Abd al-Quddus, *al-Rusasa la Tazal fi Jaybi* (Cairo: Dar al-Ma'arif, 1974). This novel was turned into a popular romantic/war movie in the same year.

79. Robert Springborg, "Professional Syndicates in Egyptian Politics, 1952–1970," *International Journal of Middle Eastern Studies* 9 (October 1978): 287.

80. Ibid.

81. Majdi Hammad, "al-Mu'assasa al-'Askariyya wa-l-Nizam al-Siyasi al-Misri, 1952–1970," in Abd Allah, *al-Jaysh wa-l-Dimuqratiyya fi Misr*, 33.

82. Ayubi, *Over-Stating the Arab State*, 258.

83. 'Amir's army won only two battles against the Israeli Army during the triple attack. It was U.S. and Soviet pressure, along with the fierce grassroots resistance of civilian volunteers, rather than 'Amir's defense, that forced the three countries to withdraw from the occupied lands. See Field Marshal Abd al-Ghani al-Jamasi, *Mudhakkirat al-Jamasi: Harb Uktubar 1973* (Cairo: al-Hay'a al-Misriyya al-'Amma li-l-Kitab, 1998), 25–26; Ayubi, *al-Dawla al-Markaziyya fi Misr*, 115.

84. Kandil, *Soldiers, Spies, and Statesmen*, 45–54; Ayubi, *al-Dawla al-Markaziyya fi Misr*, 116; Stephens, *Nasser: A Political Biography*, 359–60.

85. Stephens, *Nasser*, 359–60.

86. al-Baghdadi, *Mudhakkirat*, part 2, 170.

87. Kandil, *Soldiers, Spies, and Statesmen*, 57.

88. Cf. Roman Kolkowicz, *The Soviet Military and the Communist Party* (Princeton, N.J.: Princeton University Press, 1967).

89. Berger, *Military Elite and Social Change*, 25–26.

90. *al-Qarart al-Kubra li-Thawrat 23 Yuliu*, 92, 117.

91. Ayubi, *al-Dawla al-Markaziyya*, 118.

92. Imam, *Ali Sabri Yatadhakkar*, 81–88.

93. al-Sadat, *Al-Bahth 'an al-Dhat*, 175–83.

94. Ibid., 179, 183.

95. Aziz Sidqi interview, EBHRC.

96. Yasir Ayyub, "al-'Askar Yahkumun al-Kura fi Jumhuriyyat Misr al-Karawiyya," *al-Ahram al-Riyadi*, 27 July 2011.

97. Ayubi, *al-Dawla al-Markaziyya*, 118–120. Also see Kandil, *Soldiers, Spies, and Statesmen*, 58–61; Ghanim, *Zaynab wa-l-'Arsh*, part 2, 214–18.

98. Muhammad Abd al-Wahab interview, EBHRC, AUC, March and April 2004.

99. Adil Jazarin interview.

100. Nazli Madkour, "Egyptian Defense Programmes and Their Impact on Social and Economic Development of Egypt" (M.A. thesis, American University in Cairo, 1980), 192.

101. Michael N. Barnett, in *Confronting the Costs of War: Military Power, State, and Society in Egypt and Israel* (Princeton, N.J.: Princeton University Press, 1992), 80–103. The author's table of Egyptian military spending between 1950 and 1976 on p. 81 cites Ali E. Hillal Dessouki and Adel al-Labban, "Arms Race, Defense Expenditures, and Development: The Egyptian Case, 1952–1973," *Journal of South Asian and Middle Eastern Studies* 4 (Spring 1981): 65–77.

102. Madkour, "Egyptian Defense Programmes," 3, 5, 177–205.

103. Barnett, *Confronting the Costs of War*, 99. Also see pp. 100–101 on Soviets and Egyptian military industries.

104. For detailed statistics of each kind of industry and state-owned enterprise between 1952 and the 1970s, see Abd al-Fadil, *al-Iqtisad al-Misri bayna al-Takhtit al-Markazi wa-l-Infitah al-Iqtisadi* (Beirut: Ma'had al-Inma' al-'Arabi, 1980), 65–82.

105. Alan Richards and John Waterbury, *Political Economy of the Middle East* (Boulder, Colo.: Westview Press, 1996), 183–84.

106. Cooper, "Egyptian State Capitalism in Crisis," 481; Cooper, "Demilitarization of Egyptian Cabinet," 204–5.

107. See full text of Nasser's statement of March 30, 1968, in *al-Qarart al-Kubra li-Thawrat 23 Yuliu*, 142–48.

108. Cooper, "Egyptian State Capitalism in Crisis," 484–94.

109. David Bullard Smith, "Egyptian Military Elite: An Operational Code" (M.A. thesis, Naval Postgraduate School, 1977), 49–50.

110. Barnett, *Confronting the Costs of War*, 104.

111. Cooper, "Demilitarization of the Egyptian Cabinet," 205–8.

112. For details, see Kandil, *Soldiers, Spies, and Statesmen*, 100.

113. Ibid., 107.

114. Imam, *Ali Sabri Yatadhakkar*, 123; also 114, 120–21, 123–24.

115. Ibid., 129.

116. Robert Springborg, "al-Ra'is wa-l-Mushir: al-'Alaqat al-Madaniyya al-'Askariyya fi Misr al-Yawm," in *al-Jaysh wa-l-Dimuqraitiyya fi Misr*, ed. Ahmad Abd Allah (Cairo: Sina li-l-Nashr, 1990), 66.

117. Cooper, "Demilitarization of the Egyptian Cabinet," 208, 210.

118. Anwar al-Sadat, "Nahnu wa-l-Ikhwan al-Muslimin," *al-Jumhuriyya*, 19 January 1954.

119. See, for instance, "Istiqbal Sha'bi Ra'i' li-Abd al-Nasir fi al-Iskandariyya: Nahnu Nuharib al-Isti'mar al-Fikri bi-Ta'min Huriyyat al-Fard. li-l-'Amil Haqq wa li-Sahib al-'Amal Haqq wa-Nahnu Nahmi Huquqahuma," *al-Jumhuriyya*, 14 December 1953. The news of the arrest of Tahiyya Kariokka, a famous belly dancer and film star who was detained for joining a communist organization, was published in *al-Jumhuriyya* in 1954.

120. Anwar El Sadat, *Revolt on the Nile* (New York: John Day, 1957), 145.

121. Imam, *Ali Sabri Yatadhakkar*, 120–21.

122. al-Sadat, *al-Bahth 'an al-Dhat*, 179–80.

123. Ibid., 185. Translation quoted from Anwar el-Sadat, *In Search of Identity: An Autobiography* (New York: Harper & Row, 1978), 171.

124. al-Sadat, *al-Bahth 'an al-Dhat*, 61. Translation quoted from el-Sadat, *In Search of Identity*, 50.

125. See Hinnebusch, *Egyptian Politics Under Sadat*, 132–38.

126. Ibid., 132.

127. The full list of Sadat's prime ministers (all of whom held top positions under Nasser) included Mahmud Fawzi (1970–1972; vice president until 1974), a civilian diplomat who studied law and served as Nasser's minister of foreign affairs from 1952 to 1964 and as presidential assistant for political affairs after defeat in 1967; Aziz Sidqi (1972–1973), civilian engineer and Nasser's long-serving minister of industry who rejected infitah; Sadat himself during the war year (1973–1974); Abd al-Aziz Hijazi (1974–1975); Mamduh Salim (1975–1978); Mustafa Khalil (1978–1980); and Sadat himself again (1981).

128. Suhayr Hilmi, "Dr. Abd al-Aziz Hijazi: Lastu Mas'ulan 'an Infitah 'al-Sadah Madah'!," *al-Ahram*, 1 September 2010.

129. See Springborg, *Family, Power, and Politics*. For details about Sadat's administrative elite, see Hinnebusch, *Egyptian Politics Under Sadat*, 78–121.

130. Adil Jazarin interview. He generally thought that a role for workers in management is a positive thing, provided that it is indirect, through an advisory board, as in Germany and Japan. Meanwhile, he also believed that infitah was applied in the wrong way without strategic planning, which hurt the process of industrialization.

131. Sonallah Ibrahim, *al-Jalid* (Cairo: Dar al-Thaqafa al-Jadida, 2011), 132.

132. Hinnebusch, *Egyptian Politics Under Sadat*, 134–35.

133. See *al-Jumhuriyya*'s issues of 18–21 January 1977.

2. The Good 1980s

1. Sonallah Ibrahim, *Zaat*, trans. Anthony Calderbank (Cairo: American University in Cairo Press, 2004).
2. Ibrahim al-'Isawi, *Fi Islah ma Afsadahu al-Infitah* (Cairo: Kitab al-Ahali, Jaridat al-Ahali, Hizb al-Tajammu' al-Watani al-Taqaddumi al-Wahdawi, 1984), 65–78, 189–212.
3. See *Al-Malaff al-Watha'iqi li-l-Mushir Muhammad 'Abd al-Halim Abu Ghazala* (Cairo: Markaz al-Ahram li-l-Tanzim wa-l-Microfilm, 1981–1989), part 1.
4. For the definition of parastatal, see Kevan Harris, "The Rise of the Subcontractor State: Politics of Pseudo-Privatization in the Islamic Republic of Iran," *International Journal of Middle East Studies* 45 (2013): 45–70.
5. Michel Foucault, *Discipline and Punish*, trans. Alan Sheridan (New York: Vintage Books, 1979), 168.
6. Michel Foucault, *Society Must Be Defended*, trans. David Macey (New York: Picador, 2003), 15–16.
7. Ibid., 169.
8. Bernard Gwertzman, "C-130 Sale to Egypt Near Approval," *New York Times*, 3 April 1976.
9. *Proposed Sale of C-130's to Egypt: Hearings and Makeup Before the Subcommittee on International Political and Military Affairs of the Committee on International Relations, House of Representatives, Ninety-Fourth Congress, Second Session April 6 and 12, 1976*, 94th Cong. 12 (1976) (Opening Statement, from the *Trenton Times*, 27 March 1976, and Important Quotes on Military Sales to Egypt); (statement of Lt. Gen. Howard M. Fish, U.S. Air Force, director, Defense Security Assistance Agency, Department of Defense).
10. *Proposed Sale of C-130's to Egypt*; Joe Stork and Danny Reachard, "Chronology: US-Military Relationship," *MERIP Reports* 90 (September 1980): 29.
11. See *Proposed Sales of Military Equipment and Services to Egypt: Hearings Before the Subcommittee on Europe and the Middle East of the Committee on International Relations, House of Representatives, Ninety-Fifth Congress, First Session, September, 1977*, 95th Cong. (Washington, D.C.: U.S. Government Printing Office, 1977.)
12. See *Proposed Aircraft Sales to Israel, Egypt, and Saudi Arabia: Hearings Before the Committee on International Relations, House of Representatives, Ninety-Fifth Congress, Second Session, May 8, 9, 10, and 16, 1978*, 95th Cong. (Washington, D.C.: U.S. Government Printing Office, 1977).
13. Graham Hovey, "U.S. Puts off Jet Sale to Egypt After Saudis Delay on Paying Costs," *New York Times*, 7 July 1979.
14. International Demographic Data Center, United States Bureau of the Census, *World Population 1979: Recent Demographic Estimates for the Countries and Regions of the World* (Washington, D.C.: U.S. Government Printing Office, 1980), 25–26.

15. *Supplemental 1979 Middle East Aid Package for Israel and Egypt Hearings and Makeup Before the Committee on Foreign Affairs and Its Subcommittee on International Security and Scientific Affairs and on Europe and the Middle East, House of Representatives, Ninety-Sixth Congress, First Session April 26; May 1, 2, 8, and 9, 1979*, 96th Cong. 1–17, 35–36 (1979).

16. Christopher S. Wren, "U.S. Treads Lightly in Tacit Alliance with Egypt That Has Risks and Benefits for Both . . . ," *New York Times*, 27 July 1980.

17. *Supplemental 1979 Middle East Aid Package for Israel and Egypt*, 96th Cong. 115.

18. *Hearings on H.R. 2920 (H.R. 3455): To Authorize Certain Construction at Military Installations for FY82, Subcommittee on Military Installations and Facilities, Committee on Armed Services. House; Committee on Armed Services. House, Mar. 25–27, Apr. 1–2, 8, 29, 1981*, 126; *Hearings on H.R. 212 [H.R 3947], Military Construction Authorization Act, 1980, H.R. 2122 [H.R. 2556], Supplemental Military Construction Authorization Act, 1979, Before Military Installations and Facilities Subcommittee of the Committee on Armed Services House of Representatives, Ninety-Sixth Congress, First Session, February 14, March 1, 26, 27, 28, 29, April 2,4,5, and May 2, 1979*, 96th Cong. 464 (1979).

19. See, for example, David Shipler, "Egypt's Chief Sends Message to Reassure Israel on Peace," *New York Times*, 10 October 1981; Leslie H. Gelb, "Egypt Reaffirms Peace with Israel," *New York Times*, 28 December 1981.

20. *Foreign Assistance Legislation for Fiscal Year 1983 (Part 3): Hearings and Markup Before the Subcommittee on Europe and the Middle East of the Committee on Foreign Affairs, House of Representatives, Ninety-Seventh Congress, Second Session, March 15, 23, 30; April 1 and 27, 1982*, 97th Cong. 10–9 (1982) (summary of recommendations); *Foreign Assistance Legislation for Fiscal Years 1984–85 (Part 3): Hearings and Markup Before the Subcommittee on Europe and the Middle East of the Committee on Foreign Affairs, House of Representatives, Ninety-Eighth Congress, First Session, February 28, March 3, 9, 10, 14, 16 and April 12, 1983*, 98th Cong. 12 (1983) (general recommendations).

21. The actual figures refer to 23 percent. See table 2.

22. Muhammad Abd al-Halim Abu Ghazala, *Al-Mushir Abu Ghazala wa-l-Sahafa* (Interviews with Abu Ghazala) (Cairo, 1996), 211.

23. *Foreign Assistance Legislation for Fiscal Years 1984–85 (Part 3)* (statement of Maj. Gen. Richard V. Secord, deputy assistant secretary for Near East and South Asian affairs, Department of Defense); *Military Construction Appropriations for 1985: Hearings Before a Subcommittee of the Committee on Appropriations, House of Representatives, Ninety-Eighth Congress, Second Session*, 98th Cong. 523 (1984) (Chairman W. G. (Bill) Hefner opening statement); *Foreign Assistance Legislation for Fiscal Year 1983 (Part 3)*, 97th Cong. 19 (1982) (statement of David Ransom, director, Near East and South Asian Region, International Security Affairs, Department of Defense); Leslie Gelb, "Egypt Portrayed Itself as Major U.S. Asset," *New York Times*, 16 January 1985.

24. *Foreign Assistance Legislation for Fiscal Year 1986–87 (Part 3): Hearings and Markup Before the Subcommittee on Europe and the Middle East of the Committee on Foreign Affairs, House of Representatives, Ninety-Ninth Congress, First Session, February 21, 26, 28; March 6, 7, and 20, 1985*, 99th Cong. 136 (1985) (prepared statement of Hon. Richard W. Murphy, assistant secretary, Bureau of Near Eastern and South Asian Affairs, Department of State).

25. Ralph Sanders, "Arms Industries: New Supplies and Regional Security [National Security Implications]," *DISAM Journal* 13 (1990–91): 106.

26. Abu Ghazala, *Al-Mushir Abu Ghazala wa-l-Sahafa*, 250.

27. *Foreign Assistance Legislation for Fiscal Year 1986–87 (Part 3)*, 99th Cong. 161 (1985) (statement of Hon. Richard W. Murphy, assistant secretary, Bureau of Near Eastern and South Asian Affairs, Department of State).

28. *Supplemental 1979 Middle East Aid Package for Israel and Egypt*, 96th Cong. 152; *Foreign Assistance Legislation for Fiscal Year 1983 (Part 3)*, 97th Cong. 14–15 (statement of Morris Draper, deputy assistant secretary, Bureau of Near Eastern and South Asian Affairs, Department of State). Also see *Foreign Assistance Legislation for Fiscal Year 1988–89 (Part 3): Hearings and Markup Before the Subcommittee on Europe and the Middle East of the Committee on Foreign Affairs, House of Representatives, One Hundredth Congress, First Session, February 3, 10, 23, 25; March 3, 11, and 19, 1987*, 100th Cong. (Washington, D.C.: U.S. Government Printing Office, 1987).

29. Alan Cowell, "Egyptians Facing Squeeze Over Debts to U.S.," *New York Times*, 28 May 1989.

30. Senator John H. Chaff Speaking, speaking on October 19, 1990, 101st Cong., 2nd sess., *Congressional Record* 136, part 22:31304; *101 Bill Profile S. Cong. Res. 148—Forgiving Military Aid Debt to U.S. by Egypt*, Senate Foreign Relations Committee, 101st Congress—1989–1990, Session 2, U.S. Senate, 28 September 1990.

31. Judith Miller, "Gulf Crisis Produces Surge of Egyptian Confidence," *New York Times*, 11 November 1990; Steven Greenhouse, "Half of Egypt's $20.2 Billion Debt Being Forgiven by U.S. and Allies," *New York Times*, 27 May 1991.

32. *Foreign Assistance Legislation for Fiscal Year 1988–89 (Part 3)*, 100th Cong. 140–41 (statement of Robert Pelletreau, deputy assistant secretary for Near Eastern and South Asian affairs, Department of Defense).

33. Tony Walker, "US Sweeten the Pot for Defense Projects in Egypt," *Financial Times*, 7 May 1987.

34. Patrick E. Tyler, "Pentagon Agrees to Let Egypt Produce M1 Tank; Move Expected to Draw Fire in Washington," *Washington Post*, 29 June 1987. Also see Michael Gordon, "U.S. May Allow Egyptians to Buy and Assemble M-1 Tanks," *New York Times*, 30 June 1987; Barbara Slavin, "A Tankful of Trouble for Egypt? Critics Say Co-producing M-1 Tanks Is Misguided Show of Friendship," *St. Petersburg Times*, 23 January 1988.

35. "Export Briefs . . . Egypt, US Sign Pact," *Journal of Commerce*, 4 November 1988. Also see "Egypt and U.S. Agree on a Joint Tank Plan," *New York Times*, 2 November 1988.

36. Patrick E. Tyler, "Egypt May Drop Plans for U.S. Tanks; M-1 Production Line Seen as Too Costly," *Washington Post*, 12 May 1989; Cowell, "Egyptians Facing Squeeze Over Debts to U.S."

37. *Military Aid to Egypt, Tank Production Raised Costs and May Not Meet Many Program Goals*, Report to Chairman, Subcommittee on Foreign Operations, Export Financing and Related Programs, Committee on Appropriations, House of Representatives, United States General Accounting Office (GAO), July 1993 (GAO/NSIAD-93–203) (Washington, D.C.: U.S. Government Accountability Office, 1993), 2.

38. Ibid., 1–2, 15.

39. Jim Paul, "The Egyptian Arms Industry," *MERIP Reports* 112 (February 1983): 26–28.

40. Lieutenant Colonel Stephen H. Gotowicki (U.S. Army), "The Role of the Egyptian Military in Domestic Society," Department of Defense, Foreign Military Studies Office (FMSO), National Defense University, 1997, http://fmso .leavenworth.army.mil/documents/egypt/egypt.htm.

41. Joe Stork, "Arms Industries of the Middle East," *MERIP Report* 144 (January–February, 1987): 12–16.

42. "Egypt Wins Right to Export Arms to the U.S.," *New York Times*, 24 March 1988.

43. See Joe Stork and James Paul, "Arms Sales and Militarizing the Middle East," *MERIP* 3 (January–February 1983), http://www.merip.org/mer/mer112/arms -sales-militarization-middle-east.

44. Philip H. Stoddard, "Egypt and the Iran-Iraq War," in *Gulf Security and the Iran-Iraq War*, ed. Thomas Naff (Washington, D.C.: National Defense University Press, 1985), 36–37.

45. Gotowicki, "The Role of the Egyptian Military in Domestic Society."

46. Ralph Sanders, "Arms Industries: New Supplies and Regional Security [National Security Implications]," *DISAM Journal* 13 (Winter 1990–1991): 105.

47. See John Kifner, "Egypt Silent Over U.S. Charges of Smuggling," *New York Times*, 26 June 1988; Richard W. Stevenson, "U.S. Studying Cairo, Links to Smuggling Plot," *New York Times*, 4 September 1988; Richard Stevenson, "Egyptian Minister Named in Missile-Parts Scheme," *New York Times*, 25 October 1988; Patrick E. Tyler, "High Link Seen in Cairo Spy Case: References Heard to Defense Minister," *Washington Post*, 20 August 1988; "U.S. Rocket Expert Pleads Guilty in Egyptian Smuggling Case," *New York Times*, 11 June 1989.

48. See, for example, Patrick E. Tyler, "Mubarak Reassigns Key Deputy; Move Said Face-Off with Defense Chief," *Washington Post*, 16 April 1989; Alan Cowell,

"Cairo Aide's Ouster Tied to Efforts to Get Missile Parts in U.S.," *New York Times*, 18 April 1989; Carol Berger, "Egyptian Minister Became a Liability," *Independent*, 18 April 1989; "Egyptian Knife Tricks," *The Times*, 29 April 1989.

49. See Kifner, "Egypt Silent over U.S. Charges of Smuggling"; Stevenson, "Egyptian Minister Named in Missile-Parts Scheme"; "U.S. Rocket Expert Pleads Guilty in Egyptian Smuggling Case"; Tyler, "Mubarak Reassigns Key Deputy."

50. Antony Walker, "Egypt in Missile Program: Evidence of Collaboration with Argentina Over Past Five Years," *Sydney Morning Herald*, 19 December 1987; Patrick Tyler, "Mubarak Seeks Easing Doubts on Poison Gas, Aid During U.S. Visit," *Washington Post*, 1 April 1989; Deborah Pugh, "Egypt's Minister of Defense Told to Step Down," *Guardian*, 17 April 1989; David Ottaway, "Egypt Drops out of Missile Project: State Department Official Offers No Details on Iraqi Program," *Washington Post*, 20 September 1989.

51. Patrick E. Tyler, "Cairo Prisoner Called Espionage Pawn; Other Links Son's Case to U.S. Trial of Egyptian Rocket Scientist," *Washington Post*, 26 July 1989. Also see Carol Berger, "Defence Lawyers Seek to Arrange Swap for 'CIA Spy,'" *Independent*, 25 July 1989.

52. *Military Sales to Israel and Egypt, DOD Needs Stronger Control Over U.S. Financed Procurements*, United States General Accounting Office (GAO), Report to Chairman, Subcommittee on Foreign Operations, Export Financing and Related Programs, Committee on Appropriations, House of Representatives, July 1993 (GAO/NSIAD-93–184) (Washington, D.C.: U.S. Government Accountability Office, 1993), 1–5, 24–27. Also see David Rogers, "Fees Questioned in U.S. Sales of Arms to Cairo," *Wall Street Journal*, 10 April 1993.

53. "Wazarat al-Difa' wa-l-Intaj al-Harbi, Qarar Raqam 65 li-Sanat 1979 bi-Sha'n al-Nizam al-Asasi li-Jihaz Mashru'at al-Khidma al-Wataniyya," *Al-Waqa'i' al-Misriyya*, no. 172, 25 July 1979.

54. "Wazarat al-Difa' wa-l-Intaj al-Harbi, Qarar Raqam 24 li-Sanat 1979," *Al-Waqa'i'al-Misriyya*, no. 172, 25 July 1979.

55. "Qarar Ra'is Jumhuriyyat Misr al-'Arabiyya Raqam 583 li-Sanat 1980 bi-Ta'dil Ba'd Ahkam al-Qarar al-Jumhuri Raqam 32 li-Sanat 1979 bi-Insha' Jihaz Mashru'at al-Khidma al-Wataniyya," *Al-Jarida al-Rasmiyya*, no. 48, 27 November 1979.

56. "Wazarat al-Difa' wa-l-Intaj al-Harbi, Qarar Raqam 23 li-Sanat 1982 bi-Sha'n Ta'dil Ba'd Ahkam al-Nizam al-Asasi li-Jihaz Mashru'at al-Khidma al-Wataniyya," *Al-Waqa'i' al-Misriyya*, no. 86, 12 April 1982.

57. Robert Springborg, *Mubarak's Egypt: Fragmentation of the Political Order* (London: Westview Press, 1989), 112–13.

58. *Al-Malaff al-Watha'iqi li-l-Mushir*, part 2, 425, 434, 494.

59. For detailed examples, see ibid., 421–38, 456.

60. "Qarar Ra'is Jumhuriyyat Misr al-'Arabiyya Raqam 253 li-Sanat 1985 bi-Takhsis Juz' min 'A'id al-Bitrul li-Tamwil 'Uqud al-Quwwat al-Musallaha," *al-Jarida al-Rasmiyya*, no. 28, 11 July 1985.

61. *Al-Malaff al-Watha'iqi li-l-Mushir*, part 2, 425, 469–70.

62. Springborg, *Mubarak's Egypt*, 105.

63. *Al-Malaff al-Watha'iqi li-l-Mushir*, part 2, 431; see also 426.

64. Ibid., 494.

65. Ibid., 452.

66. Springborg, *Mubarak's Egypt*, 105.

67. Mona Abaza, "Egyptianizing the American Dream: Nasr City's Shopping Malls, Public Order, and the Privatized Military," in *Cairo Cosmopolitan: Politics Culture, and Urban Space in the New Globalized Middle East*, ed. Diane Singerman and Paul Amar (Cairo: American University in Cairo Press, 2006), 202–3.

68. *Al-Malaff al-Watha'iqi li-l-Mushir*, part 2, 423, 432–33, 480, 487.

69. Galal Amin, *Madha Hadath li-l-Masriyyin: Tatawwur al-Mujtama' al-Misri fi Nisf Qarn, 1945–1995* (Cairo: al-Hay'a al-'Amma li-l-Kitab, 1999), 185–87.

70. Ibrahim Shakib, "Shukran Ayyuha al-Sada," *al-Ahalai*, 7 November 1984; Abd Aallah, *al-Jaysh wa-l-Dimuqratiyya fi Misr*, 96–99.

71. "Arab American Vehicles Corporation," *Infocredit Group Business Information Reports—Egypt*, 2 June 2011, http://www.aav.com.eg/Pathtosuccess.html.

72. Springborg, *Mubarak's Egypt*, 110; Ahmad Abd Allah, ed., *al-Jaysh wa-l-Dimuqratiyya fi Misr* (Cairo: Sina li-l-Nashr, 1990), 16. Also see "General Motors, Egypt," *Globe and Mail* (Toronto), 18 June 1986.

73. Springborg, *Mubarak's Egypt*, 110; Abd Allah, *al-Jaysh wa-l-Dimuqratiyya fi Misr*, 16.

74. "GM Egypt to Build Cars," Gazette (Montreal), 3 July 1991.

75. *Al-Malaff al-Watha'iqi li-l-Mushir*, part 2, 439, 463; Hani Badr al-Din, "Mustashfa Kubri al-Qubba al-'Askari . . . Madina Tibiyya Mutakamila," *al-Ahram*, 5 October 2011.

76. "Qanun Raqam 91 li-Sanat 1983 bi-Tanzim al-I'fa'at al-Jumrukiyya," *al-Jarida al-Rasmiyya*, no. 30, 28 July 1983; "Qanun Raqam 2 li-Sanat 1984 bi-Ighfal al-Hay'at wa-l-Sharikat wa-l-Wahadat al-Tabi'a li-Wazarat al-Intaj al-Harbi min Ba'd Anwa' al-Dara'ib wa-l-Rusum," *al-Jarida al-Rasmiyya*, no. 3, 19 January 1984; "Qarar Ra'is Jumhuriyyat Misr al-'Arabiyya bi-l-Qanun Raqam 186 li-Sanat 1986 bi-Isdar Qanun Tanzim al-I'fa'at al-Jumrukiyya," *al-Jarida al-Rasmiyya*, no. 34 (tabi'), 21 August 1986.

77. Springborg, *Mubarak's Egypt*, 115.

78. Ibid., 118.

79. Gotowicki, "The Role of the Egyptian Military in Domestic Society."

80. Judith Miller, "Cairo's Army Has a New Job: Milk the Cow," *New York Times*, 29 November 1985.

81. Abd Allah, *al-Jaysh wa-l-Dimuqratiyya fi Misr*, 97.

82. *Al-Malaff al-Watha'iqi li-l-Mushir*, part 2, 434 450.

83. Ibid., 455, 488.

84. "Wazarat al-Difa' wa-l-Intaj al-Harbi, Qarar Raqam 143 li-Sanat 1980," *al-Waqa'i' al-Misriyya*, no. 296, 31 December 1980.

85. *Al-Malaff al-Watha'iqi li-l-Mushir*, part 2, 441–44.

86. Ibid., 425, 466.

87. Muhammad Nur Farahat, "al-Hiwar Mustamir Hawla Dawr al-Mu'assasa al-'Askariyya fi Hayatina," *al-Ahalai*, 19 December 1984, in Abd Allah, *al-Jaysh wa-l-Dimuqratiyya fi Misr*, 107–10.

88. "Qarar Ra'is Jumhuriyyat Misr al-'Arabiyya Raqam 531 li-Sanat 1981 bi-Sha'n Qawa'id al-Tasarruf fi al-Aradi wa-l-'Aqarat allati Tukhliha al-Quwwat al-Musallaha wa-Takhsis 'A'idha li-Insha' Mudun wa-Manatiq 'Askariyya Badila," *al-Jarida al-Rasmiyya*, no. 42, 15 October 1981.

89. "Qarar Ra'is Jumhuriyyat Misr al-'Arabiyya Raqam 224 li-Sanat 1982 fi Sha'n Tanzim wa-Ikhtisasat Jihaz Mashru'a Aradi al-Quwwat al-Musallaha," *al-Jarida al-Rasmiyya*, no. 21, 27 May 1982.

90. "Qarar Ra'is Jumhuriyyat Misr al-'Arabiyya Raqam 403 li-Sanat 1990 bi-Sha'n Qawa'id al-Tasarruf fi al-'Aqarat al-Mashghula bi-Wadi'i al-Yadd min Khilal Jihaz Aradi al-Quwwat al-Musallaha," *al-Jarida al-Rasmiyya*, no. 41, 11 October 1990.

91. "Qanun Raqam 143 li-Sanat 1981 fi Sha'n al-Aradi al-Sahrawiyya," *al-Jarida al-Rasmiyya*, no. 35 (mukarrar), 31 August 1981.

92. "Wazarat al-Difa' wa-l-Intaj al-Harbi, Qarar Na'ib Ra'is Majlis al-Wuzara' wa-Wazir al-Difa' wa-l-Intaj al-Harbi Raqam 367 li-Sanat 1986 bi-Sha'n Tahdid al-Manatiq al-Istratijiyya Dhat al-Ahamiyya al-'Askariyya min al-Aradi al-Sahrawiyya allati la Yajuz Tamalukkuha," *al-Waqa'i' al-Misriyya*, no. 2, 3 January 1987.

93. Wajih Ra'fat, "Nahnu Narfud Hadhihi al-Zawahir wa-Nuhadhdhir min 'Awaqibiha," *al-Wafd*, 21 August 1986, in Abd Allah, *al-Jaysh wa-l-Dimuqratiyya fi Misr*, 157–60; EgyCo, http://www.egyco-egypt.com/depdetails_ar.aspx?ID=101, accessed 1 December 2014; Sahil Online, http://www.sa7elonline.com/ar/maps.php?resort=10, accessed 1 December 2014.

94. Amin Huwaydi, "Ta'ammulat: Kalima li-Wajh Allah," *al-Ahali*, 30 July 1986, in Abd Allah, *al-Jaysh wa-l-Dimuqratiyya fi Misr*, 145–46.

95. Ra'fat, "Nahnu Narfud Hadhihi al-Zawahir."

96. Abd Allah, *al-Jaysh wa-l-Dimuqratiyya fi Misr*, 15.

97. David W. Carr, "The Possibility of Rapid Adjustment to Severe Budget-Deficit and Other Economic Problems in Egypt," *Journal of Developing Areas* 1 (January 1990): 231; Muhammad Ahmad Labib, "Hiwar Hadi' Hawla Mawdu' Sakhin.

2- al-Ahdaf al-'Askariyya," *al-Wafd*, 21 August 1986, in Abd Allah, *al-Jaysh wa-l-Dimuqratiyya fi Misr*, 161–62.

98. Ibrahim Dusuqi Abaza, "La Tusadiru 'ala al-Matlub," *al-Wafd*, 3 July 1986, in Abd Allah, *al-Jaysh wa-l-Dimuqratiyya fi Misr*, 120–21.

99. See Abd Allah, *al-Jaysh wa-l-Dimuqratiyya fi Misr*, 120–41, 157–83.

100. "Wazarat al-Difa' wa-l-Intaj al-Harbi, Qarar Raqam 262 li-Sanat 1984 fi Sha'n Idafat Anshitat Jihaz Mashru'at al-Khidma al-Wataniyya bi-Wazarat al-Difa' ila al-Jadwal al-Murfaq bi-l-Qarar al-Wazari Raqam 105 li-Sanat 1974 bi-Sha'n al-Munsha'at wa-l-Wahadat al-Siriyya al-Mustathna min Riqabat wa-Taftish al-Jihaz al-Markazi li-l-Muhasabat," *Al-Waqa'i' al-Misriyya*, no. 46, 23 February 1985; "Wazarat al-Difa' wa-l-Intaj al-Harbi, Qarar Raqam 193 li-Sanat 1986 bi-Ilgha' al-'Amal bi-Qarar Na'ib Ra'is Majlis al-Wuzara' wa-Wazir al-Intaj al-Harbi bi-Sha'n Idafat Anshitat Jihaz Mashru'at al-Khidma al-Wataniyya bi-Wazarat al-Difa' ila al-Jadwal al-Murfaq bi-l-Qarar al-Wazari Raqam 105 li-Sanat 1974 bi-Sha'n al-Munsha'at wa-l-Wahadat al-Siriyya al-Mustathna min Riqabat wa-Taftish al-Jihaz al-Markazi li-l-Muhasabat," *Al-Waqa'i' al-Misriyya*, no. 161, 16 July 1986.

101. Abd Allah, *al-Jaysh wa-l-Dimuqratiyya fi Misr*, 15–16.

102. Amira Fikri, *al-Mushir Abu Ghazala: Zalamathu al-Siyasa wa-Ansafahu al-Tarikh* (Cairo: Maktabat Jazirat al-Ward, 2012), 241.

103. See Muhammad al-Baz, *al-Mushir: Qissat al-Sira' bayna Mubarak wa-Abu Ghazala* (Cairo: Kunuz li-l-Nashr, 2006), 27, 47–48; Fikri, *al-Mushir Abu Ghazala*, 242–43.

104. See Springborg, *Mubarak's Egypt*, 47–50, 63–65; Ibrahim, *Zaat*, 184–85, 251–70.

105. Springborg, *Mubarak's Egypt*, 121; al-Baz, *al-Mushir*, 27.

106. Midhat al-Zahid, "Mulahazat Hawla Hudur wa-Bayan al-Mushir Abu Ghazala li-Mu'tamar al-Hizb al-Watani," *al-Ahali*, 6 August 1986, in Abd Allah, *al-Jaysh wa-l-Dimuqratiyya fi Misr*, 152–54; Filib Jallab, "al-Mushir Abu Ghazala wa-'Adam al-Inhiyaz," *al-Ahali*, 19 May 1982; al-'Isawi, *Fi Islah Ma Afsadahu al-Infitah*, 147–57.

107. See Jihad 'Uda, "al-Mu'assasa al-'Askariyya wa-l-Siyasa al-Kharijiyya fi Fatrat al-Ra'is Mubarak, 1981–1987," in Abd Allah, *al-Jaysh wa-l-Dimuqratiyya fi Misr*, 51–63; Abd al-Qadir Shuhayb, "Hall Mushkilat al-Duyun al-Amrikiyya wa-l-Suviytiyya," *Ruz al-Yusuf*, 22 December 1986; *Al-Malaff al-Watha'iqi li-l-Mushir*, part 1, 334–403; part 3, 853–918.

108. al-Baz, *al-Mushir*, 48, 88; Springborg, *Mubarak's Egypt*, 99; *Al-Malaff al-Watha'iqi li-l-Mushir*, part 1, 380; Fikri, *al-Mushir Abu Ghazala*, 222–24.

109. *Al-Malaff al-Watha'iqi li-l-Mushir*, part 1, 382.

110. Ibid., part 2, 490; and Ministry of Defense website, http://www.mod.gov.eg/Mod/Mod_MilMuse01.aspx, accessed 10 January 2015.

III. See *Ruz al-Yusuf*, 3 and 10 March 1986; Sawsan al-Jayyar, "Qa'id Quwwat al-Amn al-Markazi li-Ruz al-Yusuf: al-Dubbat wa-l-Junud Ya'ishun fi Munakh Wahid," *Ruz al-Yusuf*, 16 February 1987; Christopher Dickey, "Mubarak Ends Curfew in Cairo; Riots May Have Enhanced Defense Minister's Standing," *Washington Post*, 9 March 1986.

112. Ghada Ghalib, "26 Ma'luma 'an Abu Ghazala," *al-Masry al-Youm*, 16 January 2015; Muhammad Adil and Agharid Mustafa, "al-Muqattam Tarikh min al-Af'al al-Fadiha," *Ruz al-Yusuf*, 23 March 2013.

113. The script writer was Usama Anwar 'Ukasha and the producer was state-owned Egyptian TV. *Layali al-Hilmiyya*'s dates of production are 1987 (first season), 1988 (second season), 1989 (third season), 1992 (fourth season), and 1995 (fifth season).

114. See, for example, Alan Cowell, "A Parade in Egypt Marks '73 Fighting: Military Observance Is First Since the Killing of Sadat by Islamic Militants," *New York Times*, 6 October 1988; Miller, "Cairo's Army Has a New Job: Milk the Cow"; Berger, "Egyptian Minister Became a Liability"; Alan Cowell, "Mubarak Ousts Defense Chief, Making Him Aid," *New York Times*, 16 April 1989; Tyler, "Mubarak Reassigns Key Deputy"; Pugh, "Egypt's Minister of Defence Told to Step Down."

115. See, for example, Mahmud al-Tuhami, "al-Qa'id al-A'la li-l-Quwwat al-Musallaha," *Ruz al-Yusuf*, 24 April 1989.

116. al-Baz, *al-Mushir*, 30–31.

117. Ibid.

3. Neoliberal Officers Make Big Money (1990s–2000s)

1. Mamduh Sha'ban, "Mash'al: Mabi'at Qita' al-Intaj al-Harbi Balaghat 3.6 Miliyar Junayh," *al-Ahram*, 24 October 2009; Ibtisam Ta'lab, "Dr. Sayyid Mash'al Wazir al-Intaj al-Harbi li-l-Masry al-Youm (2–2): Tasdir al-Asliha Yakhda' li-Hisabat Siyasiyya . . . ," *al-Masry al-Youm*, 15 May 2010; "Mash'al Yarqus bi-l-'Asa ma'a Ansarihi fi Hilwan . . . ," *El-Badil*, 12 November 2010; Jamil 'Afifi, "Mash'al fi al-Ihtifal bi-'Id al-Intaj al-Harbi: al-'Amil al-Rakiza al-Asasiyya li-Tatwir al-Intaj," *al-Ahram*, 20 October 2003; Egyptian Center for Social and Economic Rights, "Ghadan . . . al-Hukm fi Qadiyyat 'Ummal 99 Harbi," 29 August 2010, http://ecesr.org/?p=1031.

2. Cf. Jörn Brömmelhörster and Wolf-Christian Paes, eds., *The Military as an Economic Actor: Soldiers in Business* (Basingstoke: Palgrave Macmillan, 2003).

3. Ibid., 9.

4. Kristina Mani, "Militaries in Business: State-Making and Entrepreneurship in the Developing Countries," *Armed Forces and Society* 33 (July 2007): 607, 592.

5. Philippe Droz-Vincent, "From Political to Economic Actors: The Changing Role of Middle Eastern Armies," in *Debating Arab Authoritarianism: Dynamics and Durability in Non-Democratic Regimes*, ed. Oliver Schlumberger (Stanford: Stanford University Press, 2008), 201, 203.

6. Stephen Graham, *Cities Under Siege: The New Military Urbanism* (London: Verso, 2010), 380, 77, 74.

7. See Holger Albrecht, "Does Coup-Proofing Work? Political-Military Relations in Authoritarian Regimes Amid the Arab Uprisings," *Mediterranean Politics* 20 (2015).

8. Salah Abd al-'Aziz and Jamal al-Khuli, "Mubarak Yaftatih Ma'rad al-Quwwat al-Musallaha," *Al-Ahram*, 28 April 1999.

9. Yezid Sayigh, *Arab Military Industry: Capability, Performance, and Impact* (London: Brassey's Putnam Aeronautical 1992), 45.

10. Business Monitor International Ltd, *Egypt Defence and Security Report*, quarter 4, issue 4 (2011): 59.

11. Joe Stork, "Arms Industries of the Middle East," *MERIP* 17, no. 144 (January/February 1987): 14.

12. "CRS Report for Congress. Middle East Arms Control and Related Issues. Foreign Affairs and Nation Defense Division," Congressional Research Service, May 1, 1991, 14.

13. "White House Fact Sheet on the Middle East Arms Control Initiative," May 29, 1991, 579–80, http://www.presidency.ucsb.edu/ws/?pid=19637.

14. United States General Accounting Office (GAO), "Report to Chairman, Subcommittee on Foreign Operations, Export Financing and Related Programs, Committee on Appropriations, House of Representatives. Military Aid to Egypt. Tank Coproduction Raised Costs and May Not Meet Many Program Goals," July 27, 1993, 3.

15. See the Russian examples in Ksenia Gonchar, "The Largest European Army in Business: The Case of Russia," in *The Military as an Economic Actor: Soldiers in Business* (Basingstoke: Palgrave Macmillan, 2003), ed. Jörn Brömmelhörster and Wolf-Christian Paes, 178–80. Chinese examples are in Tai Ming Cheung, "The Rise and Fall of the Chinese Military Business Complex," in ibid., 56–58.

16. Abd al-'Aziz and al-Khuli, "Mubarak Yaftatih Ma'rad al-Quwwat al-Musallaha."

17. Sayigh, *Arab Military Industry*, 55–57; MoMP website, http://www.momp.gov.eg/Ar/Facts.aspx, accessed 15 January 2014.

18. Sayigh, *Arab Military Industry*, 57–60; AOI website, http://www.aoi.com.eg/aoiarab/factories/abdinfo.html; http://www.aoi.com.eg/aoiarab/factories/acfinfo.html; and http://www.aoi.com.eg/aoiarab/factories/sakrinfo.html, all accessed 15 January 2014.

19. For example, see the case of Russia in Julian Cooper, "Soviet Military Has a Finger in Every Pie," *Bulletin of Atomic Scientists* 46 (1990): 22–25.

20. Ahmad Abd al-'Azim, "al-Fariq Hamdi Wahiba- Ra'is al-Hay'a al-'Arabiyya li-l-Tasni' fi Hiwar ma'a Ruz al-Yusuf," *Ruz al-Yusuf,* 3 November 2009.

21. Ibtisam Ta'lab, "Dr. Sayyid Mash'al Wazir al-Intaj al-Harbi li-l-Masry al-Youm (2–2)," *al-Masry al-Youm,* 15 September 2010.

22. See Karima Korayem, *Egypt's Economic Reform and Structural Adjustment* (Cairo: Egyptian Center for Economic Studies, 1997); Dieter Weiss and Ulrich Wurzel, *The Economics and Politics of Transition to an Open Market Economy. Egypt* (Paris: OECD, 1998), 44–51.

23. Jamal Mazlum, *al-Quwwat al-Musallaha wa-l-Tanmiya al-Iqtisadiyya* (Cairo: Markaz Dirasat wa-Buhuth al-Duwal al-Namiya, 1999), 106.

24. "Qanun Raqam 11 li-Sanat 1991 bi-Isdar Qanun al-Dariba al-'Amma 'ala al-Mabi'at," *al-Jarida al-Rasmiyyai,* no. 18 (abi' alif), 2 May 1991.

25. "Wazarat al-Maliyya, Qarar Raqam 161 li-Sanat 1991 bi-Isdar al-La'iha al-Tanfidhiyya li-Qanun al-Dariba al-'Amma 'ala al-Mabi'at," *al-Waqa'i' al-Misriyya,* no. 123 (tabi'), 1 June 1991.

26. Brömmelhörster and Paes, *The Military as an Economic Actor,* 9.

27. Seymour Melman and Lloyd Dumas, "Planning for Economic Conversion," *Nation,* 16 April 1990: 526. Also see Seymour Melman, *The Demilitarized Society: Disarmament and Conversion* (Montreal: Harvest House, 1990).

28. Cooper, "Soviet Military Has a Finger in Every Pie," 22, 23–25.

29. United States General Accounting Office (GAO), "Report to Chairman, Subcommittee on Foreign Operations, Export Financing and Related Programs, Committee on Appropriations, House of Representatives. Cooperative Threat Reduction. Status of Defense Conversion Efforts in the Former Soviet Union," April 1997; Lisa Bergstrom, "Reevaluating U.S. Defense Conversion Assistance to Russia," *Georgetown Security Studies Review,* 26 December 2013.

30. Gonchar, "The Largest European Army in Business," 174.

31. Dongmin Lee, "Swords to Ploughshares: China's Defence Conversion Policy," *Defence Studies* 11 (March 2011): 1–4, 20.

32. Kenneth L. Adelman and Norman R. Augustine, "Defense Conversion: Bulldozing the Management," *Foreign Affairs* 71 (Spring 1992): 27, 33.

33. For more details about general characteristics in global cases of conversion, see ibid., 27–28; and the chapters on Russia, Argentina, Pakistan, Central America, and Indonesia in Brömmelhörster and Paes, *The Military as an Economic Actor.*

34. Walid Majdi, "Da'wa Tutalib bi-l-Tahqiq ma'a 50 Mas'ul baynahum Tantawi wa-l-Janzuri wa-Musa fi Fasad al-Khaskhasa," *al-Masry al-Youm,* 8 January 2012.

35. Paul Betts, "French Rail Group Awarded Cairo Order," *Financial Times,* 7 January 1986.

36. See the factory's official website, http://www.aoi.com.eg/aoiarab/aoi/semaf /pages/AboutA.html, accessed 15 January 2014; Abd al-Fattah Ibrahim, "800 'Arabat Qitar Jadida bi-'Istithmarat 1.5 Milyar Junayh," *al-Ahram,* 26 May 2004.

37. Mona al-Sayyid, "Tasni' al-Mukawwinat al-Dakhiliyya li-l-Qitarat Mahaliyyan Badalan min Istiradiha," *al-Ahram*, 28 August 2002.

38. Abd al-Fattah Ibrahim, "Bi-Hadaf Ta'miq al-Tasni' al-Mahalli al-Hay'a al-'Arabiyya li-l-Tasni' Tusharik li-'Awwal Marra fi Tahdith Ustul 'Arabat al-Sikka al-Hadid,'" *al-Ahram*, 2 June 2003; Abd al-Fattah Ibrahim, "3 'Uqud li-Tatwir 'Aarabat al-Sikak al-Hadidiyya wa-'Intaj al-Faramil Mahaliyyan," *al-Ahram*, 15 June 2003.

39. "Itfaqiyya ma'a al-Yaban li-Tasni' Qitarat al-Khatt al-Thalith li-Mitru al-'Anfaq Mahliyyan," *al-Ahram*, 11 November 2008.

40. "Trade Fairs Bring Together Industrial Insiders," *Daily News Egypt*, 25 October 2009.

41. "Total Orders Placed So Far with Mitsubishi of Japan for the Rolling Stock to Serve Different Cairo Metro Lines Valued L.E. 1.7 Billion," *AmCham Egypt Project News*, 21 September 2010.

42. For example, Muhammad Lutfi Mansur resigned in 2009 after a train accident in the rural area of 'Ayyat, near Giza. This minister was one of the business tycoons in Gamal Mubarak's circle.

43. Khayr Raghib, "Taqrir Hukumi: 82% min Khutut al-Sikak al-Hadidiyya Aqall Amanan," *al-Masry al-Youm*, 12 September 2010.

44. Personal observations and interviews with passengers at the Upper Egyptian train stops of Sohag, Qina, and Luxor, 3–4 April 2012.

45. "al-Jihaz al-Markazi li-l-Muhasabat: 'Ihdar 1.5 Milyar Junayh bi-Sharikat al-Nasr li-Sina'at al-Sayyarat," *Masrwy*, 26 June 2011.

46. "Hafiz Yu'lin fi al-Shura Tafasil Damm al-Nasr li-l-Sayyarat li-Wazaratih," *al-Bawwaba News*, 2 April 2013.

47. Amira Salah-Ahmed, "One on One: What Bailout? Chrysler Egypt Sales Surge in 2008," *Daily News Egypt*, 21 January 2009.

48. Shuruq Husayn, "Safqat Toyota wa-Sina'at al-Sayyarat al-Mahaliyya," al-Ahram, 31 October 2010.

49. Facebook page "Didd Fasad al-Hay'a al-'Arabiyya li-l-Tasni' AAV," https://www.facebook.com/pages/AAV-ضد-فساد-الهيئة-العربية-للتصنيع/ 163930696955240, accessed 20 March 2012. The same group of workers also created a blog for the same cause, http://aav-corruption.blogspot.com/2011/03/aav.html, accessed 20 March 2012.

50. Company profile of AAV generated from Graham & Whiteside Ltd., 15 October 2009; AVV company profile generated from Infocredit Group Business Information Reports—Egypt, 2 June 2011; "DaimlerChrysler Subsidiary List according to § 313 para. 4 of the German Commercial Law (HGB) as of December 31, 2002," http://www.cms.daimler.com/Projects/c2c/channel/documents/2095329 _DCX_Subsidiary_List_Group_2002_____313_HBG_.pdf, accessed 30 November 2012; Salah-Ahmed, "One on One."

51. "News in Brief," *Daily News Egypt*, 17 December 2008; Ahmed, "One on One"; AAV company profile generated from Infocredit Group Business Information Reports—Egypt, 2 June 2011.

52. Muhammad Amin, "al-Liwa' Bahari Ibrahim Jabir al-Dusuqi: Hadafuna Tatwir wa-Raf' Kafa'at Tirsanat al-Iskandariyya," *Uktubar*, 23 January 2011.

53. "Bay' Sharikat al-Nil li-l-Naql al-Nahri ila Jihaz al-Sina'at al-Bahriyya," *al-Ahram*, 3 October 2008; "Wazarat al-Difa' wa-l-Intaj al-Harbi. Qarar Raqam 3 li-Sanat 2010 bi-Sha'n Insha' Sharikat al-Nil li-l-Naql al-Nahri," *al-Waqa'i' al-Rasmiyya*, no. 66, year 182, 21 March 2010.

54. Du'a' Najib and Ahmad al-Dimirdash, "al-Intiha' min Tatwir Tirsanat al-Iskandariyya," *Amwal al-Ghadd*, 18 March 2013; Alexandria Shipyard website, http://www.alexyard.com.eg/ar%20first%20stage.html, accessed 15 April 2014. Mamduh Sha'ban and Jamal al-Khuli, "Tirsanat al-Iskandariyya Tahtafil bi-Tadshin 'al-Huriyya 3,'" *al-Ahram*, 28 December 2010; Rubban Muhammad Bahyy al-Dina Mandur, "Takhalluf Sina'at Bina' Sufun A'ali al-Bihar fi Misr," *International* (London), http://www.international-mag.com/index.php?option=com_content&view=article&id=651:2011–12–11–12–50–20&catid=37:getaways&Itemid=532, accessed 15 April 2014; China Shipbuilding Trading Co. website indicating sources of technology, http://www.cstc.com.cn, accessed 15 April 2014; Muhammad Amin, "al-Liwa' Bahari Ibrahim Jabir al-Dusuqi: Hadafuna Tatwir wa-Raf' Kafa'at Tirsanat al-Iskandariyya," *Masress*, 23 January 2011, http://www.masress.com/october/110405. The French company is Bureau Veritas.

55. "Alexandria Shipyard, Acquired Earlier by the Military Production Sector, Delivering Two Large Sized Barges, Part of a L.E. Billion Order for 16 Barges Issued by Citadel Group's Affiliate Handling Land River Transport Investments at Home," *AmCham Egypt Project News*, 10 August 2010.

56. See the company's website, http://nationalniletrans.com, accessed 15 April 2014.

57. See the company's website, http://www.ezzsteel.com/main.asp?pageid=119, accessed 15 April 2014.

58. 'Usama 'Abd al-'Aziz and Mukhtar Shu'ayb, "al-Ra'is Yaftatih Masna' Darfalat al-Sulb al-Makhsus al-Tabi' li-Wazart al-'Intaj al-Harbi bi-Abu Za'bal," *al-Ahram*, 7 December 2005.

59. Saygh, *Arab Military Industry*, 54.

60. "Mash'al: Mashru' 'Imlaq li-'Intaj wa-Darfalat al-Sulb," *al-Ahram*, 16 March 2004; Mamduh Sha'ban, "Ba'd Najah 'Intaj 'Awwal Lawh min al-Sulb bi-l-Darfala, Mash'al: al-'Intaj al-Harbi Yusahim fi Tatwir al-Sina'at al-Thaqila," *al-Ahram*, 23 September 2005; 'Abd al-'Aziz and Shu'ayb, "al-Ra'is Yaftatih Masna' Darfalat al-Sulb al-Makhsus."

61. Minister Ali Sabri stated this in an interview in March 2012. Zeinab Abul-Magd, "Siyadat al-Liwa' Sayuqatil al-Sha'b," *al-Masry al-Youm*, 3 April 2012.

62. Ghurfat al-Sina'at al-Ma'daniyya, "Nubdha 'an Sina'at al-Sulb fi Misr," http://www.cmiegypt.org/Pages/Overall/Article.aspx?Id=82, accessed 11 April 2014.

63. See the company's website, http://queenservicealex.blogspot.com, accessed 13 April 2014.

64. "Egypt's Construction Boom to Buoy Steel Production," *Daily News Egypt*, 14 December 2010; "Experts Talk Real Estate at al-Ahram," *Daily News Egypt*, 14 July 2009; "Ahmad 'Izz Yatakhalla 'an Wu'udih wa-Yarfa' As'ar Hadid al-Taslih," *al-Youm al-Sabi'*, 9 December 2010.

65. *Al-Waqa'i' al-Misriyya*, no. 160, year 183, 12 July 2010.

66. Dalia 'Uthman, "al-Mushir Yaftatih Masna' 'Asmant al-'Arish," *al-Masry al-Youm*, 1 May 2012; Amira Ibrahim, "al-Mushir Yaftatih 'Awwal Masna' Asmant 'Asakari bi-Taqat 3.2 Tann Sanawiyyan bi-Taklufa 174 Milyun Yuru," *al-Dostor al-Asly*, 30 April 2012; Sinoma, "Kiln Inlet Steel Tower of GOE Project Line 1 in Egypt Contracted by TCDRI Installed," http://en.sinoma.cn/news/ShowArticle.asp?ArticleID=989, accessed 13 April 2014. The Chinese company's name is TCDRI, part of state-owned Sinoma Group, and its website is http://www.tcdri.com.cn/english/intro.asp, accessed 13 April 2014.

67. Ibrahim, "al-Mushir Yaftatih 'Awwal Masna' Asmant 'Asakari."

68. Amira Hisham, "al-Ihsa': Irtifa' As'ar al-Asmant wa-Taraju' As'ar al-Hdid Khilal Shahr Yunyah al-Madi," *al-Ahram*, 22 July 2012; "al-Ihsa': Irtifa' As'ar al-Asmant wa-l-Zalat wa-Taraju' al-Hadid Khilal Shahr Sibtambir," *al-Masry al-Youm*, 22 October 2012.

69. Cement prices in the local Egyptian market are available at http://cementegypt.com/price, accessed 15 July 2012, 10 February 2013, and 13 April 2014.

70. AOI's electronics factory website, http://www.aoi.com.eg/aoiarab/factories/electinfo.html, accessed 16 April 2014.

71. See Nile Sat's company profile at http://www.nilesat.com.eg/AboutUs/CompanyProfile.aspx, accessed 16 April 2014.

72. See Egyptian Center for Social and Economic Rights, "al-Mudhakkira al-'Ula al-Muqaddama min al-Markaz al-Masri fi Qadiyyat 'Ummal Hilwan," http://ecesr.org/?p=1018; "al-Mudhakkira al-Thniya al-Muqaddama min al-Markaz al-Masri fi Qadiyyat 'Ummal Hilwan," http://ecesr.org/?p=1014; "al-Mudhakkira al-Thalitha al-Muqaddama in al-Markaz al-Masri fi Qadiyyat 'Ummal Hilwan," http://ecesr.org/?p=1021, all accessed 1 June 2014; Dar al-Khadamat al-Niqabiyya, "Waqa'i' Muhakamat 'Ummal Masna' 99 al-Harbi," 22 August 2010, http://www.ctuws.com/?item=511.

73. Interviews with anonymous workers at the MoMP, April 2012.

74. "Istighatha min 'Ummal al-Sharika al-Misriyya li-Islah wa-Bina' al-Sufun," *Tadamun Misr*, 23 July 2008, https://tadamonmasr.wordpress.com/2008/07/23; Jaklin Munir, "'Awdat Azmat 'Ummal al-Misriyya li-Islah al-Sufun li-Ta'annut al-Idara fi Tanfidh Matalibahum," *al-Youm al-Sabi'*, 1 May 2014; "Ihdar Huqu

'Ummal al-Misriyya li-l-Sufun wa-l-Sijn al-'Askari li-l-Mu'tarid," *El-Badil*, 6 April 2015.

75. Interview with Hamdi Wahiba and a group of protesting workers, March 2012. I obtained the internal document "Laws, Decrees, and Statutes Regulations of AOI" from the interviewed workers.

76. See chapter 2 for details on law no. 91 of 1983, law no. 2 of 1984, and law no. 186 of 1986. On AOI, see Presidential Decree no. 150 of 1976, *al-Jarida al-Rasmiyya*, no. 48, 25 November 1976.

77. "Qanun Raqam 91 li-Sanat 2005 bi-Isdar Qanun al-Dariba 'ala al-Dakhl," *al-Jarida al-Rasmiyyai*, no. 23 (tabi'), 9 June 2005.

78. "Wazarat al-Maliyya, Qarar Raqam 861 li-Sanat 2005 bi-Isdar al-La'iha al-Tanfidhiyya li-Qanun Tanzim al-I'fa'at al-Jumrukiyya," *al-Jarida al-Rasmiyya*, no. 249 (tabi'), 31 October 2005.

79. "Qanun Raqam 9 li-Sanat 2005 bi-Ta'dil ba'd Ahkam Qanun al-Dariba al-'Amma 'ala al-Mabi'at al-Sadir bi-Qanun Raqam 11 li-Sanat 1991," *al-Jarida al-Rasmiyya*, no. 13 (tabi'), 13 March 2005.

80. Cassation Court, session of 24 June 2003, "al-Ta'n Raqam 78 li-Sanat 72 al-Qada'iyya," published on the court's website, http://www.cc.gov.eg/Courts/Cassation_Court/All/Cassation_Court_Images.aspx?ID=111129441.

81. Cassation Court, session of 28 April 1993, "al-Ta'n Raqam 2018 li-Sanat 58 Qada'iyya," http://www.cc.gov.eg/Courts/Cassation_Court/All/Cassation_Court_Images.aspx?ID=111113254.

82. See, for instance, Cassation Court, session of 26 January 2003, "al-Ta'n Raqam 2233 li-Sanat 68 Qada'iyya," session of 24 June 2003, "al-Ta'n Raqam 75 li-Sanat 71 Qada'iyya," http://www.cc.gov.eg/Courts/Cassation_Court/All/Cassation_Court_Images.aspx?ID=111129104; http://www.cc.gov.eg/Courts/Cassation_Court/All/Cassation_Court_Images.aspx?ID=111129436.

83. See chapter 2.

84. Their full names are Tourism Development Authority (created in 1991 by the same law), General Authority for Reconstruction Projects and Agricultural Development, and New Urban Communities Authority.

85. "Qarar Ra'is Jumhuriyyat Misr al-'Arabiyya Raqam 407 li-Sanat 1994 bi-Takhsis ba'd al-Aradi li-l-Quwwat al-Musallaha," *al-Jarida al-Rasmiyya*, no. 49, 8 December 1994.

86. "Qarar Ra'is Jumhuriyyat Misr al-'Arabiyya Raqam 153 li-Sanat 2001 bi-Insha' al-Markaz al-Watani li-Takhtit Istikhdamat Aradi al-Dawla," *al-Jarida al-Rasmiyya*, no. 22, 31 March 2001.

87. See chapter 4 on retired generals in government positions.

88. "Wazarat al-Difa' wa-l-Intaj al-Harbi, Qarar Raqam 146 li-Sanat 2002 . . . ," *al-Waqa'i' al-Misriyya*, no. 20, 25 January 2003.

89. Interview with anonymous original owners of the land, Aswan, 2 July 2013.

90. Prices are given on the women's Internet forum at http://forums.fatakat.com/thread5037039, accessed 17 June 2014.

91. See public advertisements at http://egypt.aqar-estate.com/property-view -89326-فرصه_____في_الـ_البيع_بقرية_سيدي_كرير_للقوات_ رتم_%D9%A0%D9%A0%D9%A0١_حلـ_المسلحا and http://www.4orsa.com/re-alestate/80848/Chalet-for-sale-in-northern-coast/, both accessed 17 June 2014.

92. "Presidential Decree No. 330 of 2003 Bisha'n Takhsis Aradi Sahrawiyya li-Wazarat al-Difa' wa-I'tibariha min al-Manatiq al-Istratijiyya Dhat al-Ahamiyya al-'Askariyya," *al-Jarida al-Rasmiyya*, no. 52, 25 December 2003.

93. See Mustafa al-Miliji, "al-Qatamiyya al-'Ayn al-Sukhna Awwal Tariq Yatim Tanfidhahu min Kharij al-Muwazana," *al-Ahram*, 29 September 2004; 'Umar al-Shaykh, "Mubarak Yaftatih Tariq al-Kuraymat-Bani Suwayf ba'd Tashghilahu bi-Shahrayn," *al-Masry al-Youm*, 14 October 2008.

94. Al-Hay'a al-'Amma li-l-Isti'lamat, "al-Quwwat al-Musallaha wa-l-Tanmiya al-Shamila," http://www.sis.gov.eg/Ar/Templates/Articles/tmpArticles.aspx ?ArtID=67648#.U2K8BfogpD0, accessed 1 May 2014. On controlling billboards, see Yasmin Karam, "Sidam bayn Sharikat I'lanat al-Turuq al-Sahrawiyya wa-Jihaz al-Khidma al-Wataniyya," *al-Masry al-Youm*, 9 April 2014. (Media mistakenly think that there are two companies by the name Wataniyya, one for construction and the other for management and operations, but there is actually only one company.)

95. The subsidiary that undertook the project is the General Nile Company for Road Construction and Paving, http://www.holdroads.com/AR/index.php ?Page=Subjects&MID=79, accessed 1 May 2014. The parent holding company states that the project took eighteen months and cost LE48 million.

96. "Sidam Bayna Sharikat al-I'lanat al-Turuq al-Sahrawiyya wa-Jihaz al-Khidma al-Wataniyya," *al-Masry al-Youm*, 9 April 2014.

97. Islam 'Atris and Rihab Sabir, "al-Wataniyya Tuwasil Fard al-Rusum 'ala al-Turuq al-Sari'a . . . ," *Alborsanews*, 6 March 2014.

98. "Qarar Ra'is Jumhuriyyat Misr al-'Arabiyya Raqam 13 li-Sanat 2011," *al-Jarida al-Rasmiyya*, no. 3 (mukarrar), 23 January 2011.

99. Sami Kamil and 'Amr Jalal, "al-Mushir Yaftatih Tariq al-Jaysh Sharq al-Nil bi-l-Sa'id bi-Istithmarat 2.4 Milyar Junayh," *Akhbar al-Yawm*, 3 October 2011.

100. See al-Hay'a al-'Amma li-l-Isti'lamat, "al-Quwwat al-Musallaha wa-l-Tanmiya al-Shamila;" "Awad al-Haras, "Tawaqquf al-'Amal Faj'a bi-l-Mazra'a al-Wataniyya li-Sharq al-'Uwaynat," *al-Dostor*, 16 February 2014; Shahinda al-Bajuri," al-Quwwat al-Musallaha Tastaslih 100 Alf Faddan bi-Sharq al-'Uwaynat," *Sabah al-Khayr*, 2 November 2010.

101. Hasan 'Ashur, "Jawlat Mubarak fi Sharq al-'Uwaynat Tashmal Mazari' Wazart al-Zira'a wa-l-Quwwat al-Musallaha wa-Kliubatra," *al-Ahram*, 30 March 2005; Muhammad Ali, "Wazir al-Zira'a: Mashru'at al-Quwwat al-Musallaha wa-Abu

al-'Aynayn fi Sharq al-'Uwaynat Tushim fi Taqlis al-Fajwa al-Ghidha'iyya," *Sada El-Blalad*, 21 September 2013.

102. Muhammad Maqlad, "Muhami 'Ummal Kliubatra Yuharir Mahdr li-Hifz Huquq al-'Ummal . . . ," *El-Watan News*, 11 July 2012.

103. Lajnat al-Tadamun al-Fllahi-Misr, "Hal Yuraqib al-Majlis al-'Askari Jihaz Mashru'at al-Khidma al-Wataniyya?," *al-Hiwar al-Mutamaddin*, 5 April 2012.

104. "Qarar Ra'is Jumhuriyyat Misr al-'Arabiyya Raqam 403 li-Sanat 2009 bi-Sha'n I'adat Takhsis al-Ard al-Mashghula bi-l-Hay'a al-'Amma li-l-Naql al-Nahri . . . li-Salih Wazarat al-Difa'," *al-Jarida al-Rasmiyya*, no. 52 (mukarrar), 27 December 2009.

105. Lajnat al-Tadamun al-Fllahi-Misr, "Hal Yuraqib al-Majlis al-'Askari Jihaz Mashru'at al-Khidma al-Wataniyya?"

106. Sayyid Mahfuz, "al-Quwwat al-Musalahha Tabda' fi Istislah 17 Alf Faddan bi-Tushka," *al-Youm al-Sabi'*, 19 April 2011.

107. Jamil 'Afifi, "Wazir al-Intaj al-Harbi li-l-Ahram: Nusharik fi al-Tanmiya al-Shamila li-l-Dawla min Fa'id Taqatina wa-l-Musharaka fi Zira'at 23 Alf Faddan fi Mashru' Tushka," *al-Ahram*, 27 September 2003.

108. Ahmad Fu'ad and Jamal al-Khuli, "Fi al-Mantiqa al-Gharbiyya al-'Askariyya: Istislah 100 Alf Faddan . . . ," *al-Ahram*, 20 June 2000.

109. "Anzimat Rayy Sathi min al-Intaj al-Harbi li-Istislah 3.7 million Faddan," *al-Ahram*, 6 July 2003.

110. "al-Muhandisin Tastarrid 140 Faddan min al-'Iskan," *Alborsanews*, 10 January 2013.

111. Field research and personal communication with inhabitants, Greater Cairo, June 2014.

112. Supreme Constitutional Court, case no. 8 of judicial year 32, session 15 January 2013.

113. 'Awad Salim, "Jihaz Khadamat al-Quwwat al-Musallaha Yashab Manjam min Sharikat al-Nasr li-l-Ta'din bi-Aswan," *al-Dostor al-Asly*, 15 May 2013.

114. Fatima Mansur, "Shu'bat al-Mahajir Tunashid al-Quwwat al-Musallaha Khafd As'ar Mawad al-Tafjir," *al-Ahram*, 3 May 2011.

115. Muhammad Ibrahim, "Harb al-Mahajir..Tabda' Hadha al-Kharif," *al-Ahram al-Iqtisadi*, September 2008.

116. Ibid.

117. Mustafa 'Ubayd, "Qanun al-Mahajir al-Jadid Yuwaffir 6 Milyarat Junayh 'A'idat Sanawiyyan," *al-Wafd*, 4 June 2012.

118. South Center for Rights, Aswan, August report (unpublished), August 2013.

119. Wala' Abd al-Karim, "Shu'bat al-Mahajir Tutalib bi-I'adat al-Nazar fi As'ar al-Mutafajjirat wa-Takhfid Rusum al-Murur 'ala al-Turuq," *Sada El-Balad*, 16 October 2012, http://www.el-balad.com/289982.

120. "Wazir al-Intaj al-Harbi: Khita li-l-Masani' al-Harbiyya li-Tawfir al-Naqd al-Ajnabi. Al-Tawassu' fi Intaj al-Makhabiz al-Aliyya," *al-Ahram*, 8 March 2003; Jamil 'Afifi, "Mubarak Yaftatih Mashru'at Sihiyya wa-Ghidha'iyya Aqamataha al-Quwwat al-Musallaha li-Khidmat Janub al-Wadi," *al-Ahram*, 17 October 2003; "Wazarata al-Intaj al-Harbi wa-l-Tadamun al-Ijtima'i Yahtafilan bi-Taslim al-Duf'a al-'Ula min Akshak al-Khubz," *al-Ahram*, 15 February 2008; "10 Mujamma'at li-Intaj al-Khubz al-Muda'am bi-l-Qahira a-Kubra wa 249 Makhbaz fi al-Qura al-Mahruma wa 500 Manfadh li-l-Bay'," *al-Ahram*, 14 March 2008.

121. For instance, the bread outlet outside the Third Field Army camp in Nasr City, personal observation, Cairo, June 2014.

122. "Mubarak Yukallif Jihaz al-Khidma al-Wataniyya wa-Wazarat al-Dakhiliyya bi-Inha' Azmat Raghif al-Khubz," *al-Ahram*, 17 March 2008; Amina Khayri, "al-Raghif al-Masry Musqit al-Nizam Lam Yasta'id Karamatih," *al-Hayat*, 15 September 2012.

123. Ahmad Abd al-Khaliq, "al-Qwwuat al-Musallaha Tahtafil bi-Tafawwuq al-Hay'a al-Handasiyya," *al-Ahram al-Masa'i*, 31 October 2010; Daliya 'Uthman, "al-Liwa' Tahir Abd Allah Ra'is 'al-Hay'a al-Handasiyya': Nusahim fi Taqdim Khadamat li-Mutadarriri al-Kawarith wa-l-Siyul..wa-Insha' 12 Qariyah fi Sayna' wa-Halaib wa-Shalatin," *al-Masry al-Youm*, 27 March 2010.

124. Abd al-Khaliq, "al-Quwwuat al-Musallaha Tahtafil bi-Tafawwuq al-Hay'a al-Handasiyya."

125. For instance, EAAF collaborates with the Arab Contractors and al-Ragheb General Contractors Co.: Iman Ibrahim, "al-Mujtama'at al-'Umraniyya Tatala'ab fi Makittat al-Iskan al-'A'ili," *Dostor*, 1 July 2012; http://www.alraghebrcc.com/index.php?option=com_content&view=article&id=155%3A2012 –01–06–01–17–03&catid=50%3Acerrent-project&Itemid=53.

126. For example, Amin 'Abd al-'Azim, "I'tilaf al-Mujtama'at al-'Umraniyya Yutalib bi-Iqalat al-Qiyadat al-'Askariyya min al-Hay'a," *Sada al-Balad*, 19 August 2012; Ibrahim, "al-Mujtama'at al-'Umraniyya Tatala'ab fi Makittat al-Iskan al-'A'ili."

127. See the list of military hospitals on the MoD website, http://www.mod.gov.eg/Mod/Mod_Hosp.aspx, and the Military Medical Academy website, http://www.mma.edu.eg/History.aspx, both accessed 3 May 2015.

128. "Mubarak Yaftatih al-Markaz al-Tibbi al-'Aalami al-Tabi' li-l-Quwwat al-Musallaha bi-Munasabat Ihtifalat Uktubar," *al-Ahram*, 5 October 2004; Aram Roston and David Rhode, "Egyptian Army's Business Side Blurs Lines of U.S. Military Aid," *New York Times*, 5 March 2011.

129. Salah Abd al-'Aziz and Jamal al-Khuli, "Mubarak Yaftatih Ma'rad al-Quwwat al-Musallaha," *al-Ahram*, 28 April 1999.

130. See, for example, "al-'Arabiyya li-l-Tasni': Sanatasadda li-Istirad Haddanat al-Atfal li-Tawafurha Mahaliyyan," *al-Youm al-Sabi'*, 25 January 2012; Faruq Abd

al-Majid, "Fi Ta'awun bayna Wazarat al-Sihha wa-l-Hay'a al-'Arabiyya li-l-Tasni': 'Iyadat Mutanaqqila . . . ," *al-Ahram*, 18 February 2003.

131. "Brutkul Ta'awun Bayna Wazarat al-Istithmar wa-l-Hay'a al-'Arabiyya li-l-Tasni'," *al-Ahram*, 17 June 2005; see AOI's Engineering Factory website, http://www.enginefactory.com.eg/arabic/pages/Civil/Grain%20Air%20 Conveyor%20system/Grain%20Air%20Conveyor/Grain%20Air%20Conveyor .html, accessed 15 July 2014.

132. Ahmad Fu'ad, "Iftitah Mashru'at Mu'aljat Miyah al-Sarf al-Sina'i bi-l-Mahlla," *al-Ahram*, 11 March 2000.

133. Adil al-Laqqani, "Brutukul li-l-Ta'awun bayna Hay'at al-Tasni' wa-l-Ma'had al-Qawmi li-l-Ittisalat," *al-Ahram*, 29 July 2004.

134. Adil al-Dib, "70 Milyun Junayh li-Da'm Hay'at al-Nazafa," *al-Ahram*, 6 July 2010.

135. Jamil 'Afif, "bi-l-Ta'awun bayna Wazarati al-Intaj al-Harbi wa-l-Tanmiya al-Mahaliyya Tawqi' 'Aqd al-Marhala al-Rabi'a li-Tadwir al-Qimama fi 7 Muha-fazat bi-Taklufa 55 Miliun Junayh," *al-Ahram*, 28 April 2003; Sharif Jab Allah, "Wazir al-Tanmiya al-Mahaliyya: 40 Milyun Junayh li-Insha' 10 Masani' Tadwir Mukhallafat wa-Intaj al-Asmida," 28 February 2007; Sharif Jab Allah, "322,7 Milyun Junayh li-Mashru'at Tadwir al-Qimama," *al-Ahram*, 8 November 2007; Mamduh Sha'ban, "Wazir al-Intaj al-Harbi wa-l-Tanmiya al-Mahaliyya fi Ihti-fal bi-Taslim 85 'Arabat Itfa' Jadida," *al-Ahram*, 28 October 2009.

136. Sali Wafa'i, "bi-l-Ta'awun bayna Wazarati al-Bi'a wa-l-Intaj al-Harbi: Tasni' Mahariq li-l-Mukhallafat al-Tibiyya wa-l-Khatira . . . ," *al-Ahram*, 3 July 2003.

137. Mamduh Sha'ban, "Khutut bi-Masani' Mu'alajat al-Mukhallafat al-Zira'iyya li-Shabab al-Khirrijin," *al-Ahram*, 20 April 2005; "Tasni' Mu'iddat Haditha li-Qama'in al-Tub li-l-Hifaz 'Ala al-Bi'a," *al-Ahram*, 6 January 2001.

138. Al-Sayyid Hijazi, "Tasni' al-'Addadat al-Iliktruniyya Mahaliyyan bi-l-Ta'awun ma'a al-Intaj al-Harbi," *al-Ahram*, 19 September 2002; Samiya Zayn al-'Abidin, "al-Duktur Sayyid Mash'al fi Hiwar Muhimm ma'a al-Masa': Nahdat al-Intaj al-Harbi Ja'at bi-Da'm al-Ra'is Mubarak," *al-Masa'*, 27 November 2010.

139. "Min Khilal al-Intaj al-Harbi: Shabaka Jadida li-Taghyir Nizam al-Rayy . . . ," *al-Ahram*, 14 August 2003.

140. "Tawqi' Brutukul li-Tawfir Ajhizat al-Hasib al-Ali li-Tullab al-Jami'at," *al-Ahram*, 17 August 2000; "100 Alf Jihaz Kumbutar bi-As'ar Mukhaffada wa-Khadamat Majjaniyya min al-Sharikat al-'Alamiyya li-Tullab al-Jami'at," *al-Ahram*, 22 March 2000.

141. Amin al-Mahdi, "Baha' al-Din: Tawzi' Ajhizat Kumbutar 'ala Milyun Mu'allim wa-Idari bi-l-Ta'lim," *al-Ahram*, 28 January 2001; Muwaffaq Abu al-Nil, "Masna' li-l-Wajabat al-Madrasiyya wa 26 Madrasa Jadida bi-Aswan," *al-Ahram*, 1 September 2009.

142. Sa'id Halawi, "4 Alaf Jihaz li-Tawhid al-Adhan bi-Masajid al-Qahira al-Kubra," *al-Ahram*, 18 April 2006.

143. Manal al-'Isawi, "bi-l-Suwar . . . Mash'al Yakhtub Widd Ahalai Da'iratih bi-Hilwan bi-Qafila Tibyya Mjanaiyya," *al-Youm al-Sabi'*, 22 November 2010; "Fi Takrim al-Ummahat al-Mithaliyyat bi-Hilwan: Sayyid Mash'al Yad'u li-l-Musharak fi-l-Istifta'," *al-Ahram*, 25 March 2007; Mamduh Sha'ban, "Mash'al wa-'A'isha fi Ihtifal bi-'Id al-'Ummal: la Sihha lima Yatraddad hawla Khaskhasat Sharikat wa-Masani' al-Intaj al-Harbi," *al-Ahram*, 5 May 2006.

144. Mamduh Sha'ban, "Jack Warner Yaltaqi Mash'al wa-Yushid bi-Istad al-Intaj al-Harbi," *al-Ahram*, 2 November 2008.

4. The Republic of Retired Generals (1990s–2000s)

1. Muhammad Tahir, "Muhafiz al-Daqahliyya: Ma Tshamitush al-Kilab fina," *al-Wafd*, 29 July 2014; Salih Ramadan, "al-Liwa' 'Umar al-Shawadfi Muhafiz al-Daqahliyya . . . al-Rumansi alladhi Ya'ish fi al-Madina al-Fadila," *al-Watan*, 14 August 2013; "Azma Barlamaniyya wa-Ittihamat Mutabadala li-Husul Sharika 'ala 26 Alf Faddan," *al-Jumhuriyya*, 21 June 2010.

2. Holger Albrecht, "Does Coup-Proofing Work? Political-Military Relations in Authoritarian Regimes Amid the Arab Uprisings," *Mediterranean Politics* 20 (2015).

3. Personal communication, anonymous officer, Marine Corps University, Quantico, 21 October 2015.

4. Michel Foucault, *Security, Territory, and Population*, trans. Graham Burchell (Basingstoke: Palgrave, Macmillan, 2007), 36.

5. Stephen Graham, "When Life Itself Is War: On the Urbanization of Military and Security Doctrines," *International Journal of Urban and Regional Research* 36 (January 2012): 137.

6. C.f. LMDC's website, http://lmdc.gov.eg/en/about-us/clients.html, accessed 1 January 2013.

7. See, for example, Khalid Miri, "Mafia Mukhalafat al-Bina' fi a-Iskandariyya. Al-Niyaba Tuhaqqiq fi Balagh did Labib wa-l-Mahjub . . . ," *al-Akhbar*, 26 March 2013.

8. Amira 'Awad, "Ahali al-Nasiriyya Yantazirun al-Mawt . . . wa-l-Muhafaza Tutalibhum bi-l-Muta'akhirat," *al-Wafd*, 26 June 2014.

9. Shirin Tahir, "al-Niyaba Tastakmil al-Tahqiq ma'a Labib wa-l-Mahjub," *al-Wafd*, 8 March 2011; Shirin Tahir, "Ilgha' al-Tahaffuz 'ala Amwal al-Mahjub wa-Usratihi," *al-Wafd*, 19 June 2011.

10. Ibid.

11. Mahmud al-Mamluk and Ahmad Mitwalli, "Balagh Yattahim al-Mahjub wa-l-Nu'mani bi-l-Tala'ub fi Musa'adat al-Umam al-Muttahida," *al-Youm a-Sabi'*, 9 June 2011.

12. For his dissertation defense, see Samir Faraj's YouTube channel, https://www.youtube.com/watch?v=EqH82cTRCSQ, accessed 19 February 2016.

13. See Samir Faraj's website, http://samirfarag.com/index_ar.html, accessed 19 February 2016; "Qarar Ra'is Jumhuriyyat Misr al-'Aarabiyya Raqam 2 li-Sanat 2006," *al-Jarida al-Rasmiyya*, no. 52 (mukarrar) (B), 1 January 2006.

14. Nasr al-Qusi, "Raf' al-Aqsur min Kharitat al-Turath al-'Alami li-Munazammat al-Yunisko," *Aqbat Muttahidun*, 14 August 2010.

15. "Al-Majlis al-'A'ala li-l-Quwwat al-Musallaha, Marsum bi-Qanun Raqam 45 li-Sanat 2011 bi-Ta'dil ba'd Ahkam Qanun al-Qada' al-'Askari al-Sadir bi-l-Qanun Raqam 25 li-Sanat 1966," *al-Jarida al-Rasmiyya*, no. 18 (mukarrar alif), year 54, 10 May 2011; "Tashri'iyyat al-Sha'b Tubqi 'ala Mada Taqsir Muhakamat al-Dubbat al-Fasidin 'ala al-Qada' al-'Askari Hatta ba'd Taqa'udihim," *El-Badil*, 22 April 2012.

16. Najwa Abd al-Aziz, "Samir Faraj Yandamm li-Nazif fi Qadaya al-Fasad," *al-Wafd*, 16 April 2011; Iman al-Hawwari, "Muhami Niyabat al-Aksur Yanfi Qiyamihi bi-l-Tahqiq fi Mukhalafat Fasad Nazif wa-Samir Faraj," *al-Ahram*, 19 February 2012; Ahmad Finjan, "al-Niyaba al-'Askariyya Tahbis Faraj 15 Yawm," *al-Wafd*, 21 April 2011.

17. Karim Abd al-Mu'in, "Muzaharat bi-l-Suways Tutalib bi-Rahil al-Muhafiz wa-Tahsin al-Awda'," *al-Masa'*, 9 February, 2011; Abd Allah Dayf, "Muzahart fi al-Suways li-Muhakamat al-Muhafiz," *al-Wafd*, 22 April 2011; also see this local blog: http://nagyheikal122.blogspot.com/2011/08/blog-post_1273.htm, accessed 2 October 2012.

18. See this local blog: http://nagyheikal122.blogspot.com/2011/08/blog-post_1273.html, accessed 2 October 2012.

19. Ilhami al-Marghani, "Muhammad Abu al-'Aynayn Mustathmir min Dawlat al-Fasad," *al-Hiwar al-Mutamaddin*, no. 3794, 20 July 2012; Faraj Abu al-'Izz, "al-Akhbar Takshif Haqiqat al-Mukhalafat bi-Mantikat Shamal Gharb Khalij al-Suwys," *Akhbar al-Yawm*, 14 March 2011; Faraj Abu al-'Izz, "al-Akhbar Takshif Haqiqat al-Mukhalafat bi-Mintaqat Shamal Gharb Khalij al-Suways," *Akhbar al-Yawm*, 14 March 2011.

20. Muhammad al-'Ajrudi, "'Ummal Siramika Cleopatra Yantazi'un Huquqahum min Abu al-'Aynayn," *al-Ahram*, 17 March 2012; Walid Majdi, "'Ummal Cleopatra Yujbirun Abu al-'Aynayn 'ala al-Istijaba li-Matalibihim ba'd Muhasaratihi li-Sa'at," *al-Masry al-Youm*, 16 March 2012.

21. Suhayla Nazmi, "Fi Nadwa bi-Handasat al-Iskandariyya: al-Muhandisun al-'Askariyyun Azalu 1 Milyun Lagham fi Sina'," *al-Ahram*, 28 November 1998.

22. Muhammad Mustafa, Tazahur 300 min Ahali Kafr al-Shaykh li-l-Mutalaba bi-Iqalat 'Abdin," *al-Ahram*, 3 May 2011.

23. 'Ala' Abd Allah, "Intiha' Mushkilat Miyah al-Shurb bi-Kafr al-Shaykh," *al-Ahram*, 10 December 2008; 'Ala' Abd Allah, "Muhafiz Kafr al-Shaykh Yushakkil Lajna li-Bahth Mushkilat Miyah al-Shurb . . . ," *al-Ahram*, 11 July 2014.

24. "Zaqzuq wa 'Abdin Yada'an Hajar Asas Madina Sakaniyya bi-Kafr al-Shaykh," *al-Ahram*, 26 November 2008.

25. 'Ala' Abd Allah, "12 Da'wa Qada'iyya Didd Muhafiz Kafr al-Shaykh," 24 June 2010.

26. Salah Sharabi, "Kafr al-Shaykh Tutalib bi-Iqalat 'Abdin," *al-Wafd*, 31 July 2011.

27. 'Ala' Abd Allah; "Idrab Ashab Wakalat al-Fawakih wa-l-Khudrawat bi-Kafr al-Shaykh," *al-Ahram*, 30 March 2010; Muhammad Sulayman, "Idrab Ashab Wakalat al-Fawakih wa-l-Khudrawat bi-Kafr al-Shaykh," *al-Youm al-Sabi'*, 24 March 2010.

28. Hamdi al-Sa'id Salim, "Hal min al-Nahda an Yakhtar Mursi Muhafizan Baltajiyyan li-Wazarat al-Tanmiya al-Mahaliyya?," *al-Hiwar al-Mutamaddin*, 3 August 2012; Muhammad Nassar, "Irtiyah li-Tark Muhafiz Kafr al-Shaykh li-Mahammih wa-Sakhat li-Tawallih al-Hukm al-Mahalli," *al-Shorouk*, 1 August 2012. While governor of Beni Suief, he issued decree no. 1797 of 2006 allotting 1365 square meters by the Nile to the National Security Council to build a headquarters. See Hamdi al-Sa'id Salim, "Hal min al-Nahda an Yakhtar Mursi Muhafizan Baltajiyyan li-Wazarat al-Tanmiya al-Mahaliyya?"

29. Muhammad Mustafa, "Tazahur 300 min Ahali Kafr al-Shaykh l-Iqalat 'Abdin," *al-Ahram*, 3 May 2011.

30. Farida al-Qadi, "Ghadan Mu'tamar Muwassa' li-Da'm al-Dustur," *Masrawy*, 8 January 2014.

31. Interview with General Fu'ad Sa'd al-Din: Abd al-Aswani, "al-Liwa' Fu'ad Sa'd al-Din Muhafiz al-Minya li-l-Masry al-Youm: Antazir Tashri' Yamnah al-Muhafizin Mazid min al-Salahiyyat," *al-Masry al-Youm*, 27 May 2006; Ashraf Kamal, "Miyah al-Sarf al-Sihhi Taqtahim Manzil al-Minya," *al-Wafd*, 16 August 2011; also see local blog http://shamalelsa3ed.blogspot.com/2009/11/00.html, accessed 5 December 2012.

32. "Msra' 4 Ashkhas fi Hadith Gharaq bi-l-Minya," *Akhbar Misr*, 15 October 2007.

33. Muhammad Abd al-Shafi, "Shahid 'Iyan 'ala Fasad al-Mahaliyyat . . . fi Hadith al-Mi'adiyya . . . ," *al-Ahram*, 26 December 2007; "Msra' 4 Ashkhas fi Hadith Gharaq bi-l-Minya," *Akhbar Misr*, 15 October 2007; Sa'id Nafi' wa-Tiriza Kamal, "Irtifa' Dahaya Mi'adiyyat Dir Mawwas bi-l-Minya . . . ," *al-Masry al-Youm*, 24 December 2007.

34. The Mallawi High Bridge opened in 2012.

35. "Dallu'at Mubarak al-Tha'ir Muhammad Anwar al-Sadat Batal 'Isabat al-Mafiya allati Nahbat Misr," *Sout al-Omma*, 13 February 2013; Ayman Sha'ban, "Bakri:

Tal'at al-Sadat wa-Ashiqqa'uh Kawwanu 10 Milyar Junayh bi-Tariq Ghayr Mashru'," *Masrawy*, 14 August 2011; Muhammad Sa'd Khattab, "'Ismat al-Sadat Hut Takhsis al-Aradi . . . ," *Sout al-Omma*, 3 Februray 2013.

36. Muhammad Allam, "al-Markazi li-l-Muhasabat: 'Izz Ishtara 21 Milyun Mitr fi Gharb Khalij al-Suways bi 5 Junayhat li-l-Mitr," *El-Badil*, 17 April 2011.

37. Muhammad al-Bahnasawi, "al-Liwa' Mustafa 'Afifi Qa'id al-Haras al-Jumhuri al-Asbaq: al-Siyada li-l-Qanun wa-l-Nizam al-Sabiq Adkhalana fi Ghaybuba," *al-Akhbar*, 13 April 2011.

38. Karim Yahiya, "Qissat Rajul A'mal min Zaman Ra'smaliyyat al-Mahasib . . . ," *al-Ahram*, 27 June 2011; Muhammad 'Awad, "Masir Tharwat Mubarak . . . ," *al-Youm al-Sabi'*, 22 June 2012.

39. Interview with an anonymous local citizen working in Sharm al-Shaykh, Cairo, 15 June 2014.

40. Muntasir al-Zayyat, "Fasad al-Bahr al-Ahmar li-l-Rukab (2)," *al-Masry al-Youm*, 10 March 2010; Mamhumd al-Dab', "al-Fasad Yabda' Ahyanan bi-Sura ma'a Ahmad Nazif . . . Asrar al-Qabd 'ala Imbratur al-Iskan fi al-Bahr al-Ahmar," *Sout al-Omma*, 20 February 2010; Yusuf al-'Umi and Hisham Yasin, "Man' Ibnat Muhafiz al-Bahr al-Ahmar al-Sabiq min al-Safar li-Ittihamiha fi Qadyyat Kasb Ghayr Mashru'," *al-Masry al-Youm*, 21 April 2013.

41. Amr Hasan, "Bawwabat al-Ahram Tufatish fi Dhakirat Idrab al-Mahalla 'an Mashru' Thawra lam Yaktamil," *al-Ahram Gate*, 9 February 2012.

42. Sayyid 'Abdin, "Muhafiz Suhaj Yuhil Malaffat Fasad al-Nu'mani li-l-Niyaba," *al-Wafd*, 30 June 2012; interview with an anonymous local citizen, 13 March 2012.

43. Muhammad Zaki, "al-Nu'mani Yastab'id Hall al-Majalis al-Mahaliyya Haliyan," *al-Wafd*, 2 March 2011; Muhammad Ali, "Lajna Qanuniyya li-l-Khuruj min Wartat al-Majalis al-Mahaliyya," *al-Ahram*, 12 March 2011; ECESR, "al-Haythiyyat al-Kamila li-Hukm Hall al-Majalis al-Mahaliyya al-Sha'biyya," http://ecesr.org/?p=4051, accessed 30 January 2013.

44. Nahid Nasr, "Muhafiz Aswan: Manazil al-Siyul Satabta'id 'an al-Makharrat," *al-Youm al-Sabi'*, 21 January 2010; Mahmud al-Malla, "Mutadarriru al-Siyul fi Aswan: al-Hukuma Fathat al-Makharrat 'ala Manazilina," *al-Masry al-Youm*, 9 August 2010.

45. 'Izz al-Din Abd al-'Aziz, "al-Talawwuth Yuhasir Buhayrat Nasir," *al-Ahram al-Masa'i*, 3 September 2012; 'Izz al-Din Abd al-'Aziz, "al-Hay'a Wahida wa-l-Taqarir Mutadriba . . . wa-l-Talawwuth Yanhash fi Buhayrat Nasir," *al-Ahram al-Masa'i*, 13 December 2014.

46. The list of colonels in control of quarries in 2011 included Yusuf Bakir, 'Ala' Muhammad Isma'il, Abd al-Rahim Abd al-Raziq Ahmad, and al-Sabbahi Ahmad. "Aswan's August Report" (unpublished), August 2013.

47. "Tahdid Asma' al-Murashshahin li-l-Shura min al-Hizb al-Watani bi-l-Qahira al-Yawm," *al-Ahram*, 9 April 2001.

48. Ibtisam Sa'd, "Matlub Bank Ma'lumat li-Da'm al-Sina'at al-Mughadhiya . . . ," *al-Ahram*, 29 June 1999.

49. "Tarh 120 Sharika Hukumiyya Misriyya li-l-Bay'," *al-Bawwaba*, 14 September 2000.

50. "Intel to Manufacture Computer Chips in Egypt," *IPR Strategic Information Database*, 6 November 2000.

51. Muhyi al-Din Fathi, "Hay'at al-Istithmar Tuwafiq 'ala Mashru' Misri Kuwayti Bahrini Imarati li-l-Asmida al-Kimawiyya bi-Istithmar 300 Milyun Dular," *al-Ahram*, 13 October 2003; Nur al-Qarmuti, "Bi-Kulfa Istithmariyya 330 Milyun Dular Mashru' Masri-Imarati-Bahrini-Kuwayti li-Intaj al-Asmida al-Kimawiyya wa-Mushtaqqatiha fi Abu Qir," *al-Hayat*, 13 October 2003.

52. AlexFert Company profile generated from Zoom Company Information, 22 August 2014; AlexFert company profile generated from InfoCredit Group, 27 April 2013; AlexFert website, http://www.alexfert.com/new/abouts/view/2 /menuid:8, accessed 22 August 2014; Egypt Kuwait Holding (EKH) website, http://www.ekholding.com/Portfolio/Fertilizers—Petrochemicals/AlexFert .aspx, accessed 27 April 2013.

53. Muhyi al-Din Fathi, "Ta'sis 1120 Sharika bi-Istithmarat 10.1 Milyar Junayh fi 6 Ashhur," *al-Ahram*, 27 February 2004.

54. UNCTAD WID Country Profile: Egypt, posted November 2006, http://unctad .org/sections/dite_fdistat/docs/wid_cp_eg_en.pdf. The figure for 2005 includes the petroleum sector. See table 3 and 6 for the period 1980–2005.

55. Ibid., table 6; Muhyi al-Din Fathi, "Bahth Jadhb al-Istithmarat al-Italiyya ila Mu- hafazat al-Minya," *al-Ahram*, 3 April 2004; Muhyi al-Din Fathi, "2 Milyar Junayh Istithmarat Yabaniyya fi Misr," *al-Ahram*, 29 January 2002.

56. "Chinese Investment in Free Zone Valued," IPR Strategic Information Data- base, 2 June 2004.

57. Yasir Subhi, "Fi Munaqasha Sakhina Hawla Ta'dil Qanun Hawafiz al-Istithmar, al-Ghamrawi: al-Ta'dilat Talbiya li-Matalib al-Mustathmirin . . . ," *al-Ahram*, 5 March 2004; Amr Fawzi et al., "Wazir al-Maliyya wa-Ra'isa Hay'at Suq al-Mal wa-l-Istithmar fi Mu'tamar al-Bursa . . . ," *al-Ahram*, 30 December 2003; "Qanun Raqam 162 li-Sanat 2000 bi-Ta'dil ba'd Ahkam Qanun wa-Damanat Hawfiz al-Istithmar al-Sadir bi-l-Qanun Raqam 8 li-Sanat 1997," *al-Jarida al-Rasmiyya*, no. 24 (mukarrar), 18 June 2000.

58. UNCTAD WID Country Profile: Egypt.

59. 'Ali Khalid and Basil Basha, "Da'wa Qada'iyya Tutalib bi-Nadb Qadi li-l- Tahqiq ma'a 50 Waziran baynahum Tantawi wa-l-Janzuri wa-'Ubayd fi Fasad al-Khaskhasa," *El-Badil*, 8 January 2012.

60. Tadamun, "al-Markaz al-Watani li-Takhtit Istakhdamat Aradi al-Dawla," http:// www.tadamun.info/?post_type=gov-entity&p=2745, accessed 10 May 2013.

61. Zeinab Abul-Magd, "Dawalat Qanun Wazarat al-Difa'," *al-Masry al-Youm*, 6 May 2012.

62. Muhammad Sa'd Khattab, "Safqat Ard al-'Ayat Tafdah Istimrar Nufudh al-Hizb al-Watani," *Sout al-Omma*, 12 February 2012.

63. "Al-Istithmar: I'adat Tarh Qadiyyat al-Misriyya al-Kuwaytiyya al-Khassa bi-Ard al-'Ayyat amam Fadd al-Munaza'at," *Mubashir*, 30 July 2014; "al-Shawadfi: Rusum Taghir Nashat Ard al-Sharika al-Kuwaytiyya fi al-'Ayyat 30 Miliyar Junayh," *al-Masry al-Youm*, 4 August 2010; Muhammad Sa'd Khattab, "Safqat Ard al-'Ayat Tafdah Istimrar Nufudh al-Hizb al-Watani," *Sout al-Omma*, 12 February 2012; Amr Abd al-Hamid et al., "Mihlib Yaltaqi Mas'uli al-Misriyya al-Kuwaytiyya al-Usbu' al-Muqbil," *al-Borsa News*, 2 April 2014; Ahmad 'Ashur and Yusuf Majdi, "al-Masriyya al-Kuwaytiyya Tatlub Mufaqat al-Quwwat al-Musallaha li-Iqamat Matar fi al-'Ayyat," *al-Mal News*, 14 May 2014.

64. Muhammad Tahir, "Muhafiz al-Daqahliyya: 'ma tshammitush al-kilab fina,'" *al-Wafd*, 29 July 2014.

65. See TDA website, http://www.tda.gov.eg/AboutTDA/TDAConstruction.aspx, accessed 20 February 2015.

66. 'Arafat 'Ali, "Nazif al-Aradi al-Siyahiyya Yatawasal bi-l-Bahr al-Ahmar," *al-Ahram*, 18 October 2011.

67. Nadiya Mansur, "al-Hilm al-Da'i' fi Mashru' al-Ittihad al-Ta'awuni," *al-Ahram*, 26 August 2009; Muhammad Sa'd Khattab, "Khal' al-Misiri wa A'wanuh min Majlis Idarat al-Ittihad," *Sout El-Omma*, 20 May 2014; Minna Islam, "Hall Majlis Idarat al-Ittihad al-Taw'auni al-Iskani wa-Ta'yin Akhar Mu'aqqat," *al-Bawwaba News*, 20 February 2014.

68. Ministry of Housing website, http://www.moh.gov.eg/Affiliates/Affiliates_mission.aspx, accessed 20 October 2015.

69. 'Umar Sahwki et al., "Sarf Sihhi . . . Masdud," *al-Misa*, 1 November 2013. http://www.almessa.net.eg/main_messa.asp?v_article_id=11952#.VBX8di6Szzc.

70. For instance, Muhammad al-'Isawi, "Infijar Mawasir al-Miyah wa-l-Sarf Yghriq Sibin al-Kum," *al-Ahram*, 13 December 2010; Abd al-Mun'im Hijazi, "Sami 'Imara..Muhandis Takhrib al-Munufiyya," *al-Wafd*, 8 April 2011.

71. See the ministry's website, http://www.moh.gov.eg/Affiliates/Affiliates.aspx, accessed 10 October 2014.

72. Ahmad al-Buhayri et al., "Shawari' al-Qahira Tashta'il bi-'Asharat al-Muzaharat li-Raf' al-'Ujur wa-l-Tathbit wa-'Iqsa' al-Fasidin," *al-Masry al-Youm*, 13 February 2011; Wa'il Fikri, "Muhafiz al-Jiza wa-Na'ibahu wa-Ra'is al-Mutaba'a . . . Irhalu," *Masrawy*, 27 February 2011.

73. Abd al-Azim Basil, "Ra'is Hay'at al-Nazafa wa-Tajmil al-Qahira: Mqalib al-Qimama taht al-Riqaba," *al-Ahram*, 26 October 1999.

74. Yusri Ahmad 'Abawi, "al-Nazafa bayna al-Sharikat al-Khassa wa-Fawatir al-Kahraba'," *Ahwal Masriyya*, 1 October 2003; "Jami'u al-Qimama Yatazaharun

Ihtijajan 'ala Isnad Sharq al-Qahir li-Sharkia Wahdia," *al-Masry al-Youm*, 30 April 2009; Nadia al-Mallakh, "Lu'bat al-Qitt wa-l-Fa'r Bayna al-Muhafaza wa-Sharikat al-Nazafa," *al-Ahram*, 6 July 2009; Muhammad al-Khuli, "Ta'aththur Mufawadat Ta'dil 'Uqud Sharkiat al-Nazafa al-Ajnabiyya ma'a Muhafazat al-Qahira," *al-Dusur al-Asli*, 31 May 2011.

75. See the Survey Authority's website, http://www.esa.gov.eg/history.aspx, accessed 10 December 2013.

76. Videos showing workers' reactions against him in 2011, https://www.youtube.com/watch?v=6LSZaXfB1Q0, accessed 20 February 2016.

77. Hamada Sa'd, "al-Liwa' Muhammad Abd al-Latif Ra'is Hay'at al-Misaha al-Sabiq Muhafizan li-Dumyat wa-Rudud Af'al Ghadiba bayna Abna' Dumyat li-Ta'ynahu," *Shabakat Dumyat al-Ikhbariyya*, 13 August 2013.

78. See the Ministry of Trade Industry website, http://www.mti.gov.eg/affiliates/industry/pvtd/about.htm, accessed 10 December 2013; Ahmad al-'Attar, "Mashru' li-Tahsin Intajiyyat al-Masani' bi-l-Ta'awun ma'a al-Yaban," *al-Ahram*, 28 April 2004.

79. Interview with Sayyid Abd al-Qadir Sayyid by Wa'il Isma'il and Nuha Rushdi, Economic and Business History Research Center, American University in Cairo, 26 September 2006.

80. See the organization's website, http://www.goeic.gov.eg/briefindex.asp, 10 December 2013.

81. Samah Labib, "Khubara': Kashf Jihaz Himayat al-Mustahlik 'an Asma' al-Bada'i' al-Amrikiyya al-Fasida Yadurr al-'Ilaqa bayna al-Baladin," *al-Youm al-Sabi'*, 16 February 2009; Salah al-Sa'dani, "al-Wafd Takshif bi-l-Mustandat Manabi' al-Fasad fi al-Sadirat wa-l-Waridat," *al-Wafd*, 21 February 2011.

82. Except for the first year, 1956–57, its head was law professor and judge Muhammad Hilmi Bahjat Badawi.

83. Khidr Khudayr, "Al-Fariq Fadil fi Dhikra Murur 34 'Am 'ala I'dadat al-Tashghil: Qanat al-Suways Satuhaqqiq Thani Akbar Irad fi Tarikhiha Raghm al-'Alamiyya," *al-Ahram*, 8 June 2009; Sayyid Ibrahim, "2.84% Mutawassit Ziyada fi Rusum 'Ubur Qanat al-Suways Bidaya min April," *al-Ahram*, 28 December 2006.

84. Wala' Wahid, "Ishti'al Muzaharat Qanat al-Suways," *al-Wafd*, 24 June 2011; Azza Khalil, "'Ummal Sharikat Qanat al-Suways amam Maktab al-Irshad 28 June 2011," *Tadamun*, 6 July 2011, accessed 1 December 2014, https://tadamonmasr.wordpress.com/category/عامل-نقل-عام-الشركات-التابعة-لهيئة-قناة-السويس/.

85. See the Egyptian Authority for Maritime Security website, http://www.eams.gov.eg, accessed 1 December 2014.

86. See the River Transport Authority website, http://www.rta-egypt.com/services.html, accessed 1 December 2014; Muwaffaq Abu al-Nil, "Yatfaqqadha al-Ra'is Mubarak fi Ziyaratihi li-Aswan: Tatwir Mahattat Kahraba' wa-Mina' al-Sadd

al-'Ali," *al-Ahram*, 10 January 2005. General Kamal Maghribi was appointed as the head of the High Dam Port Authority in 2011.

87. "Qarar Ra'is Majlis al-Wuzara' Raqam 898 li-Sanat 2002 bi-Insha' Jihaz Riqabat al-Dawla 'ala al-Mawani al-Misriyya," *al-Jarida al-Rasmiyya*, no. 22, 30 May 2002.

88. Maritime Safety Committee, "71 Countries Make IMO's Initial STCW White List," 73rd session: 27 November—6 December 2000, http://www.imo.org/blast/contents.asp?topic_id=68&doc_id=513, accessed 20 February 2016; see also Baltic and International Maritime Council, "2010 Shipping Industry Flag State Performance Table," https://www.bimco.org/News/2010/11/~/media/A9617EA297FD442E88138E1443C5CA8B.ashx, accessed 20 February 2016; Khayr Raghib, "Taqrir Dawli: Misr fi al-Qa'ima al-Sawda' li-l-Naql al-Bahri," *al-Masry al-Youm*, 7 April 2011.

89. See MTS workers' Facebook page, "La li-'Askarat al-Naql al-Bahri," 12 April 2012, https://mbasic.facebook.com/LaLskrtAlnqlAlbhry/photos/a.346917295360213.90887.346895428695733/356052124446730/?type=1&source=46&refid=17; "Qita' al-Naql al-Bahri didd al-'Askara," 28 July 2012, https://elthawry.wordpress.com.

90. Adil al-Bahnasawi, "Fath al-Bab amam a-Mustathmirin al-'Arab wa-l-Ajanib li-Idarat wa-Tashghil al-Mawani' fi Misr," *al-Sharq al-Awsat*, 15 May 2005; Salah Abd al-'Aziz, "Misr Tastadif Awwal Majlis li-l-Ru'ah li-Tarwij al-Istithmar fi Mashru'at al-Naql al-Bahri," *al-Ahram*, 29 January 2006; Najla' Kamal, "al-Liwa' Shirin Hasan Yuhadhir min Istihwadh al-Ajanib 'ala Sharikat al-Naql," *al-Youm al-Sabi'*, 21 June 2009.

91. Rami Ibrahim, "al-Sirsawi li-l-Mashhad lam Atalqqa Ayy Ittisal Rasmi li-Tawwali Wazarat al-Naql," *al-Mashhad*, 27 November 2011; MENA, "al-Mahkama al-Ta'dibiyya Tudin 58 Mas'ul bi-Tuhmat al-Tasabbub fi Gharaq al-'Abbara al-Salam 98," *al-Dostor al-Asly*, 21 April 2010; Hanan Hajjaj, "Fasad Wazari wa-Sariqa 'Alaniyya bi-Mina' Sharq al-Tafri'a," *al-Ahram*, 9 April 2011.

92. Hani Qilwina, "al-Liwa' Hisham al-Sirsawi . . . li-International Review," *International Review*, http://www.inter-review.com/magazine-show-7-ar.html, accessed 1 February 2014; Mahmud al-Zahi et al., "al-'A'idun min 'Umrat Rajab Yuhadhdhirun: Ra'ayna Shabah al-Salam 98 . . . wa-l-Karitha Qad Tatakrrar," *al-Masry al-Youm*, 7 August 2007.

93. Ibrahim, "al-Sirsawi li-l-Mashhad am Atalqqa Ayy Ittisal Rasmi . . . ."

94. "Ahad Ahali Dahaya al-'Abbara Yarudd 'ala Husayn al-Harmil," *al-Masry al-Youm*, 31 October 2007.

95. Ashraf Hajjaj, "Ilgha' 'Aqd Mina' al-Iskandariyya ma'a al-Hawiyat al-Siniyya," *al-Jumhuriyya*, 30 December 2012; Amira 'Awad, "Tazahur Hay'at al-Mina' wa-Sharikat Tadawul al-Hawiyat bi-l-Iskandariyya," *al-Wafd*, 24 September 2012; Siddiq al-'Isawi, "al-Tahrir Takshif . . . 21 Jinral Yatahakkmun fi Qita' al-Naql fi Misr," *al-Tahrir*, 10 November 2015.

96. Khayr Raghib, "Mahkama Injliziyya Taqdi bi-Taghrim Misr 900 Milyun Junayh wa-l-Hajz 'ala Amlak Bank Misr fi Paris," *al-Masry al-Youm*, 9 May 2011.

97. Mahmud Dawud, "Qarar Jumhuri bi-Ta'dil Salahiyyat Hay'at al-Naql al-Nahri . . . ," *al-Ahram*, 21 June 2008.

98. Husam al-Zarqani, "al-Tawassu' fi al-Mawani' al-Nahriyya Yad'am Manzumat al-Naql," *al-Mal News*, 10 August 2009; "Ra'is Hay'at al-Naql al-Nahri: Tarh Mawani Nahriyya fi Khams Muhafzat amam al-Mustathmirin al-Misriyyin Qariban," *al-Ahram*, 10 December 2008.

99. al-Borsa, "EgyTrans Tukhattit li-Naql 75 Alf Hawiya Nahriyyan ba'd al-Intiha' min Insha' Mina'iha al-Awwal," *al-Borsa News*, 5 January 2013.

100. IIP Digital, "USTDA to Fund Study of Nile River Transport," 17 September 2003, http://iipdigital.usembassy.gov/st/english/texttrans/2003/09/200309171 71420namfuakso.7855341.html#axzz40pgMeIB5.

101. "al-Naql al-Nahri..Ghariq fi Bahr al-Nisyan wasila Amina wa-Rakhisa Tahtaj li-l-Nuhud Biha," *al-Masa'*, 23 September 2011; "Muhafiz al-Minya Yata'ahhad bi-'Adam Tikrar Mashhad Gharaq al-Mi'adiyyat," *al-Mashhad*, 2 November 2011.

102. Yasir Abu al-Nil, "al-Sadd al-'Ali Mina' al-Ghalaba . . . Ruwwaduh min Tujjar al-Shanta," *al-Ahram*, 21 August 2013; Samah Abd al-'Ati and Sarah Nur al-Din, "Misr wa-l-Sudan: Tariq al-Tijara . . . al-Shuryan al-Masdud (1–3)," *al-Masry al-Youm*, 28 September 2011.

103. Rida Hubayshai, "Wazir al-Naql Yu'ayyin Hijazi Ra'isan li-Hay'at al-Mawani' al-Bariyya wa-l-Jaffa," *al-Youm al-Sabi'*, 31 October 2012; Muhammad al-Abnudi, "al-'Amilun bi-Ma'bar Rafah al-Barri Ya'tasimun Didd 'Askarat al-Hay'a . . . wa-Yuhaddidun bi-Ighlaq al-Ma'bar," *El-Watan News*, 26 August 2012.

104. Hisham al-Shami, "24 Ittiahm Didd Shafiq bi-Ihdar al-Mal al-'Am wa-Muhabat 'Ala' wa-Jamal Mubarak fi Sharikat Mövenpick," *al-Ahram*, 12 March 2011.

105. Mustafa Sami, "al-Istiqala . . . wa-l-Sadma," *al-Ahram*, 25 February 2003; Ahmad Shalabi, "Bara'at Abd al-Fattah Katu wa-7 min Mas'uli Hay'at al-Tayaran al-Madani wa-Habs Biritaniyyin fi Ittihamihm bi-Ihdar 6 Milyar Junayh," *al-Masry al-Youm*, 3 September 2006; "Ghadan 'Ula Jalasat Muhakamat al-Liwa' Katu li-Ittihamih bi-l-Idrar bi-l-Mal al-'Am," *El-Balad*, 5 January 2013; Samira Ali Ayyad, "Bara'at Katu fi Qadiyyat Ittihamih bi-l-Idrar bi-Amwal Sharikat Misr li-l-Tayarn," *al-Ahram*, 5 September 2013.

106. "Istid'a' Tayyar Mubarak li-Ittihamihi bi-l-Tazwir," *al-Wafd*, 3 September 2012; Majida Salih, "Asrar 'Izbat Shafiq wa-Jamal fi al-Tayaran," *al-Wafd*, 24 July 2011.

107. Such as General Mamduh Abu al-'Azim, assistant of the minister of investment for the holding companies affairs in 2007, and General Muhammad Basyuni, chairman of the Egypt Company to Manage Real Estate Assets (a subsidiary of Egypt Insurance) in 2010. Other examples are in Muhammad Mujahid,

"Mukhalfat Idariyya Sarikha li-Ra'is al-Qabida li-l-Naql al-Barri wa-l-Bahri," *al-Masry al-Youm*, 19 March 2006.

108. See HCMLT website for a list of its subsidiaries, http://www.hcmlt.com/a_comp.htm, accessed 21 February 2016.

109. "Push for Privatizing Transportation Grows, Though Tempered by Some Worries," *Daily News Egypt*, 2 November 2008.

110. Such other generals include Mansur al-Hilbawi, taking a leading role in land transport in the holding company from 2006 to the present, and Majid Faraj, chairman of the National Company for River Ports. Salwa Ghunaym, "Ra'is al-Qabida li-l-Naql: Fadd Mazarif Muzaydat al-Handasiyya li-l-Sayyarat al-Shahr al-Muqbil," *al-Ahram*, 14 January 2006; al-Sayyid Fu'ad, "Najah al-Mawani' al-Nahriyya Marhun bi-l-Tansiq Bayna al-Qita' al-Khass wa-Wazarat al-Naql," *al-Mal News*, 30 July 2009.

111. Salwa Ghunaym, "Ra'is al-Qabida li-l-Naql: Fadd Mazarif Muzaydat al-Handasiyya li-l-Sayyarat al-Shahr al-Muqbil," *al-Ahram*, 14 January 2006; See EAMCO website, http://eamco-eg.com/, accessed 20 March 2013; "Tawqi' 'Aqd Bayn IDI wa-l-Sharika al-Handasiyya li-l-Sayyarat EAMCO li-Intaj wa-Tasni' Was'il al-Naql," 26 December 2013; al-Borsa, "FAW Tabda' Intaj Sayyarat Tijariyya bi-Masani' al-Intaj al-Harbi," *al-Borsa News*, 16 December 2014.

112. See Damietta for Container and Cargo Handling Company website, http://www.dchc-egdam.com/profile.php, accessed 20 March 2013; Alex Cont website, http://www.alexcont.com/ar/about/2010-08-18-09-41-45.html, accessed 20 March 2013; Sharif al-Sabah, "Fi Dimiyat: Awnash al-Fasad," *al-Ahram*, 6 September 2009.

113. Hilmi Yasin, "Tawqi' 'Aqd Ta'miq al-Mamar al-Milahi li-Mina' Dimiyat . . . ," *al-Shorouk*, 4 August 2015; Rami Ibrahim, "bi-l-Mustandat: Wazir al-Naql Yuhdir 700 Milyun Junahy fi Mina' Dimyat," *al-Mashhad*, 18 February 2014.

114. "al-Islah al-Haykali li-Tirsanat al-Iskandariyya Yu'ahilha ila Insha' Sufun Humulat 6 Alaf Tinn . . . ," *al-Ahram*, 26 May 2002.

115. Salwa Ghunaym, "Wazir al-Istithmar fi Ijtima' al-Jam'iyya al-'Umumiyya li-l-Naql: Naql Milkiyyat Usul Sharikat Tirsanat al-Iskandariyya li-Wazarat al-Difa'," *al-Ahram*, 15 June 2006.

116. Ali Zalat, "'Ummal al-Naql al-Nahri Yu'alliqun al-I'tisam . . . wa-Qarar min al-Qabida bi-l-Muwafaqa 'ala al-Khuruj li-l-Ma'ash al-Mubakkir," *al-Masry al-Youm*, 28 December 2007. The two cases are detailed in chap. 3.

117. Rabab al-Jali, "Intiqad Ziyadat 'Ujrat 'Utubis al-Wajh al-Qibli bi-l-Fayyum," *al-Youm al-Sabi'*, 25 February 2010; "Bay' Sharikat al-Nil li-l-Naql al-Nahri ila Jihaz al-Sina'at al-Bahriyya," *al-Ahram*, 3 October 2008; personal observations in Qina and Sohag, June 2014.

118. See, for example, "22 Musaba wa Qatil fi Hadith 'Ala al-Tariq al-Dawli," *al-Youm al-Sabi'*, 6 August 2008; Khalid Hijzai and Hasan 'Afifi, "Inqilab 'Utubis

li-Gharb wa-Wasat al-Dilta bi-l-Mansura," *al-Youm al-Sabi'*, 12 December 2011; Personal Observations in Gharbiyya, July 2014; Jaklin Munir, "'Ummal 'Utubis Gharb al-Dilta Yaqta'un al-Tariq Ihtijajan 'ala al-Khasm min Murattabatihim," *al-Youm al-Sabi'*, 28 July 2010.

119. "Ra'is 'al-Turuq wa-l-Kabari' Mashari' Sanawiyya bi-1.8 Milyar Junayh . . . ," *al-Masry al-Youm*, 24 January 2009; Mirvat Rashad et al., "4 Milyar Junayh Taklufat Hawadith al-Turuq Sanawiyyan," *al-Youm al-Sabi'*, 7 June 2009.

120. World Bank, "Egypt: Airports Development. Capacity Boost at Airports Paves Wayfor Stronger Economic Growth," http://go.worldbank.org/ NC5IKKW990, accessed 21 February 2016; World Bank, "Egypt and the World Bank Sign Two New Agreements," 25 October 2010, http://go.worldbank. org/UDBNM1UEV0; Amira Muhammad, "Sharikat Taf al-Turkiyya Tafuz bi-'Aqd Insha' Mabna al-Rukkab al-Jadid bi-Matar al-Qahira bi-Qimat 350 Milyun Dular," *al-Sharq al-Awsat*, 5 December 2004; Mahir Maqlad, "al-Yawm I'lan Tafasil 'Uqud al-Sharikat al-Ajnabiyya li-Idarat al-Matarat al-Masriyya," *al-Ahram*, 26 December 2004; "Bidders Selected for Cairo Airport Terminal Two Deal," *Middle East Economic Digest*, 6 August 2010.

121. Layla Abd al-Hamid, "Li-Waqf Nazif Khasa'ir Tashghil al-Khutut Ighlaq 13 Maktaba li-Misr li-l-Tayaran fi 'Awasim al-'Alam," *al-Ahram*, 29 May 2004.

5. Angry Workers, Islamic Grocers, and Revolutionary Generals (2011–2014)

1. Facebook page of the NoMilCivilPositions campaign, https://www.facebook .com/nomocp, accessed 22 December 2012; Basma al-Mahdi, "Kharita Iliktru-niyya li-Hukm al-'Askar Tarsud 438 'Askari Sabiq Yatawallun Manasib Mada-niyya," *al-Masry al-Youm*, 2 August 2012.

2. See, for instance, Wala' Wahid, "I'tisam al-'Asharat bi-Hay'at Qanat al-Suways," *al-Wafd*, 5 March 2011; Yusri Muhammad, "Isabat 3 min al-'Amilin bi-Qanat al-Suways bi-l-'I'iya' ba'd Idrabihim 'an al-Ta'am," *al-Dustur al-Asli*, 14 March 2011; Wala' Wahid, "Idrab al-'Imala al-Mu'aqatta bi-Qanat al-Suways," *al-Wafd*, 8 March 2011; Hiba Subayh, "Li-Tahsin Murattabatihim . . . 'Ummal al-Rabat wa-l-Anwar Yudribun 'an al-'Amal," *Sawt al-Umma*, 20 March 2011; "Fadil Yar-fud Matalib 'Ummal Tirsanat al-Suways," *al-Youm al-Sabi'*, 7 April 2011; Yusri Muhammad, "Fashal al-Mufawadat bayna 'Ummal Sharikat Qanat al-Suways wa-l-Fariq Fadil," *al-Muraqib*, 14 April 2011; Yusri Muhammad, "Tasa'ud Saqf Matalib 'Ummal Qanat al-Suways Raddan 'Ala Tanassul Fadil min Ittifaq April," *al-Dustur al-Asli,* 19 June 2011; Wala' Wahid, "'Ummal Qanat al-Suways Yaqta'un al-Sikka al-Hadid," *al-Wafd*, 4 July 2011.

3. Muhammad, "Tasa'ud Saqf Matalib 'Ummal Qanat al-Suways . . . "; Wahid, "'Ummal Qanat al-Suways Yaqta'un al-Sikka al-Hadid . . . "; Yusri Muhammad, "'Ummal Sharikat Qanat al-Suways Yaqta'un al-Tariq al-Mu'adiya ila Idarat al-Qana," *al-Dustur al-Asli*, 28 June 2011; "Al-Quwwat al-Musallaha Tamna' Iqtiham 'Ummal Sharikat Qanat al-Suways li-Mabna al-Hay'a," *Akhbar Misr*, 18 June 2011; Siham Shawda, "al-Niyaba al-'Askariyya Tastad'i 5 min 'Ummal Qanat al-Suways al-Mu'tasimin li-l-Tahqiq wa-Tarfud al-Samah bi-Hudur al-Muhamin," *El-Badil*, 4 July 2011; Siham Shawda, "al-Niyaba al-'Askariyya Tuqarrir Habs 4 Niqabiyyn bi-Sharikat Qanat al-Suways 4 Ayyam," *El-Badil*, 5 July 2011.

4. 'Abdu Khalil, "Istimrar I'tisam 'Ummal Mina' Dumiyat li-Tard Fulayfl," *al-Wafd*, 13 December 2011; Muhammad al-Khuli, "Wazir al-Naql Yastardi 'Ummal Mina' Dumiyat wa-Yuqarir Iqalat Ra'is al-Mina'," *al-Tahrir*, 15 December 2011; https://www.youtube.com/watch?v=rpT-fDOfz_0, accessed 1 January 2012.

5. Rami Ibrahim, "Muzaharat bi-l-Salama al-Bahriyya Tutalib bi-Iqalat Ra'ys al-Hay'a wa-l-Qasas al-Qanuni," *al-Mashhad*, 15 July 2012; "Al-Markazi li-l-Muhasabat Yakshif Mukhalaft bi-l-Jumla fi Hay'at al-Salama al-Bahriyya," *Ruz al-Yusuf al-Usbu'iyya*, 23 June 2012.

6. Sayyid Hasan, "Ihtiwa' Azmat al-'Amilin bi-Sharikat Dimiyat li-Tadawul al-Hawiyat," *al-Ahram*, 3 July 2011; Suhad al-Khudari, "Mumaththilu al-'Amilin bi-Hawiyat Dimyat Yadkhulun fi I'tisam Maftuh 'amam Majlis al-Wuzara'," *al-Watan*, 3 September 2012.

7. Amina Abd al-'Azim, "I'tilaf al-Mujtama'at al-'Umraniyya Yas'a li-Taghyir Siyasat al-Hay'a 'abr al-Facebook," *al-Youm al-Sabi'*, 11 September 2011; Amina Abd al-'Azim, "I'tilaf al-Mujtama'at al-'Umraniyya Yutalib bi-Iqalat al-Qiyadat al-'Askariyya," *Sada al-Balad*, 19 August 2012.

8. Sayyid Abd Illah, "Idrab 'Ummal Mawani' al-Bahr al-Ahmar bi-l-Suwayz Ihtijajan 'ala 'Askarat al-Waza'if," 29 February 2012.

9. Shakawa Baladna, "Hudumna li-l-Bay'bi-Amr Ra'is al-Misaha," 17 January 2011, http://shakawi.masreat.com/2570/; video showing workers' reaction against him in 2011, https://www.youtube.com/watch?v=6LSZaXfB1Qo, accessed 1 January 2012.

10. Al-Ishtiraki, "Idrab al-'Amilin fi Matarat al-Uksur wa-Aswan wa-l-Ghardaqa wa-Sharm al-Shaykh wa-Taba wa-Sant Katrin wa-Hitafat Didd 'Askarat al-Tayaran," 31 December 2011, http://revsoc.me/-5226; Ahmad Mas'ud, "Istiqalat Fath Allah Ra'is al-Sharika al-Qabida li-l-Matarat wa-l-Milaha al-Jawiyya," *al-Ahram*, 24 July 2011; "'Asharat al-'Amilin bi-Matar al-Qahira Yatazahrun li-l-Mutalaba bi-Tahsin Awda'ihim," *al-Ahram*, 9 February 2011; Mahir Abd al-Wahid, "Muzaharat 600 min Muwazzafi al-Khadamt al-Jawiyya bi-l-Matar," *al-Youm al-Sabi'*, 10 February 2011; Muhammad al-Shawadfi, "Muwazzafu Mina' al-Qahira al-Jawwi Yandammun ila I'tisamat al-Matar," *al-Ahram*, 1 January 2012.

11. Siham Shawada, "Idrab 5 Alaf 'Amil bi-l-Masani' al-Harbiyya li-l-Mutalaba bi-l-Ta'yin wa-Waqf Ihalatihim li-l-Muhakamat al-'Askariyya," *El-Badil*, 7 March 2012.

12. Egyptian Center for Social and Economic Rights, "'Umal Masna' Harbi 63 Ya'tasimun li-l-Mutalaba bi-Ziyadat al-Hawafiz," 16 March 2011, http://ecesr.org/?p=3256.

13. Mahmud Badr, "I'tisam 3 Aalaf 'Amil fi Masna' 200 li-l-Intaj al-Harbi li-l-Mutalaba bi-l-Tahqiq ma'a Sayyid Mash'al, *al-Dustur al-Asli*, 1 March 2011; Fathiyya al-Dib, "Waqfa Ihtijajiyya li-'Ummal Masna' 200 al-Harbi amam Majlis al-Wuzara' Ghadan," *al-Youm al-Sabi'*, 9 April 2011.

14. Tadamon Masr, "'Ummal Masna' 9 al-Harbi Yarfa'un Da'wa Qada'iyya li-Ilgha' Sunduq al-Zamala," 3 March 2011, https://tadamonmasr.wordpress.com.

15. "Military Factory Workers Strike for Paying Increase," *Egypt Independent*, 7 March 2012; Ahmad Fathi, "Idrab Maftuh li-'Ummal Masani' Muhimmat al-Tajnid bi-Tanta," *Sada El-Balad*, 10 March 2012.

16. I'tilaf Shabab Masni' al-Intaj al-Harbi Facebook page, https://www.facebook.com/alentagal7arby, accessed 9 May 2012.

17. Mamduh Sha'ban, "Aqib Iftitah, al-Marhala al-Thaniya li-Mujamma' Intaj al-Kimawiyyat bi-l-Fayyum, al-Mushir Tantawi: Misr lam wa-lan Tasqut wa-Nuwaffir laha Kull al-'Imkanat li-Tanmiyatiha," *al-Ahram*, 3 October 2011; Thawra Didd al-Fasad bi-Sharkiat al-Nasr li-l-Kimawiyyat al-Wasita bi-l-Fayyum," *al-Shorouk*, 5 May 2012; Sayyid al-Shura, "Inha' Azmat 'Ummal Sharikat al-Nasr li-l-Kimawiyyat bi-l-Fayyum," *al-Wafd*, 24 February 2012; Amr Taha, "Nanshur Tafasil 'Inha' Azmat al-Jaysh ma'a 'Ummal Sharikat al-Nasr li-l-Kimawiyyat," *Moheet*, 24 February 2012.

18. ONA, "Takaddus Mi'at al-Sayyarat bi-l-Suways bi-Sabab Qat' Sa'iqi al-Naql Tariq al-Qatamiyya-al-'Ayn al-Sukhna," *ONA News Agency*, 31 May 2012, http://onaeg.com/?p=137248.

19. Rida Hubayshi, "al-'Amilun bi-l-Wataniyya li-l-Naql al-Nahri Ya'tasimun wa-Yuhadiddun bi-Ighlaq Majra al-Nil," *al-Youm al-Sabi'*, 5 March 2012.

20. The prime minister particularly complained about the pressure these protests placed on the public sector. See 'Isam Abd al-Karim and Mahmud Hilmi, "Fi Awwal Tasrihatih Muhammad Yusuf: Hall Mushkilat Qita' al-Ghazl wa-Masadir Jadida li-Tamwil Sharikatih," *al-Ahram*, 26 March 2012.

21. The Public Business Sector then contained nine gigantic holding companies with hundreds of subsidiaries and affiliated enterprises in the sectors of transport, petrochemicals, tourism, food, drugs, textile, metals, insurance, water and sewage, and electricity.

22. Manal al-'Isawi, "'Ummal al-Sharika al-Qawmiyya li-l-Asmant Yu'awidun I'tisamahum ba'd Ilgha' Ziyadat al-Murattabat," *al-Youm al-Sabi'*, 11 April 2011; Rim 'Id, "I'tisam al-Sharika al-Qawmiyya li-l-Asmant Hqqaq Matlib al-'Ummal,"

al-Ahali, 30 April 2011; Ramiz Subhi, "al-Majlis al-'Askari Yulghi 'Alawat 'Ummal al-Qawmiyya li-l-Asmant," *El-Badil*, 27 July 2011; National Cement Company website, http://ncc-eg.com/cemant/co3.html, accessed 29 March 2015.

23. "Fasad bi-l-Sharika al-'Amma li-l-Sawami' wa-l-Takhzin," 23 March 2012, http://shakawi.masreat.com/32110/; Mu'taz al-Shirbini, "Ta'liq I'tisam al-'Amilin bi-Sawma'at Mina' Dimyat li-Muddat Thalathat Asabi'," *al-Youm al-Sabi'*, 19 April 2012; Sayyid Hasan, "Ta'liq Idrab 'Ummal Sharikat al-Sawami' li-Muddat 3 Asabi'," *al-Ahram*, 20 April 2012; video of an officer negotiating with striking workers, https://www.youtube.com/watch?v=3Z43AkjatWo, accessed 28 March 2015; employees' Facebook page, Silo News, https://www.facebook.com/pages/%D8%A3%D9%86%D8%A8%D8%A7%D8%A1-%D8%A7%D9%84%D8%B5%D9%88%D8%A7%D9%85%D8%B9/298271426952593?fref=nf, accessed 25 December 2012.

24. "Al-Majlis al-A'la li-l-Quwwat al-Musallaha, Marsum bi-Qanun Raqam 34 li-Sanat 2011 bi-Tajrim al-I'tida 'ala Huriyyat al-'Amal wa-Takhrib al-Munsha'at," *al-Jarida al-Rasmiyya*, no. 14 (mukarrar alif), year 54, 12 April 2011.

25. Rania Fahmi, "'Ummal al-Bitrul Yahtajjun amam Wazaratihim," *al-Wafd*, 2 February 2011.

26. See the blog of a Petrotrade worker, post of 10 March 2010 on the strike, and another of 25 December on the company's military chairman, https://btro.wordpress.com/.

27. Tadamon Masr, "'Ummal Sharikat Petrogas Qina Yata'arradun li-l-Fasl bi-Sabab Iblaghihim 'an al-Fasad," 22 April 2011, https://tadamonmasr.wordpress.com/2011/04/22/petrogaz/.

28. Sayyid Abd al-Nabi, "I'tisam Alf 'Amil bi-Pterojet ba'd Tardihim min Mashru'at al-Sharika," *al-Ahram*, 20 March 2011; Egyptian Center for Social and Economic Rights (ECSER), "Fi Mu'tamar Sahafi bi-l-Markaz al-Masri: Matalib Huquqiyya wa-'Ummaliyya bi-Ilgha' al-Muhakamat al-'Askariyya," 6 July 2011, http://ecesr.org/?p=4065.

29. In March 2011 Minister of Labor Forces and Migration Ahmad Hasan al-Bura'i allowed independent labor unions to be created by only notifying the ministry. Hanafi Abu al-Su'ud, "Fi Hudur Mudir Munazzamat al-'Amal al-Dawliyya al-Bura'i Yu'lin Insha' al-Naqabata al-'Ummaliyya bi-l-Ikhtar," *al-Masa'*, 13 March 2011.

30. Jaklin Munir, "'Ummal al-Iskandariyya li-Tadawul a-Hawiyat Yatazaharun bi-Sabab Hifz Balaghahum," *al-Youm al-Sabi'*, 4 May 2011; Marwa al-Shafi'i, "Mu'aradat al-Hukm al-Sadir bi-Habs 5 min Qiyadat al-Niqaba al-Mustqilla li-Tadawul al-Hawiyat 14 Uktubar," *al-Shorouk*, 26 September 2012.

31. Yusuf Jabir, "'Ummal 'Wahat Paris' Yastanjidun bi-Ghurab: Tasarrufat al-Idara al-'Ashwa'iyya Tu'adi ila Inhiyar al-Sharika Khilal Shahr," *al-Ahram*, 10 February 2012.

32. Mahmud Muqbil, "Rahil al-Muhafiz wa-Mudir al-Amn Ahamm Matalib Mu-tazahiri Suhaj," *al-Youm al-Sabi'*, 15 July 2011; Isma'il Ra'fat, "al-Nu'mani: Laysa min al-Mantiqi ann Nattahim 3 Malayin Muwatin bi-l-Fasad," *al-Youm al-Sabi'*, 29 June 2011; "Tawarrut Muhafiz Suhaj al-Sabiq fi Tahsil 15 Miliun Junayh bi-Mkhalafat al-Qanun," *al-Tahrir*, 27 July 2012.

33. "Shillat Jamal Mubarak allati Afsadat Misr," *al-Wafd*, 4 March 2011; Sayyid Abd al-Ghani, "Qarar bi-Man' Dukhul al-Muhafiz Sayf Jalal al-Suways Niha'iyyan . . . wa Rahil Mudir al-'Amn," *al-Ahram*, 25 February 2011; Abd Allah Dayf, "Muza-harat bi-l-Suways ba'd Takrim al-Muhafiz al-Sabiq," *al-Wafd*, 20 April 2011.

34. Muhammad al-Juhari, "Muzaharat fi al-Uksur Tutalib bi Rahil Samir Faraj," *al-Ahram*, 1 April 2011; "al-Niyaba al-'Askariyya Tabda' al-Tahqiq ma'a Samir Faraj fi Tuhmat Ihdar al-Mal al-'Am," *al-Masry al-Youm*, 21 April 2011.

35. Husam Ali, "Masha'ir Mutabayina min Istimrar al-Qubaysi Muhafizan li-l-Bahr al-Ahmar," *al-Ahram*, 15 April 2011; Hind Mukhtar, "Thuwwar al-Bahr al-Ahmar: Mutafa'ilun bi-l-Muhafiz al-Jadid," *al-Youm al-Sabi'*, 6 August 2011.

36. See, for instance, "Tabur al-Muhafizin Yantazir amam al-Kasb Ghayr al-Mshru'," *Uktubar*, 24 April 2011; Sharif Abu al-Fadl, "Balagh li-l-Na'ib al-'Am Yattahim Ra'is al-Riqaba al-Idariyya bi-l-Tasattur 'ala Fasad Mubarak wa-Hashyatih," *al-Ahram*, 14 August 2012.

37. "Al-Majlis al-'Ala li-l-Qwuuat al-Musallaha, Marsum bi-Qanun Raqam 45 li-Sanat 2011 bi-Ta'dil ba'd Ahkam Qanun al-Qada' al-'Askari al-Sadir bi-l-Qanun Raqam 25 li-Sanat 1966," *al-Jarida al-Rasmiyya*, no. 18 (mukarrar alif), year 54, 10 May 2011; "Tashri'iyyat al-Sha'b Tubqi 'ala Mada Taqsir Muhakamat al-Dubbat al-Fasidin 'ala al-Qada' al-'Askari Hatta ba'd Taqa'udahum," *El-Badil*, 22 April 2012.

38. "Al-Niyaba al-'Askariyya Tabda' al-Tahqiq ma'a Samir Faraj fi Tuhmat Ihdar al-Mal al-'Am," *al-Masry al-Youm*, 21 April 2011; 'Isam 'Ajami, "Jaridat Ahwal Masr Tanshur Ahamm Injazat al-Duktur Samir Faraj Muhafiz al-Uksur al-Sabiq," *Ah-wal Masr*, 11 December 2013, http://a7walmasr.com/print.php?id=12312.

39. Samah Mansur, "Ihalat Balagh Didd Mash'al li-l-Niyaba al-'Askariyya," *al-Ahram*, 25 February 2011.

40. Robert Springborg, "Is Tantawi Reading the Public Pulse Correctly?," *Egypt Independent*, 6 December 2011.

41. On Jadaliyya.com, under the name Mohamed al-Khalsan, later changed. Zeinab Abul-Magd, "al-Jaysh wa-l-Iqtisad fi Barr Masr," *Jadaliyya*, 21 December 2011.

42. Interview with workers, 24 and 25 March 2012; "Didd fasad al-Hay' al-'Arabiyya li-l-Tasni' A.A.V," http://www.aav-corruption.blogspot.com, accessed 31 March 2015; Buss wa-Tull, "al-Hay'a al-'Arabiyya li-l-Tasni' Tusdir Qarar bi-Waqf al-'Amilin alladhin Kharaju fi Tazahurat Tutalib bi-l-Islah," 8 September 2011, http://boswtol.com/politics/reports/11/September/08/26191/?ref=1.

43. For a full account of the visit, see Zeinab Abul-Magd, "al-'Askar fi Maslahat al-Miyah wa-l-Sarf al-Sihhi," *al-Masry al-Youm*, 26 March 2012; and English

translation, Zeinab Abul-Magd, "Time for a Civilian Handover," *Egypt Independent*, 1 April 2012.

44. Fatima al-Sayyid Ahmad, "Ra'is al-Hay'a al-'Arabiyya li-l-Tasni': al-Hay'a Sakhkharat 70% min Hajm Taqatiha li-l-Intaj al-Madani," *al-Youm al-Sabi'*, 2 November 2010.

45. Wael Gamal, "al-'Askarai: Mashru'atuna 'Araq Wazarat al-Difa' . . . wa-lan Nasmah li-l-Dawla bi-l-Tadakhkhul Fiha," *al-Shorouk*, 27 March 2012.

46. Rime Naguib, "Boycott Them: Activists Raise Awareness About Military's Economic Empire," *Egypt Independent*, 12 February 2012; Wala' Mursi, "Nushata' Yutliqun Hamla li-Muqata'at Muntajat al-Quwwat al-Musallaha . . . wa-Khubara' Iqtisadiyyun Yuhadhdhirun minha," *al-Ahram*, 5 February 2012. The campaign's Facebook page is titled Boycott SCAF Products.

47. The 'Askar Kadhibun campaign's Facebook page, https://www.facebook.com /3askar.Kazeboon, accessed 1 May 2013.

48. Amira Hisham, "Radwan: La Taraju' 'an Siyasat al-Suq al-Hurra wa-l-Islah al-Iqtisadi," *al-Ahram*, 8 June 2011; Amal 'Allam, "Mumtaz al-Sa'id: Tarh Barnamag al-Islah al-Iqtisadi 'ala al-Mujtama' li-l-Tawafuq 'ala Bunudih," *al-Ahram*, 11 March 2012.

49. See such court rulings at the ECSER website: "Isdar Kitab 'bi-Ism al-Sha'b': Ahamm Ahkam al-Tqadi al-Istratiji li-l-Markaz al-Misri," 1 May 2014, 2 March 2016, http://ecesr.org/?tag=rulings; Hadir Yusuf, "Markaz Huquqi: al-Qada' Kashaf Mukhattat 'Ihdar al-Mal fi Khaskhasat al-Sharikat," *al-Wafd*, 17 December 2011

50. Yusuf Wahbi, "Fayza Abu al-Naja: La Yumkin Tanfidh Hukm al-Qada' bi-'Awdat Sharikat al-Khaskhasa ila al-Qita' al-'Am," *al-Shorouk*, 28 January 2012; Ahmad 'Ashur, "al-Masri al-Sa'udi Yujammid Mufawadat Taswiyat al-Munaza'at ma'a Sharikat al-Khaskhasa," *al-Mal News*, 4 May 2012. "Qarar Ra'is Majlis al-Wuzara' Raqam 32 li-Sanat 2012 bi-Sha'n Tashkil al-Majmu'a al-Wazariyya li-Fadd al-Munaza'at al-Khassa bi-l-Istithmar," *al-Jarida al-Rasmiyya*, no. 2, year 55, 12 January 2012. Investors were to sue the Egyptian government at the International Center for Settlement of Investment Disputes.

51. Mansur Kamil et al., "al-Hukuma Tu'lin Ilgha' Wazarat al-'Istithmar wa-Inha' Barnmaj al-Khaskhasa," *al-Masry al-Youm*, 19 July 2011.

52. "Statement by an IMF Spokesperson on the Arab Republic of Egypt," IMF Press Release no. 11/174, 12 May 2011; Mariam Fam, "IMF Agrees to $3 Billion Egypt Loan for Post-Mubarak Transition," *Bloomberg*, 5 June 2011; "Egypt Drops Plans for IMF Loan Amid Popular Distrust," *BBC*, 25 June 2011; "Khubara' Misriyyun Yurahhibun bi-Rafd al-Hukuma Qard al-Bank wa-Sunduq al-Naqd al-Dawliyyin," *al-Arabiya*, 27 June 2011; Alaa Shahin, "Egypt May Seek $3 Billion Loan from IMF as Debt Costs Soar," *Bloomberg*, 18 November 2011.

53. The campaign was called "The Public Campaign to Drop Egypt's Debt" (al-Hamla al-Sha'biyya li-'Isqat Duyun Misr). Bassem Abo Alabbas, "Egypt's Economic Reform Proposals Ignore Social Justice: Civil Group," *al-Ahram Online,* 24 March 2012.

54. The firm is Tianjin Cement Industry Design and Research Institution Co., part of public-sector company Sinoma International Engineering. "Egyptian Defense Minister Tantawi Inspect GOE EPC Project," 13 July 2012, http://www.tcdri .com.cn/English/vinfo.asp?id=450; "Kiln Intel Steel of GOE Project Line 1 in Egypt Contracted by TCDRI Installed," http://en.sinoma.cn/news/Show Article.asp?ArticleID=989, accessed 3 April 2015.

55. Ali Sham, "al-Mushir Tantawi: 250 Milyun Junayh min al-Quwwat al-Musallaha li-l-Mashru'at al-'Ajila bi-Sayna'," *al-Ahram,* 1 May 2012; Daliya 'Uthman, "al-Mushir Yaftatih Masna'' al-'Arish wa-Yu'akkid 'Ala Tanmiyat Sayna' li-Dur Abna'iha fi Himayat al-Watan," *al-Masry al-Youm,* 1 May 2012.

56. Amira Hisham, "al-Ihsa': 'Irtifa' As'ar al-Asmant wa-Taraju' al-Hadid Khilal Shahr Yunya al-Madi," *al-Ahram,* 22 July 2012. For national prices of cement, see http://cementegypt.com/price, accessed 2 March 2016.

57. Muhammad al-Bahnasawi, "al-Mushir Yaftatih al-Marhala al-Thaniya li-Majma' 'Intaj al-Kimawiyyat bi-l-Fayyum bi-'Istithmarat 500 Miliun Junayh," *al-Akhbar,* 2 October 2011. See the company's website, http://www.nasrchemicals.com /ArMain.html, accessed 2 March 2016; Ashraf Fikri, " 'As'ar al-Asmida Tashta'il ma'a Naqs al-Ma'rud . . . wa-l-Hukuma Tadrus Nizam Jadid li-l-Tawzi'," *al-Masry al-Youm,* 9 January 2012; "30% 'Ajz fi 'Intaj al-Asmida bi-Misr . . . wa-'Inti'ash bi-l-Suq al-Sawda' . . . wa-Naqib al-Fallahin: Ihtikar al-Samad Yu-haddid Misr bi-Thawrat Jiya'," *Sada al-Balad,* 26 February 2012; http://cement egypt.com/price, accessed 7 June 2015.

58. Ahmed Zaki Osman, "Military-Owned Factories Threaten Farmers' Livelihood in Fayyum," *Egypt Independent,* 19 December 2011.

59. "Toyota Marks Start of SUV Assembly in Egypt," Toyota Motor Corporation and Toyota Tsusho, 9 April 2012, http://www2.toyota.co.jp/en/news/12/04 /0409_2.html; "ABR: Toyota Starts Fortuner Assembly in Egypt," *Egypt Business Directory,* 10 April 2012, http://www.egypt-business.com/Web/details/1215 -xg-Toyota-starts-Fortuner-assembly-in-Egypt/4744.

60. Sahar Zahran, "3.6 Milyar Junayh li-Tajdid Qitarat wa-Mahattat Sikak Hadid Misr," *al-Ahram,* 22 April 2012; "al-Janzuri Yashhad Tawqi' 'Aqd Tasni' wa-Tawrid 212 'Arabat Rukkab Sikak Hadid," *al-Ahram,* 21 April 2012.

61. "L.E. 21 Million Contract Endorsed to Semaf Co., Reporting to the A.O.I. Arab Organization for Industrialization in Cooperation with Mitsubishi of Japan, to Build and Supply Three Metro Coaches," *AmCham Egypt Project News,* 17 November 2011.

62. Hani Badr al-Din, "Iftitah Mahattatayn li-Tahliyat Miyah al-Bahr li-Muhafazat Matruh min Intaj al-Hay'a al-'Arabiyya li-l-Tasni'," *al-Ahram*, 18 October 2011.

63. Sami Kamal and 'Amr Jalal, "al-Mushir Yaftatih Tariq al-Jaysh Sharq al-Nil bi-l-Sa'id bi-Istithmarat 2.4 Milyar Junayh," *Akhbar al-Youm*, 3 October 2011; "Qarar Ra'is Jumhuriyyat Misr al-'Arabiyya Raqam 13 li-Sanat 2011 bi-Sha'n Takhsis Aradi Sahrawiya li-Wazarat al-Difa' wa-I'tibariha min al-Manatiq al-Istratijiyya Dhat al-Ahmiyya al-'Askariyya," *al-Jarida al-Rasmiyya*, no. 3 (mukarrar), 23 January 2011.

64. Wafa' Bakri, "al-Quwwat al-Musallaha wa-Jahaz al-Ta'mir Yabda'an Mashru' al-Iskan al-Ijtima'i al-Jadid . . . wa-Insha' 6 Alaf Wahda bi 15 Mayu," *al-Masry al-Youm*, 30 December 2011; Badawi al-Syyid Nujayla, "bi-Taklufat Milyarayy Junayh al-Quwwat al-Musallaha Tusallim Madinat al-Jaysh wa-l-Sha'b fi Disambir," *al-Ahram*, 5 March 2012.

65. For example, Abu Sri' Imam, "Li-Khidmat Nisf Milyun Muwatin Iftitath Kubri Mushah bi-Gharb Shubra al-Khayma bi-Taklufa 1.5 Milyun Junayh," *al-Ahram*, 16 January 2012; Layla Mustafa, "Tantawi Yaftatih Mashru' Tatwir Mayadin al-Shahid wa-Wataniyya wa-l-Wafa' wa-l-Amal," *al-Ahram*, 11 May 2012; Badawi al-Sayyid Nujayla, "Ba'd Ittihamih li-l-Jaysh bi-Sariqat Tasmimatih al-Qada' al-'Askari Yastad'i Mamduh Hamza," *al-Ahram*, 5 March 2012; see prices of wedding halls at http://vb.onstek.com/t16658.html, accessed 4 April 2015.

66. See http://el3askarmap.kazeboon.com/, accessed 10 July 2012; https://www.facebook.com/el3askarMap; Issander El Amrani, "Awesome Google Maps Mashup of Egypt's Retired Army Generals and Where They've Landed," *Arabist*, 7 July 2012, http://arabist.net/blog/2012/7/7/awesome-google-maps-mashup-of-egypts-retired-army-generals-a.html.

67. See video of Salafi preacher Muahmamd Huasyn Ya'qub at https://www.youtube.com/watch?v=tnOxAQGFSHU, accessed 28 February 2016.

68. For the full text of the March 2011 constitutional declaration, see http://gateold.ahram.org.eg/Malafat/170/1066/Borsa.aspx.

69. Ahmad Mustafa and Rihab Abdillah, "Taqrir Lajnat Taqassi Haqa'iq Huquq al-Insan fi Ahdath al-'Unf bi-Majlis al-Wuzara' wa-Muhammad Mahmud," *al-Youm al-Sabi'*, 31 January 2012.

70. See, for example, al-Jam'iyya al-Misriyya li-l-Nuhud bi-l-Musharaka al-Mujtama'iyya, al-'Itilaf al-Mustaqqil li-Muraqabat al-Intikhabat, "Taqrir al-Marhala al-'Ula li-Intikhabat Majlis al-Sha'b 2011, 28–29 November 2011. Taqrir al-Muraqaba al-Maydaniyya," 1 December 2012, http://www.mosharka.org/index.php?newsid=417.

71. See an interview with Ahmad al-Bur'i: Mahmud Musallam and Mahmud Sabri, "Ahmad al-Bur'i: Sharaf Thar 'ala al-Isawi bi-Sabab 'Adam Ikhbarih bi-Qarar Ikhla' Midan al-Tahrir . . . fa-Ajabahu: 'Ya'ni Ana illi Kunt A'raf," *al-Watan*, 21 October 2012.

72. For an interview with Juda Abd al-Khaliq, see Mahmud Musallam, "al-Duktur Juda Abd Khaliq: 'al-'Askari' Sallam al-Sulta li-l-Ikhwan Mundhu Tashkil 'Lajnat al-Bishri'," *al-Watan*, 2 October 2012.

73. "Haykal: Morsi lam Yastab'id Tantawi lakin al-Majlis al-'Askari Wajad Nafsah Amam Mas'uliyya Kabira," *al-Shorouk*, 6 December 2012.

74. "Jama'at al-Ikhwan Tafsil Abu al-Futuh," *al-Jazeera*, 19 June 2011.

75. 'Ala' Ahmad, "Muhammad Mursi Ta'liqan 'ala Wasfihi bi-l-Murashshah al-Istibn: Abu Tirika Ahraz 3 Ahdaf Raghm Annahu Kan Ihtitati," *al-Ahram*, 19 May 2012.

76. See the press releases of the Supreme Electoral Committee for the 2012 presidential elections at http://pres2012.elections.eg/index.php/the-media/media-releases, accessed 9 April 2015. About issue of demilitarization in platforms of candidates, see Zeinab Abul-Magd, "al-'Askar wa-Mu'dilat al-Murashshah al-'Abit," *al-Masry al-Youm*, 30 April 2012.

77. "Hurra Naziha: Morsi Yatasaddar Intihakat al-Yawm al-Awwal bi 57% . . . ," *El-Badil*, 23 May 2012; Khalaf Ali Hasan and Mu'taz Nadi, "Hurra Naziha: Ansar Mursi fi Qina Yuwazzi'un Zayt wa-Lahma wa-Sukkar 'ala al-Nakhibin," *al-Masry al-Youm*, 24 May 2012.

78. See the video of the speech at http://www.youtube.com/watch?v=pzs7R3l UeUQ, accessed 2 March 2016.

79. "I'lan Dusturi," *al-Jarida al-Rasmiyya*, no. 24 (mukarrar), year 55, 17 June 2012.

80. English translation from http://www.egyptindependent.com/news/egypt-s-draft-constitution-translated. For the full Arabic text, see http://www.almasryalyoum.com/news/details/255182.

81. Baha' Mubashir, "Wazir al-Intaj al-Harbi Yu'lin Tafasil I'adat Tashghil Sharikat al-Nasr li-l-Sayyarat wa-Tatwir al-Masani' li-Intaj Sayyara Misriyya," *al-Ahram*, 3 April 2012; Muhammad Abd al-'Ati, "Tafa'ul bi-Intiqal Sharikat bi-Qita' al-'Amal li-l-Intaj al-Harbi wa-Tawaqqu'at bi-Najah al-Nasr li-l-Sayyarat," *al-Masry al-Youm*, 15 April 2013; Nadya Mansur, "Ba'd 'Awdat al-Nasr li-l-'Amal Taht Ishraf al-Intaj al-Harbi: al-Sayyara al-Misriyya Tataharrak," *al-Ahram*, 16 April 2013; "Tafasil Damj al-Nasr li-l-Sayyarat fi-l-Intaj al-Harbi," *al-Mal News*, 18 February 2014; "al-Nasr li-l-Sayyarat Tatfawad ma'a Sharikat 'Alamiyya li-Tamwil I'data Tashghiliha," *al-Mal News*, 26 January 2015.

82. "Nur Ali and Nura Fakhri, "Lajna Barlamniyya bi-l-Shura Tuwafiq 'ala Ziyadat Ma'ashat al-'Askariyyin," *al-Youm al-Sabi'*, 23 February 2013; "Waslat Madh Bayna al-Jaysh wa-Nuwwab al-Shura Khilal Iqrar Qanun Ziyadat al-Ma'ashat al-'Askariyyin," *al-Youm al-Sabi'*, 24 February 2013; "Al-Majlis al-'Ala li-l-Quwwat al-Musallaha, Marsum bi-Qanun Raqam 3 li-Sanat 2011 bi-Ziyadat al-Ma'ashat al-'Askariyya wa-Ta'dil Ba'd Ahkam Qanun al-Taqa'ud wa-l-Ta'min wa-l-Ma'ashat li-l-Quwwat al-Musallaha al-Sadir bi-l-Qanun Raqam 90 li-Sanat 1975," *al-Jarida al-Rasmiyya*, no. 6 (mukarrar jim), 16 February 2011.

83. "Al-Shura Yuwafiq 'ala Insha' Kuliyyat Tibb Tabi'a li-l-Quwwat al-Musallaha," *al-Dostor*, 27 June 2013, Nur Ali, Nura Fakhri, et al., "al-Shura Yuwafiq Mabda'iyyan 'ala Insha' Kuliyyat Tibb 'Askariyya," *al-Youm al-Sabi'*, 27 June 2013.

84. Muhammad Abd al-Qadir and Muahmmad Gharib, "al-Shura Yuwafiq Naha'iyyan 'ala Mashru' Qanun Insha' Mu'assasat Qurud li-l-Quwwat al-Musallaha," *al-Masry al-Youm*, 14 May 2013; Nur Ali, Nura Fakhri, et al., "al-Shura Yuwafiq bi-l-Ijam' 'ala Ta'dil Qanun Qurud Dubbat al-Quwwat al-Musallaha," *al-Youm al-Sabi'*, 14 May 2013.

85. "Iskan al-Shura Tushid bi-Dawr al-Quwwat al-Musallaha fi Da'm al-Mashru'at al-Qawmiyya," *al-Borsa News*, 28 March 2013.

86. Ahmad Abd al-Khaliq and Salim Abd al-Ghani, "Mursi wa-l-Sisi Yaftatihan 'Adad min al-Mashru'at al-Istratijiyya," *al-Ahram al-Masa'i*, 3 May 2013.

87. Iman Ibrahim, "Mursi li-Ra'is al-Hay'a al-Handasiyya: 'Hayyi Qandil 'Ashan Yisaliklak al-Umur'," *al-Dostor*, 2 May 2013.

88. "Al-Bursa Tanshur al-Mashru'at allati Kallaf al-Ra'is al-Quwwat al-Musallaha bi-Tanfidhiha . . . wa-l-Hay'a al-Handasiyya: Sanunafidhuha Qabl Ihtifalat Uktubar," *al-Borsa News*, 6 May 2013; Ahmad Abd al-'Azim, "al-Quwwat al-Musallaha . . . Dawlat al-Khadamat al-Baqiya fi Ghiyab Dawlat al-Mu'assasat," *al-Watan*, 6 May 2013.

89. Khalid Hijazi, "Iftitah Wazir al-Intaj al-Harbi wa-l-Ittisalat wa-Muhafiz al-Qaliyubiyya Khutut Intaj Awwal Tablit Misri," *al-Youm al-Sabi'*, 4 June 2013.

90. Maha Salim, "Munafasa Misriyya . . . al-'Arabiyya li-l-Tasni' Tatrah Tablit Blutu.. wa-al-Intaj al-Harbi Tatrah al-Isdar al-Thani min Inar," *al-Ahram*, 26 September 2013.

91. Hisham 'Umar Abd al-Halim, "Ittifaqiyyat Ta'awun bayna al-Kahraba' wa-l-'Arabiyya li-l-Tasni' fi Majal al-Taqa al-Mutajaddida," *al-Masry al-Youm*, 7 April 2013.

92. Abu Sri' Muhammad, "Manh Insha' wa-Idarat wa-Tashghil wa-Siyanat Tariq 'al-Jaysh-al-Tanmiya' li-l-Sharika al-Wataniyya li-Muddat 50 'Am," *Sada al-Balad*, 1 June 2013.

93. Minna Majdi, "bi-l-Video: Muzaharat bi-l-Nu'ush Tarfud Ziyarat Mursi li-Suhaj . . . wa-Ra'is al-Jami'a Yansahib Khilal Kalimatih," *Albedaiah*, 16 March 2013; Karim Hasan, "Majlis al-Wuzara': Tawzi' Makaruna Mu'abba'a wa-Munaqasa 'Amma li-Tawrid Ful li-Tawzi'ihima Majjanan 'ala al-Batqat al-Tamuwiniyya Khilal Ramadan," *al-Ahram*, 26 June 2013.

94. Document on FJP Youth Anticoup Facebook page, Belbies al-An, in Bilbis, Sharqiyya, 18 March 2013, https://www.facebook.com/Shabab.FJ.Belbies/photos/a.497355183652008.1073741827.414590995261761/497355210318672/; 'Ammar al-Nisr, "Bi-l-Suwar: Mul Tijari Kabir li-Jihaz Khadamt al-Quwwat al-Musalaha bi-Bilbis," *Sha'b Misr*, 18 March 2013.

95. Rami Qinawi and Nivin Abd al-Ghani, "bi-l-Suwar . . . Ihtiraq 3 Manazil fi Ishtibakat al-Amn wa-l-Ahali bi-Sabab Ard al-Jaysh bi-l-Mansura," *al-Dostor*, 14 April 2013. The video, made by a group of activists called "Mosireen," is at https://www.youtube.com/watch?v=i14jSlDTfEA, accessed 2 March 2016.

96. See more details about the progress of the case at the Egyptian Center for Economic and Social Rights website, http://ecesr.org/?p=766151, accessed 11 April 2015.

97. 'Atif Abd al-Aziz, "al-Nadim: al-Jaysh Yu'adhdhib 25 Mu'taqal fi Ahdath al-Qurasaya bi-l-'Isi wa-l-Kahraba' . . . wa-l-Niyaba al-'Askariyya Tahbisahum 15 Yawm," *Albedaiah*, 18 November 2012; "al-Jaysh: al-Qurasaya Milk al-Quwwat al-Musallaha wa-Sanatasadda bi-Kull Hasm li-l-Mu'tadin 'Alayha Mahma Kallafana min Tadhiyyat," *Albedaiah*, 18 November 2012 ; Ahmad Abd al-'Azim, "al-Mutahaddith al-'Askari: Ard al-Qurasaya Mamluka li-l-Quwwat al-Musallaha wa-Tustakhdam ka-Manatiq 'Irtikaz li-Ta'min al-'Asima," *al-Watan*, 18 November 2012.

98. "Mursi: la Ta'thir 'ala Amwal wa-Mukhassasat wa-Muddakharat al-Quwwat al-Musallaha," *al-Tahrir*, 18 October 2012.

99. "Junayna: al-Markazi li-l-Muhasabat 'Ajiz hatta al-An 'an Riqabat al-Munsha'at al-Iqtisadiyya li-l-Quwwat al-Musallaha hatta Qa'at al-Afrah," *Albedaia*, 4 November 2012.

100. "al-Quwwat al-Musallaha Tanfi al-Muwafqa 'ala Idraj Anshitatiha Taht Ishraf al-Markazi li-l-Muhasabat wa-l-Ajhiza al-Riqabiyya al-Ukhra," *al-Ahram*, 22 April 2013.

101. For full report, see Transparency International, "Government Defence Anti-Corruption Index 2013," http://transparencyschool.org/wp-content/uploads/GI-main-report.pdf, accessed 11 April 2015.

102. Ahmad 'Umar, "Ta'yinat Muhafizi al-Ikhwan Tuthir Ghadab Sha'bi wa-Siyasi fi Misr," *BBC* Cairo, 18 June 2013.

103. See, for example, 'Umar Abd al-Aziz, Mustafa al-Marsafawi, and Ayat al-Habbal, "al-Masri al-Yum Tarsud 'Amaliyyat Akhwanat al-Dawla fi 8 Shuhur min Hukm Mursi (Malaff Khass)," *al-Masry al-Youm*, 14 February 2013.

104. Muhammad Abd al-Jawwad, "'Awajiz al-Tanizm al-Niqabi Istaslamu li-Qanun al-Azhari," *al-Ahram al-Iqtisadi*, 3 December 2012.

105. Muhammad Abdu Hasanayn, "Qard Sunduq al-Naqd al-Dawli Yubaddil Mawaqif al-Quwa al-Siyasiyaa fi Misr," *al-Sharq al-Awsat*, 29 August 2012.

106. See full text of FJP's platform at its website, http://www.fj-p.com/Party_Program.aspx, accessed 12 April 2015.

107. Mustafa al-Marsafawi, "bi-l-Arqam . . . Imbraturiyyat Khayrat al-Shatir," *al-Masry al-Youm*, 13 April 2012; Zeinab Abul-Magd, "the Brotherhood's Businessmen," *Egypt Independent*, 13 February 2012, Avi Asher-Schapiro, "The GOP Brotherhood of Egypt," *Salon*, 25 January 2012.

108. Zeinab Abul-Magd, "al-Brins wa-l-Jiniral wa-l-Baqqal," *al-Tahrir*, 22 September 2012; Nadine Marroushi, "Cheap Food No End," *Egypt Independent*, 2 August 2012.

109. Muhammad Rabi' "Munahidu al-Ikhwan Yanshurun Qa'ima bi-Mahillat al-Ikhwan al-Murashshaha li-l-Musadara,"*Almesryoon*, 19 June 2014.

110. Rida 'Awad, "Jam'iyyat Ibda' al-Ikhwaniyya Tadumm fi 'Udwiyyatiha Fulul al-Watani," *Sout al-Omma,* 21 March 2012.

111. Ahmad Mansur, "Hasan Malik Yashtari Misr?!," *Al-Watan*, 29 July 2012; Mahmud Karim, "Rihlat al-Sin Shahidat 14 Safqa Muhimma li-Misr," *Sada al-Balad*, 30 August 2012.

112. Ghada Muhammad al-Sharif, "al-Brins: Mursi Aqal Ra'is al-Hay'a al-'Arabiyya li-l-Tasni' li-Takhsisih 5% min al-Arbah li-Nafsih," *al-Masry al-Youm*, 8 September 2012; "al-Ra'is Yutalib bi-Sur'at 'I'timad Mizaniyyat al-Hay'a al-'Arabiyya li-Tasni' wa-Sarf Mustahaqqat al-'Amilin biha," *al-Ahram*, 11 September 2012; Muhammad al-Masri, "al-Brins Ya'tadhir li-Wahbia Hawla Amwal Mubarak," *al-Wafd*, 12 September 2012.

113. Dalia 'Uthman, "Mudir al-Kuliyya al-Harbiyya: Qabilna Tullab min al-Ikhwan fi Duf'at Hadha al-'Am," *al-Masry al-Youm*, 18 March 2013; Maha Salim, "Mudir al-Kuliyya al-Harbiyya: Lam Nata'arrad li-Dughut li-Qabul Abna' Qadat al-Huriyya wa-l-'Adala . . . ," *al-Ahram*, 20 November 2012.

114. http://morsimeter.com/, accessed 19 April 2015.

115. Alison Pargeter is quoted in Farah Halime, "Egypt's Long-Term Economic Recovery Plan Stalls," *New York Times*, 2 May 2013.

116. See, for example, Rachel Shabi, "Egyptians Are Being Held Back by Neoliberalism, Not Religion," Guardian, 21 December 2012; Matthias Sailer, "Poverty, Disillusionment Drive Egypt's Protests," *Deutsche Welle*, 3 February 2013; Gilbert Achcar, "Extreme Capitalism of the Muslim Brothers," *Le Monde Diplomatique* (English edition), June 2013.

117. Khaild Lutfi et al., "al-Muhafazat Tatamarrad 'ala al-'Ashira Masa'an'," *al-Ahram al-Masa'i,* 16 October 2012; Zeinab Abul-Magd, "Egypt's Mock Authoritarianism," *Atlantic Council,* 13 February 2013.

118. "Jihan al-Sadat: Bakayt 'Indama Ihtafal Mursi bi-6 Uktubar fi Hudur Qatalat Zawji," *al-Masry al-Youm*, 28 September 2014.

119. Muhammad 'Ashur, "Mursi Yasil Istad al-Qahira li-l-Musharaka fi Mu'tamar al-Quwa al-Islamiyya li-Nusrat Surya," *El-Watan*, 15 June 2013.

120. "Hadithat al-Shi'a Hasan Shihata . . . Dahiyyat Tahrid Hassan wa-'Abd al-Maqsud fi Hudur al-Ra'is," *al-Masry al-Youm*, 5 July 2013.

121. Qanat al-'Arabiyya: Mu'assis al-Firqa 777: Ikhtitaf al-Junud Musalsal Batalahu al-Ikhwan wa-Hamas," *al-Arabiya*, 22 May 2013.

122. For main figures, political parties, and movements that formed NSF, see "Profile: Egypt's National Salvation Front," *BBC*, 10 December 2012.

123. "Egypt's National Salvation Front Rejects Dialogue with Morsi," *Ahram Online*, 28 January 2013.

124. See, for example, Matthias Sailer, "Egyptian Police Brutality Continues Under Morsi," *Deutsche Welle*, 2 February 2013; "Egyptian Police Torture 88, Kill 34 Under President Morsi," *Ahram Online*, 15 October 2012.

125. Amira Ibrahim, "al-Sisi Yuhadhdhir min Istidraj al-Jaysh li-l-Sira' al-Siyasi . . . wa-Wala'una al-Wahid li-l-Sha'b," *al-Tahrir*, 25 November 2012.

126. Sa'id Hijazi, "Burhami: Ittafaqt ana wa-l-Shatir 'ala Tadayyun al-Sisi wa-Hubb al-Nas lahu," *al-Watan*, 2 February 2014; "Video . . . al-Shatir: al-Sisi Mutadayyin Sawwam Qawwam," *Almesryoon*, 19 October 2013.

127. Ahmad Abd al-Khalik, "Niyabatan 'an al-Ra'is- al-Sisi Yada' Akalil al-Zuhur 'ala Darih Abd al-Nasir," *al-Ahram al-Masa'i*, 28 September 2012; Samar Nabih, "al-Sisi Yazur Darih Abd al-Nasir bi-Hudur Haykal wa-Abna' al-Za'im al-Rahil," *al-Watan*, 28 September 2013.

128. See, for example, Abd al-Jawwad Tawfiq, "Mursi Yaftatih Mashru'at Turuq Naffadhatha al-Quwwat al-Musallaha," *al-Ahram*, 3 May 2013.

129. Yasir Rizq, "al-Sisi li-l-Masri al-Yum: Adrakt ann Mursi Laysa Ra'isan li-Kull al-Masryyin wa-Qult lahu Laqad Fashaltum," *al-Masry al-Youm*, 7 October 2013.

130. Ahmad Hamdi, "20 Mahatta fi Hayat Mahmud Badr Sani' Azmat al-Baskawit," *al-Masry al-Youm*, 20 December 2014.

131. Mu'taz Nadi, "Bi-l-Video . . . Film al-Jaysh: 30 Yunyu laysa Inqilab wa Mursi Inhaz li-l-Ikhwan," *al-Masry al-Youm*, 14 July 2013.

132. Bel Trew, "Welcome to the Department of Morale Affairs: Belly Dancers, Billboards, and Egypt's Military Propaganda Machine," *Foreign Policy*, 15 January 2013.

133. For instance, Hasan Abd al-Barr and Hajar 'Uthman, "Ta'irat al-Jaysh Tulqi Bunat Hadaya 'ala Mutazahiri al-Tahrir," *El-Badil*, 20 July 2013; Aya Fathi, "al-Jaysh Yulqi A'lam wa-Kubunat Hadaya 'ala Mutazahiri al-Tahrir," *al-Dostor*, 18 February 2014.

134. Iman Hilal and Majdi Abu al-'Aynayn, "20 Alf Kartunat Mawad Ghidha'iyya min al-Jaysh li-Fuqara' Kafr al-Shaykh," *al-Masry al-Youm*, 29 November 2013; "20 Alf Kartunat Mawad Ghidha'iyya min al-Quwwat al-Musallaha li-l-'Amilin bi-Sharikat Misr bi-l-Mahalla al-Kubra," *Moheet*, 11 November 2013.

135. Sa'id Nafi' and 'Ammar Abd al-Wahid, "al-Ziham 'ala Kartunat Ramdan Yaqtul Sayyidatayn bi-Suhaj," *al-Masry al-Youm*, 17 July 2013.

136. Maha Salim, "al-Jaysh Yanjah fi Isti'adat Kafa'at Jisr Madinat al-Saff al-Munhar . . . ," *al-Ahram*, 16 October 2013.

137. Mansur Kamil and Daliya 'Uthman, "Intifadat al-'Ummal Tutih bi-Hukumat al-Biblaw," *al-Masry al-Youm*, 25 February 2014; Kamal 'Abbas, "al-'Ummal Iktashafu Ann al-Hadd al-Adna li-l-'Ujur Wahm Siyasi," *al-Masry al-Youm*, 25 June 2014.

138. Muhammad Yusuf and Muhammad Hamdi, "Tasa'ud al-Khilafat bayna Lajnat al-Khamsin wa-l-Jaysh Hawl al-Amn al-Qawmi wa-l-Muhakamat al-'Askariyya wa-Habs al-Sahafyyin," *al-Watan*, 3 November 2013; Wala' Ni'ma et al., "Insihab Mumaththil al-Quwwat al-Musallaha bi-al-50 Ba'd Khilaf Hawla Mada Siriyyat al-Ma'lumat," *al-Watan*, 28 October 2013; "'Udu bi-Lajnat al-Khamsin Yutalib bi-Ikhda' Anshitat al-Jasyh al-Iqtisadiyya li-l-Qawanin al-'Adiyya wa-l-Dara'ib," *Aswat Misriyya*, 8 October 2013.

139. Ghada Ali, "Bi-Amr al-Dustur . . . Shabb Madani Amam al-Qada' al-'Askari ba'd Mushajara ma'a Mujannadin fi Wataniyya," *al-Watan*, 3 August 2014.

140. Quote from Maggie Fick, "Egyptian Army Extends Power by Taking Charge of Gulf Aid," *Reuters*, 27 March 2014.

141. "Qarar Ra'is Jumhuriyyat Misr al-'Aarabiyya bi-l-Qanun Raqam 82 li-Sanat 2013 fi Sha'n Ta'dil Ba'd Ahkam al-Qanun Raqam 89 li-Sanat 1998 bi-Isdar Qanun Tanzim al-Munaqasat wa-l-Muzayadat . . . ," *al-Jarida al-Rasmiyya*, no. 36 (Mukarrar alif), uear 56, 11 September 2013; "Qarar Ra'is Jumhuriyyat Misr al-'Aarabiyya bi-l-Qanun Raqam 48 li-Sanat 2014 bi-Ta'dil Ba'd Ahkam al-Qanun Tanzim al-Munaqasat wa-l-Muzayadat al-Sadir bi-l-Qanun Raqam 89 li-Sanat 1998," *al-Jarida al-Rasmiyya*, no. 23 (tabi'), year 57, 5 June 2014; Karim Hasan, "Mihlib: al-Muwafqa 'ala Indimam al-'Arabiyya li-l-Tasni' li-l-Hay'at al-Tabi'a li-Dawla wa-Taklifaha bi-Mashari' Qawmiyya," *al-Ahram*, 14 April 2014.

142. Mohamed El-Dahshan, "The Egyptian Army Collects Billions in Government Contracts," 3 January 2014, http://eldahshan.com/2014/01/03/army-contracts/.

143. Arshad Mohammed, "U.S. Shifts to Closer Contact with Egypt Islamists," *Reuters*, 30 June 2011;

144. Reena Ninan and Dana Hughes, "Egypt's President Morsi Wins U.S. and Israeli Gratitude in Gaza Deal," *ABC News*, 21 November 2012, http://abcnews.go.com/International/egypts-president-morsi-wins-us-israeli-gratitude-gaza/story?id=17780177.

145. "IMF Discuss New Loan Program with Egypt, Says Lagarde," *IMF Survey Magazine*, 22 August 2012, http://www.imf.org/external/pubs/ft/survey/so/2012/car082212a.htm.

146. See: Zeinab Abul-Magd, "U.S. Military Aid to Egypt Lost Value," *Jadaliyya*, July 25 2013; Robert Rampton and Arshad Mohammed, "Obama Ends Freeze on U.S. Military Aid to Egypt," *Reuters*, 31 March 2015.

147. "Egypt's Sissi Negotiates Arms Deal in Russia," *Times of Israel*, 13 Februay 2014; "KSA, UAE to Finance Russian Arms Deal with Egypt," *Egypt Independent*, 7 February 2014; "Putin Backs Sisi 'Bid for Egypt Presidency,'" *BBC*, 13 Februrary 2014.

148. Ahmad Rajab, "'Adli Mansur Yuqarrir Raf' Muwazanat Jihaz al-Khadamat bi-Wazarat al-Difa' 517 Milyun Junayh," *al-Masry al-Youm*, 8 December 2013.

149. Muhammad Basal, "Nanshur Qarar Jumhuri li-Mansur bi-Naql Mina' al-'Arish li-l-Quwwat al-Musallaha," *al-Shorouk*, 9 June 2014.

150. Muhmmad Basal, "Mihlib Yusdir Qarar bi-Manh Iltizam Tariq Shubra-Banha li-l-Quwwat al-Musallaha li-Muddat 99 'Am," *al-Shorouk,* 6 April 2014; "Manh al-Quwwat al-Musallaha Haqq Istikmal wa-Idarat Tariq al-Qahira-al-Iskandariyya al-Sahrawi li-Muddat 50 'Am," *al-Borsa News*, 31 October 2013.

151. Muhammad Tahir, "Muhafiz al-Daqahliyya: Ma Tshammitush al-Kilab fina," *al-Wafd,* 29 July 2014; Salih Ramadan, "al-Liwa' 'Umar al-Shawadfi Muhafiz al-Daqahliyya . . . al-Rumansi alladhi Ya'ish fi al-Madina al-Fadila," *al-Watan*, 14 August 2013; Mai al-Kanani, "Bi-l-Arqam . . . Kashf Hisab li-l-Shawadfi Khilal Fatrat Tawwalih Muhafazat al-Daqahliyya," *Wilad El-Balad*, 7 February 2015.

152. Muhsin 'Ashri "bi-l-Suwar . . . Muhafiz Bursa'id Yada' Yadahu 'ala Famm Tajir li-Man'ih min al-Hadith 'an al-Fasad," *Shorouk*, 18 March 2014.

153. Hani 'Imara, "al-Mashhad al-An: Fulayfil wa-Hay'at al-Nadama," *al-Ahram,* 17 December 2013.

Conclusion

1. Stephen Graham, "When Life Itself Is War: On the Urbanization of Military and Security Doctrine," *International Journal of Urban and Regional Research* 36 (January 2012): 138–39.

2. Salwa al-'Antari, "al-Inhiyazat al-Ijtima'iyya li-l-Qrarat al-Iqtisadiyya," *Majallat al-Dimuqratiyya*, 29 September 2014; MENA, "Muhafiz Qina: Takhsis 22 Alf Kartuna Ramadaniyya li-Tawzi'iha 'ala al-Fuqara'," *al-Masry al-Youm*, 19 May 2015; Amani Abu al-Naja, "al-Sisi: Lan Astati' Talbiyat Matlab Fi'awi Wahid . . . ," *al-Shorouk*, 24 June 2014; "Prime Minister's Decision no. 1455 of 2014," *al-Jarida al-Rasmiyya*, no. 37, 11 September 2014; Rajab Jalal, "Wazir al-Difa' Ya'fi 574 Munsha'a li-l-Jaysh min al-Dariba al-'Aqariyya," *al-Masry al-Youm*, 3 June 2015; see also state budget on Ministry of Finance website, http://www.mof.gov.eg, accessed 9 September 2015.

3. Sahar Zahran and Muhammad Fu'ad, "al-Hukuma al-Jadida Khilal Sa'at . . . ," *al-Ahram*, 14 September 2015.

4. Muhammad Hasan, "Ra'is al-Hay'a al-Handasiyya li-l-Ahram: 850 Mashru' Tusharik Fiha al-Quwwat al-Musallaha li-Khidamt al-Sha'b al-Misri," *al-Ahram*, 20 August 2014; Mahir Abu Nur, "Mihlib Yatafaqqad 10 Alaf Faddan bi-l-Farafira Tastaslihum al-Quwwat al-Musallaha," *al-Youm al-Sabi'*, 14 September 2014.

5. "Wazarat al-Intaj al-Harbi, Qarar Raqam 64 li-Sanat 2015," *al-Waqa'i' al-Misriyya*, no. 113 (tabi'), year 188, 18 May 2015.

6. Muhammad Fu'ad, "al-Shorouk Tarsud Kawalis Istiqalat al-Misiri," *al-Shorouk*, 26 October 2015.

7. Ahmad Ramadan, "Nushata' Yutliqun Da'wa li-l-Tazahur 30 Uktubar li-l-Mutalaba bi-Iqalat Ru'asa' Ahya' al-Iskandariyya," *Albedaiah*, 27 October 2015; "Al-Liwa' Tariq al-Mahdi Muhafiz al-Iskandariyya fi Diyafat Nadwat al-Ahram," *al-Ahram*, 4 December 2014; Khayr Raghib and Muhammad al-Buhayri, "Ta'yin Liwa' Sabiq Khalafan li-Ra'is Sarf al-Iskandriyya al-Mustaqil," *al-Masry al-Youm*, 30 October 2015.

8. See https://www.facebook.com/events/1662626983979717/, accessed 27 October 2015.

9. See general critique of economic crisis in Ziyad Baha' al-Din, "Iqtirahat li-l-Ta'amul ma'a al-Azma al-Iqtisadiyya," *al-Shorouk*, 20 October 2015. On the Suez Canal extension, see Sharif Siraj and Ahmad Farahat, "Muhab Mimmish: al-Taraju' fi Iradat Qanat al-Suways Yarji' li-Tabatu' al-Intaj al-'Alami," *al-Borsa News*, 17 October 2015.

10. See, for example, "al-Quwwat al-Musallaha Tuwazi' 66 Alf Kartuna ka-'Idiyyat 'Id al-Adha li-l-Fuqara'," *al-Shorouk*, 22 September 2015.

11. Galal Amin, "Tanmiya Iqtisadiyya am Tanmiya 'Aqariyya," *al-Shorouk*, 14 April 2015; Raniya Badawi, "Galal Amin Ustadh al-Iqtisad bi-l-Jami'a al-Amrikiyya: Tajdid al-Khitab al-Dini fi Balad Ja'i' Madya'a li-l-Waqt," *al-Masry al-Youm*, 5 May 2015.

12. Mahmud Abd al-Fadil, "Hal Satashhad Misr Nuskha Mu'addala min Nasiriyyat al-Khamistnat," *al-Shorouk*, 10 March 2014; Mahmud Abd al-Fadil, "Awlawiyyat al-Nuhud al-Iqtisadi wa-Istratijiyyat al-Sayr 'ala Qadamayn," *al-Shorouk*, 15 April 2015.

13. 'Abir al-'Arabi and Salama 'Amir, "Mamish: 'A'id Qanat al-Suways sa-Yartafi' ila 200 Milyar Junayh Khilal 5 Sanawat," *El-Watan News*, 28 September 2014; Ayman Ramadan, "Muhab Mamish: Dakhl Qanat al-Suways sa-Yasil li-Akthar min 200 Milyar Junayh Khilal 5 Sanawat," *al-Youm al-Sabi'*, 16 September 2014.

14. Jamal Hiraji, "Muhab Mamish: Taraju' Dakhl Qanat al-Suways la-'Alaqa lahu bi-Qanat al-Suways al-Jadida," *al-Youm al-Sabi'*, 25 October 2015; 'Abir al-'Arabi, "Inkhifad Dakhl Qanat al-Suways . . . wa-Mamish: al-Sabab Taraju' al-Tijara fi Kull al-'Alam," *El-Watan*, 26 October 2015.

15. Reuters, "Inkhifad Iradat Misr min Qanat al-Suways ila 5.175 Milyar Dular fi 2015," *Reuters*, 13 January 2016.

16. Isma'il Hammad, "al-Watan Tu'id Nashr Akhir Hiwar li-Muhafiz al-Bank al-Markazi," *El-Watan News,* 18 October 2015.

17. Muhammad Basal, "al-Sisi Yumaris Sultat al-Tashri' . . . al-Sisi Yusdir 263 Qanun fi 420 Yawm," *al-Shorouk*, 4 August 2015.

18. Reuters, "Sisi Loyalists Sweep List Seats in Egypt's Election," *Reuters*, 25 November 2015.

19. Fatima al-Khatib, "bi-l-Asma' . . . 51 Maq'ad Hasilat al-Jinralat Dakhil Majlis al-Nuwwab," *al-Tahrir*, 7 December 2015.

20. "Full Text of IMF's Lagarde Speech at Egypt Economic Development Conference," *Ahram Online*, 13 March 2015.

21. U.S. Department of State, "Remarks at the Opening Plenary of the Egypt Economic Development Conference. John Kerry, Secretary of State, Sharm el-Sheikh, Egypt, 13 March 2015," http://www.state.gov/secretary/remarks/2015/03/238872.htm; Kevin Liptak, "Obama Lifts Freeze, Ships Arms to Egypt," *CNN*, 31 March 2015.

22. On UAE support, see Simeon Kerr and Heba Saleh, "UAE Focuses on Economic Reform in Egypt in Battle Against Islamism," *Financial Times*, 19 June 2014.

23. Philippe Droz-Vincent, "Civilianizing the State: Reflections on the Egyptian Conundrum," Middle East Institute, 14 May 2014.

24. Robert Springborg, "President Sisi's Delegative Authoritarianism," *Istituto Affari Internazionai Working Papers* 15, 26 July 2015, 1.

25. Ibid., 11–12.

26. Tai Mig Cheung, "The Rise and Fall of the Chinese Military Business Complex," in Jörn Brömmelhörster and Wolf-Christian Paes, *The Military as an Economic Actor: Soldiers in Business* (Basingstoke: Palgrave Macmillan, 2003), 52–73.

27. Thomas Scheetz, "Military Business in Argentina," in Brömmelhörster and Paes, *The Military as an Economic Actor*, 18–31.

28. Terence Lee, "The Military's Corporate Interests: The Main Reason for Intervention in Indonesia and the Philippines," *Armed Forces and Society* 34 (April 2008): 491–502; Human Rights Watch "Indonesia: Military Business Reforms 'Totally Inadequate,'" 12 January 2010, https://www.hrw.org/news/2010/01/12/indonesia-military-business-reforms-totally-inadequate.

29. Wael Gamal, "al-'Askarai: Mashru'atuna 'Araq Wazarat al-Difa' . . . wa-lan Nasmah li-l-Dawla bi-l-Tadakhkhul Fiha," *al-Shorouk*, 27 March 2012.

30. Maggie Fick, "Egyptian Army Extends Power by Taking Charge of Gulf Aid," *Reuters*, 27 March 2014.

31. Michael Georgy and Stephen Kalin, "Gulf Arab Allied Pledge $12 billion to Egypt at Summit," *Reuters*, 13 March 2015; Kerr and Saleh, "UAE Focuses on Economic Reform in Egypt."

32. IMF Press Release no. 15/422, "IMF Staff Concludes Visit to Egypt," 17 September 2015, http://www.imf.org/external/np/sec/pr/2015/pr15422.htm.

33. Lin Noueihed and Michael Georgy, "Egypt Expects $1.5 Billion in Aid by Year-end, Eying IMF," *Reuters*, 8 December 2015; Bloomberg News, "IMF Loan Could be Back on the Table for Egypt," *National UAE*, http://www.thenational.ae/business/economy/imf-loan-could-be-back-on-the-table-for-egypt, accessed 6 March 2016.

Index

National Salvation Front (NSF, Jabhat al-Inqadh al-Watani), 219

National Service Projects Organization (NSPO), 14, 81, 93–96, 100, 104, 116, 118, 120, 122, 130, 132–34, 136, 140–42, 144, 146–47, 150, 192, 201, 211, 226; the Nile Wataniyya Company for River Transport, 192

nationalization, 53, 56, 58, 67, 74

NATO, 26

navy, 9, 15, 85, 130, 156, 177–78, 180, 189, 208, 231; admiral, 190, 195, 193, 236; navy officers, 177

Naval Postgraduate School, 9

neoliberalism, 2, 4, 6, 20–24, 32, 80, 111–51, 155–85, 188, 214, 196, 200, 213, 218, 225, 229–32, 235, 239

nepotism, 9, 56, 165

newspapers, 29, 30, 31, 33, 43, 48, 104, 109, 110, 157, 188, 189, 197, 210

Nile transport: 142; ferryboats, 153, 165, 180; Wataniyya River Transport, 184

Non-Aligned Movement, 48

nongovernmental organizations (NGOs), 173, 238

oil, 4, 12, 22–28, 47, 78, 80, 87, 90, 95, 97, 106, 119, 194, 195, 204, 208, 218, 230, 237, 240

Osman, Osman Ahmed, 100

Pakistan, 20, 50, 124, 239

Palestine, 41, 47, 87, 158; Gaza, 24, 166, 181, 225, 233; Hamas, 225

paramilitary, 8, 10, 23–24, 108

parastatal, 14, 23, 31, 81–82, 93, 117, 146, 210, 230, 234

parliament: socialist parliament, 45, 52–56, 59, 64, 66, 71, 73; Sadat's parliament, 75, 83; Mubarak's parliament, 99, 102–3, 105, 110, 112, 129, 132, 145, 150, 152, 171; post-2011 parliaments, 191, 194, 197,

199, 205, 207, 209; parliamentary elections, 52, 106, 160, 168, 170, 236; Shura Council, 206, 209–11

peasants, 46, 48, 52, 53, 59–60, 68, 73, 142, 202, 224. See also lower classes

Pentagon, 48, 54, 148, 225

Peru, 16, 17, 38

petrochemicals, 120

petroleum, 50–51, 64, 70, 131. See also oil

pharmaceuticals, 22, 70, 92, 125

political parties, 44, 74, 220–21, 224, 236

population control, 2, 7, 8, 27, 38, 81–82, 84, 100, 115, 151, 155, 203, 205, 228, 232

ports, 15, 32, 99, 114, 131, 151, 156, 176–85, 190, 211, 228, 231, 234; airports, 91, 95, 97, 113, 141, 147, 168, 172, 176, 181, 184–185, 191, 211; al-'Arish, 201, 226; Alexandria, 179; High Dam Port, 169, 181; Port Said, 158, 177–78, 182, 213, 227

postcolonial, 2, 8, 9, 15, 16, 28, 36, 38, 79, 109, 229

presidential elections, 159, 165, 181, 188, 204–5, 208–9, 218, 220–21, 232

private business, 23, 30, 52, 56, 73, 77, 96, 98, 100, 116, 140–41, 144–45, 147, 153, 160, 178, 214, 231

private sector, 22, 53, 67, 70, 100, 138, 147, 149, 180–84, 201

private capital, 36, 47, 49, 94, 182, 235; private investment, 48, 75, 141, 169, 177, 182, 235

privatization, 22–23, 32, 56, 73, 97, 115–16, 122–23, 126–27, 129–30, 156, 168, 170, 172, 176, 180, 182–84, 193, 200, 210, 230–31, 239

propaganda, 5, 8, 15, 57, 188, 217, 222, 232, 238

protests, 2, 26–29, 32, 45, 48, 72, 76, 141, 159–69, 172–77, 186, 189–99, 206, 220–27, 232; 2011 protests, 186–217; 2013 protests, 217–27. See also uprisings provincial Egypt. *See* governorates

public authorities, 64, 153, 169–76, 203, 213, 234, government authorities, 15, 32, 138, 151, 153, 156, 186, 225, 231; Accountability State Authority (ASA), 129, 166, 213; Administrative Control Authority, 196, 203; Agricultural Development Authority, 172; Authority of Tourism Development, 203; Authority of Civil Aviation, 181, 185; Cairo Agency for Sewage Projects, 174; Central Agency for Urban Development, 174; Central Agency of Public Mobilization and Statistics, 201; Customer Protection Agency, 176; Department of Production Sufficiency and Vocational Training, 175; General Authority for Agricultural Development Projects, 203; General Authority for Investment and Free Zones (GAFI), 170; General Organization for Export and Import Control, 176, 203; High Dam Port Authority, 169, 177; Industrial Development Authority, 203; Land Survey Authority, 175; Maritime Public Authority, 227; Maritime Safety Authority, 177–79, 190; National Authority of Potable Water and Sewage, 174; River Transport Authority, 177, 180; Suez Canal Authority, 177, 208; the New Urban Communities Authority, 148, 172, 203, 213; the Tourism Development Authority, 172–73

public complaints, 32, 64, 103, 157, 161, 167, 172–173, 195–97

Public Defense Forces, 175

public expenditure, 76, 104, 115; public spending, 11, 104, 113, 122–24, 231, 239. *See also* state budget

public sector, 3, 23, 32, 36–37, 46, 50, 55, 57, 61, 64–66, 70–76, 94, 98, 100, 103, 109–10, 113, 116, 127, 129–30, 140, 144, 147, 151, 156, 168, 170, 175, 178–79, 183, 194, 200–201, 229–30

public projects, 23, 94, 96, 104, 153, 184

public prosecutor, 161

public services, 6, 31–32, 93, 116, 152–85, 218, 226

public tenders, 102, 129, 143, 147, 162, 167, 173, 180–81, 183, 210–11, 225

Qatar, 27, 90

quarries, 14, 117, 133, 137, 144–46, 169, 172, 192

railway wagons, 126, 127

Reagan, Ronald, 107; Reagan administration, 80, 85, 86, 88

real estate, 22, 78, 101, 103, 132, 152, 161, 234–35

Red Sea, 85, 103, 139, 140, 158, 166, 174, 177, 178, 179, 190, 196, 204

Republican Guard, 25, 97, 159, 166

revolution: 25–30, 33, 36, 38, 42, 44, 51, 54, 61, 65, 67, 71, 73, 158, 185–88, 222, 229, 238; 1952 revolution, 35, 54, 61, 67, 69, 153; 2011 uprisings, 26, 29, 32, 112, 116, 128, 133, 135, 145, 149, 154, 156, 158, 160–85, 186–204, 218–20, 234; revolutionary youth, 190, 185–86, 189, 209, 219; *'Askar Kadhibun*, 199; social revolution, 38

riots: 1977 bread riots, 69, 75–76, 81, 159; 1986 riots of the Central Security Forces, 108

River Transport, 113, 130–31, 177, 180, 184, 192

rural areas, 37, 40, 46, 52, 55, 59, 61, 65, 68, 71, 73, 128, 149, 158, 169, 172, 206, 219, 236; countryside, 52, 73, 100. *See also* village

Russia, 4, 13, 20, 124–25, 226, 239, 241

GPSR Authorized Representative: Easy Access System Europe, Mustamäe tee 50, 10621 Tallinn, Estonia, gpsr.requests@easproject.com

www.ingramcontent.com/pod-product-compliance
Lightning Source LLC
Chambersburg PA
CBHW022136020426
42334CB00015B/925